AGRICULTURE IN CRISIS: PEOPLE, COMMODITIES AND NATURAL RESOURCES IN INDONESIA, 1996-2000

AGRICULTURE IN CRISIS: PEOPLE, COMMODITIES AND NATURAL RESOURCES IN INDONESIA, 1996-2000

Edited by
Françoise Gérard and *François Ruf*

LONDON AND NEW YORK

First published in 2001 by Curzon Press

This edition published 2013 by Routledge
2 Park Square, Milton Park, Abingdon, Oxfordshire OX14 4RN
711 Third Avenue, New York, NY 10017

First issued in paperback 2014

Routledge is an imprint of the Taylor & Francis Group, an informa business

ISBN 978-0-700-71465-0 (hbk)
ISBN 978-1-138-86259-3 (pbk)

Contents

Preface

Bernard Bachelier

Director-General of the Centre de coopération internationale en recherche agronomique pour le développement (CIRAD)

This book is the work of a team of Indonesian and European agricultural economists and agronomists. Its basic idea and themes were conceived by its scientific editors, Françoise Gérard and François Ruf, but all the book's authors are committed to improving agriculture in developing countries. This they seek to do not only through their own research but also by drawing on the resources and dynamism inherent in resource-poor farming communities.

Indonesia's crisis, which took economists largely by surprise, was at once environmental, economic and political. It affected a country with the world's fifth largest human population, some 200 million people—a predominantly rural country still struggling to identify a workable model for its future development. The unprecedented scale, duration and severity of the crisis call into question many of the assumptions that underpin the development models of the 1990s.

Agriculture has contributed much to the, until recently, widely feted Asian model of economic growth and social progress. Although different subsectors have been affected to different degrees, Indonesia's agriculture has been deeply hurt by the crisis. At the same time, the country looks to its agriculture to lead it out of crisis.

There is no doubt that Indonesia's farmers are capable of the hard work needed to pull the economy into recovery. The increases in production achieved over the past 30 years testify to their impressive abilities. Over this period the production of rice and soya bean has risen fourfold. Similarly, the country has experienced a remarkable cocoa boom in which production has risen from zero to over 400 000 tonnes per year in less than a quarter of a century as some 200 000 migrant families have adopted the crop spontaneously.

Today, however, while mineral prices have been rising for the past 2 years, those of agricultural commodities have sunk to record lows. One by one, cocoa, coffee, rubber and palm oil have been affected. Even pepper—a crop that symbolises tropical and Indonesian agriculture and one of the last bastions to hold out against the slump—has now succumbed.

In early 1998, Indonesia's export crops producers and exporters actually benefitted from the fall of the rupiah and international prices of cocoa, coffee, palm oil and coconut rose slightly. The incomes of the rural families producing these crops increased four- or fivefold. Their spending went up sharply, helping to offset the early impact of the crisis. But now those days are past, and just when new efforts are being demanded of them, Indonesia's farmers find they have few, if any, options for improving their lot. They are trapped in a world remote from that of the international decision makers who determine the rise and fall of global markets. And their national representatives often have no alternative but to accept the dictates of the global economy.

This book does not argue against globalisation, nor even against economic liberalism. It is an empirical study of the experiences of Indonesia's farmers and how these relate to macro-economic events, of the relationship between the local circumstances that shape agriculture and the global system of trade that determines its profitability. As such it should provoke much thought in its readers.

The French scientists responsible for the study have spent many years working with national Indonesian scientists and farming communities. Despite rising political tensions, they did not turn their backs on these partners during this time of crisis but instead remained strongly in sympathy with them. Their observations of the crisis are, then, based on a solid grasp of the situation on the ground, as revealed through surveys and interviews. By conveying this situation, and the results of their analysis, to decision makers in the developed world who influence global trends, the French team can perform a valuable service for its national colleagues.

The authors show how the environmental, economic and political strands of Indonesia's crisis are interwoven, often to devastating effect. Their treatment is political, since they have decided to speak plainly about the factors that seem to them to have most influenced events. Indeed, it would have been impossible to discuss Indonesia's development, both in the 30 years preceding the crisis and during the crisis itself, without taking the political context into account. This does not mean that the hypotheses of cause and effect advanced by the authors should be accepted without questioning. They should be questioned, and they will be. The methods of economic analysis used in this study also need further debate.

The fundamental issue raised by the study concerns the measures that should be taken to support agriculture as it grapples with the effects of the globalisation of markets, the liberalisation of trade and the currency fluctuations that, increasingly, accompany these trends. These measures should lie at the heart of the new international aid policies that are, we hope, now taking shape in donor countries and institutions. One could argue that the need for these measures is analogous to the need to apply the precautionary principle in the field of public health. The ethical dimension of the two cases is broadly similar, especially as regards the implications for relationships between rich and poor countries. But even without recourse to this argument, the need for greater coherence and effectiveness in agricultural policy making at the national level, including decisions as to which commodities a country should seek to specialise in, makes supportive measures highly desirable. On this and other issues, the authors—especially Françoise Gérard and François Ruf—advance several new ideas. In so doing they are playing their part, as scientists, in a debate that will shape society over the next century.

The authors believe that the Indonesian crisis was triggered by the sudden liberalisation of financial markets at a time when neither traders nor their institutions were ready for it. They raise the question of whether unregulated markets can ever achieve a stable equilibrium. That free markets are self-regulating is, of course, one of the basic tenets of economic theory. But the hypothetical conditions under which self-regulation is assumed to place—perfect market information, immediate production responses to price signals, matching supply and demand, independent decision making by entrepreneurs—are far from those of the real world, especially the world faced by poor countries and producers. Indeed, studies by economists have shown that the characteristics of real markets, in which information is difficult to obtain and production responses are delayed, are virtually bound to lead to large fluctuations in prices and in the volume of goods traded. Under these conditions, the hasty liberalisation of agricultural and food commodity markets can be highly damaging not only to producers but also to consumers, both nationally and internationally.

It is the authors' hope that they have contributed usefully to the international debate on these issues. Their ideas, as researchers, will often contrast with those of politicians. Each side in the debate shares an awareness that the ultimate purpose of agricultural research, like that of development aid, is to bring about a lasting improvement in the lives of the world's poorest producers and consumers.

30 October 2000

Acknowledgements

Our thanks go first to the CIRAD Director-General, Bernard Bachelier. Right from the start of the Asian crisis, he, like us, was convinced that Indonesian farmers' entrepreneurship could help the country to recover. He also believed that 20 years of CIRAD cooperation with Indonesian Research and Development partners almost naturally commanded us to testify how Indonesian farmers reacted courageously to the crisis, and how agriculture can help the country, despite the potential negative impact of monetary depreciation on world prices of most agricultural commodities. His support and consequently that of the CIRAD publications service were decisive.

As this book was written and scientifically edited by non-English researchers, an enormous debt is owed to our English editors. It was a long process, with Mrs Wheale and Dr Sandy Williams doing a great job in carefully reading and improving the first drafts. We then benefited greatly from very creative editing by Simon Chater to achieve the current state of these 12 chapters.

Many thanks to all our co-authors for their prompt cooperation and for sharing their considerable expertise shared in the book. The debate between co-authors proved to be very useful for the whole book.

As often happens, editing the book proved a more arduous task than we bargained for, and we would like to thank our respective husband and wife, Thierry Seys and Anisha Ruf, not to mention our children, for their patience during the long weekends devoted to the book at the expense of family life.

Françoise Gérard and François Ruf

Contributors

Baslian K. Yoza is a researcher in the field of transmigration settlement techniques. He is currently carrying out studies on the development of a population and transmigration information system at the Agency for Population and Population Mobility. Between 1987 and 1999 he was actively involved in socio-economic studies at the Centre for Research and Development of the Ministry of Transmigration and Forest Squatter Resettlement of the Republic of Indonesia.

Robin Bourgeois is a French agro-economist currently based at the UN-ESCAP CGPRT Centre in Bogor, Indonesia, where he is working on methods to help define sound local agricultural development policies in Indonesia and Vietnam. He worked from 1988 to 1992 at ISNAR in the Netherlands as a researcher on linkages between agricultural research and technology transfer and also provided advisory services for agricultural research management. On assignment to IICA in Costa Rica from 1992 to 1996, he developed and published a participatory method based on research and stakeholder interaction for the development of agricultural commodity systems.

Kees Burger graduated in econometrics at the University of Amsterdam. In 1984 he joined the Economic and Social Institute, Free University, Amsterdam, where he is now head of the Division for Economic Research, which he combines with a teaching assignment in the Faculty of Economics. From 1977 to 1984, he was with the Agricultural Economics Research Institute in The Hague. Main fields of research are commodity markets, with emphasis on jute, natural rubber, cocoa and pepper, and the micro-economic analysis of rural households. Among his publications are *The Natural Rubber Market* (1997), *International Commodity Policy* (1993) and, as co-editor, *Agricultural Economics and Policy: International Challenges for the Ninetie* (1991). From 1981 to 1989 he was the Editor of the *European Review of Agricultural Economics.*

Etty Diana is a researcher in the field of transmigration, particularly in socio-economic and environmental studies. She was with the Ministry of Transmigration and Forest Squatter Resettlement of the Republic of Indonesia between 1991 to 1999, and is currently carrying out studies in the field of population administration at the Agency for Population and Population Mobility.

Erwidodo has a doctorate in Economics from the University of Michigan (USA). He joined the Centre for Socio-Economic Research (CASER) in 1990, and was appointed its Deputy Director in 1994. He has worked on numerous topics related to Indonesian agriculture and forests, and has contributed to international research on the liberalization of the Indonesian agricultural sector. Since 1998, he has been Director of the Centre for Socio-Economic Research on Forestry and Estate Crops in Indonesia.

Françoise Gérard has a doctorate in Economics from the University of Paris I Panthéon-Sorbonne, and primarily works on issues associated with agricultural market regulation. She has been a researcher with CIRAD-AMIS (ECOPOL programme) since 1992, and from 1994 to 1997, led a programme covering food crops in Indonesia, Vietnam and Thailand, based at the CGPRT CENTRE, a UN centre in Bogor (Indonesia). She has published *Measuring the Effects of Trade Liberalization: Multilevel Analysis Tool for Agriculture* (1998, CGPRT Centre), and is currently heading a CIRAD research project aimed at shedding a new light on international negotiations on trade liberalization, based on an original calculable model of global equilibrium. She is also supervisor of a research seminar at the University of Paris I.

Anne Gouyon is an independent consultant specializing in socio-economics applied to agricultural development. After graduating from the main French school for agricultural science, INA-PG (Paris), she worked for CIRAD for nine years, mostly in Southeast Asia. She spent three consecutive years in Sumatra, Indonesia, analysing smallholder systems from a socio-economic point of view, and used the results of this fieldwork to write her PhD thesis, again at INA-PG. She is now an independent consultant, doing socio-economic and institutional analyses for agricultural development projects in Asia with her firm Idé-Force, which has worked with CIRAD on many projects in Indonesia.

Haryati is a researcher in the field of agricultural development. Between 1991 and 1999, she was actively involved in socio-economic studies at the Centre for Research and Development of the Ministry of Transmigration and Forest Squatter Resettlement of the Republic of Indonesia. She is currently carrying out studies in the field of population administration at the Agency for Population and Population Mobility.

Alain Karsenty, an economist, is a researcher with CIRAD's Forestry Department. He is a land tenure specialist, and has also led several projects on forest policies in developing countries and the international tropical timber market. He studied the economic implications of reduced-impact logging in a pilot project in East Kalimantan in 1993. His last book, *Economic Instruments for Tropical Forests*, published in early 2000 by CIFOR, CIRAD and IIED, addresses issues such as taxation regimes, log export bans, forest-based industrialization and path dependence, and carbon crediting through forest activities.

Patrice Levang is senior agronomist at the Institut de Recherche pour le Développement (IRD, ex-ORSTOM), and currently IRD Representative for Indonesia. Since 1980 he has been involved in numerous studies on the conversion of tropical forests into new agricultural land in Indonesia. His studies focus not only on technical but also on socio-economic matters, on policy impacts and on the cultural differences between local populations and migrants (spontaneous and government-sponsored). He is the author of La Terre d'en Face (The Land Beyond), an original insight into the Indonesian transmigration programme.

Isabelle Marty is an agronomist who has been working with CIRAD since 1992. She has published *Prospective des déséquilibres environnementaux liés à l'agriculture* (CIRAD, 1993). In 1994, she became an associate of the CGPRT Centre, a UN centre in Bogor (Indonesia), and is currently writing a thesis in conjunction with CIRAD-AMIS (ECOPOL programme), on Thai agriculture and trade with Europe.

Eric Penot is an agro-economist who has worked in Indonesia (Bogor), on secondment to ICRAF, for six years. He created and implemented the Smallholder Rubber Agroforestry Project. Its main activities were farm characterization through socio-economic surveys, implementation of an on-farm trial network and monitoring of farmer strategies between 1992 and 2000. He organized a seminar on rubber agroforestry systems in Bogor in 1997. He is currently completing a PhD in Economics in Montpellier and is considered a world expert in rubber farming systems.

Marie-Gabrielle Piketty, who initially trained as an agronomist, was awarded a doctorate in Economic Sciences from the University of Paris I Panthéon-Sorbonne in 1999. Part of her work concerns the analysis of the determining factors of regional development and their environmental consequences. This issue, applied to the case of development of the outer islands of Indonesia and its impact on deforestation, led her to conduct several study missions in Indonesia between 1995 and 1998. Having been recruited by CIRAD, she is now working more specifically on the same issue in the Amazon basin, and on the consequences of trade liberalization for agricultural markets.

François Ruf is an economist with CIRAD, graduated from the University of Paris X-Nanterre, and has been working on the cocoa and coffee economies for 20 years. He was first based in Côte d'Ivoire from 1979 to 1985 and then travelled throughout the major cocoa producing countries from 1986 to 1988. He launched a programme in Indonesia on cocoa farmers' investment, and lived in Jakarta from 1990 to 1997. He is now back in Côte d'Ivoire and West Africa, and has extended his comparative research to other major tree crops. He is the author of numerous articles on cocoa, co-editor of *Cocoa Cycles. The Economics of Cocoa Supply* (1995) and author of *Booms et crises du cacao. Les vertiges de l'or brun* (1995). He is co-editor of the forthcoming *From Slash-and-Burn to replanting. Green Revolutions in the Indonesian Uplands?*, produced by CIRAD for the World Bank (2001). Since 1999, he has been supervising a multi-institutional research programme involving around a dozen researchers and students, looking at tree crop diversification in Côte d'Ivoire.

Hidde P. Smit is Managing Director of the Economic and Social Institute, Free University, Amsterdam, which he joined in 1979. From 1970 until 1986 he also held an associate professorship at the Faculty of Economics. From 1976 to 1978, he interrupted his university career to work as an expert with ESCAP in Bangkok, where he started his work on natural rubber. Since then he worked on many commodities, and on macro-models of developing countries. Major publications include *The Natural Rubber Market* (1997), *International Commodity Policy* (1993), *International Commodity Development Strategies* (1993) and *Economic Modelling and Policy Analysis* (1991).

Tancrède Voituriez, who has a doctorate in Economics, is currently working for CIRAD-AMIS (ECOPOL programme) on modelling the effects of free trade on the economy of developing countries, and particularly on the rural sector. His doctorate thesis, which he defended in 1999, concerned the modelling of changes in price volatility on agricultural commodity markets, with particular emphasis on palm oil, of which Indonesia is currently the world's second largest producer.

Yoddang is an agronomist who graduated from Hasanuddin University (Ujung Pandang, Indonesia). Since 1990, he has been working as a research assistant on the joint CIRAD/ASKINDO (Indonesian Cocoa Association) programme on the cocoa economy in Indonesia. He is co-author of several papers and chapters of books, including *Smallholder cocoa in Indonesia: why a cocoa boom in Sulawesi?* in Clarence-Smith (ed.), *Cocoa pioneer fronts since 1800* (1996) and *Price and non-price factors in a green revolution* in F. Ruf and F. Lançon (eds.), *From Slash-and-Burn to Replanting. Green Revolutions in the Indonesian Uplands?* (2001).

Waris Ardhy graduated in English from the University of Hasanuddin and participated for several years in the joint CIRAD/ASKINDO (Indonesian Cocoa Association) programme on the cocoa economy in Indonesia. He is currently a specialist in pod counting, working for a private company. He is co-author of *The Spectacular Efficiency of Bugis Smallholders; Why? Until when?* in F. Ruf and P.S. Siswoputranto (eds.), *Cocoa Cycles. The Economics of Cocoa Supply* (1995).

List of Figures and Tables

Figures

Tables

Introduction

Southeast Asia's economic crisis, which began in July 1997 with a panic on the Thai financial market and quickly spread throughout the region, surprised everyone by its severity in countries that had for so long been considered so successful.

Until then, Indonesia was considered by most economists to have one of the strongest economies in the region. It was even complimented on its performance a few months before the crisis. The few analysts who spotted the underlying weaknesses—growth based on increased use of inputs rather than the pursuit of greater efficiency (Krugman, 1994), the country's growing indebtedness (World Bank, 1996) and its flawed political system—did not dampen the general optimism. Indonesia's past economic performance was indeed impressive. In the 30 years since 1967, average annual per capita income had risen from US$ 50 to over US$ 1000, poverty had been massively reduced and life expectancy at birth had increased by 20 years. Whereas around 70 million people or 60% of the population lived below the poverty line in 1970, only 20 million or 10% did so just before the crisis struck (World Bank, 1998). The rupiah was stable and inflation was under 10%.

That was why, when the financial crisis began in July 1997, experts at first remained optimistic. They were confident of the country's ability to overcome what they saw as a temporary correction in the value of its currency, a natural reaction to previous overvaluation. Six months later, it was clear that Indonesia was experiencing one of the most catastrophic economic collapses of all time, accompanied by a deep social and political crisis. The number of rupiahs needed to buy a US dollar had risen at least threefold and, in the feverish rushes out of the currency that characterised the deepening crisis, up to tenfold. The prices of imported goods escalated, leading to thousands of bankruptcies and wholesale economic and social melt-down.

The financial crisis, or *krismon* as it became known in Bahasa Indonesia, the national language, was far more severe in Indonesia than in other countries of the region. The reasons were several. First, its opening stages coincided with an El Niño event that had a devastating effect on Indonesia's agriculture. In 1997-98 the country experienced its most severe drought in over 50 years, leading to widespread crop failure. At the height of the drought, huge fires raged in the countryside, especially around the concessions of large logging companies and corporate estates. These fires, which were partly induced by the weather and partly man-made, caused a pall of smog that led to severe health problems in addition to disrupting transport and communications. The drought was followed by flooding, as La Niña—the reversal of winds and sea-currents that follows El Niño—brought torrential rains in the second half of 1998. In contrast, Thailand and Vietnam received enough rain in 1998 to produce a record rice harvest. Second, the crisis also coincided with a period of low oil prices, which in 1998 fell by 30% over those of the previous year (World Bank, 1998). The fall deprived Indonesia of badly needed foreign exchange, undermining any hopes the government might have had of spending its way out of recession. Third, the financial crisis quickly led to a political crisis which further sapped confidence and paralysed efforts to recover. The announcement of a new provisional government in May 1998 was a stop-gap measure that did little to restore confidence, undermined as it was by 30 years of nepotism and corruption. Indonesians needed democratic elections and a new President before they were able to start hoping again. As this book went to press in early 2000, social and ethnic tensions across the country remained high, with a heavy military or police presence often exacerbating the problems rather than solving them.

Nineteen ninety-eight and most of 1999 were, indeed, unimaginably bad years for Indonesia and for the vast majority of Indonesians. The rupiah's exchange rate against the US dollar plunged from Rp 2500 in June 1997 to Rp 15 000 a year later, then, at the end of 1998, stabilised at around Rp 8000, a level it held until the elections of 20 October 1999 (Figure 1). The fall led to steep hikes in the prices of imported goods at a time when climatic conditions made huge food imports necessary, pushing food prices up for all consumers and especially for the poor. The rate of inflation rose to around 80% in 1998, causing severe difficulties in all sectors of the economy. The combination of plummeting demand and soaring prices bankrupted thousands of businesses, while the banking system collapsed altogether. Unemployment shot up, by 20.6% in 1998 according to the country's Central Bureau of Statistics (CBS). Growth was first checked, then sent sharply into reverse, with Indonesia's gross domestic product (GDP), which had risen by 7.8% in 1996, rising by a further 4.65% in 1997 before shrinking by 14% in 1998. Real GDP per capita fell from over US$ 1000 to US$ 450. Skyrocketing food prices led to riots and looting, producing an unbearable level of uncertainty and risk that further depressed economic activity. Foreign capital fled the country, which is now highly indebted. The number of poor people increased sharply and their lot became—and remains—pitiful.

Figure 1 Rupiah-dollar exchange rates, 1997-99 (©IRD 1999)

From the beginning of the currency's slide in mid-1997, it took 2 years for the financial crisis to lead to real political change, which finally came with the independence of Timor and the election of Gus Dur and Megawati as president and vice-president respectively on 20 and 21 October 1999. The political U-turn led to a U-turn in the fortunes of Indonesia's beleagured currency. As the vice-president received the congratulations of President Clinton, the rupiah strengthened to Rp 6700 against the dollar, compared with Rp 8000 only 3 days earlier. But although a few international investors seemed to have decided it was time to come back to Indonesia, this did not mean the crisis was over. By May 2000, the exchange rate had weakened again to Rp 8500 and there are fears that it may return to Rp 10 000 by the time this book is published. Unlike its neighbours in Southeast Asia, who are now enjoying a healthy recovery, Indonesia seems set to experience severe economic pain for some time to come.

The events of 1998 and 1999 led to a spate of economic and political studies about the causes and effects of the crisis and the best route to recovery. Most of these studies were conducted at a macro-economic level, using aggregate data.

The approach taken in this book is radically different. Its authors paint a more detailed picture, focussing on individual households and enterprises, specifically those involved in or affected by agriculture. The picture is built up using a combination of micro-economic data, observations, interviews and first-hand information collected in village surveys, both before and during the crisis. Each chapter covers a commodity or group of commodities in a different location: cocoa in South and Central Sulawesi, coffee and food crops in southern Sumatra, rubber in Kalimantan, oil palm in Sumatra and Kalimantan, food crops in Java (Figure 2).

In each case we ask how producers were affected by the crisis. Who were the winners and losers? How did the winners spend or re-invest their profits? What were the survival strategies of the losers, especially those impoverished by the crisis? Did smallholders respond to the rising nominal rupiah prices of export commodities by increasing production for the export market? If so, did that increase supplies to the point at which prices on international markets started to fall?

These questions matter because, under certain conditions, agriculture could play a central role in Indonesia's economic recovery. As it has been known to do elsewhere in the past, the sector could trigger strong export-led growth, leading to job creation, renewed investment and increased demand for other goods and services. However, in Indonesia's case this rosy scenario is by no means guaranteed. New institutions, policies and technologies will have to be put in place first, especially

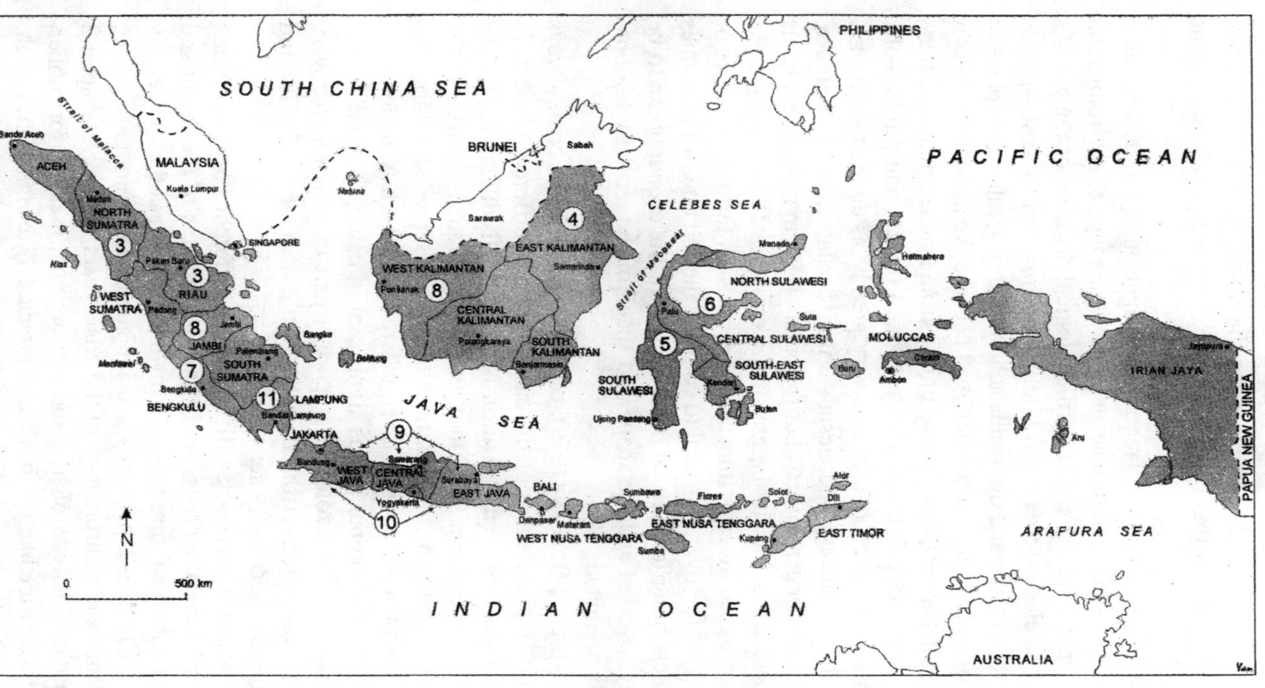

Figure 2 The islands and provinces of Indonesia. The circled numbers denote the areas covered by each chapter

if poor producers are to participate in the recovery. In particular, the land tenure conflicts that currently bedevil the sector will have to be addressed.

Answering these questions requires a disaggregated approach because agricultural producers in Indonesia face a wide range of environmental and economic conditions. The agro-ecological diversity of the world's largest archipelago—over 5000 kilometres from east to west—means that the crops grown and the yields achieved vary greatly from place to place as well as from year to year. And because the agricultural sector comprises all manner of production units—from landless rural labourers, through smallholders, to large estates both private and public—the constraints faced by producers also vary greatly, as do their solutions.

For some producers, Indonesia's crisis translated, as we shall see, into a fall into deeper poverty, but for others it led to remarkable gains in incomes, at least at the height of the crisis, in 1998. Under these circumstances the average impact of the crisis on farmers has little or no meaning. Moreover, it is vital to consider the full range of outcomes if the effects of agriculture on other sectors of the economy are to be accurately assessed and the shape and speed of the recovery to come accurately predicted.

In the words of Braudel (1979), economic and political crisis always results in a "redistribution of the cards" held by different players. In Indonesia's case this redistribution is dramatically illustrated by the hard-won independence of Timor and by the radical changes in the country's leadership that have now taken place. But redistribution also occurs at the micro-economic level, where it may be less obvious and less highly publicised but just as significant in its implications for the future. Since Braudel wrote, the important part in economic recovery played by small production units by virtue of their flexibility and adaptability has become better known.

Each chapter in this book will, then, tell a different story, describing conditions before the crisis, analysing the impacts of the crisis and outlining a possible future for those involved in each of the sub-sectors we cover. Chapter 1 provides a brief account of Indonesia since independence and a chronology of the crisis years, 1997-99. Chapter 2 is a theoretical analysis of how the international markets for rubber, cocoa and coffee are likely to have been affected by the fall of the rupiah. Chapters 3 to 8 deal in detail with the country's major export commodities—palm oil, timber, cocoa, coffee and rubber—while Chapters 9 to 11 examine the domestic food crop sector. Lastly, in Chapter 12, we summarise our findings and present our overall conclusions.

References

Braudel, F. 1979. *Le temps du monde: Civilisation matérielle, économie et capitalisme, XVe-XVIIIe siècle*, vol. 3. Armand Colin, Paris, France.

Krugman, P. 1994. The Myth of the Asian Miracle. Website: http://www.mit.edu/krugman

World Bank. 1996. Indonesia: Dimensions of Growth. Washington DC, USA.

World Bank. 1998. Indonesia in Crisis: A Macro-economic Update. Washington DC, USA.

Chapter 1

Indonesia's Crisis

Françoise Gérard and François Ruf

Indonesia's crisis was a multiple one, social and political as well as financial and economic. It was also deeper and longer lasting than those of its neighbours. The purpose of this book is to describe how Indonesia's crisis affected its agriculture and to assess the contribution this sector can make to the country's economic recovery. But to do that we must first understand the nature of the crisis and how it unfolded.

For this reason, we provide, in the first section, a brief account of the half century that elapsed between the country's independence in 1946 and the externally triggered currency collapse of mid-1997, focussing on the events and policies that sowed the seeds of future disaster. The second section is a chronology of the crisis years, 1997-99. Here we pay no particular attention to agriculture but are rather concerned with the "contagion phenomena"—how the crisis caught on, spread and was magnified, like one of Indonesia's huge forest fires—and with the enormous scale on which it then did its damage. We also analyse Indonesia's simultaneous political crisis and how that influenced events. Lastly, in the third section, we offer some conclusions.

Indonesia since Independence

Indonesia is an archipelago of more than 13 000 islands. At its core lie Java and its neighbour Bali, known as the inner islands. These account for only 7% of the country's land area, yet are home to 60% of its population. They are its economic powerhouse, producing 63% of GNP. They are also the seat of government. The rest of the islands, including such giants as Irian Jaya, Kalimatan, Sumatra and Sulawesi alongside a multitude of medium-sized and smaller islands, are referred to as the outer islands, which are much less developed. These fundamental inequalities in population densities and levels of development are a source of tensions that undermine the country's unity—tensions that have often been exacerbated by the policy decisions of an authoritarian central government.

Indonesia gained independence from its Dutch colonial masters after the end of the Second World war. From then until 1965, the country was ruled by President Sukarno, the man known as the "father of independence" and who is chiefly credited with building today's nation state. The main priority during these years was national unity. Separatist rebellions in Sumatra, Sulawesi and the Moluccas were suppressed by the army, which began playing a growing part in the political and economic life of the country—a part it still plays today.

In 1960 Sukarno invited the Communist Party, which was growing in popularity, to join the government. Relations with the West deteriorated and the economy fell into decline. On 11-12 March 1966, military commanders under the leadership of General Suharto took over the executive power, in obscured circumstances. The Communist Party was immediately outlawed.

The Suharto government announced the "New Order", marking the start of an obsessive campaign against Indonesians who were supposed to have been members of, or sympathetic to, the Communist Party. Between 400 000 and 1 million people are thought to have died during the purge (Aarsse, 1993; Dorléans, 1992). Thousands fled Jakarta and other major cities of the inner islands, taking refuge in neighbouring southern Sumatra or further afield. Twenty years later, in the mid-1980s, the campaign was still a major force driving policy decisions, including the expulsion of successful coffee farmers from the hills of southern Sumatra to the swampy plains, where they could not but fail to grow any crops at all (see Chapter 11).

In the early period of his rule, from 1966 onwards, Suharto concentrated on exploiting the country's oil resources. Exploration and extraction were encouraged through a massive programme of investment by foreign companies. The regime struck lucky: the 1973 oil price hike came at the right time, just as the country was reaching its full potential for production, at around 65 million tonnes per year. Among the non-Middle East countries, Indonesia is recognised as having profited from the boom more than most others (Losch et al, 1997).

Indonesia did not waste its oil revenues, sensibly deciding to invest at least some of them in developing agriculture. Suharto knew the importance of feeding the country's vast population as a means of ensuring stability and consolidating his power base. Modern irrigation systems in the plains were developed alongside the traditional terraced irrigation systems of the hills. New, short-stemmed rice varieties responsive to inputs were developed and introduced. A floor price set by the Badan Urusan Logistik (BULOG), the government agency responsible for food policy, provided an incentive to farmers. Subsidised fertilisers, introduced in 1971, also helped to increase rice production. These investments ensured that the country experienced a classical Green Revolution, culminating in the achievement of self-sufficiency in rice by 1984.

The islands benefitting most from the Green Revolution were Java and Sulawesi. In Sulawesi, the development of irrigated rice was closely associated with transmigration schemes, whose occupants came mostly from Java and Bali. One of independent Indonesia's first major decisions was to adopt and develop the policy of transmigration. Originally started by the Dutch in 1905 for the purpose of bringing cheap labour to the new rubber and palm oil plantations on the outer islands, the transmigration programme rapidly became, under the new government, the largest resettlement programme ever undertaken by a state, resettling some six million transmigrants over the period 1951-93. The programme's original objective was to redress the strong demographic imbalance between "overcrowded" Java and the "underpopulated" outer islands. Later, the emphasis changed to one of agricultural development of the outer islands and their integration into the Indonesian nation state (Levang, 1997).

Once rice self-sufficiency had been achieved, it was time to diversify into non-oil exports. The regime turned its attention to the manufacturing sector and to intensifying the production of export-oriented tree crops. In manufacturing, plants producing textiles, paper, electrical goods and fertilisers were established. Automobile assembly and ship building were also developed. Attempts to develop tree crops focussed mostly on the outer islands, especially Sumatra and Kalimantan. Here efforts to introduce clonal rubber, launched in the late 1970s, were intensified. Oil palm production on large-scale estates also began receiving massive investment.

Most government investment in tree and other export crops benefitted large-scale producers, often at the expense of smallholders or indigenous forest dwellers. The government introduced the nucleus/plasma concept, in which a central private or public estate and a factory—the nucleus—were established to grow and process a commercial crop such as rubber, oil palm or sugar. The plasma consisted of small family farms, which were then established round the outside of the estate to increase supplies to the factory. These projects were often associated with transmigration schemes, with transmigrants being settled on the new farms.

A few tree crops, including coffee and cocoa, were, however, left entirely in the hands of smallholders. Development of these crops accelerated throughout the 1960s, 1970s and 1980s, as successive waves of migrants colonised and cleared new areas of forest, mainly on the outer islands. Most of the migrants were spontaneous, but a sizeable minority were refugees from failed food crop transmigration schemes.

With the diversification of the 1980s and 1990s came intensive deforestation. More and more land was allocated to logging concessions, estates and transmigration schemes, adding to the pressures exerted by smallholders. Around 1-1.3 million hectares of forest are estimated to have been lost each year during this period (Durand, 1995). The fires used to clear large areas caused widespread smoke pollution—a problem the government attempted to pin on smallholders practising slash-and-burn agriculture. These accusations persisted until satellite imagery established conclusively that the main culprits were large-scale estates and transmigration schemes.

The 1990s were also characterised by a growing inequity in the distribution of the benefits of development. The inequity took two main forms: money and other resources flowed away from the poor into the hands of the president's family and friends; and they flowed away from the less developed outer islands into Java, where the wealthier urban classes began enjoying a high standard of living (Box 1.1). The granting of forest concessions to estates or logging companies was a lucrative source of income for the few. Earmarked for land officially classifed as "empty", the estates often displaced smallholders and forest dwellers, whose traditional land tenure rights were flouted and who were subject to punishment beatings or even murdered if they protested. The estates are the major source of the conflicts over land that plague huge areas of Indonesia today. Many farmers now openly squat on state forest or undeveloped estate land.

Box 1.1 The exploitation of Aceh

The region of Aceh, on the nortwestern tip of Sumatra, lies 1500 kilometres from Jakarta. Its annual per capita income in the pre-crisis years was US$ 500, compared with an average of US$ 1000 for Indonesia as a whole.

In the early 1970s, Acehnese entrepreneurs initiated contacts with overseas investors with a view to exploiting the region's oil and natural gas fields. Jakarta responded by initiating its own contacts, cutting the Acehnese out of the negotiations, a step it took with the backing of the military. Once contracts had been signed and operations were ready to begin, work crews were brought in from Java. Almost no Acehnese were recruited.

The revenue generated by Acehnese oil and gas went into public and private coffers in Jakarta. Aceh received only a standard regional budget, itself determined entirely in Jakarta. Rough calculations suggest that, if the region had received only 50% of the revenue from its oil and gas fields, it would have been able to offer free education and a free health service to its entire population of four million. Instead, these services remain poorly developed. In addition, a vast area of Aceh's 55 390 square kilometres remains inaccessible because of poor infrastructure.

Not surprisingly, Aceh took advantage of the crisis years to make a bid for independence from Indonesia. The region today is characterised by increasing violence as secessionist groups gain in strength and confidence.

Source: Tiwon (1999).

Stories of the greed and corruption of the regime during this period are legion. The president's family and friends owned extensive business interests, through which they amassed fortunes at the expense of ordinary citizens (Box 1.2). Import bans on goods ranging from cars to cloves effectively shielded these interests from competition, allowing their owners to monopolise domestic and export trade. The government's "policy" towards the clove industry provides a classic example of the state's plundering of the country's resources and of the way in which it blighted the lives of ordinary people (Box 1.3). Many banks were part of family conglomerates, to which they provided loans on easy terms, laying the basis for the bank failures of the crisis years. Foreign investors in Indonesia at this time were alleged to have to allow for an extra 20% on top of their normal costs in order to pay the bribes and kick-backs demanded by corrupt politicians, a burden that severely hampered the development of sectors such as mining and manufacturing. It became impossible to start a business in the country without sharing the profits with the president's family. The government's stranglehold over the media meant that, while the rumour machine worked overtime, few of the scandals surrounding the regime ever broke. And the lack of democracy ensured that the regime could not be held to account for its sins.

In the mid-1990s came the first signs of approaching nemesis. Rice self-sufficiency, a real policy success of the 1980s, came to an end in 1994, the victim of a mixture of factors including population growth, a plateau in yields, rising fertiliser prices and lack of attention to farmers' needs, and the speculative seizure of land ripe for urban development. Its passing, little lamented at the time, was symbolic of the contradictions inherent in the Suharto model of development, as people turned increasingly to speculative rather than productive investments. A few voices began warning that Indonesia's economic miracle was not all it seemed. It was too dependent on the one-off consumption of non-renewable assets such as minerals and tropical forests and therefore could not be sustained indefinitely. And it was profoundly inequitable, exploiting cheap labour to enrich the clique of landowners and businessmen surrounding Suharto. But these voices went largely unheeded. As speculative foreign capital poured into the country, the price of land and other assets soared. A surge in imports of rice and coffee from Vietnam demonstrated that Indonesia was losing its competitive edge in the production of basic commodities (Losch et al, 1997). In 1997 came a last-ditch attempt by the regime to clear forests in huge swampy areas of Kalimantan and turn thousands of hectares of peat into green rice fields. Everybody knew that this project was doomed to fail for technical reasons, but nobody dared tell the president.

Box 1.2 Family business

The business interests of President Suharto's children show the extent to which Indonesia's wealth was concentrated in a few hands.

In 1980 Suharto's eldest daughter, Tutut, set up the Citra Lamtoro Gung group, a conglomerate with interests in construction, toll-roads, telecommunications, television broadcasting, the oil industry and banking. By the mid-1990s, this group was valued at around US$ 2 billion. Tutut was also one of the eight presidents of Golkar, Suharto's political party. Suharto's son Bambang Trihatmojo presided over the Bimantara group, thought to be worth around US$ 3 billion. This group was involved in the petrochemical industry, telecommunications and television, banking and the car industry. In 1984 Suharto's youngest son, Tommy, created the Humpuss group, worth around US$ 600 million. This group is active in petrochemicals, airlines, telecommunications, the car and building industries, and toll-roads.

Although they still deny it, the Suharto family is known to have benefitted from preferential treatment from a wide range of national companies, including Garuda, the national airline, and Pertamina, a company which held the monopoly on the importation and distribution of petroleum oil. The favours meted out to the family included discounted prices for goods and services, extensive credit and the awarding of contracts to family companies.

The policies of market liberalisation and privatisation adopted by Indonesia in the early 1980s served as yet more grist to the family mill. Large public concerns, such as PT Telkom, were distributed to the family through the privatisation process.

In about 1995, the citizens of Bali found they were subject to a special tax on beer and other alcoholic drinks. The tax had been instigated by one of Suharto's grandsons, indicating that the third generation was impatient to get its slice of the cake too. In the end the tax was abandoned after the president intervened. Suharto's intervention showed less regard for the law than for the interests of the second-generation Suhartos, who owned the hotels and bars of Bali in which alcohol was consumed.

Box 1.3 **The clove saga**

Indonesians have a taste for clove cigarettes that forms the basis of what should be a flourishing domestic clove industry. The country accounts for 75% of world demand for cloves.

In 1990-91, one of Suharto's sons persuaded his father that clove farmers needed protecting against the price fluctuations to which this commodity became subject after a ban on imports. He was given permission to establish a clove marketing board, the Badan Penyangga dan Pemasaran Cengkeh (BPPC), with a monopoly on domestic trade. In 1991-92, the board cut the producer price of cloves by more than 50% while raising its selling price to cigarette factories. Throughout most of the 1990s, the official producer price remained at a historic low of around Rp 3000 per kilogramme, while the selling price was around Rp 8000 per kilogramme, well above the international price. Thus farmers, factories and the Indonesian consumer were all subsidising the BPPC. In theory, the board was supposed to pay part of its profits into a special fund to support farmers in the future. In practice, it bought luxury cars for a small circle of friends and relations.

Farmers stopped planting new orchards and gave up taking care of their existing trees. Eventually, they could no longer be bothered even to harvest. On the steep slopes of the Toli Toli hills in Central Sulawesi, harvesting, done from wooden ladders, is both precarious and laborious. Now in their fifties, the migrants who had come there in the late 1960s and early 1970s found the work an unappealing way of preparing for their old age and switched to off-farm labour instead. Many farmers began intercropping cocoa between their clove trees. Others abandoned their clove farms altogether and migrated a few dozen kilometres away, where they acquired relatively cheap land on which to plant cocoa. Among the abandoned clove orchards diseases spread, weakening the trees' resistance to the 1997 drought, which decimated the remaining population. Some farmers were so disgusted by the board and its works that they accelerated the natural rate of tree mortality by cutting down their trees. On the once thickly clad slopes of Toli Toli, grey vertical stripes of dead clone trees appeared.

The result of the government's "policy" on cloves was a growing shortage of the product, both domestically and globally. In late 1998, the international price began recovering, rising first to Rp 10 000-12 000 per kilogramme. Farmers felt frustrated. Having sold their ladders and scissors and all the other tools necessary for harvesting and maintenance, they were not prepared to reinvest in them. In July 1999, the price of cloves rocketed to Rp 30 000 per kilogramme, but this was during the low season, when few farmers could harvest. Most remained sceptical, suspecting a trick by middlemen. After a decade of exploitation at the hands of the board, they could not believe that the price of cloves could rise. And even if what they heard were true, they had accumulated too much frustration and rage against the Suharto regime and the marketing system to respond to the rise by returning to cloves. For those who had cut down their trees in disgust in the mid-1990s, it was unthinkable to replant. They perceived the new high prices as a mockery and an attempt to manipulate them like puppets once again. Many are so disgusted that they find it difficult to even talk about cloves. When they do talk, it soon becomes clear that their politics have become radical.

In the El Niño year of 1997, a huge pall of smoke blotted out the sun over large areas of both Indonesia and its neighbours for weeks on end, as a prolonged drought delayed the start of the rains and allowed forest fires to rage out of control. It was a fittingly apocalyptic harbinger of the turmoil that was to come.

From *Krismon* to *Kristal*

Indonesia's crisis began outside the country, with a rapid depreciation of the Thai baht. Through "contagion effects" the run on currencies quickly spread to all Asian financial markets. This early panic soon became known as *krismon* by the Indonesians, an abbreviation of "monetary crisis". The progressive contagion of the financial sector prefigured disturbances throughout the whole economy, all sectors of which were gradually infected one by one over a period of about

9 months. The financial crisis thus became a terrible economic crisis, called kristal (total crisis). It unfolded in five stages, which roughly correspond to the movements of the rupiah against the US dollar over the period July 1997-June 1999.

Until July 1997, the Indonesian rupiah fluctuated around a band of permitted values. It was generally considered to be overvalued, as were other currencies in Southeast Asia (World Bank, 1998a, 1998b). Overvaluation was mainly due to the increasing flow of foreign investment into the country. It penalised domestically produced commodities subject to international trade, especially agricultural products.

July 1997-November 1997: Experts believe the crisis will be short-lived

In July 1997, after other Asian currencies had depreciated sharply, the rupiah's band was first widened (from 8% before the crisis to 12%, on 11 July 1997). Continuing pressure on the currency led to its flotation on 14 August. At this stage, Indonesian monetary authorities were able to act successfully to maintain the value of the rupiah. It was hoped that the psychologically important threshold of Rp 3000 = US$ 1.00 would not be crossed. However, this happened in early October, and on 13 October the Government of Indonesia asked for assistance from the International Monetary Fund (IMF).

By this time, the impact of the crisis on the economy was still limited. Consumer prices had increased, but only moderately, by around 10%. Overall economic growth had halved, but all sectors still exhibited positive growth. However, the banking system and those sectors deeply in debt, such as construction, were badly affected. This led to the first wave of workers being fired.

In the outer islands, the most striking events during this period were huge fires, especially in Sumatra and Kalimantan, where large logging companies and estates are numerous. For the first time, the direct responsibility of these companies for lighting fires was publicly acknowledged by the Ministry of Forestry.

November 1997-February 1998:
The rupiah tips into free fall and the crisis spreads

The crisis deepened with the first package of reforms imposed by the IMF (31 October 1997), which was subject to much criticism inside and outside the country. Along with the usual conditions of tight monetary policy and drastic cuts in public expenditure, the IMF insisted that 16 banks be liquidated. The aim was to show determination in dealing with this financially troubled sector. But the move backfired, leading to monetary panic. Funds were swiftly withdrawn from domestic banks and re-deposited in foreign banks with branches in Indonesia. In this process rupiah were converted into dollars, placing further pressure on the currency.

On 9 December 1997, following President Suharto's cancellation of his trip to a meeting of the Association of South East Asian Nations (ASEAN) on the grounds of ill-health, the rupiah began depreciating much more rapidly than the currencies of other Southeast Asian countries. Its headlong fall reflects the important part played by political instability in the fate of Indonesia during the Asian crisis. In November, the rupiah was trading at about Rp 3500 = US$ 1.00; by mid-December the rate was Rp 6000 = US$ 1.00. The "succession crisis", which is a characteristic of autocratic regimes such as Indonesia's, compounded the financial crisis, leading to considerable uncertainty and adding still further pressure to the rupiah. The failure of the government to adopt credible reforms quickly, coupled with the failure of the private sector to negotiate with international debtors, did nothing to restore confidence. In some other Southeast Asian countries most affected by the crisis, the government fell at an early stage, after financial scandals had been revealed by the press. Political change gave people hope that things would improve. Only in Indonesia, whose political system was tainted by authoritarianism, censorship and violence, did the monetary crisis lead to a major political crisis. Worse was to come...

The budget announced on 6 January 1998, deemed unrealistic by foreign observers and found unacceptable by the IMF, caused strong market reactions. The value of the rupiah immediately plunged to over Rp 9000 = US$ 1.00. As the World Bank (1998a) noted, during this period "Indonesia saw widespread capital flight for the first time." In the first 3 weeks of January the fall continued, reaching

Rp 13 600 = US$ 1.00 and at one point touching Rp 17 000 = US$ 1.00. In mid-January, further negotiations with the IMF led to a budget revision on the basis of Rp 5000 = US$ 1.00, but by 10 February the rupiah was still trading at Rp 10 000 = US$ 1.00.

During the first 6 months of the crisis the inflation rate was still contained at 1-2% monthly[1]. In January 1988, it entered a more harmful phase, rising to 6.88%. By the end of January the year-on rise in the cost of living was about 15%, but by the end of February it was almost 30%, according to Indonesia's Central Bureau of Statistics (CBS). Despite government intervention, food prices rose even faster, pushing down real wages. The lack of credit and the sharp increase in imported good, combined with the slump in domestic demand meant that the economic crisis spread to all sectors of the economy, triggering a steep rise in unemployment. At the same time, the drought of 1997 led to widespread crop failure, resulting in severe food shortages in some areas. As prices rose inexorably, riots and religious or ethnic conflicts broke out in several parts of the archipelago, including Sumbawa, Flores, Sulawesi and Jakarta. The Chinese, who represent only 3.5% of the population but are highly active in the retail sector, were blamed for the price rises and were often the victims of looting. Together with the high interest rates, the frequent rioting and looting increased the risk of trading, forcing shop-keepers to operate on a cash-only basis and to keep stocks low. The resulting inability of the market to function properly hampered the whole economic activity and led to severe shortages of basic commodities.

Economic growth was drastically curtailed. The worst affected sectors were those that had grown strongly in the 5 years before the crisis, namely construction and trade. The manufacturing sector was also badly affected. Agriculture, however, appeared to be an exception. Indeed, the statistics suggest that agriculture was barely affected bythe crisis and was a haven of stability. In the 5 years before the crisis it grew more slowly than all other sectors, registering an increase in GDP of only 1% in the first quarter of 1997. Whereas the GDP of the construction and hotel sectors was 35% and 10% lower in the first quarter of 1998 than in the first quarter of 1997, agricultural GDP actually rose by 2%. However, this aggregate performance masks considerable diversity at the household level.

March-April 1998: Calm before the storm...

The announcement of plans to deal with private-sector debt, new banking sector reforms and a third IMF package worth US$ 43 billion (10 April 1998) calmed the foreign exchange market. Nevertheless, capital flows intensified and interest rates remained exceptionally high. The rupiah was still trading at Rp 7500-8500 = US$ 1.00—three to four times the level of 8 months earlier. Inflation continued to take its toll, standing at 22.95% over the February-April period. External debt was estimated at US$ 140 billion, US$ 74 billion of which was owed by the private sector, half of that being short-term debt (Cayrac-Blanchard, 1998). By way of comparison, the Suharto fortune has been valued at US$ 16 billion, but is much greater than this if family business interests are included (see Box 1.2).

Relationships with international institutions, and particularly with the IMF, remained difficult. The government was reluctant to implement an agreement which implied breaking up monopolies and state enterprises owned by Suharto's relatives. The IMF suspended its second tranche of funding (US$ 3 billion) because this agreement had not been acted on. The World Bank and the Asian Development Bank followed suit. However, the IMF agreed that the government could keep in place its interventions in basic commodity markets, in order to maintain social order.

What began as economic protests became political protests directed against Suharto's regime. Inside the country and outside it, people spoke out against the lack of political freedom, the regime's use of violence and its corruption. Nevertheless and despite his age (he was 76) Suharto was re-elected for the seventh time by the Consultative Assembly (11 March 1998). With the benefit of hindsight, this seems astonishing. But at the time the regime's brutal past record in dealing with its opponents made proposing alternative leaders inconceivable[2]. The sudden realization by the international community of just how illiberal the Suharto regime was, after 30 years of its misrule, played an important part in deepening the Indonesian crisis compared to that of neighbouring countries.

Market liberalisation in agriculture was part of the second IMF plan. Nevertheless, the need to protect the urban poor from sharp increases in the price of staple foods was widely understood from the beginning of Indonesia's crisis, perhaps because of the rising levels of poverty that had resulted from previous experiences of structural adjustment in Africa. The depreciation of the rupiah meant that the price of imported food had by this time risen around threefold. However willing the government was to protect the poor, food price rises were therefore inevitable, since large amounts of expensive rice and other staples had to be imported following the drought. Even so, by April, the domestic price of rice was only 60% of the import parity price (Tabor et al, 1999). Given international prices and the financial difficulties of the government, this was not a sustainable level, despite the special funding provided by the World Bank.

The drought brought food insecurity and hunger to large areas of Irian Jaya, Central Sulawesi, South Moluccas, East Timor and Kalimatan. But where its impact was not so great, agriculture performed relatively well. The crisis made itself felt much more severely in other sectors: in the second quarter of 1998, manufacturing shrank by 13% while services collapsed altogether[3]. Unemployment rose even faster, following the severe contraction of all economic activity. In April 1998, four million jobs were lost in the manufacturing sector alone.

Nine months into the crisis, the last vestiges of optimism about Indonesia's future had been extinguished. It was clear that the country would experience far more difficulty than its neighbours in weathering the storm. The cities were deeply affected. However, the rural areas did seem to provide a ray of hope amidst the gloom. The late and light impact of the crisis on agriculture was due to a number of factors which will be discussed in more detail in subsequent chapters. Essentially, this sector was not in debt when the crisis struck (except in the case of palm oil, see below). It had not participated in the "bubble" of the mid-1990s and so suffered less when the bubble burst.

May-September 1998: Indonesia hits rock-bottom

In May, the political and social crisis intensified. Unrest again broke out, in protest against the absence of political reform and the failure to promise democratic elections. In mid-May Suharto's regime reacted with violence, its army shooting students protesting against price rises in Jakarta. In the following weeks, riots, looting and arson occurred all over the country, especially in Jakarta. Some 1200 people died in the violence. The financial market reacted sharply, the exchange rate plunging from Rp 8000 = US$ 1.00 in early May to over Rp 16 000 = US$ 1.00 in mid-June. This further fall pushed the import parity price of rice up to Rp 4600 per kilogramme. President Suharto resigned at last, on 20 May. However, his designation of Habibie, the former vice-president, as interim president did not resolve matters. Habibie promised free elections before the end of 1999. In early June, discussions with the IMF started up again.

In the third quarter of 1998, the economy plunged even deeper into crisis[4]. Inflation reached 80%. In July, unemployment rose to 15.4 million or 17% of the workforce and was expected to rise to over 20 millions or 22% of the workforce (FAO/WFP, 1998). Riots and looting continued, adding to the international pressures on the rupiah. In Jakarta, the Chinese quarter was almost completely destroyed, leading to shortages of many commodities throughout the country. Continuing depreciation put further pressure on food prices, stretching to breaking point the government's ability to contain price rises. Panic buying became widespread as prices soared during the summer. In September, the price of rice was 230% higher than in the same month in 1996 and well above the import parity price.

The high rate of inflation sharply reduced consumer purchasing power and triggered an alarming rise in the number of families going hungry. Estimates of those below the poverty line (defined as an income of US$ 0.50 per day per person) stood at 100 million (ILO/UNDP, 1998).

In early September 1998, following IMF recommendations, the monopolies held by BULOG on imports of sugar, soybean and wheat flour were revoked and subsidies on these commodities were lifted.

October 1998-December 1999: Towards recovery?

Signs of macro-economic stability at last began to reappear towards the end of 1998 and persisted throughout 1999. The exchange rate became less volatile, with the rupiah fluctuating within a much narrower band, Rp 7400-8000 = US$ 1.00. Inflation slowed down, even turning briefly negative in November 1998. However, real wages fell by a further 20-40% in the manufacturing sector. Towards the end of 1998, in response to renewed protests from 11 to 13 November, the government announced several important reforms and set a date for the 1999 elections[5]. In addition, newspapers were granted more freedom of speech. Unrest, however, continued, and several secessionist movements intensified their activities. Also in late 1998, the government lifted fertiliser subsidies and revoked BULOG's monopoly on rice imports, bringing to long-awaited completion the process of agricultural liberalisation begun in the late 1980s.

According to official statistics, agriculture was the only sector in which jobs were created in 1998[6]. Nevertheless, real agricultural wages continued to fall, reaching a level inadequate to meet basic needs. Agricultural commodities began playing an active part in economic recovery through increased exports, but these were limited by reduced regional demand, reflecting the crisis in other countries. Nevertheless, in September-November 1998, exports were 40% higher in volume terms than their level a year previously, although their value fell slightly.

In the first quarter of 1999, growth in GDP was up by 1.3% over its level a year earlier. However, the economy was still in a state of collapse. In the second quarter, higher petrol and oil prices had a positive effect on the balance of trade. Most investors spent the first half of the year waiting for the election results, then assessing the ability of the new government to deal with the social turmoil unleashed by the crisis.

On 7 June 1999, parliamentary elections gave Indonesians their first taste of democracy after 40 years of autocratic rule. They were able to choose from among 48 political parties, some of them Islamic and others populist groups that pandered to one or more of Indonesia's many ethnic minorities. International observers were sent to guard against electoral fraud. Some irregularities were reported, including unexplained delays in the counting of votes, which postponed the announcement of the final election returns until July. The results showed the success of the Indonesian Democratic Party of Struggle (PDIP), led by the popular Megawati Sukarnoputri, which got 32% of the votes cast. The new parliament met in October and elected a new president the same month.

At last, some good had come of the crisis. In 1999 the restraints placed on the free expression of ideas and dissent were largely lifted and most political detainees were released. However, the tragic events in Timor, which occurred just before the presidential election, were a grim reminder of the power of the army and the fragility of the reform movement as it sought to shake off the legacy of 35 years of dictatorship and corruption.

On 20 October, the moderate Muslim Abdurrahman Wahid ("Gus Dur") was elected Indonesia's new president. He referred to Indonesia's first president, Sukarno, as "the keeper of Indonesian unity" and called Sukarno's daughter, who had stood against him in the election, his "good friend". On the following day, she was elected vice-president, signalling the new leader's desire to heal the country's wounds through consensus politics and the skilful crafting of new alliances. The change of leadership was a major turning point for Indonesia, allowing its 210 million people to live in hope once more. There were also fears, however, especially on the outer islands, including Sulawesi where ex-President Habibie came from. One of the first protest demonstrations against Gus Dur's election occurred in Ujung Pandang, the capital of South Sulawesi, whose people objected to having a Christian vice-president. But this was nothing compared to the tensions in Aceh, at the western edge of the archipelago, or in the Moluccas, in the east, where Muslim migrants are now clashing with indigenous Christians and violence is on the increase.

Despite the new regime's wily handling of the country's problems, it could not greatly alter the basic facts. The 1998 political crisis laid bare the full extent of the problems Indonesia has to overcome before it can recover. These include several secessionist movements, widespread conflicts over land and a near total lack of confidence in the country's institutions.

Conclusions

In conclusion, for Indonesia's farmers the crisis consisted not only of unfavourable weather conditions and sharp fluctuations in prices but the total breakdown of the country's economy, accompanied by mounting insecurity.

Indonesia's many institutional and political shortcomings go a long way towards explaining the scale and depth of the country's crisis, even if they were not its direct cause. Nevertheless, as Stiglitz (1999) has emphasised, it would be wrong to attribute Indonesia's crisis to the faults of the regime alone. An element of hypocrisy has been apparent in the way the international community has responded to the crisis. For 30 years it turned a blind eye to the dark side of Suharto's dictatorship as the price of the economic miracle and the regional stability his rule was thought to be delivering, yet it now lays responsibility for the crisis entirely at the door of the regime and its corruption. Certainly, the crisis took the lid off the tensions that seethed beneath the surface calm hitherto maintained by the regime's iron fist. But the severity of Indonesia's crisis is also explained by overreaction on the part of the international financial markets. Their new volatility, which is associated with the liberalisation and globalisation of the 1990s, is something for which ordinary Indonesians have paid dearly. The crisis therefore raises questions as to what mechanisms can be put in place to regulate these markets.

References

Aarsse, R. 1993. *L'Indonésie*. Karthala, Paris, France.

Cayrac-Blanchard, F. 1998. Faillite fracassante pour la dictature Indonésienne. *Le Monde Diplomatique*, February 1998.

Dorléans, B. 1992. *L'Indonésie: Les incertitudes du décollage économique.* La Documentation Française, Paris, France.

Durand, F. 1994. *Les forêts en Asie du Sud-est: Recul et exploitation: Le cas de l'Indonésie*. L'Harmattan, Paris, France.

FAO/WFP (Food and Agriculture Organization/World Food Programme). 1998. Crop and food supply assessment mission to Indonesia. *Journal of Humanitarian Assistance*. Website: http://www.jha.sps.cam.ac.uk/b/b127.pdf

ILO/UNDP (International Labour Organization/United Nations Development Programme). 1998. Employment Challenges of the Indonesian Economic Crisis. ILO, Jakarta, Indonesia.

Levang, P. 1995. Tanah Sabrang: La transmigration en Indonésie: Permanence d'une politique agraire contrainte. PhD Thesis, Ecole nationale supérieure d'agriculture (ENSA), Institut français de la recherche scientifique pour le développement en coopération (ORSTOM), Montpellier, France.

Losch, B., Laudié, C., Varlet, F., and Ruf, F. 1997. *Politiques publiques et agriculture: Une mise en perspective des cas mexicain, camerounais et indonesien.* Collection Repères, CIRAD, Montpellier, France.

Stiglitz, J.E. 1999. Lessons from East Asia. *Journal of Policy Modelling* 21 (3): 311-380.

Tabor, S.R., Dillon, H.S. and Husein Sawit, M. 1999. Understanding the 1998 food crisis: Supply, demand or policy failure? Paper presented at the International Seminar on the Agricultural Sector during the Turbulence of Economic Crisis: Lessons and Future Directions. Center for Agro-Socioeconomic Research, Agency for Agricultural Research and Development, Ministry of Agriculture, Bogor, Indonesia.

Tiwon, S. 1999. East Timor and the "disintegration of Indonesia". Paper presented at the Berkeley Indonesia Forum, 17 September 1999, Berkeley, California, USA.

World Bank. 1998a. Indonesia in Crisis: A Macro-economic Update. Washington DC, USA.

World Bank. 1998b. East Asia: The Road to Recovery. Washington DC, USA.

Notes

1 However, even this low rate was a threefold increase on pre-crisis levels.

2 On re-election, Suharto acted true to past form by dismissing reformists from his government and appointing Bob Hasan, a timber baron, as the Minister of Industry and Trade, and Tutut, his eldest daughter, as the Minister for Social Affairs.

3 Agricultural GDP contracted by 2% during this period, whereas the building sector shrank by a massive 43%.

4 Year-on GDP fell by 43% in construction, 40% in financial and business services and around 20% each for the hotel/restaurant, transportation and manufacturing sectors, according to the CBS.

5 Among the measures announced were that: new political parties would be allowed seats in parliament, the president and vice-president would be limited to a maximum of a two 5-year terms, parliamentary elections would be held in May or June 1999, all parties meeting the legal requirement to compete in the election would be permitted to do so, parliamentary representation of the military would be reduced, and an independent commission would be established to oversee the elections.

6 The statistics do not include parts of the informal sector, which grew during the crisis.

PART ONE

THE INTERNATIONAL CONTEXT

Chapter 2

International Market Responses to the Asian Crisis for Rubber, Cocoa and Coffee

Kees Burger and Hidde P. Smit

The Asian crisis has many faces. In this chapter we focus on the effects of the crisis on Indonesia's position in the world markets for natural rubber, cocoa and coffee. Especially for natural rubber and to some extent for cocoa and coffee, US dollar prices have become very low recently. A weakening of demand may have been a factor in some cases, notably cocoa. But there has certainly not been a collapse in world demand. The consumption of natural rubber, for example, grew by almost 2% in 1998.

We therefore need to look at the supply side for an explanation. Since the major factor implicated on the supply side is what has happened to exchange rates, their movements are examined first, in the first section. This is followed by a theoretical discussion of how commodity markets are likely to have been affected by these movements. We then examine national and regional supplies of the three commodities, in the third, fourth, and fifth sections. The last section gives our conclusions. Unless indicated otherwise, all the data we have used are from the Monthly Commodity Price Bulletin of the United Nations Conference on Trade and Development (UNCTAD).

Exchange Rate Movements

Figure 2.1 shows exchange rate movements for the three major Southeast Asian currencies affected by the crisis—the Indonesian rupiah, the Thai baht and the Malaysian ringgit—over the period 1997-98.

Thailand stopped supporting the baht on 1 July 1997. The baht then fell against the US dollar and the other currencies, and the ringgit and rupiah closely followed it. For Indonesia, one of the worst months of the crisis was December 1997, when the rupiah went into free fall. During the first quarter of 1998 the three currencies appreciated, after which the baht and the ringgit remained relatively stable and close to one another in value. The rupiah, in contrast, remained extremely volatile, with relative stability achieved only in the last quarter of 1998.

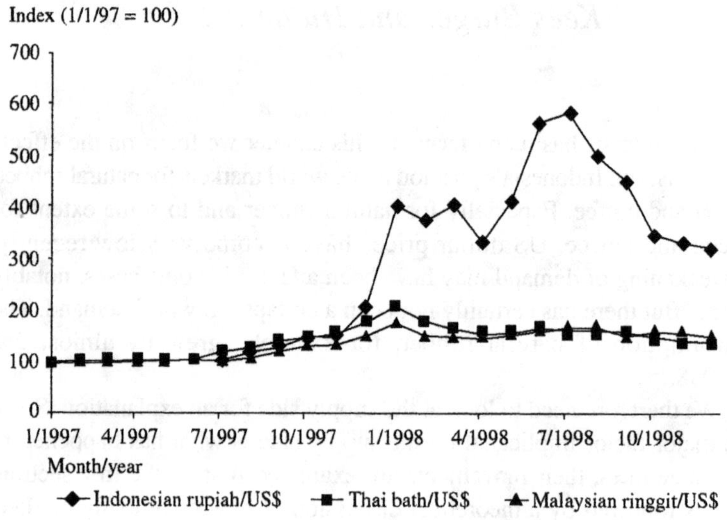

Figure 2.1 Exchange rate movements of three Southeast Asian currencies, 1997-98

Theoretical Effect on World Market Prices

Theoretically, the immediate impact of a fall in a country's currency is to make exports more profitable and imports less so. The standard analysis does not cover the effects that exchange rate movements might have on world market prices. Some global commodity markets are significantly affected by Indonesian supplies, so we cannot simply ignore this possible effect, especially since the devaluation of the rupiah coincided with changes in the rates of the baht and the ringgit, whose countries export some of the same commodities. What this means in theoretical terms is explained below. The relevant graphs and mathematical details can be found in Burger and Smit (1999a), whose analysis can be used as a tool to estimate the past or the possible future effect of currency devaluations on world commodity prices.

A fall in the rupiah against the US dollar means that Indonesian producers receive more money in rupiahs if the world price is expressed in US dollars. The first factor that matters is how producers react to this increase in the local price. The parameter describing this reaction is called supply elasticity. Suppose, for example, that the rupiah devalues by 10%. Local producers would initially receive 10% more for their commodity. If the supply elasticity is 0.3, this means that they would supply 0.3 x 10% more, so supply from Indonesia would initially rise by 3%.

This increase would then have a negative effect on world prices in US dollars. The next question is: at what price would the market return to equilibrium? This depends on consumers' reactions. Here what is known as demand elasticity plays a role. If the price in US dollars falls by 25% and demand elasticity is -0.2, this means that demand will increase by 0.2 x 25%, or 5%. We assume for present purposes that all consumers are aggregated; in other words, all have the same demand elasticity.

However, there are other suppliers apart from Indonesia. Another factor that affects how the world market reacts is therefore Indonesia's share in world supply. Obviously, the effect of an increase in Indonesian supply on the world market price will be stronger if Indonesia's share is larger.

Yet another factor is that Thailand and Malaysia saw their currency depreciate at the same time as Indonesia. The analysis should therefore include the effect of any potential increases in supplies coming from them. So, in the analysis we distinguish Indonesian supply, supplies from other parts of the region (Thailand, Malaysia and the Philippines) and supplies from outside the region. These data enable us to calculate the balance of supply and demand. Some algebraic manipulation leads to a fairly straightforward expression in which the change in the world market price in US dollars is expressed in terms of:

- The shares of each region in world supply
- The supply elasticities for the various regions, and
- The demand elasticity for the world.

Thus, for example, when only the Indonesian exchange rate doubles, all elasticities are 0.2, the share of Indonesia is 25% and that of the rest of the region is 50%, it can be calculated that the world market price goes down by about 8%.

Actual exchange rate changes are shown in Table 2.1. Taking 1997, first quarter as basis, the changes in each of the currencies by the end of 1998 amount to 230% for the rupiah, 45% for the baht and 60% for the ringgit.

Table 2.1 Local currencies per US$ (first quarter 1997 = 1.00)

Quarter	*Rupiah*	*Baht*	*Ringgit*
1997-I	1.00	1.00	1.00
1997-II	1.01	1.00	1.01
1997-III	1.16	1.28	1.12
1997-IV	1.67	1.57	1.40
1998-I	3.93	1.82	1.61
1998-II	4.35	1.56	1.55
1998-III	5.10	1.59	1.63
1998- IV	3.31	1.43	1.58

What actually happened in the cases of natural rubber, cocoa and coffee is discussed in detail in the following sections. The elasticities used in these sections are either our own estimates or estimates based on elasticities published by others.

Natural Rubber

Indonesia has produced natural rubber ever since this commodity reached the country. On 30 August 1876, 18 of the seedlings that Henry Wickham had brought from Brazil to Kew Gardens in London were shipped to the Botanical Garden in Bogor (Baulkwill, 1989). The crop spread first to Java, later to Sumatra, and by 1910 some

245 000 hectares were being cultivated. Research in Indonesia during the early decades of the twentieth century led to the development of bud-grafting, a technique that greatly raised productivity. At that time rubber was largely an estate crop. Smallholders grew only some 8100 hectares in 1914 (Baulkwill, 1989), but their share in total area cultivated expanded rapidly in later years. By 1940, a national tree count in what was then the Netherlands' East Indies came to a provisional figure of 1.3 million hectares for smallholdings (MacFadyean, 1944), an area roughly equal to what was thought until then to be the total area under rubber. The estate area at that time stood at 0.6 million hectares.

The smallholder sector has gained still further in importance since then. Figures for 1990 indicate that 2.6 million hectares of rubber are believed to be grown on smallholdings, while around 0.5 million hectares are on estates. However, the figures for smallholdings are highly unreliable. The traditional smallholder sector is described as inefficient, producing low yields and taking no advantage either of technical innovations or of advice as to planting densities and tapping practices. The sector is, however, thought to be quite responsive to prices. Rubber is often interplanted with other crops and, if not well managed, tends to be overgrown by secondary forest or weeds once the other crops have been harvested. What actually is rubber area is therefore difficult to define, complicating the already difficult task of collecting accurate statistics.

In the late 1970s, the government launched comprehensive programmes for the resettlement of many farmers on outer islands and the rehabilitation of their old rubber land. The resettlement programmes include the Nucleus Estate Scheme or Perkebunan Inti Rakyat (NES/PIR), which settles formerly landless transmigrants close to a nucleus estate that provides them with guidelines on how to grow and tap rubber and purchases their latex, paying a price net of any outstanding credit. The Smallholder Rehabilitation and Development Programme (SRDP) is directed at rubber smallholders and provides them with advice, clonal planting materials, fertiliser and credit. Farmers in both these programmes should be distinguished from traditional growers, as their yields are higher and their management is more intensive. However, an increasing number of traditional growers are adopting clonal planting materials.

Indonesian rubber growers compete in the world market with producers from Thailand, Malaysia and several other countries. Until 1990, Malaysia was the world's major producer. Since then, Thailand has taken the lead, while Indonesia has maintained second place. Together the three countries produce about three-quarters of world supplies. Malaysia's loss of the lead can be ascribed to industrialisation. Over time, labour productivity in the manufacturing and services sectors has improved and wages have gone up by more than in the primary natural rubber sector. This has happened despite the sizeable yield gains made possible by the development and dissemination of improved rubber clones. The gradual drift of workers away from the sector, often coinciding with the ageing of the trees and of the farmers themselves, contributed to a fall in production of some 30% in the period 1990-98. It was predicted that Thailand would follow suit, as its agricultural wages soared in the 1990s (Burger and Smit, 1995). Indeed, many farmers in the south of Thailand complained about the shortage of hired tappers. The cost of production rose and, with the Thai baht strengthening against the US dollar, the profitability of rubber cultivation came under increasing pressure. However, the outcome in Thailand was different to that in Malaysia. Thai farmers voiced their discontent and were heard in Bangkok, where the government released funds to support the local price of rubber. This intervention made the government unhappy with the performance of the international stabilisation fund, a mechanism that had been set up by the International Natural Rubber Organisation (INRO) to support world market prices when they were low. Unfortunately, the agreement on which the mechanism is based has no provisions for interventions made necessary by movements in exchange rates.

When, on 1 July 1997, Thailand announced its decision to stop supporting the baht, with the immediate result that it fell by 10% against the US dollar, it did not take more than a day for the international rubber market to react. On 2 July, the US dollar price fell by exactly the same amount. And when the Malaysian and Indonesian currencies followed the Thai devaluation some months later, US dollar prices were again adjusted downwards.

The region's currency devaluations thus had two unfortunate corollaries. One was that, even in the very first country to devaluate, Thailand, farmers did not benefit at all from the devaluation, as their

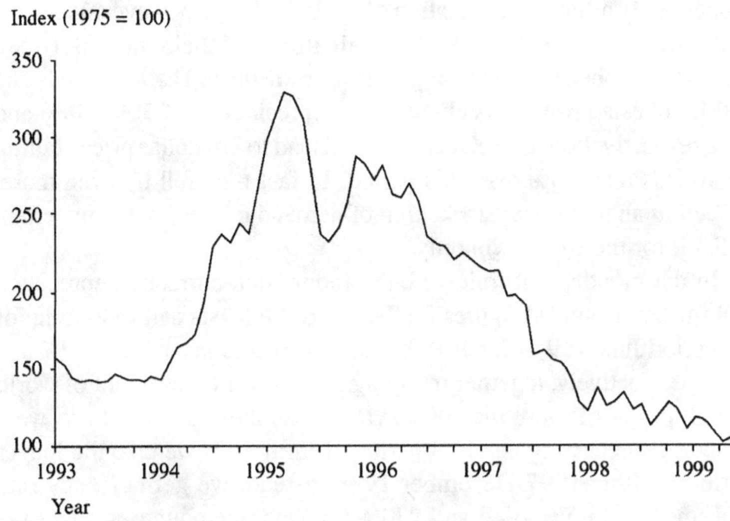

Figure 2.2 World natural rubber prices (US$), 1993-99

selling prices in baht remained virtually unchanged for several months and even fell in the longer term. The other was that the INRO was unable to intervene in the market, because its reference price was expressed in the average currencies of Malaysia and Singapore and therefore did not decline when the US dollar price fell.

Figure 2.2 shows the trend in natural rubber prices during the 1990s. The differences between the various grades have been eliminated, as they cancel each other out in the long run. The slide in prices during 1997 is clearly observable, especially during the first half of the year. Prices then bottom out at a level much lower than in previous cyclical troughs. If the trend had been in line with past troughs, we would have expected a low of 175 in the index value.

The formula discussed above helps understand how this price response came about. Initially, it was assumed that Thailand would devaluate the baht without other countries following suit. Given demand elasticity of 0.05, supply elasticity of 0.2 in Thailand and the region and of 0.1 elsewhere, a depreciation of 25% in the baht and a Thai share in the world market of 30%, world market prices should have come down by around 9% in US dollar terms—close to what actually happened immediately after the devaluation of the baht. Soon, however, Malaysia and Indonesia responded with devaluations of their own. Between June and October 1997, exchange rate movements in Thailand, Malaysia and Indonesia brought local currency depreciations of 50%, 30% and 20% respectively. These changes should lead to US dollar prices falling by no less than 23% over this period. In fact they fell by even more, reflecting an additional slackening of demand caused by the uncertain outlook for the world economy.

In the months that followed, the Indonesian currency depreciated still further. Rounded figures for Thailand, Malaysia and Indonesia for the period June 1997-March 1998 show depreciations of 80%, 60% and 300% respectively, together implying a downward movement of world market prices of more than 40%. Of course, these depreciations were temporary, occurring amidst a period of turmoil. If we take the longer period of June 1997-December 1998 instead, we get currency rate movements of 45%, 60% and 230% for the three countries. Over the same period, the world market price of natural rubber in US dollars fell by 36%. This implies that Malaysian producers are facing more or less unchanged prices in local currency (0.64 x 1.6), while Thai farmers have seen prices fall by 10% (0.64 x 1.45) and Indonesian farmers should have experienced a doubling of local prices (0.64 x 3.30).

However, in Indonesia the rapid adjustments made in the rupiah prices of agricultural inputs and other goods used by farmers soon eroded this gain. The initial lack of change in Malaysian prices meant that INRO could not intervene in the market, as the prices in its reference currency did not fall into the "Amay-buy" zone. They did so only later, in 1998, when the Malaysian currency was fixed at RM 3.8 = US$ 1.00. But by this time Malaysia had announced her withdrawal from INRO. Thailand later followed suit. In October 1999, INRO decided to terminate the agreement.

Figure 2.3 compares actual local Indonesian rubber prices with theoretical local prices derived from changes in world market prices and official exchange rates (shown as "world market"). The local prices used here are taken from the website of Indonesia's Ministry of Agriculture. The figure shows that local prices did eventually reflect world market prices, but after some delay. Budiman (1998) reports similar but more consistent changes in prices. His findings are that local prices tripled over the period to September 1998. But so did the

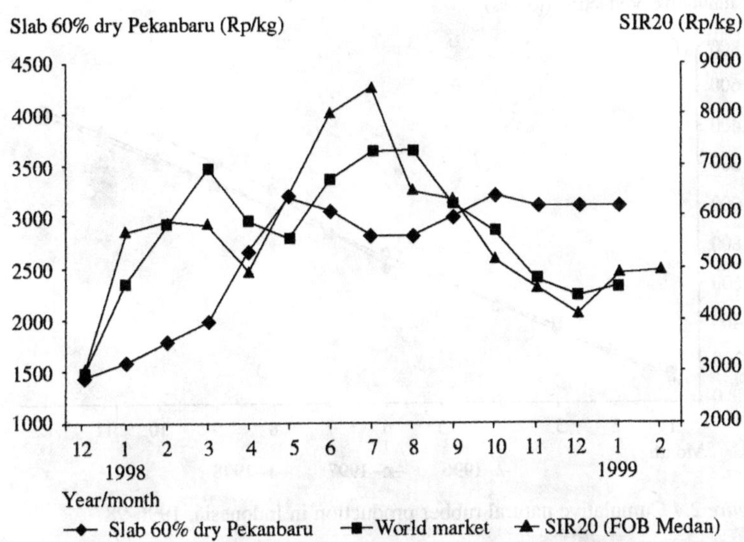

Figure 2.3 Actual and theoretical local prices of natural rubber in Indonesia, 1998

price of rice! In Chapter 8 more evidence will be provided to show that the crisis has equally affected the prices of inputs used by rubber growers. In addition, processing costs have increased in rupiah terms, due to higher nominal wages, higher costs of imported inputs and—an interesting corollary of the crisis—the scarcity of containers.

Figure 2.4 shows the impact of these price changes on domestic supplies, to the extent that this can be measured from the statistics currently available. The supply response is observable in the production figures for the second half of 1998. The response came somewhat late, as world market prices in rupiah terms had shot up since January. The delay can be attributed to the fact that middlemen were slow to transfer a share of the high export prices back to local producers. For slabs, the form in which smallholders most commonly sell rubber, prices reached their highest levels only in May 1998. Some time-lag is to be expected, as production can be recorded only some time after crude latex has been tapped. Not too much weight should be attached to these data, however, as Indonesian production statistics are notoriously unreliable.

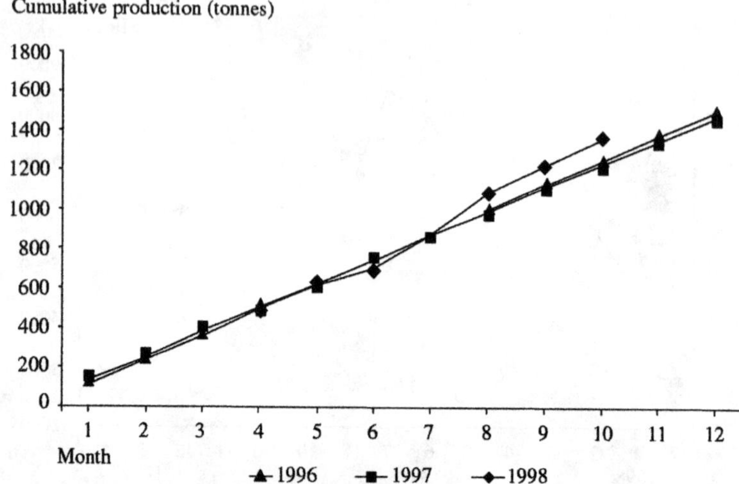

Figure 2.4 Cumulative natural rubber production in Indonesia, 1996-98

Exporters may have responded more promptly than smallholders. Figure 2.5 shows a decisive shift towards exports, away from selling into the domestic market. This reflects an immediate response by stockholders as well as an overall response to slackening domestic demand.

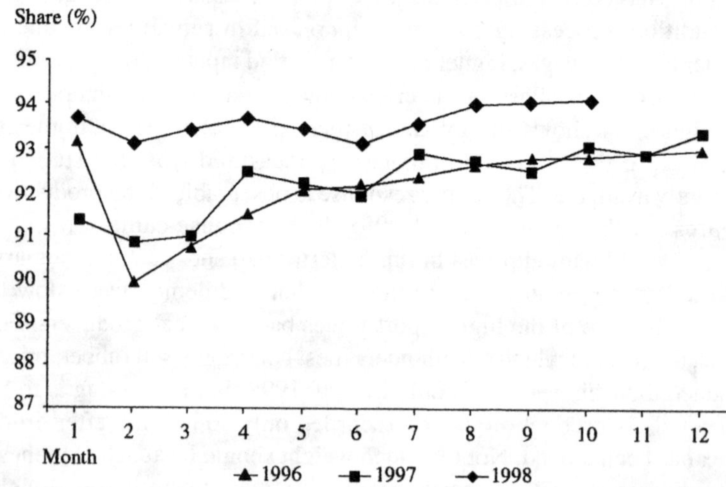

Figure 2.5 Share of natural rubber exports in total production in Indonesia, 1996-98

The impact of the Southeast Asian crisis on the world market for natural rubber has, then, been substantial. Not only did the crisis spell the end of the last of the international commodity agreements that actually meant something for the market, but it also established Indonesia as the region's most competitive future supplier of natural rubber.

Cocoa

Cocoa growing in Southeast Asia dates back to the seventeenth century, when the Spanish introduced the crop to the Philippines. Production in Indonesia is mentioned as early as 1778, when a prize was announced for the first successful cocoa plantation (Toxopeus and Wessel, 1983), so the crop must have been introduced there much earlier (Durand, 1995). For the next 200 years, diseases, notably the cocoa pod borer, considerably constrained production, which began rising again only in the 1970s. It was during this decade that the large-scale expansion of production in Sulawesi took place. Forest land was converted into cocoa land by farmers, who benefitted by the Malaysian example, which they learned about either through social networks or through direct experience of working there. Other factors promoting production for export were the devaluation of the rupiah and the availability of subsidised fertiliser (Ruf et al, 1995). Indonesian production increased from under 2000 tonnes in 1970 to over 300 000 tonnes in 1995. Most Indonesian cocoa comes from Sulawesi, but North Sumatra and East Java are also important producers. Smallholders generate more than three-quarters of total production. Their yields are generally quite high and use of modern inputs such as fertilisers and pesticides is widespread. The Indonesian Government subsidised these inputs until shortly before the crisis.

Indonesia's share in world production is still only 11%, but is rising rapidly (it was 2% in 1985). The world's major producer is still Côte d'Ivoire, which accounts for some 40% of world production, followed by Ghana with 15%. Although Malaysia served as the example for Indonesian cocoa production, its production has fallen, from nearly 250 000 tonnes in 1989 to 150 000 tonnes in 1995 and around 80 000 tonnes in 1998. The reason most often cited for this decline is the conversion of cocoa land to oil palm, which has become more

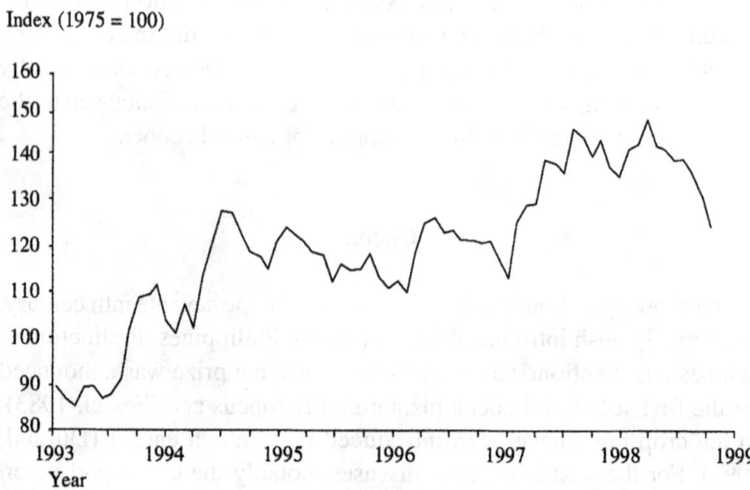

Figure 2.6 World cocoa prices (US$), 1993-98

profitable because it requires less labour at a time when wages have been rising rapidly. Figure 2.6 shows how cocoa prices have moved in the recent past.

Prices do not appear to have fallen during the early stages of the Asian crisis (mid-1997). Indeed, they rose during this period. Some downward pressure on prices should nevertheless be expected, even if only at a later stage, since Malaysia and Indonesia together account for 20% of the global market. To calculate the theoretical impact, we employ the formula used earlier, with a demand elasticity of -0.175, a world supply elasticity of 0.3 and a regional supply elasticity (Indonesia and Malaysia) of 0.5. These elasticities are taken from Burger (1996) and Burger and Smit (1999b) and are comparable to those used by the International Cocoa Organization (ICCO, 1993). The theoretical impact of exchange rate movements on world cocoa prices would then be a fall of around 15%. Recent prices do indeed show such a trend. In mid-1998 they stood at around US$ 1500 per tonne, but by March 1999 they had fallen to below US$ 1200 per tonne. This decrease of over 20% can thus be attributed largely to the Asian crisis.

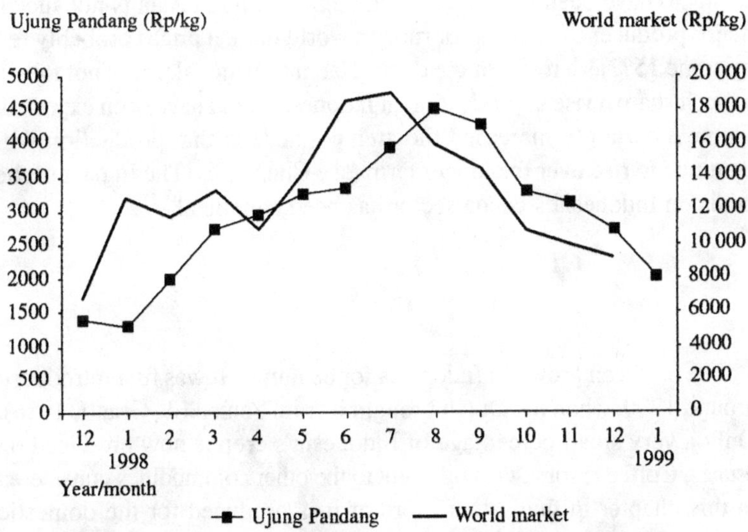

Figure 2.7 Actual and theoretical local prices of cocoa in Indonesia, 1998

Prices within Indonesia (Fintrac, website) have followed world market prices and exchange rate movements without much of a time-lag—no more than 1 month (Figure 2.7). Prices rose until around mid-1998, when they were three to four times higher than a year earlier.

World market prices seem to have moved in such a way as to take Indonesian supply responses into account. Is there evidence of local responses to the short-term rise in domestic prices? The answer is, only some. The total area planted to cocoa is estimated to have risen from 420 000 hectares in 1997 to 467 000 hectares in 1998, while total production is also estimated to have risen slightly, from 305 000 tonnes in 1997 to 307 080 tonnes in 1998. A further increase was expected in 1999, according to the US Department of Agriculture (USDA, website) and indeed occurred (see Chapter 5). In considering these figures it should be noted that Indonesian production suffered from a drought in early 1998. In addition, some diversion of cocoa from the local to the international market probably added to the increase in exports. On a world scale this effect is, however, likely to be small.

To sum up, the impact of the Asian crisis on world cocoa prices seems to have been substantial. Although Southeast Asia is not such a major producer of cocoa as of rubber, world market prices probably fell by some 15% as a result of the crisis. Had international prices not fallen, a much sharper rise in production in Indonesia could have been expected. Farmers certainly increased the area planted, so that production will continue to rise over the longer term (see Chapter 5). The impact of the crisis on Indonesia's cocoa sector has been beneficial.

Coffee

Coffee has been grown in Indonesia for centuries. It was first introduced around 1700, when the Dutch brought it from Yemen (de Graaff, 1986). Only a very small percentage of Indonesia's crop is now produced on estates. Coffee is somewhat different to the other commodities considered in this chapter in that rather more of it is produced for the domestic market. In the early 1970s domestic consumption was about 40% of total production, according to statistics produced by the Directorate General for Estate Crops (DGE). Intensive efforts were then made to increase production, which doubled to around 300 000 tonnes per year by the early 1980s. A similar increase was achieved in the early 1990s, raising production to an all-time high of around 450 000 tonnes per year. Since then it has hovered around 7 million bags or 420 000 tonnes per year. As a result, domestic consumption, which has grown only slowly, now accounts for only 20% of production.

World production is distributed over many countries. The two largest producers are Brazil (25-30%) and Colombia (10-15%). Indonesia is now the third largest, providing around 7% of world production in 1997-98. Vietnam's production is growing rapidly, approaching that of Indonesia. There are numerous medium-sized producers (in the 2-5 million bags range), including Mexico, Guatemala, Honduras, Costa Rica, Nicaragua, India, Côte d'Ivoire, Uganda and Ethiopia. Production in Thailand and Malaysia is negligible from a global perspective. Weather is a major factor behind fluctuations in production.

The 1996-97 season saw a peak in Indonesian production, which rose to 7.9 million bags, an increase of 35% over the previous year. This was followed by a fall to 7.2 million bags in 1997-98, caused by

El Niño. In the 1998-99 season, production declined still further to some 6.8 million bags, again because of adverse weather conditions. Production has thus fallen by 15% over a 2-year period. The depreciation of the rupiah should more than compensate for this fall. However, world production is estimated to have reached a record of 107 million bags in 1998-99, an increase of 9% over the previous year, and this has allowed world prices to decline.

Given the small share of Indonesia, Thailand and Malaysia in the world market, the devaluation of their currencies cannot be expected to have had a sizeable effect on world prices, especially since Indonesian supplies have actually fallen since devaluation. Using the formula as before and assuming elasticities of demand and supply of 0.3 and around 0.15 respectively (Akiyama and Varangis, 1990), we calculate a decline in prices of only 2.5%. In fact, no effect at all can be discerned in Figures 2.8 and 2.9, which show world and domestic coffee prices during the 1990s. If the fall in the rupiah had had a depressing effect on prices, this should have started showing up by late 1997. Instead, the world market index converted into rupiah rose dramatically in January 1998. The overall decline in world market prices may have

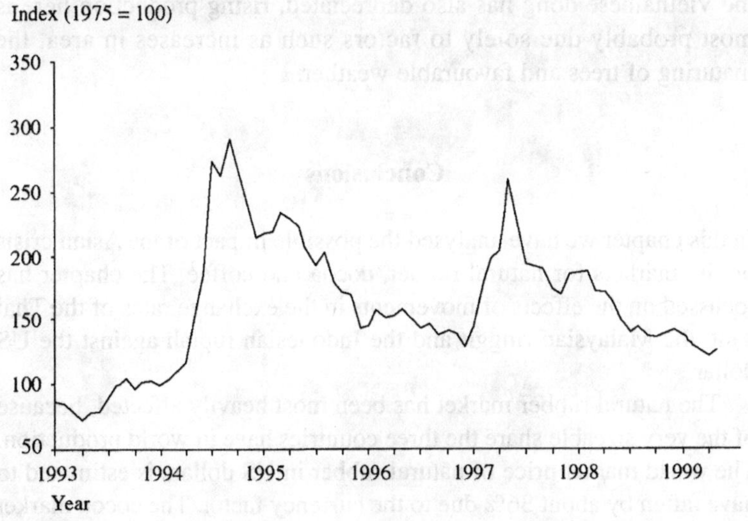

Figure 2.8 World coffee prices (US$), 1993-99

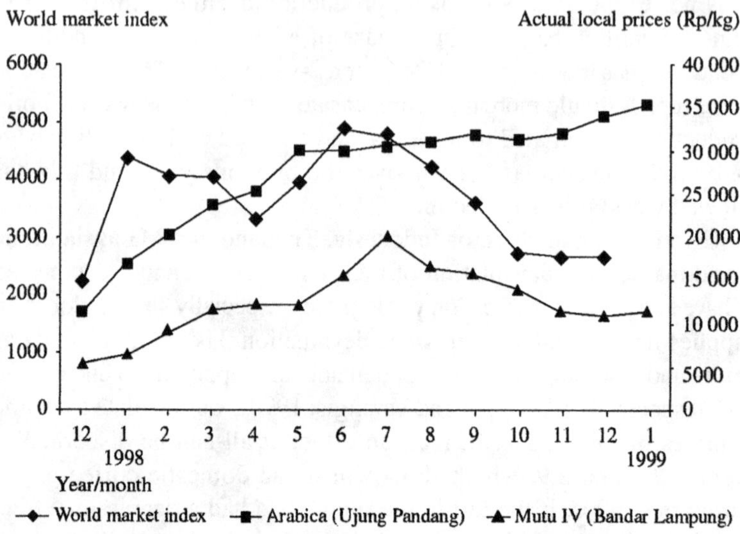

Figure 2.9 Actual and theoretical local prices of coffee in Indonesia, 1998

been partly influenced by the surge in production in Vietnam. Although the Vietnamese dong has also depreciated, rising production here is most probably due solely to factors such as increases in area, the maturing of trees and favourable weather.

Conclusions

In this chapter we have analysed the possible impact of the Asian crisis on the markets for natural rubber, cocoa and coffee. The chapter has focussed on the effects of movements in the exchange rates of the Thai baht, the Malaysian ringgit and the Indonesian rupiah against the US dollar.

The natural rubber market has been most heavily affected, because of the very sizeable share the three countries have in world production. The world market price of natural rubber in US dollars is estimated to have fallen by about 36% due to the currency factor. The cocoa market has also been affected, but not as heavily because the three countries provide a much smaller share of world production, some 20%, leading to a decline in world market prices of around 15%. The case of coffee is quite different. Indonesia provides only around 7% of global supplies, while other countries in the region provide negligible amounts. In addition, production has fallen in recent years owing to adverse weather conditions. No significant effect on world prices can therefore be expected.

References

Akiyama, T. and Varangis, P. 1990. The impact of the International Coffee Agreement on producing countries. *World Bank Economic Review* 4 (2): 157-173.

Baulkwill, W.J. 1989. The history of natural rubber production. In: Webster, C.C. and Baulkwill, W.J. (eds), *Rubber*. Tropical Agriculture Series. Longman, London, UK.

Budiman, A.F.S. 1998. The rubber industry of Indonesia amidst the current economic crisis. Paper presented at the International Rubber Forum, 38th Assembly of the International Rubber Study Group (IRSG), 28-29 October 1998, Bali, Indonesia.

Burger, K. 1996. The European Chocolate Market and the Effects of the Proposed EU Directive. Economic and Social Institute, Free University of Amsterdam, the Netherlands.

Burger, K. and Smit, H.P. 1995. Smallholders and their interest in future natural rubber production. Paper presented at the International Rubber Forum, 36th Assembly of the International Rubber Study Group (IRSG), 27 February-3 March 1995, Tokyo, Japan.

Burger, K. and Smit, H.P. 1999a. Exchange Rate Devaluation and Commodity Price Developments: Indonesian Rubber, Cocoa and Coffee. Economic and Social Institute, Free University of Amsterdam, the Netherlands.

Burger, K. and Smit, H.P. 1999b. Modelling and Forecasting the Market for Cocoa and Chocolate: Supply of Cocoa. Background paper No. 1, Economic and Social Institute, Free University of Amsterdam, the Netherlands.

de Graaff, J. 1986. *The Economics of Coffee*. Pudoc. Wageningen Agricultural University, the Netherlands.

Durand, F. 1995. Farmer strategies and agricultural development: The choice of cocoa in eastern Indonesia. In: Ruf, F. and Siswoputranto, P.S. (eds), *Cocoa Cycles: The Economics of Cocoa Supply*. Woodhead, Cambridge, UK.

Fintrac. Website: http://www.fintrac.com/indoag/prices

ICCO (International Cocoa Organization). 1993. The World Cocoa Market: An Analysis of Recent Trends and of Prospects to the Year 2000. London, UK.

MacFadyean, A. 1944. *The History of Rubber Regulation 1934-1943*. Allen and Unwin, London, UK.

Ruf, F., Jamaluddin, Yoddang and Waris Ardhy. 1995. The "spectacular" efficiency of cocoa smallholders in Sulawesi: Why? Until when? In: Ruf, F. and Siswoputranto, P.S. *Cocoa Cycles: The Economics of Cocoa Supply*. Woodhead, Cambridge, UK.

Toxopeus, H. and Wessel, P.C. 1983. Cocoa Research in Indonesia, 1900-1950. American Cocoa Research Institute, Washington DC, USA.

USDA (United States Department of Agriculture). Website: http://www.fas.usda.gov/htp/ tropical

Chapter 3

Palm Oil and the Crisis: A Macro View

Tancrède Voituriez

Exchange rates movements in 1997-98, together with rising interest rates, had an impact on both the world market and the Indonesian domestic market for palm oil. The effects on the world market were transitory. The domestic market, however, suffered serious disruption that continues to this day.

Three essential features should be borne in mind when considering the *krismon* and its impact on palm oil markets. The first, discussed in further detail in the section entitled "Substitution of Oils and Fats", is the exchangeability of oils and fats in world industry. At least 17 oils and fats are commonly traded in the world. Substitutions in the industrial processes they enter as inputs—for the making of soap, margarine and confectionery or the cooking of fast foods, for example—allow consumers to switch between many different oils depending on their relative prices. Substitution has neutralised the depressing effect on world prices that might have been expected from currency devaluations in the major palm oil exporting countries, Malaysia and Indonesia. This neutralising effect occurs because world demand turns to a particular oil as long as its prices are attractive. A sudden upsurge in supply can, therefore, be absorbed. The main household process for which oils and fats are used is, of course, cooking. Substitution is also possible here, provided alternatives are available to individual consumers in the domestic market. Indonesian households, however, are highly dependent on palm oil for cooking, and in their case there is no available substitute. As a result, domestic palm oil prices soared during the *krismon*.

The second essential feature, discussed in Section "Demand-driver Market", is the unprecedented part played by Chinese and Indian demand in the growth of palm oil trade over the past decade. During the 1990s Asian markets were in transition, with consumers turning away from traditional food grains towards the consumption of other commodities, among them oils and fats. China and India did not devalue their currencies during the Southeast Asian crisis. Their purchasing power was thus left intact, whereas that of Indonesia was halved. In response, Indonesian palm oil producers diverted their produce towards other Asian countries and away from the domestic market. In so doing they exacerbated the already sharp rise in prices at home, with the result that millions of Indonesian households were unable to meet their most basic needs.

The third feature, the subject of Section "Price Volatility", is the volatile nature of palm oil prices on both world and domestic markets. Here too, the severe consequences for Indonesia, as it grappled with the *krismon*, form a contrast with the effects elsewhere. The world has the benefit of a futures market, established in Kuala Lumpur, Malaysia, where palm oil can be bought or sold at a fixed price months before delivery. This market possesses professional and competitive traders who, thanks to standard contracts and an enforcement mechanism (a clearing house), are for the most part able to cope with erratic and unpredictable movements in prices. In contrast, the Indonesian domestic market has a strongly integrated distribution chain, is burdened with an oligopoly in oil processing and selling and suffers from an absolute lack of transparency in price setting. It lacks the solid institutions, either private or public, that would allow buyers and sellers to limit their risks and the losses they incur through price fluctuations.

All three of these features suggest that the effects of the *krismon* on palm oil prices will be felt most strongly in the Indonesian domestic market. As will be shown in Section "Reponses to the Crisis", the widespread insolvency of consumers in this market, together with its illiberal distribution system, encouraged palm oil traders to divert supplies towards the export market, sometimes illegally. Section "Production Costs" concludes the analysis by shedding light on palm oil production costs. The crisis had an uneven impact on domestic production and consumption. In contrast with the devastating effect on domestic demand, production actually benefitted, owing to the persistence of relatively low production costs. In the current context of market liberalisation, the domestic effects of all three features of the palm oil market require a somewhat unfashionable remedy. Targeted public spending seems necessary to revive the domestic market that the crisis so effectively crushed.

Substitution of Oils and Fats

The mechanics of substitution provide a key to understanding price behaviour in the world market for oils and fats. In this market, seven oils account for 90% of production and 95% of trade. These oils are soybean, palm, rapeseed, sunflower, groundnut, coconut and palm kernel. At present, palm oil leads the field in volume terms in the world vegetable oil trade.

Crude vegetable oils display different chemical properties which distinguish their taste, physical state and use. They are generally divided into two distinct groups, the liquid oils—mainly soybean, rapeseed, sunflower, groundnut and olive—and the solid ones, including coconut and palm. Liquid oils are also broadly defined as food oils, only 10% of production being used in the non-food sector. So-called solid oils, which are really solid only in temperate climates, are used largely for non-food purposes, which account for approximately 40% of the world market. Palm oil is an intermediate product which should really be described as semi-solid, but which is generally classed among the solid oils and is used as such in the countries of the North.

The consistency of an oil determines its use. Liquid oils are preferred for direct consumption as table oils. Solid oils are used mainly in the food industry, for example in the manufacture of margarine, and also to make soaps and surfactants. The substitution of vegetable oils which reside in the same group, for example soybean oil for sunflower oil, is becoming increasingly common, having a lead over substitution between oils in different groups. However, processing techniques such as hydrogenation can be used to "harden" oil, allowing a naturally liquid oil to compete with a solid one. This process increases the competition faced by almost all oils, whether liquid or solid, in the world market. The world oils and fats market is still regarded as highly competitive by companies and traders. Its many products and the potential for substitution ensure that no single exporting country can be a "price maker".

The main uses of palm oil in the food sector are as:

- Cooking oil. In tropical countries, locally produced palm oil is used, without prior processing or the addition of other oils, for household cooking. When imported, it is usually blended with other local vegetable oils.
- Deep frying oil. Palm oil is used in the manufacture of food items for the catering industry, usually fried food such as rice, noodles and chips. It is blended with other frying oils in both Europe and Asia, but is also used unblended in Asia. Palm oil can be used for frying more extensively and for longer periods than other oils because it undergoes very little oxidation. This gives it an advantage in this market, which is a strong one in Asia, especially in China. Since the early 1990s China has greatly increased its consumption of palm oil, mainly to make noodles.
- Manufacture of margarine. The solid consistency of palm oil renders it the oil of choice by temperate countries for the manufacture of both table and industrial margarine. The latter product is used in cakes, shortening ingredients and vanaspati[1]. Hydrogenation and interesterification are necessary if liquid oils are used to make margarine. The temperate palm oil market centres mainly on the European Union (EU), which is still the commodity's leading importer.

In 1997, when Indonesia devalued its currency, the major importers of palm oil were the EU, with 16% of the world's imports, closely followed by China (15%), India (12%) and Pakistan (9.5%). In terms of consumption, Indonesia ranked first (16%), followed by the EU (11%), China (10%), India (8%) and Pakistan (6%). The largest exporters were Malaysia, with 46% of the world's exports, and Indonesia, with 25%. Malaysia was the primary producer (50%), followed by Indonesia (30%).

Over the past decade, Indonesia has been the largest planter of new palms. In the 4 years prior to 1997, planting reached a record average of 212 000 hectares annually. Mature planted areas are now estimated at 1.6 million hectares, compared to 2.4 million hectares in Malaysia. Worldwide, the area planted with mature oil palm rose by 77% between 1990 and 1999, due chiefly to the efforts of Indonesia and Malaysia. In comparison, the worldwide increase in planting was 23% for soybean, 30% for sunflower and 25% for rapeseed.

A Demand-driven Market

The second key feature of the oil palm market is the increasing part played by demand from India and China in the growth of world trade. To understand and assess the effect of this demand on world prices, we should place it in an historical context, comparing it with the more gradual increase in the consumption of other oils and fats in both developed and developing countries.

The first recorded imports of palm oil were to Liverpool, Great Britain in 1790, to meet demand from the soap and candle industries. Palm oil producers at this time were competing mostly with the producers of tallow in Russia, South America, Australia and the USA. The oil was produced in Africa, in or around the Gulf of Guinea, whence it was exported to the European commodities market by former slave-traders. This trade continued, on a long-term contract basis, throughout the nineteenth century. Mége Mouriès invented margarine in 1869; research by Wesson improved the refining of vegetable oils in 1900; and Norman invented hydrogenation in 1902. These events effectively opened the food market to most vegetable oils by the early twentieth century.

However, it was not until the late 1920s that palm oil, together with whale oil, began expanding its market share in the ever-growing American and European food markets. At about this time, diets in the developed countries began changing, moving away from the consumption of grains to that of fats and other high-value foods. Figure 3.1 shows how this occurred in France. Food intake per day is shown in calories on the horizontal axis, while the vertical axis shows the intake of fats in grams. The contribution of fats to daily food intake increased slowly through the 1920s, began rising during the 1930s, then rose sharply after the Second World War. This sharply rising trend has continued until the present day.

The dominance of palm oil in the world oil trade became evident in 1972, when it overtook soybean oil to reach first place, where it has remained ever since. This was made possible by record production in Malaysia and Indonesia, where yields reached 4 tonnes of palm oil per hectare. Another contributing factor was the low cost of production, which stemmed from the use of unskilled and poorly paid labourers.

Asian demand for palm oil began growing in the late 1970s, chiefly

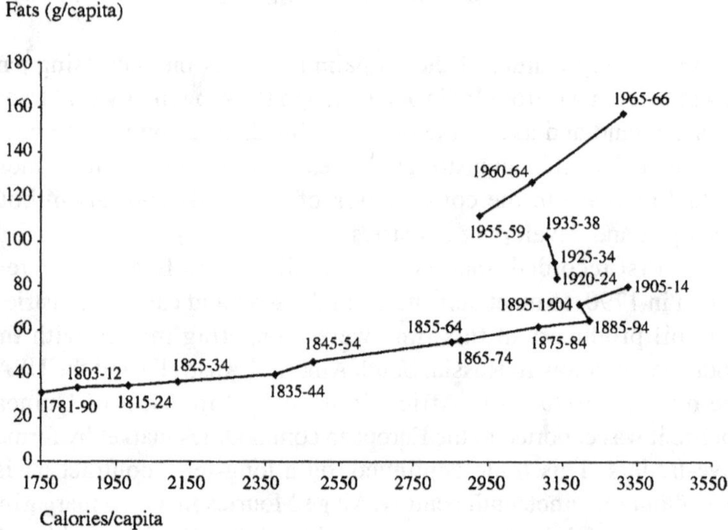

Figure 3.1 Contribution of fats and calories to daily food intake in France, 1790-1966. Source: Toutain (1971).

in China, India and Pakistan. Again, it was triggered by the trend in diets away from grains towards fats and other commodities (Figure 3.2). In the case of China and some other developing countries, recent studies have shown that this change is occurring at a much lower threshold of income than it did in the developed countries (Drewnowski and Popkin, 1997; Popkin et al, 1996). If this is also happening elsewhere in the developing world, the demand for oils and fats is likely to rise much faster in the near future than has previously been predicted.

Figure 3.3, in which oil and fat consumption is plotted against per capita income, shows what economists call the "Engel curve"—the tendency for the consumption of a given product to rise with incomes rapidly at first, but more slowly over the longer term over a certain level of wealth. The developing countries appear near the lower part of the curve, on the left, whereas the developed countries are near the upper part, on the right. According to this figure, growth in demand should shift from Europe and the developed world towards the developing countries and especially, in the short term, towards the Asian countries,

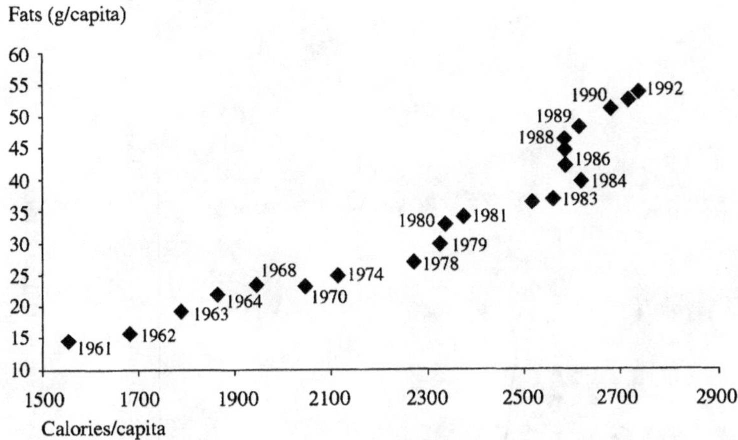

Figure 3.2 Contribution of fats and calories to daily food intake in China, 1961-92. Source: FAO.

where incomes are rising fastest[2]. These countries have admitted palm oil to their diets because of its relatively low price, determined in part by low transaction costs. The main competitor is South American soybean oil, which must be transported half way round the globe. Importing Indonesian or Malaysian palm oil into China or India takes a week, or a fortnight at most. It takes five times as long to import soybean oil from South America, forcing would-be importers to take out expensive insurance against the risk of price fluctuation during this period.

During the period 1994-97, world consumption of the 17 most widely consumed oils and fats increased by an average 4 million tonnes per annum. Fifty per cent of this increase occurred in China and India, which together represent one-third of the world's population. Barring some major economic setback, consumption in these countries, as in other rapidly growing economies of the developing world, should continue to rise rapidly in the future. A 2-kilogramme increase in per capita consumption in China and India should lead to an increase of 4 million tonnes in world demand. It is figures like these that explain the unparalleled growth enjoyed by Indonesian and Malaysian palm oil production over the past 20 years (Figure 3.4).

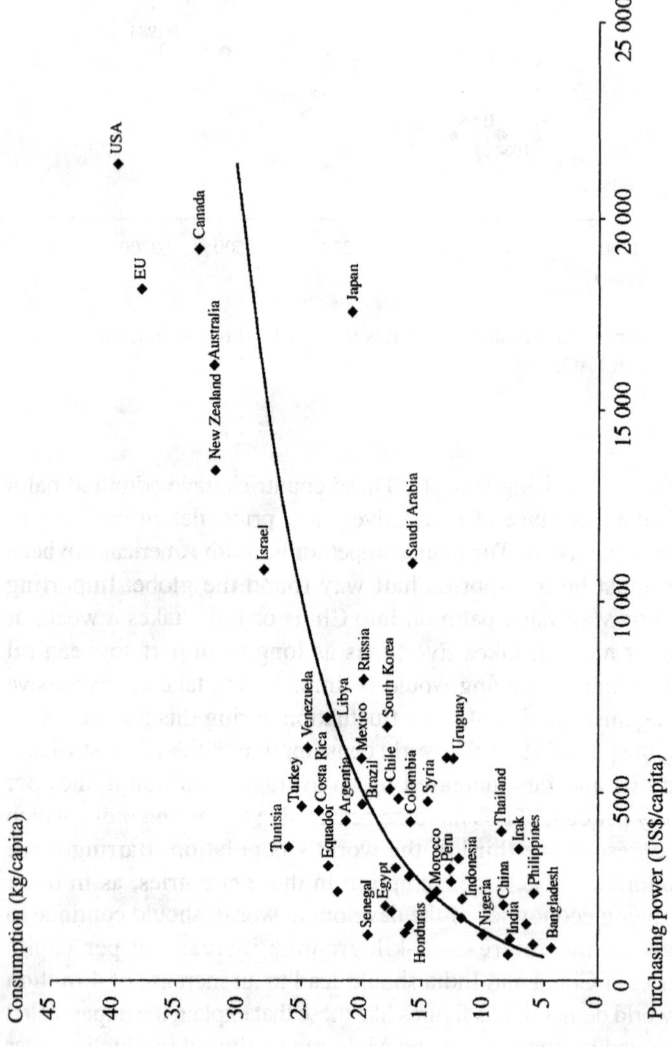

Figure 3.3 Per capita consumption of oils and fats in different countries, 1993. Sources: United Nations (1993); *Oil World* (various issues).

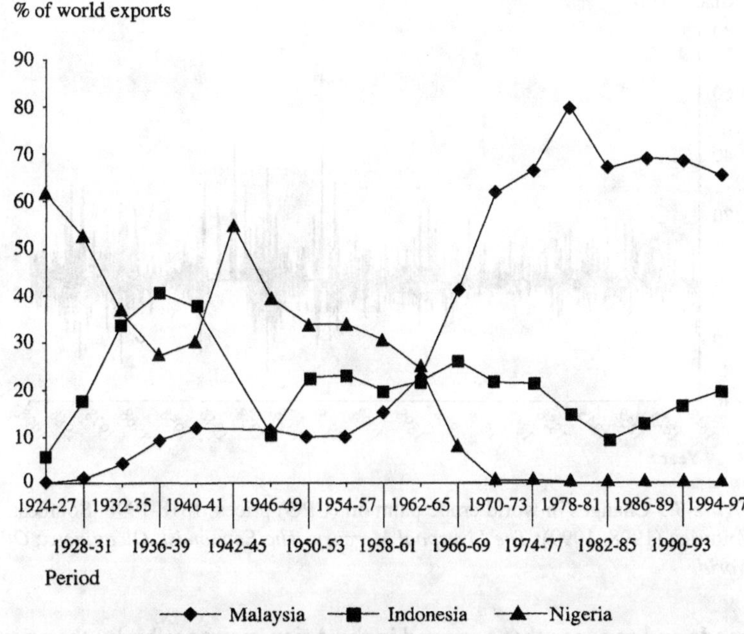

Figure 3.4 Share of different countries in world palm oil exports, 1924-97.
Sources: Hartley (1967); *Oléagineux; Oil World.*

Price Volatility

Two sources that reported early crude palm oil (CPO) prices are quoted by Latham (1978). They are *The Liverpool Mercury*, which gave cost, insurance and freight (CIF) prices in Liverpool over the period January 1818-December 1843, and the *The Economist*, which covered January 1844-December 1946. In Figure 3.5, these data are complemented by CIF Rotterdam prices obtained from *Oléagineux* and *Oil World* to give an unprecedented 182-year monthly index of prices for CPO. The figure shows that price volatility tends to coincide with periods of surging demand, such as the 1930s and 1970s, underscoring the demand-driven nature of the palm oil market.

Between May 1997 and May 1998 the Indonesian rupiah lost 80% of its value against the US dollar. The 1998 contraction of exports in

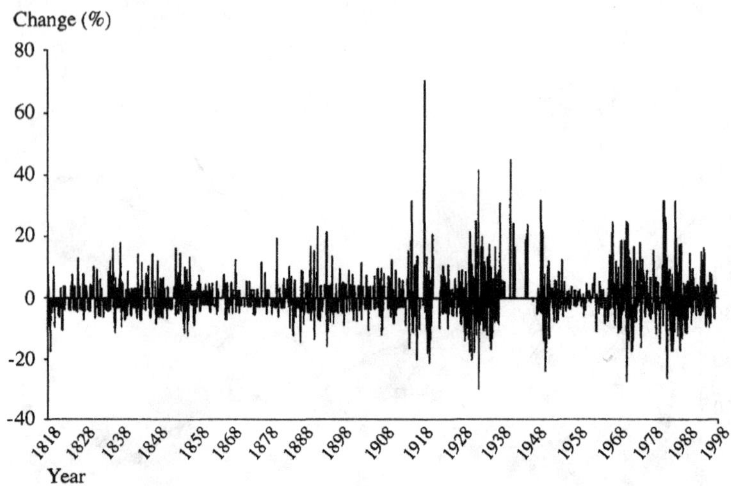

Figure 3.5 Changes in world crude palm oil (CPO) prices, 1818-1998. Sources: Voituriez (1998, 1999); *The Liverpool Mercury*; *The Economist*; *Oléagineux*; *Oil World*.

goods and services that occurred in the Asian countries hit by the crisis seems counter-intuitive, as theory suggests that the low value of their currencies should have boosted exports. However, the geography of trade is an important part of the explanation: about half the relevant trade of the most affected countries was with other Asian countries.

For both political and geographical reasons, this contraction was not apparent in the world palm oil market. CPO prices did not immediately plunge (Figure 3.6). Indeed, as early as 1997, opportunist traders began buying positions labelled in US dollars on the world palm oil market, sustaining the trend towards rising prices. Severe inflation in Indonesia, especially in the prices of staple food items, led the government to impose a ban on palm oil exports, which lasted from January to April 1998. As a result of the ban, world demand was directed towards Malaysia.

Because the currencies of India and China were not affected by the crisis, the 27% share of these countries in world palm oil imports helped avert the spread of the crisis to the rest of the sector[3]. And because Europe and the USA were not greatly affected either, the gulf between rising global demand and reduced Asian supply widened, hardening prices.

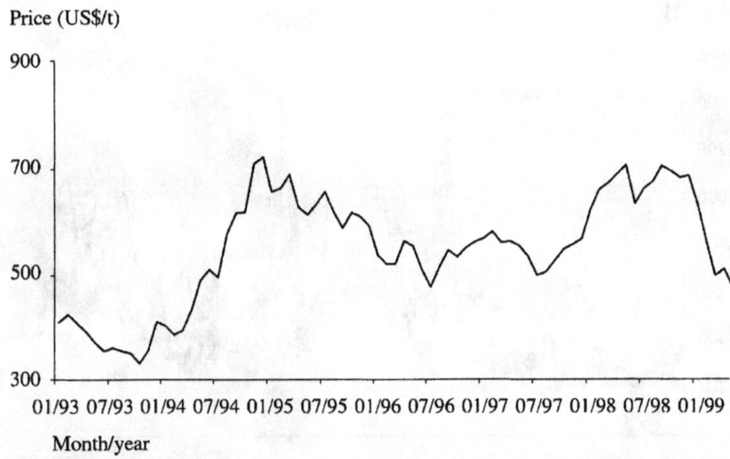

Figure 3.6 Monthly changes in crude palm oil (CPO) prices on the international market, 1993-99. Source: *Oil World.*

The subsequent fall in prices, in December 1998, was caused by factors other than the Asian crisis, primarily record soy exports from North and South America. By June 1999, prices of CPO had fallen by nearly 40% from their June 1998 level. Average 1998 CPO prices, in contrast, were nearly 20% above their 1997 level. This boom-and-bust cycle is an essential feature of the behaviour of the oils and fats market in the twentieth century, whether or not there is an accompanying financial crisis (Figures 3.5 and 3.7).

The *krismon*, then, has not so far greatly changed the behaviour of world prices. This is largely because these prices both determine and are determined by substitutions in the industry. According to *Oil Weekly* (various issues), professional traders claim that the *krismon* had no more than a transient effect on world prices. Substitution provides a "safety net" for the market, cushioning price fluctuations by allowing it to turn to the cheapest product.

However, such substitutions are not possible in the Indonesian domestic market, where the consequences of the *krismon* were felt with the utmost severity. Cooking oil is a key ingredient in the Indonesian diet and is officially listed by the government as one of nine basic commodities. During the late 1970s, the political will existed to switch

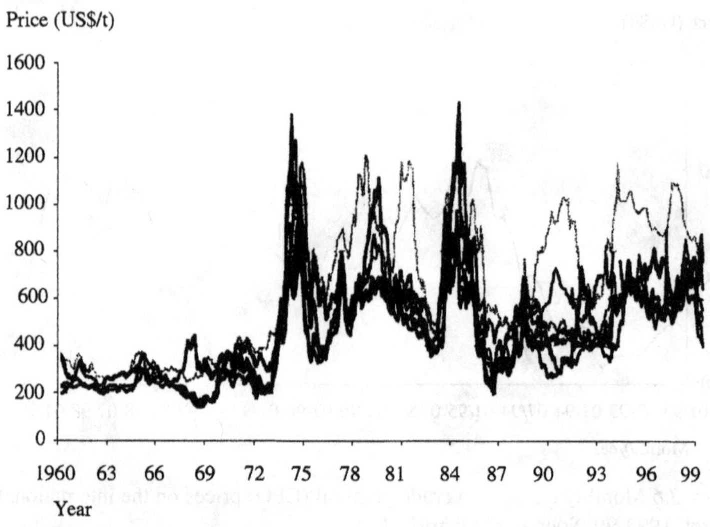

Figure 3.7 Prices of major vegetable oils (soya, cotton, groundnut, sunflower, rape, palm (CPO), palm kernel, and coconut) on the world market, 1960-99. Source: *Oil World*.

the country's oil consumption from coconut oil to the sole use of locally supplied palm oil. Along with this switch came a price stabilisation policy, designed to protect the consumer from the volatility seen on the world market. These factors gave rise to an oligopolistic domestic market, which was still operating when the crisis broke.

At that time, a few large companies bought the entire stock of Indonesian palm oil, which they then processed and resold on the domestic market without permitting any competing product to enter the country. These companies' operations, which were reinforced by political connections, had both advantages and disadvantages. On the one hand, for a considerable period they contributed to food security, supplying a staple product at an affordable price. On the other, they distorted the market, which was effectively protected from competition. Sales were often timed to coincide with peaks in demand when prices could be raised, a typical example being the end of Ramadan. Finally, when inflation soared in the wake of the rupiah's 1997 devaluation, the companies reaped huge profits while providing Indonesian households with no real protection against world price fluctuations.

Responses to the Crisis

Before the crisis, Indonesia and Malaysia displayed very different responses to price volatility. The differences reflect the different issues at stake in the palm oil sectors of each country.

Now second only to electronics in terms of export earnings, Malaysia's palm oil industry has been part of a long-term government programme to diversify exports. This programme was launched after Malaysia became independent in 1957. A key element in the strategy to counter price volatility has been adding value to the product through processing. A range of secondary products has been developed, including refined, bleached and deodorised (RBD) palm oil to higher-value products such as oleo-chemicals. By 1998, 90% of palm oil produced in Malaysia was exported, and 100% of exports consisted of processed oil. Joint ventures inside Malaysia were promoted through tax breaks, which attracted highly skilled foreign workers to strategic industries such as oleo-chemicals.

Indonesia's situation was both more complex and more challenging. Whereas there are roughly 20 million people in Malaysia, there are 200 million in Indonesia—a huge market that needed to be supplied with a low-cost product. Indonesia's answer was direct state intervention on a large scale[4]. By 1994, state-owned plantation companies, such as Perusahaan Negara Perkebunan (PNB) and Perseraan Terbatas Perkebunan (PTP), produced about 40% of Indonesian palm oil, compared with only 27% in Malaysia. In 1998, domestic consumption amounted to 55% of production.

Between 1978 and 1991, CPO domestic prices were fixed in order to protect local consumers from adverse fluctuations in world prices (Figure 3.8). This did not happen in Malaysia. Indonesia's domestic market was "deregulated" in June 1991, but export taxes were maintained. From then on, palm oil had to be officially delivered through BULOG to the major processors, who received a discount price. The processing companies, such as Salim, Sinar Mas, Astra and Musim Mas, were expected to provide the domestic market with cooking oil at a "fair, stable and reasonable price". Products such as Salim's famous "Bimoli" or "Filma", from Sinar Mas, became available throughout the country. Once the domestic market had been supplied, palm oil could be exported crude to Rotterdam.

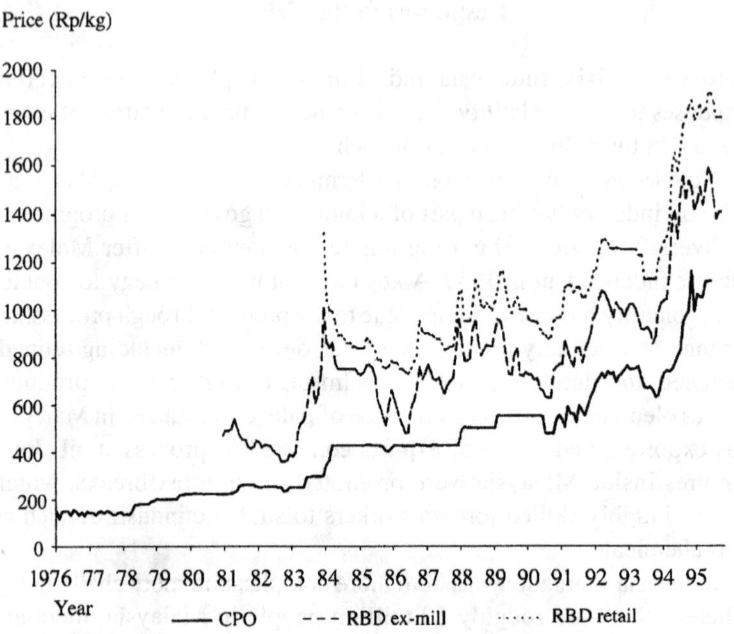

Figure 3.8 Local crude (CPO) and processed (RBD) palm oil prices in Indonesia, 1976-95. Source: Indonesian Ministry of Trade and Industry.

The government took two measures to maintain the supply of domestic cooking oil during the crisis. On 29 December 1997 it banned the export of CPO. The ban remained in place until 22 April 1998. The second measure was to raise export taxes, to 40% in April-June 1998 and then to 60% in July 1998-January 1999. The taxes were reduced to 40% again in February 1999.

These measures met with mixed success. A review of cooking oil prices shows that they nearly tripled during the first half of 1998. Despite the increase, local palm oil prices remained well below the international US dollar price. Continuing shortages and rising prices in the domestic market led to allegations of widespread smuggling[5]. The ratio of the price of unbranded cooking oil (UCO) to the CPO local price, which had allowed the oil processors a certain margin, shot up (Table 3.1). This was accompanied by a rise in export taxes, which in turn indicated that the rise in UCO prices was not commensurate with the rise in CPO prices. Indeed, the rise in CPO prices, following inflation in the price of all staple food items, was aggravated by the margins of the processing companies. In his first ministers' meeting, President Habibie announced that cartels and monopolies would henceforth be banned.

The government signed a memorandum of understanding with private-sector cooking oil processors in July 1998. The processors, however, were either unable or unwilling to abandon their vested interests. The memorandum banned smuggling but failed to inject competition into this crucial link in the chain from producers to consumers.

Table 3.1 Crude palm oil (CPO) and unbranded cooking oil (UCO) prices on the Indonesian and international markets, July 1997-October 1998

Month/year	*7/97*	*12/97*	*1/98*	*2/98*	*3/98*	*4/98*
Exchange rate	2615	5550	10 300	8950	8700	8155
CPO local	1170	2230	2500	3000	3000	2750
UCO international	1400	2700	3750	4200	3500	3850
UCO/CPO ratio %	20	21	50	40	17	40
Month/year	*5/98*	*6/98*	*7/98*	*8/98*	*9/98*	*10/98*
Exchange rate	11 200	15 100	13 300	11 150	10 850	7700
CPO local	3500	3500	3900	3900	4000	2700
UCO international	6250	5600	5600	6400	6400	4500
UCO/CPO ratio %	79	60	44	64	60	67

Sources: ING Barings survey, *Oil World* and Rabobank.

In July 1998, the government refused to accept responsibility for the rise in cooking oil prices. It accused palm oil producers of creating a domestic shortage by exporting oil, possibly under cover. The government made BULOG responsible for selling "Orange" (a special cooking oil which does not meet standard quality requirements for export) to middle and lower-income consumer groups. The oil was to be sold for Rp 3900-4000 per kilogramme, a subsidised price funded by the government with money from export tax revenues. At the same time, private-sector producers and processors were still allowed to sell high-quality cooking oil at a higher price outside BULOG's network. Two price levels, reflecting the two different qualities, would henceforth be found in the retail market. The overall structure of the distribution system did not change, but the measure taken with regard to Orange would now provide the safety net needed by consumers.

The next boom in world prices will test the efficacy of these measures. By continuing to protect the economic interests of private-sector producers and processors, the government risks further exposing BULOG to consumers' anger and to IMF and World Bank criticism. A further international price rise of the proportions experienced in the past will surely attract Indonesian palm oil onto the world market and away from the domestic one.

Production Costs

Indonesia's oil palm producing areas consist of state-owned plantations (PTPs), private and industrial plantations and smallholdings. Before the crisis, smallholder planting was either spontaneous or was carried out under a government project. In the Inti-plasma or PIR project, for example, a village created a central plantation or "nucleus", around which additional planting could be undertaken by smallholders—the "plasma". The costs of establishing the central plantation (land preparation, planting, etc) were met by government. At 4 years old the trees came into maturity, enabling production and processing to begin. The encircling plasma area was then ceded back to smallholders, henceforth referred to as settlers, whose role was to supplement the produce entering the factory from the estate. Each settler received 2 hectares for planting oil palm and a 0.5 hectare plot in the village on which to build a home and grow food crops. Settlers were given 12 years in which to pay back to the nationalised banks the cession price plus 12-16% interest.

A surge in interest rates and the collapse of the banking system (16 banks failed in late 1997 and a further 7 in April 1998) caused a credit squeeze. This led to both private- and public-sector projects being put on hold. The reduction in project activity was reflected in the sales of germinated tree seeds. Socfindo, one of the three major suppliers, reported that sales fell by 15% in 1998 over their level in 1997. This was followed by a further fall of 60% in the first half of 1999.

The decline in the planting of oil palm is generally attributed to the drastic rise in the costs of production, due mainly to the high costs of imported inputs such as fertilisers. The pre-crisis costs of Indonesian palm oil production are presented in Table 3.2, which shows values for a typically efficient and appropriately located plantation.

Table 3.2 Ex-mill costs of palm oil production in Indonesia, 1997

Operation	*Cost (US$/t)*	*Share of total (%)*
Harvesting	24.29	13
Maintenance	18.78	10
Fertiliser	38.74	21
Transportation	12.00	7
Processing	19.35	11
Overheads	22.00	12
Depreciation	47.00	26
Total	182.16	100

Note: Assumptions: production is labour-intensive, yields are 24 t/ha of fresh fruit bunches (FFB), the extraction rate is 23% and the exchange rate is Rp 2500 = US$ 1.00.
Sources: Tan Siauw Liang (1998) and P.T. Smart (personal communication).

The table shows that, before the crisis, fertiliser accounted for only one-fifth of total costs. Even if the cost of fertiliser were to rise by 80-100% (an increase not matched even during the worst throes of the *krismon*), the profitability of production and processing by the more efficient companies would not be seriously endangered. A temporary 50% increase in other production costs occurring in tandem with this hypothetical rise in the cost of fertiliser could also be absorbed without greatly affecting profitability. Total costs would still have amounted to less than US$ 300 per tonne, even at the worst moment of the crisis. The large amount of labour available after the crisis is likely to have reduced costs in many areas, particularly during 1998-99. Average daily wages in North Sumatra and West Kalimantan in 1998 were only US$ 0.50-0.61, compared with US$ 1.50 in 1996 (Tan Siauw Liang, 1998). Lower labour costs will have helped offset the higher cost of imported inputs.

Assuming, as I have done, that the only costs which really benefitted from devaluation were labour costs, Fry (1998) deduced that "today's [September 1998] Rotterdam prices are over four times greater than the ex-mill Indonesian production costs of CPO." Thus, on the basis of available production costs, Indonesian palm oil production remains highly profitable and was, unlike demand, unshaken by the crisis[6]. Nevertheless, according to *Oil World* (various issues), the establishment of new oil palm plantations has virtually come to a halt as a result of the economic crisis and the credit crunch throughout the country. Foreign investment has fallen sharply and previous expansion plans have been either cancelled or frozen. In the whole of 1998, only 20 000-30 000 hectares were newly planted, and this represented merely the completion of existing projects, not the start of any new ones. In January 1999, no new investments were made.

Conclusions

At the September 1998 International Oil Palm Conference held in Bali, the Deputy Chairman of the Planting Investment Co-ordinating Board of Indonesia (BKPM) painted an optimistic picture of the future of Indonesian palm oil production, citing a combination of favourable production costs and buoyant export demand. "It is the right time to grasp the golden opportunity to invest in Indonesia," he said, announcing a government decree under which the Ministries of Agriculture and Investment would collaborate in the development of agro-industry in general and of oil palm plantations in particular. According to the decree, foreign investment is welcome and does not have to be made in an industrial estate. The Chairman also announced that, "to improve national economic competitiveness, the Indonesian Government has presented an opportunity to foreign companies whereby they may invest in large-scale trade distribution, in the capacity of wholesaler/distributor" (Zainal Abidin, 1998). This announcement, which is clearly linked to Habibie's announcement of a ban on cartels and monopolies, reflects the pressure put on the government by the IMF and the World Bank for greater transparency. This prompts me to raise four key issues by way of conclusion.

The first issue is that of the *environmental and social impacts* of a further expansion of oil palm plantations. A recent study conducted by the Japanese International Co-operation Agency (JICA) and Indonesia's National Development Planning Agency (BAPPENAS) warned that excessive expansion, particularly in West and Central Kalimantan, could have a detrimental impact. As has occurred in previous projects, indigenous land owners might be dispossessed to accommodate land-hungry oil palm companies. In the past, land has been offered to companies by the provincial government without consulting local communities, which were then forced to surrender their land with very little compensation in return. In addition, the JICA study, together with fieldwork commissioned by the World Wildlife Fund (WWF) in West Kalimantan, revealed that smallholders involved with oil palm in the past have often received less than half the estimated returns to production and have experienced severe economic difficulties (Potter and Lee, 1998). Alarmingly, the JICA study also observed that many of the cartels notorious for logging and pulping Indonesia's forests had, in 1998, moved into oil palm. Two of the primary pulp and paper conglomerates, Raja Garuda Mas and Sinar Mas, also had vast oil palm interests. The Astra Group, which is a major logging concessionaire, was operating 39 oil palm estates via its subsidiary Sumalindo Lestari Jaya. As the WWF report points out:

"Oil palm planted by smallholders and nucleus estate companies on lands converted from traditional agriculture poses no danger to forests, though it may have other undesirable impacts. It is the cartels that have degraded the forests with whatever weapon was at hand and the negligence of government officials that has aided them. At the planning level it, seems that the desire to convert forested or "underutilised" lands to any intensified land use has been the driving force behind the spread of estates in many instances. Governors' requests for oil palm estates have far exceeded the ability of companies to raise the capital needed to set up operations. Official eagerness to attract estates, however, has allowed speculators to sidestep planning regulations, clearfell remnant vegetation and run."

Secondly, *transparency and competition* are the two principles required by international financial institutions and foreign investors as conditions for granting loans or investing in oil plantations. Policy and legal reforms, together with improved regulation of business practices, are essential if these principles are to be complied with. These reforms mean, as *The Economist* (1999) puts it, "stronger banking systems with more foreign involvement; less meddling with the local price of capital; more transparent dealings between governments and the private sector; a better system for handling bankruptcy; and incentives for people to learn more and to make less wasteful use of natural resources."

Under Suharto, money was lent by banks that did not care about credit risk, to companies that cared less still. Banks were part of large conglomerates. They often belonged to an agro-business group that controlled all or at least a large part of the distribution and imports of a given commodity, for example companies such as the Salim Group, involved in the processing and distribution of cooking oil. These companies are now, theoretically, exposed to harsher competition. The first issue to be looked at in the future is the performance of Habibie's government in improving competition and transparency in strategic business practices. The goverment professes a willingness to do this. How real is this?

The third, closely related, issue is how far the existing margins in oil palm cultivation will protect the sector from the process of *concentration* observed for years in the processing sector and especially in the cooking oil industry. The case of Malaysia is often invoked by way of comparison. With roughly similar margins, the plantation sector here is free and competitive. This may also be the outcome in Indonesia, should the BKPM prove successful in fostering foreign investment. With regard to processing, the future is much more murky. One factor likely to strengthen the market power of the largest palm oil processors in Indonesia could be the next Lomé Convention, at which the EU is likely to decide to revise its import taxes on palm oil products. The EU has favoured CPO for decades, levying an average 4% in import tax whereas a rate of 12% (recently reduced to 9%) has been applied to refined oil. Revision may mean that both crude and refined products arrive in Europe on an equal footing.

Structural adjustment in many African countries in the late 1980s led to the privatisation of oil palm plantations, the best known case probably being Côte d'Ivoire. Here the new private owners, in their attempt to increase their profits by adding value to their product, often carry out downstream activities such as the refining of palm oil on their premises. If the EU does not maintain discriminatory measures against the import of refined palm oil, Indonesia may soon follow the same path. The major Indonesian processors would thus be able to exploit their already powerful position in the domestic market, then simply shift their focus to the export market.

The fourth and last issue, then, is who will supply the Indonesian people? How will local supply and demand cope with price fluctuations once the umbrella provided by the state and its associated manufacturers is removed? The state is bankrupt and manufacturers are seeking new markets abroad. World Bank's response to risk in commodity markets is now *institution building*. This involves the setting up of credit institutions and futures markets to absorb the risk of price fluctuation by permitting buying and selling at pre-determined prices. In addition, crop assurance institutions should be formed to stabilise the price of crops, providing further protection against adverse price movements for producers.

Where the market and the state have failed to create such institutions, international financial organisations are today striving to build them, for two reasons. These are, first, to weaken the stranglehold of corrupt government, as seen in Indonesia, and second, to offset the low profits caused by lack of domestic demand. Whether or not such institutions would be sufficient to ensure the optimal allocation of resources for society, relying on the state to "rev up" demand still seems the best way to jump-start the economy and shake off the damaging hangover from the currency crisis. Restrictive fiscal policies were initially urged on many East Asian countries by the IMF. The decision to abandon these policies was seen as "crucial", even by the advocates of liberalisation. Indonesia and South Korea will thus have deficits of more than 6% of GDP this year, with Thailand and Malaysia not far behind. According to *The Economist* (1999), "The direct effects of those deficits are only now beginning to be felt, but the mere expectation of their arrival appears to have given the region a lift." The new tendency to ignore fiscal rectitude and run a short-term deficit should resurrect long-buried discussions on the respective abilities of the state and the market-place to speed economic recovery, improve social welfare and prevent future catastrophes.

In conclusion, Indonesia's palm oil sector is a microcosm of the weaknesses and strengths of its whole economy. I hope this chapter will help to throw light on the way forward for both of them.

References

Drewnowski, A. and Popkin, B.M. 1997. The nutrition transition: New trends in the global diet. *Nutrition Reviews* 55 (2): 31-43.

FAO (Food and Agriculture Organization of the United Nations). Statistical database. Website: http://www.fao.org

Fry, J. 1998. Implications of recent developments in Asian economies and in the global economy for the palm oil industry. Paper presented at the 1998 International Oil Palm Conference, 23-25 September, Bali, Indonesia.

Hartley, C.S.W. 1967. *The Oil Palm.* Tropical Agriculture Series. Longman, London, UK.

Latham, A.J.H. 1978. Price fluctuations in the early palm oil trade. *Journal of African History* 19: 213-218.

Popkin, B.M., Richards, M.K., and Monteiro, C. 1996. Stunting is associated with overweight in children of four nations that are undergoing the nutrition transition. *Journal of Nutrition* 126: 3009-3016.

Potter, L. and Lee, J. 1998. Oil Palm in Indonesia: Its Role in Forest Conversion and the Fires of 1997-98: A Report for the World Wildlife Fund. Bogor, Indonesia.

Tan Siauw Liang. 1998. Oil palm costs in Indonesia. Paper presented at the 1998 International Oil Palm Conference, 23-25 September, Bali, Indonesia.

The Economist. 1999. Asia's economies: On their feet again? 21 August, London, UK.

Tomich, T.P. and Mawardi, M.S. 1995. Evolution of palm oil trade policy in Indonesia, 1978-1991. *Elaeis* 7 (1): 87-102.

Toutain, J-C. 1971. La consommation alimentaire en France de 1789 à 1964. *Cahiers de l'ISEA* 5 (11): 1909-2049.

United Nations. 1993. Human Development Report. New York, USA.

Voituriez, T. 1998. Long-run and short-run dynamics of world palm oil prices, 1818-1998. Paper presented at the 1998 International Oil Palm Conference, 23-25 Septembre, Bali, Indonesia.

Voituriez, T. 1999. L'huile de palme et son marché: La modélisation de la volatilité. PhD thesis, University of Sorbonne, Paris, France.

Zainal Abidin. 1998. Indonesian government policy on investment. Paper presented at the 1998 International Oil Palm Conference, 23-25 September 1998, Bali, Indonesia.

Notes

[1] Shortenings and *vanaspati* are similar products: they are blends of cooking fats which have the consistency of lard. Shortenings are mainly used in the USA and *vanaspati* in India.

2 The share of Asia in world palm oil imports was less than 20% until 1972-73. Since then it has risen to 40-60%, fluctuating within this range. European palm oil imports accounted for more than 60% of world imports in 1972-73. Since the early 1980s, this has fallen to just under 20%.

3 China has been accused of being ultimately responsible for the Asian exchange crisis, due to its "competitive devaluation" of 1994, which enabled it to win market shares in the West. It has also been identified as a victim of the crisis due to the loss of competitiveness of its exports in 1997-98, which in theory should have made the devaluation of the yuan inevitable. This Asian giant either provoked the crisis or cushioned it, according to different analysts.

4 The value share of palm oil in Indonesian oil consumption was small until the 1970s, when coconut oil was predominant. Palm oil overtook coconut in 1984, on the back of large plantings in the early 1970s. Coconut production was scattered and processing was done as a cottage industry. Palm production, in contrast, was concentrated in North Sumatra, with the oil being processed in large factories. All this facilitated the rising market share of palm oil to the detriment of coconut oil. For a more detailed discussion, see Tomich and Mawardi (1995).

5 Press reports state that the volume of palm oil recorded as arriving in ports of destination during the first half of 1998 was significantly higher than the volume recorded as leaving the Indonesian ports of origin. One report indicated that the disparity at the port of Dumai in North Sumatra (a major CPO shipping terminal) was more than 300 000 tonnes.

6 Moreover, the short-term opportunity provided by falling labour costs should help the sector quickly recover its growth path. New planted areas could reach 60 000 hectares in 2000, 70 000 hectares in 2001 and 120 000 hectares in 2002, according to *Oil World*.

Chapter 4

The Asian Crisis and its Impact on the Indonesian Timber Sector

Marie-Gabrielle Piketty and Alain Karsenty

In the early 1990s Indonesia was among the three countries in the world with the largest remaining areas of tropical forest, the other two being Brazil and Zaire (now Democratic Republic of the Congo). Having depended heavily on log exports until the mid-1980s, the country rapidly became, with strong government support, the world's leading producer of plywood, producing 9-10 million cubic metres per year during the pre-crisis years of the early to mid-1990s. However, the sector's expansion, like that of timber processing as a whole, was based on highly protectionist policies. And it has led to the rapid depletion of primary forest, resulting in domestic timber shortages during the 1990s.

In this chapter, we will first review the main features and weaknesses of the Indonesian timber sector in the 1990s (first section: "Features and Weaknesses"). We will then analyse how the Asian crisis affected the sector, focussing on three key sequences of events. First, from the onset of the crisis until April 1998, the sector experienced severe setbacks (second section). Second, the crisis caused major policy and institutional upheavals (third section). Third, reforms in China, coupled with the positive effects of devaluation in Indonesia, had a positive effect on the demand for exports, leading to the sector's partial recovery (fourth section). Although it is difficult to judge the overall impact of the crisis on the forestry sector, analysis of the available data, interviews with specialists and a consideration of some aspects of natural forest exploitation allow us to discuss possible future scenarios and draw some tentative conclusions (Section "Conclusions").

Features and Weaknesses

Indonesia began developing its timber sector in the late 1960s. At first the country specialised in log production—an emphasis that persisted into the 1980s. Indonesia became the leading exporter of logs on the international market, representing 41% (25.3 million cubic metres) of world log exports in 1979. Then, through strong intervention, the government transformed the sector and its output, enabling the country to become a major exporter of plywood. In 1985 it imposed a ban on log exports, which was replaced by a high export tax in the 1990s. These measures, designed to stimulate domestic timber processing, have driven down the domestic price of timber compared with that in neighbouring countries. For example, the price of Meranti logs in Sarawak, Malaysia was regularly 20-40% higher than the domestic price in Indonesia. Bolstered by low taxation and license fees in the forestry sector, Indonesia's cheap timber policy has enabled it to shut its main competitors, Korea and Taiwan, out of the US plywood market and to take over plywood production from Japan[1], where, in the late 1980s, 98% of the processing industry was supplied with raw materials from Indonesia (Barr, 1998). Indonesia's share of the world plywood export market reached 55% by the early 1990s.

Despite this broadly successful record, the Indonesian timber sector suffered from several structural weaknesses that were apparent before the crisis struck.

The very low price of logs on the domestic market did not provide processors with the necessary incentives to increase productivity. The recovery rates[2] achieved by Indonesian plywood mills fluctuated around 40-50%, whereas they were 60% or more in Japanese mills (Barr, 1998). Moreover, the timber sector was highly specialised, dealing in a very limited number of products and markets: plywood represented 96% of export income from the timber sector, with 70% of it going to Korea and Japan (USDA, 1998). Secondary timber processing activities (moulding and furniture manufacture, for example) remained virtually non-existent until the mid-1990s. Table 4.1 and Figure 4.1 illustrate the high share of plywood in total timber exports in both value and volume terms.

Table 4.1 Values of different Indonesian timber exports, 1989 and 1993

Product	*Value*			
	1989		*1993*	
	Million US$	*%*	*Million US$*	*%*
Plywood	2709	77.5	4518	72.5
Sawn timber	228	6.5	636	10.0
Other timber products	440	12.5	593	9.5
Pulp and paper	125	3.5	493	8.0
% of non-oil exports		21.0	26.0	

Source: PDBI (1995).

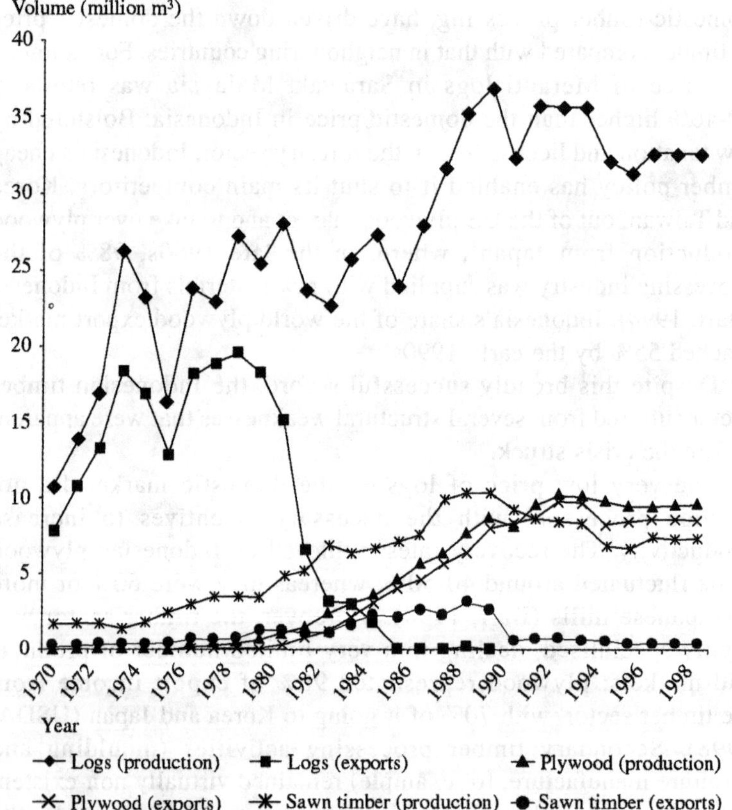

Figure 4.1 Volumes of different Indonesian timber products produced and exported, 1970-98

At the start of the crisis, Abbas Adhar, who was then the Vice-chairman of the institution responsible for regulating the plywood export market, the Indonesian Wood Panel Association (APKINDO)[3], described the industry's situation as follows: "The machinery in most of the plywood mills is already 15 years old; new machines can process logs up to 8 centimetres from the centre core while old machines can only process logs up to 20 centimetres. There is disguised unemployment in the industry: work that is supposed to be done by two persons only is often given to five people."

Mr Adhar also said that, with the exception of a few factories, most of the plywood produced in Indonesia was of low quality. Such a situation resulted from a strategy based on high volume and low prices, intended to capture market shares, and from the cheap timber policy implemented to supply the country's factories with low-cost raw material.

Another weakness associated with Indonesia's timber sector is the excessive harvesting of natural forest. In becoming the world's leading plywood producer, Indonesia has sacrificed most of its primary forest resources. Nearly all easily accessible forests, in the plains or in the coastal areas of Sumatra and Kalimantan, have already been harvested. Foresters now have either to operate in the more remote areas of these islands or to establish new concessions in the less developed outer islands and regions, such as Maluku or Irian Jaya. The shortage of timber has become a chronic problem in Indonesia and is now regularly mentioned in the press. Since 1990, "traditional" forest exploitation has increasingly given way to the conversion of over-logged forest into industrial timber plantations for the pulp and paper industry or into oil palm plantations. A study of logging activities reveals annual offtake of approximately 50 million cubic metres (Boxes 4.1 and 4.2), whereas government forecasts are that annual production will not exceed 26-32 million cubic metres over the 5-year period 1998-2003.

It might have been thought that the severe drought caused by El Niño, which was partly responsible for the huge forest fires of 1997-98, would have dealt a devastating blow to timber production by destroying a large part of the natural resources on which it depends. This does not seem to be the case, for several reasons. First, the fires occurred mainly in secondary or depleted forests, in other words those that are not at present log suppliers. Second, the main effect will be on the long-term supply of logs, because it is mainly young trees that suffered. The effects of the drought on tree growth in well established trees may be considered negligible (P. Sist, personal communication). We know that a large area of logged and secondary forests, which should have been ready for harvesting after a regrowth period of 35 years, was completely burned (Y. Laumonier, personal communication). However, most forest companies have shown little interest in harvesting these forests in the future (see below). Worse, it is highly probable that some of these companies started the fires themselves, in order to replace these sometimes very depleted forests with timber or estate crop plantations, instead of waiting for the second cut. In short, the drought and associated forest fires may have increased the probability of log shortages in the longer term, but it is difficult to demonstrate that this has in any way harmed the timber industry and its businessmen.

Box 4.1 How much timber does Indonesia produce?

Different sources give very different assessments of the amount of timber produced by Indonesia.

The Food and Agriculture Organization of the United Nations (FAO) gave a figure for *sawlogs and veneer logs* alone of 32.7 million cubic metres in 1996. According to the Indonesian Forestry Society (MPI), the total production of *industrial wood* in 1998 was 37.36 million cubic metres, including 26.16 million from productive natural forests and 11.2 million from converted forests, with a further 3 million cubic metres of fast-growing species for pulp and paper being produced in plantations. However, the International Tropical Timber Organisation (ITTO) indicates *log production* (again, sawlogs and veneer logs only) at only 28.53 million cubic metres in 1997 and estimates 1998 production at 26.5 million cubic metres.

All observers agree that illegal logging and unrecorded log exports are substantial. It seems reasonable to assume that the country's real annual output is over 40 million cubic metres, even allowing for a decrease in the late 1980s. However, much of this production comes from conversion forests, and the switch to fast-growing planted species for pulp and paper production should lead to a rapid decrease in the coming years.

According to the FAO, the output of *processed wood* in 1996 was 7.57 million cubic metres of *sawn wood* and 9.57 million cubic metres of *plywood*. To this should be added an output of 3 million cubic metres of *pulp*, mainly from fast-growing species but also from sawlogs and veneer logs, and the output of the furniture factories, which consume 1.3 million cubic metres of wood each year. Assuming a recovery rate slightly below 50%, these figures are consistent with annual production of 40 million cubic metres. The FAO's actual estimate is over 47 million cubic metres for *industrial roundwood*, including 32.5 million cubic metres for *sawlogs and veneer logs*.

After 1996, the estimates diverge more sharply. For 1997 and 1998, ITTO estimates *plywood* production at 6.07 million and 6.00 million cubic metres respectively. Plywood exports are reported as down to 5.46 million cubic metres in 1997. However, the official figures produced by the Indonesian central statistic agency (BPS, Biro Pusat Statistik), are much higher, giving production at 10.27 and exports at 8.35 million cubic metres in 1997 (USDA, 1998). The FAO gives comparable figures. For 1998, the BPS estimates plywood production and exports at 9 million and 7.1 million cubic metres respectively.

Box 4.2 Domestic log supply and demand: Estimating the difference

The Jakarta Post of 1 October 1998 states that *sawmills* are capable of producing 13.28 million cubic metres of sawn wood per year, corresponding to a log processing capacity of 26.57 million cubic metres. If this is true, it means that the current rate of utilisation is only 55% of capacity (assuming, optimistically, that wood recovery is 50%).

With regard to *plymills*, the figures are still more confusing. A 1997 Indonesian Forestry Department document (quoted by Whiteman and Scotland, 1999) tells of an annual log processing capacity of 20.8 million cubic metres, which corresponds to an annual output of around 10 million cubic metres (the average for the 1990s).

The critical question is the utilisation rate of the installed capacity. The second figure appears to be based on an assumption that the mills are operating at 100% of capacity. That would be surprising, even if it is true that plymills get priority over sawmills in terms of log supply (because they can afford higher prices). In 1998, when plywood production (whose magnitude is in any case controversial) is reported to have fallen, officials stated the operating capacities of sawmills to be around 30-40%. Log processing capacities for plywood production can thus be assumed to be over 20 million cubic metres per annum.

Adding the 1.3 million cubic metres needed for the production of *furniture* (part of which is actually being supplied by rubberwood) and of *chip wood panels* (the annual production of which is 1.9 million cubic metres), the annual demand for logs of Indonesian mills can be estimated at around 50 million cubic metres (timber for pulp excluded).

According to Titus Sarijanto, the Director of Forest Utilisation, annual log output should not exceed 26 million cubic metres over the period 1998-2003. Indeed, Sarijanto forecasted an annual domestic log shortage of 14.5 million cubic metres over this period. A few months later, the Minister of Forestry and Plantations, Muslimin Nasution, gave a maximum production figure of 31.35 million cubic metres and predicted a log shortage of 25 million cubic metres over the same 5-year period. The difference between the two estimates may reflect the inclusion of output from converted forests and/or pulp wood plantations in the Minister's figure.

The Impact of the Crisis on Demand

The effects of the Asian crisis on the timber sector began appearing in late 1997, when there was a sudden fall in the demand for timber on the international market. South Korea and Japan, which imported 639 000 and 3.3 million cubic metres of Indonesian plywood respectively in the years before the crisis, went into severe recession. The building industry in these countries was particularly badly affected. In the first half of 1998, activity in Japan's building industry was 14% lower than in the first half of 1997. Korea also suffered a major setback in this sector. Japanese log imports from Southeast Asia fell by 28% in the first half of 1998 compared with the same period in 1997, while the domestic and foreign supply of plywood fell by 32.5%. Chaos in the banking sector intensified the crisis, triggering panic in exporters when letters of trade were suspended.

The fall in North Asian demand for Indonesia's plywood could not be offset by a rapid increase in exports to Europe because of the low quality of the product and the EU's partial self-sufficiency. Consequently, export prices of plywood fell rapidly (Figure 4.2).

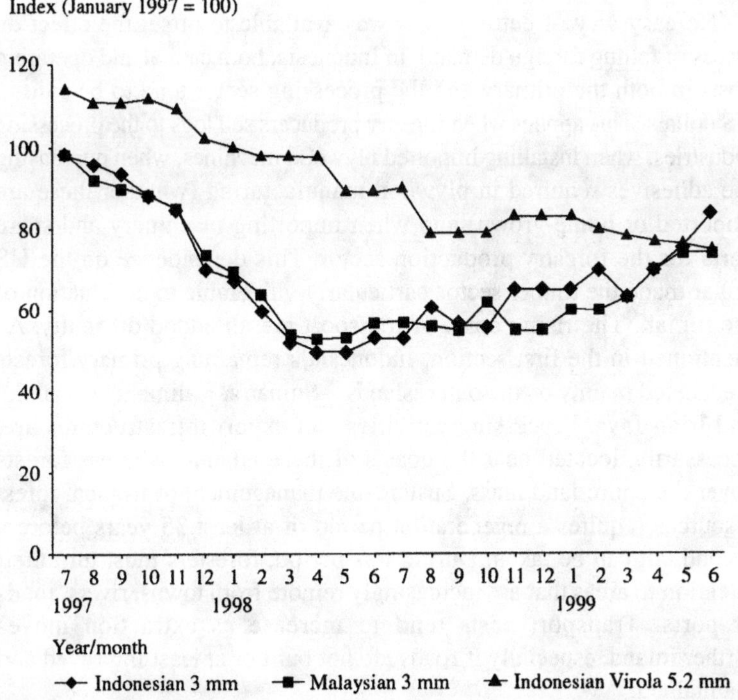

Figure 4.2 Movements of export prices for three Southeast Asian plywood types, 1997-99

In the second half of 1997 and early 1998, world plywood prices fell by half, from US$ 400 to US$ 200 per cubic metre. It is difficult to estimate the corresponding fall in production accurately. According to ITTO (1998), plywood production in 1997 reached only 6 million cubic metres, but this level is not corroborated by Indonesian official statistics, which make the total nearer 9 million cubic metres (see Box 4.2). Definitive data for 1998 are not yet available, but ITTO estimates that plywood production will not exceed 6.1 million cubic metres. The Indonesian Ministry of Forestry and Estate Crops (1999) gives figures of 10.2 million cubic metres for 1996-97 and 6.7 million cubic metres for 1997-98. The figures for plywood exports are 4.4 and 2.3 million cubic metres respectively. In 1997, the export values of all timber products fell by 25% compared with those of 1996, reaching US$ 6.34 million compared with US$ 8.3 million.

No easy way of cutting costs was available to offset the effect on prices of falling foreign demand. In Indonesia, both capital and operating costs in both the primary and the processing sector tend to be paid in US dollars. This applies when forestry producers sell logs to the processing industries, when installing imported plywood machines, when purchasing the adhesives required in plywood manufacturing (whether these are imported or home-grown) and when importing machinery and spare parts for the forestry production sector. This dependence on the US dollar made the timber sector particularly vulnerable to devaluation of the rupiah. The rising costs of transport are an added difficulty. As mentioned in the first section, Indonesia's remaining primary forests are located mainly on the outer islands—Sumatra, Kalimantan, Maluku and Irian Jaya. Processing activities and export infrastructures are, necessarily, located near the coasts of these islands, whereas forests cover the entire land mass. Sustainable management of tropical forest resources requires a regeneration period of at least 35 years before a second cut can be taken. During this period, foresters must turn their attention to areas that are increasingly remote from towns, rivers, roads or ports. Transport costs tend to increase as extraction moves further inland, especially if roads are not built or at least improved and maintained.

Reduced foreign demand for plywood and the devaluation of the rupiah have led to a major fall in the domestic price of logs, from US$ 90 per cubic metre to prices as low as US$ 30 per cubic metre, according to the chairman of APKINDO. The former Minister of Forestry, Djamaludin Suryohadikusumo, was quoted in the Jarkarta Post of 1 October 1998 as having received a report saying that "at least 5.9 million cubic metres of cut logs remain untouched because the timber estates had stopped operations".

The fall-off in logging had a knock-on effect in the processing sector, where unemployment became widespread. Several firms asked the government for permission to dismiss employees because of financial difficulties. According to Adi Warsita Adinegoro, vice-chairman of the MPI, around 30% of factories halted production because of insufficient demand and shortage of logs. But most dismissals seem to have been temporary and there have been no definitive factory closures. The fall in the wage bill allowed factories to ride out the worst period of the crisis. According to official statistics, direct employment in timber processing fell from 562 000 workers in 1996 to 560 000 in 1997. The fall was even steeper in 1998, with the total dropping to 523 000 workers (BPS, 1999)[4]. The value added in processing is thought to have fallen from Rp 5882 million in 1996 to Rp 5759 million in 1997 and Rp 4696 million in 1998, in constant 1993 value terms (BPS, 1999).

The experience of Indonesia's forestry sector during the *krismon* forms an interesting contrast to that of West/Central Africa in the wake of its 1994 currency devaluation. Box 4.3 summarises the differences.

Box 4.3 Devaluation with and without tears: Indonesia and West/Central Africa

In 1994, the CFA franc used in francophone West/Central Africa was devalued by 50%. At that time the export market for African timber was buoyant, thanks to European and Japanese demand. West and Central African freight-on-board (FOB) prices for both logs and processed timber remained unchanged and exporters received a "devaluation windfall", enabling them to increase production. The harvesting of "marginal forest" became profitable because labour and transport costs fell.

In Indonesia, the collapse of demand from Japan and Korea brought both production and prices down. Exporters were unable

to take advantage of falling labour costs to increase their share of the international market. Chaos in the banking sector caused problems throughout the timber sector, including logging, making life extremely difficult for exporters attempting to gain shares in more stable markets such as Europe or the USA. However, China's 1997 decision to import more Indonesian plywood provided some respite (see the fourth section).

Policy and Institutional Reforms

Corruption, collusion and nepotism are common in the Indonesian timber sector. The government has long controlled the allocation of forest resources. In the late 1960s it began awarding 20-year concessions, but a handful of conglomerates ended up with nearly all the permits. In 1993, five conglomerates (Barito Pacific, Kayu Lapis Indonesia, Alas Kusuma, Djajanti and Kalimanis) controlled 27% of all forest concessions, each consisting of at least 2 million hectares (PDBI, 1995). Often the chairmen of these conglomerates were, and in some cases still are, powerful Chinese tycoons. Bob Hasan, Prajogo Pangestu and Soedomo Salim are among the best-known names, all of them closely associated with the Suharto regime. Some authors argue that the president had deliberately foisted this politically sensitive area of business life on prominent members of this vulnerable ethnic minority in order to control them more efficiently: the government could use the forestry sector to whip up or damp down traditional anti-Chinese sentiments while Chinese concessionaires allegedly reciprocated the protection and favourable treatment they received from the president by accepting the penetration of his family into the forestry business (Asher, 1993). Bob Hasan's position was one of the most influential. He was a close personal friend of Suharto, a connection from which his company (Kalimanis) benefitted considerably. Hasan was the president of APKINDO, the MPI, the Association of Indonesian Foresters (APHI) and the Association of Indonesian Furniture Producers (ASMINDO). To escape Hasan's influence on the forestry business, another tycoon, Prajogo Pangestu, sought to associate with several other leading members of society, including Suharto's eldest daughter Tutut (Durand, 1994).

The IMF and the World Bank took exception to several of Indonesia's policies towards the forestry sector, especially the ban on log exports but also the near monopoly on plywood processing and exports held by organisations such as APKINDO. The ban was blamed for lowering the price of timber to domestic processing plants, thereby generating inefficiency throughout the commodity system and creating an artifical comparative advantage for Indonesian plymills entering the export market. This was based on a classical price distortion, the underpricing of a natural resource. When the IMF and the World Bank determined debtors' terms for Indonesia, they included radical policy reforms for the forestry sector (Kartodihardjo, 1999).

The main reforms proposed were the lifting of the ban and the dismantling of APKINDO. The prohibitive export tax of 200% has been reduced to 30% and will be further reduced to 10% in the year 2000. The dismantling of APKINDO has entailed the fall of Bob Hasan. As Barr (1998) has shown, APKINDO's operations and Bob Hasan's interests, as well as those of Suharto's family and friends, were strongly interconnected. For example, for every cubic metre of plywood sold, exporters had to pay a fixed fee, directly or indirectly to Bob Hasan[5]. APKINDO has ceased to control the price and export of plywood and is now just an association, the goals of which are mostly informative. Its new functions include collecting industry statistics, representing producers in discussions with government and serving as a forum for marketing the industry abroad (US Embassy, 1999).

A further set of reforms covered the regulatory system. Forestry companies must now pay their reforestation fees and forest royalties or face having their licenses revoked. This threat was relevant to no less than 33 companies in early 1999. In future, the companies will have to pay a deposit before they start operations, whereas previously fees were payable only after operations had begun. This tighter regulatory system is intended to pave the way for the introduction of a performance bond system. The hope is that requiring payments for each log cut, and holding a bond to guarantee that payment, will encourage sustainable management by removing the incentive to maximise extraction. The allocation of concessions was also reformed (see above).

Deliverance from China?

In the spring of 1998, the flooding of several of China's major rivers had disastrous ecological and socio-economic consequences. Large-scale deforestation of watersheds was identified as one of the major culprits. The Chinese government decided to take radical action.

China's new forestry policy places strict limits on the felling of natural forests, most of which are by now severely depleted, and promotes the establishment of timber plantations. The result is that, for the time being, the country must resort to imports to meet its high demand for timber. China's total demand for timber in the year 2000 is estimated at 110 million cubic metres, with a supply deficit of 40 million cubic metres, particularly affecting large-diameter logs. China was already importing 440 000 cubic metres of Indonesian plywood in 1996 and has since increased its imports significantly. In so doing it has greatly alleviated the effects of the *krismon* on this sector. In 1998, the total value of China's solid timber imports from Indonesia are thought to have reached US$ 490 million, compared with US$ 437 million in 1997. In other importing countries, the value of solid timber imports from Indonesia fell during this period. Given the fall in the US dollar price of timber in 1998, this increased value indicates a significant rise in the volume of imports.

In increasing its imports from Indonesia, China is taking advantage of the low market prices associated with the *krismon*. The country's log and sawn timber imports from Malaysia have also increased. Interest rates in South Korea and Thailand stabilised in July 1998, a further factor that may speed recovery. As the positive effects of rupiah devaluation took effect, European countries also began increasing their imports from Indonesia, at the expense of African and South American countries. Indonesia's plywood factories were able to re-hire their workers to meet this new demand (Sunderlin, 1999).

The rising demand for plywood, sawn timber and logs has led to a significant increase in their prices on the international market. Prices began rising in April 1998 and were 15-20% higher by the end of the year (Figure 4.3).

The new situation looks broadly similar to that before the crisis, except that plywood prices have remained well below their 1996 levels. Indonesia is once again experiencing its usual shortage of logs. If

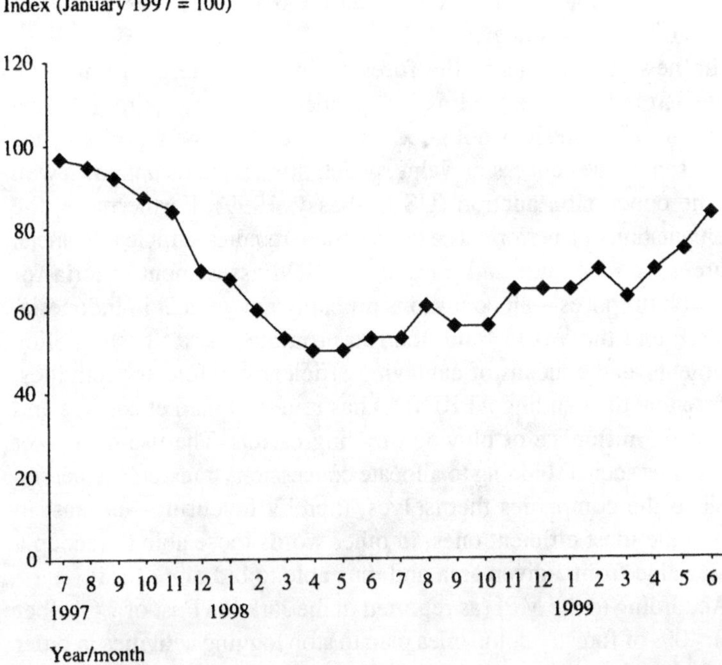

Figure 4.3 Movements of international market prices for Indonesian plywood, 1997-99

anything, firms face even greater difficulties now because the prices of imported goods are higher than before the crisis. A further difference is that the policy and institutional reforms adopted in response to the crisis have increased uncertainty throughout the sector.

Many forestry companies do not yet know if their logging contracts will be renewed. This was true before the crisis, but reforms have blurred the outlook still further. The government plans to reduce concession size considerably, in order to limit over-exploitation and rent-seeking behaviour. The logging permits that come to term this year cover 9 million hectares, only 6 million hectares of which are still harvestable. Of this, 3 million hectares may be opened to competitive bidding and it is planned that the other half will be allocated to forest cooperatives. Big companies are particularly affected by these new regulations. Until recently, they controlled concessions of over 500 000 hectares, whereas from now on they will not be able to control more than 100 000 hectares per province[6] and 400 000 hectares in all.

The new regulations in the forestry sector are largely untested. Indonesian industry, as well as independent sources, claim that data collection in Indonesia is not good enough to calculate a performance bond based on the concession value, which often remains unknown well after the concession auction (US Embassy, 1999). Furthermore, the implementation of a performance bond system requires sufficient financial resources, trained staff and measurable field assessment criteria for evaluation purposes—all conditions probably not yet met in Indonesia. The IMF and the World Bank tend to promote market-based policy instruments as the means of achieving efficiency in forestry activities. It is true that dismantling APKINDO has removed market barriers and reduced the influence of plywood trading cartels. The use of market mechanisms such as bidding to allocate concessions transfers the burden of risk to the companies themselves, thereby favouring—at least in theory—the most efficient ones, in other words those able to recoup a greater value from a given area and thus able to bid more for it.

According to the MPI (as reported in the Jarkarta Post of 7 October 1998), 40% of forestry companies plan to stop logging activities in order to invest in other activities considered more profitable or less risky, for instance timber or oil palm plantations. The increases in the prices of logs and processing equipment and the uncertain policy environment are the main reasons cited for giving up forestry. A continuing rise in the domestic price of logs seems likely in view of the growing scarcity of forest resources and the potential for exports. In 1998, at the behest of the IMF, a log export quota was instituted for the period 1998-99, in order to avoid a steep increase in domestic prices. The export market for plywood continues to fluctuate and depends greatly on the exchange rates of the Japanese yen and the Chinese yuan. Indonesia cannot raise its plywood export prices too much because of competition from Malaysia and Brazil and with non-timber products or new panel substitutes such as oriented strand board (OSB)[7] and medium density fibreboard (MDF). Finally, recent policy changes have tended to favour the establishment of timber plantations for pulp and paper and of oil palm plantations, both of which have also benefitted from devaluation.

The Industry's Future

It is too early to assess accurately the prospects for Indonesia's timber sector after the crisis. Here we discuss two possible scenarios.

The first scenario assumes a major transformation of the Indonesian forest economy, with a deep recession in plywood production benefitting other products. These products, many of which would be non-timber, would strongly affect land use. This scenario, already nascent before the crisis, could be called, in the words of David Kaimowitz (personal communication), "plywood as a sunset industry". There is growing evidence that, as accessible primary forests have been depleted, Indonesia's usable stock of high-quality and large-diameter logs (of the kind required for plywood production) has now almost all been harvested. Finding more logs of the same quality requires investment in increasingly remote provinces, such as Irian Jaya, or in the less accessible forests of Borneo, incurring higher production and transport costs. Kaimowitz says that most firms are preparing for the "post-plywood" era, transferring funds away from logging and attempting instead to convert logged forests into timber or oil palm plantations.

This process is already well under way in Sumatra and Borneo, where it appears that most forest companies are not really interested in a second felling cycle. Despite environmental regulations, forests have been badly depleted by intensive harvesting and many have been encroached on by smallholders. Forestry companies have accumulated considerable capital from the primary forest harvest, associated with the exceptional log volume of overmature trees, and this cannot be repeated. The capital is unlikely to be reinvested in "traditional" forest business.

This scenario would lead to the marginalisation of plywood and sawn timber production. The hardwood processing sector would gradually decline, to be replaced by activities based on timber plantations or the harvesting of secondary forest, such as the manufacture of pulp and paper, particle board and MDF. Domestic and foreign demand for these commodities is increasing.

By making "traditional" timber processing activities less profitable, the Asian crisis could be seen as a catalyst for this scenario. Forestry companies can use the crisis to justify investing in new types of business. The main activity benefitting from the crisis at present would appear to be the oil palm sector.

The second scenario assumes that the strong position of plywood in the Indonesian economy is maintained, following structural reforms. The sector would use remaining forest resources more efficiently, since the price of logs would no longer be artificially low, and supplies from primary forest would be supplemented from timber hardwood plantations. These are the assumptions that provide the basis for the structural reforms currently being undertaken, including liberalisation of the log trade. In this scenario, Japanese and Chinese demand for plywood remains sufficiently strong to encourage the more efficient firms to invest in new equipment and in hardwood plantations. If the plywood sector becomes more efficient, it could even afford to meet its demand for logs by importing them from neighbouring countries such as Papua New Guinea or New Zealand, just as the Japanese mills are doing at present. Two different "variations" on this scenario are possible:

- The optimistic "sustainability" variation. Forestry companies move towards the sustainable management of their natural resources. They limit harvesting in primary forests and invest in secondary forest management in order to obtain good yields from the second cut, as envisaged under the Tebang Pilih Tanam Indonesia (TPTI) provision[8]. In this variation the less efficient firms would disappear and there would be rapid restructuring of the forestry sector. Remaining firms would move towards timber products with a higher added value, such as furniture, in order to offset the higher costs of extraction. This variation could only be realised if there were strong enforcement of the new regulations negotiated with the IMF and the World Bank, whatever the short-term social costs.
- The pessimistic "degradation" variation. The lax enforcement of new forestry regulations and the uncertain prospects of the plywood market make sustainable management unprofitable. The last primary forests in remote regions of Kalimantan and the eastern islands (Irian Jaya) are harvested using the same methods as in the past, damaging the resource base irreparably. This variation involves the disappearance of nearly all smaller firms due to rising log prices and production costs. Larger firms would, however, have sufficient resources to allow them to continue harvesting logs. To avoid a major increase in domestic log prices, the government attempts to protect domestic consumers through measures of the kind seen recently, namely export

quotas and a "check price" system[9]. This second variant would only delay the realisation of the first scenario, although it is impossible to say for how long.

Three factors will have a significant effect on the future of Indonesia's forestry sector. First, most forestry companies at present are big conglomerates that are also involved in other business. Second, forest exploitation depends on the state and location of the forest resource, which mitigates against plywood manufacture in the future. Third is the kind of relationship that exists between private enterprises and the government.

The large conglomerates that have dominated Indonesia's forestry sector are still influential today, despite the recent political reforms. The companies concerned are often headed by members of the former president's family, by high-ranking army staff and by a closed circle of friends and allies. Among the allies are several leading Indo-Chinese businessmen. The Indo-Chinese may be seen as Indonesia's risk-takers—those who start investing in a new sector and test its market opportunities. They make sizeable early profits but soon have to share these and to leave part of the market to "the family", friends and army. By the time the crisis arrived, this had already happened in the plywood sector and was about to be repeated in paper and pulp (F. Ruf, personal communication). The conglomerates are often involved in other economic activities or at least can easily move their capital from one activity to another, according to profitability. In forestry, the collusion of interests has been very strong and explains much of the country's rapid forest conversion. The two most common "conversion paths" are timber harvest/oil palm plantation and timber harvest/timber plantation. Unlike the procedure for acquiring new forest concessions, land acquisition for new plantations is easy. The marketing of a timber cut is still very profitable, as demand from the timber mills is strong (Kartodihardjo and Supriano, 1998). These factors still provide strong incentives to develop timber or oil palm plantations via forest conversion.

Looking into the future, it seems unlikely that relative profitability will favour "traditional" timber processing activities such as plywood manufacture over these alternative ventures. The demand for plywood should remain strong, especially from China, but so too will the international and domestic demand for pulp and paper. Increases in the price of plywood will be limited by competition from substitutes and from other producer countries, such as Malaysia and Brazil. Indeed, competition is likely to be all the stronger since the Brazilian government has just announced its intention to make timber the country's number one export. The profitability of the oil palm sector remains high and may rise still further as a result of the *krismon*. This sector has already benefitted from low labour costs compared with its main competitor, Malaysia. Its prospects on the domestic and international markets are good to excellent. Until late 1998, oil palm development was hampered by regulations that limited oil exports in order to maintain supplies to domestic consumers, but these regulations were lifted at the behest of the IMF (see Chapter 3). The future development of both the pulp-and-paper and the oil palm sectors may, however, be constrained by the high cost of capital and imports, particularly in the case of pulp and paper. It is not yet clear how these industries can be capitalised.

No one knows how much forest is left in Indonesia. The economic and political stakes in forest exploitation are very high—which goes a long way to explain the lack of information available about this sector. The future remains dogged by difficulties and uncertainty. The current crisis has accelerated illegal logging by foresters, the army and the local population. Again, no one is willing or even able to say how much forest has been affected. What is certain, however, is that much of the remaining natural forest is located in the less developed outer islands. It seems possible, if not probable, that the social and political tensions currently afflicting these islands will continue and intensify. This political climate could hamper investment in forest exploitation.

Finally, the future of the timber sector depends greatly on future relationships between the government and the timber companies. For the time being, the IMF is in control and the government appears willing to introduce reforms. However, private-sector lobbies are still strong and may still be able to influence the government in the future. Already, there is growing pressure to restore the log export ban. It will be vital for protectionist tendencies to be firmly resisted.

Conclusions

The Asian crisis has brought change to the Indonesian timber industry. The positive effects include greater transparency in a sector where previously collusion and corruption reigned. Recent reforms and initiatives have raised the profile of the local population who, before the crisis, could not defend their rights to manage the forest and its resources. Cooperatives can now apply for forest concessions and new logging fees have been introduced (set initially at US$ 2 per cubic metre), allowing funds to be injected into local community projects. The government appears to have the will to redistribute timber profits to local people, and this is coupled with measures aimed at reducing the power of the big companies. But it is questionable whether the government can achieve economic recovery without relying on these big companies, which were the engine of economic growth before the crisis and which in many cases retain their strong connections with the government. It is significant that Chinese tycoons, such as Bob Hasan, seem to have lost some of their power. The reform process should improve the availability and flow of information about forestry in Indonesia, and this will help with planning, which was very difficult previously. The most important issue still needing resolution is land ownership in forest areas—both remaining primary forest and logged or secondary forest. Whatever the complexion of the government of the future, it cannot escape the moral and political imperative of redistributing at least some land to smallholders. The government will have to try to reduce the risk that wealthier farmers only will benefit from land tenure reforms. Land redistribution has not yet been discussed officially. And the current political situation is still too unstable to allow full and fair redistribution to be predicted as the likely outcome of any such discussion. Unfortunately, this is a situation conducive to continuing forest depletion.

Economically, increased Chinese demand for plywood enabled the industry to stave off the collapse that had seemed likely in mid-1997. The gradual recovery of the economies of North Asia may continue to postpone the collapse for a while. However, the crisis has demonstrated the limits of a plywood-based forestry export policy and highlighted Indonesia's poor performance with regard to the manufacture of other processed forestry products such as furniture. (In Malaysia, export earnings from timber products actually rose in 1998 on the strength of its furniture exports). Since plywood is mainly traded internationally in US dollars and is relatively labour-intensive to produce, this sector might have been expected to have experienced a boom during the crisis. Several features of the sector prevented such an outcome, including the narrowness of the export market, which collapsed during the first part of the crisis, and the limited options available for reducing costs.

Although forestry activities did not completely collapse during the worst period of the crisis, the industry was able to get by only by laying off labour. From 1996 to 1998, employment in the industrial timber sector fell by 7% or around 40 000 employees. (Employment may have increased in timber plantations, but data are not available for this sector.) If Indonesia had more third-stage processing activities in the timber sector, the positive effects of the crisis would have come into play sooner. The boom in Java's teak furniture sector is indicative (P. Guizol, personal communication). Such downstream products are less sensitive to market fluctuations, since they are differentiated goods with a high added value, the comparative advantages for which rely not so much on low prices as on quality, convenience, aesthetic appeal, and so on. The move from a single-product strategy backed by a cheap timber policy to a wider range of products with higher added value is one of the central challenges facing Indonesia's forestry sector.

Will "existing path dependency" in Indonesia's forestry sector prove too strong to allow the sector to evolve as it should do? The country's timber processing industry, which currently employs some 4 million people, undoubtedly suffers from severe overmanning as well as excessive productive capacity. But the sheer weight of these numbers and of past investments in the sector are strong incentives to avoid the risks associated with change. The recent return to "business as usual" in the plywood trade could hamper the reform process and undermine the prospects for more sustainable forestry.

In sum, it seems that the "traditional" timber sector can, in the short to medium term, attenuate the effects of the Indonesian crisis, but in the long term the country will have to rely more on other timber production and processing activities. These will consist largely of timber plantations for pulp and paper and palm oil plantations, both of which could continue to deplete natural forest resources. There should also be a place for diversification into a far wider range of forestry products, non-timber as well as timber, allowing sustainable forest management by forest-dwelling communities with secure land tenure.

References

Asher, W. 1993. Political Economy and Problematic Forestry Policies in Indonesia: Obstacles to Incorporating Sound Economics and Science. Report, Center for Tropical Conservation, Duke University, Durham, USA.

Barr, M. C. 1998. Bob Hasan, the Rise of APKINDO and the Shifting Dynamics of Control in Indonesia's Timber Sector. Cornell University Southeast Asia Program. *Indonesia* 65 (April): pp. 36.

BPS (Biro Pusat Statistik). 1999. Large- and Medium-scale Manufacturing Surveys. Website: http://www.cbs.go

Durand, F. 1994. *Les forêts en Asie du Sud-Est: Recul et exploitation: Le cas de l'Indonésie*. L'Harmattan, Paris, France.

ITTO (International Tropical Timber Organization). 1998. Annual Review and Assessment of the World Timber Situation. Yokohama, Japan.

Kartodihardjo, H. 1999. Toward an Environmental Adjustment: Structural Barrier of Forestry Development in Indonesia. Mimeo, IPB, Bogor, Indonesia.

Ministry of Forestry and Estate Crops. 1999. Forestry and Estate Crops Statistics of Indonesia. Bureau of Planning, Jakarta, Indonesia.

PDBI (Pusat Data Business Indonesia). 1995. Forestry in Indonesia. Jakarta, Indonesia.

Sunderlin, W. 1999. Between Danger and Opportunity: Indonesia's Forest in an Era of Economic Crisis. Website: http://www.cgiar.org/cifor

USDA (United States Department of Agriculture). 1998. Forest Product Annual Report 1998. Washington DC, USA.

US Embassy of Indonesia. 1999. If a Tree Falls in an Indonesian Forest, Who has the Export Right? Report. Jakarta, Indonesia.

Whiteman, A. and Scotland, N. 1999. Forestry policy and the development of solidwood processing industry in Indonesia. *International Forestry Review* 1 (1): 22-29.

Notes

1 Annual plywood production in Japan amounted to 7 million cubic metres until 1988, but fell to less than 4 million cubic metres in 1997. Imports exceeded national production for the first time in 1995.

2 The recovery rate is the plywood volume produced per cubic metre of log used.

3 APKINDO controlled the plywood export market until the IMF insisted on reforms that abolished its monopoly. It set the export price and specified the markets into which exporters could sell.

4 These statistics probably underestimate the loss in days paid. The reality is masked by the Indonesian tradition whereby workers accept job sharing and salary cuts in order to limit lay-offs.

5 According to the Jakarta Post (29 September 1998), Bob Hasan is alleged to have amassed a fortune of around US$ 2.04 billion by this means.

6 Except in Irian Jaya, where the limit is set at 200 000 hectares.

7 OSB is a type of wood panel with recombined wood and uniformly oriented particles, which give it good mechanical qualities.

8 TPTI, translated as the Indonesian Selective Cutting and Planting System, is the Indonesian sustainable forest management system. It is supposed to be compulsory in the productive natural forests, but is rarely, if ever, fully complied with by the companies.

9 The government issues "check prices" on all exported forest products on a periodic basis. The export taxes are applied against these check prices, not the real international price. Currently the check prices are significantly above the international prices, leading to export taxes that are in effect double or triple what they should be.

PART TWO

SMALLHOLDERS AND TREE CROPS

Chapter 5

Cocoa Migrants from Boom to Bust

François Ruf and Yoddang

The Indonesian island of Sulawesi (formerly Celebes) recently underwent one of the finest historical examples of a cocoa boom. Exports reached 300 000 tonnes per year in 1999, having risen from zero 20 years earlier. The island has been a major contributor to the rise in Indonesian production from 5000 to almost 400 000 tonnes per year over the same period. The people mainly responsible for this success story are the Bugis, who are also well known as traders and travellers (Lineton, 1975; Pelras, 1982 and 1996). The history of cocoa production elsewhere shows that most cocoa booms rely on massive migrations (Ruf, 1995). This is also the case in Sulawesi. Tens of thousands of Bugis families migrated from southern Sulawesi to the plains and forest-covered mountains of the western, central-southern, central and northern parts of the island to plant the tree. There they were joined by a growing number of families from Bali, who arrived under government food crop transmigration schemes but later switched to cocoa production.

Through cocoa, Bugis farmers have progressed from subsistence farming to relative wealth. Increasing numbers of families have been able to build substantial houses, send their children to school, buy motorcycles and satellite dishes and—last but not least—afford a pilgrimage to Mecca. Balinese migrants also have their own cocoa success stories to tell, symbolised by the presence of a beautiful Balinese temple in every backyard. These manifestations of wealth began to appear well before the *krismon*. No other country has ever achieved such rapid development of this valuable cash crop, in terms of both the amount produced and the prosperity it has brought farmers.

Price factors and access to land played a major role in Sulawesi's cocoa boom. As long as land is available, price rises always lead to a strong supply response in cocoa, as migration accelerates and new families enter the market. This phenomenon was first observed in Ghana during the 1950s (Hill, 1956 and 1963) and has since been witnessed in several other countries besides Indonesia (Ruf and Ehret, 1993; Jamal and Pomp, 1993). It leads in the medium term to increased cocoa exports (Berry, 1976; Ruf, 1995).

In theory, an increase in the real price of a commodity should also encourage the farmers who grow it to take better care of their farms and increase their use of inputs. Both yields and production should increase in the short term. If the country has a reasonable share of the international market, these positive price responses should eventually lead to lower world prices. Indonesia produces roughly 13% of world cocoa supplies and the world price of cocoa did indeed slump in 1999. Was this partly due to the Asian crisis?

To answer this question, we need to ask and answer several others. First, did production in Sulawesi actually increase during and after the crisis? In response to drastic currency depreciation, the price of cocoa in rupiah rose rapidly in mid-to-late 1997 and rocketed in 1998. Farmers can be expected to have responded by buying more fertiliser and applying it to their cocoa trees. Did they in fact do so?

In the season before the crisis reached its nadir in 1998, most farmers suffered a severe drought that took its toll on cocoa yields and tree stocks. Drought is often the factor that triggers the abandonment of old plantations and migration to a new area. Did the 1997 drought act in this way? Achieving high yields per hectare in most areas, Sulawesi's cocoa production systems were among the most intensive in the world before the crisis (Ruf and Yoddang, 1996). How did the drought of 1997 and the *krismon* of 1998 interact to affect management levels and sustainability?

A crucial question is the effect of the *krismon* on incomes in 1998. If, as we suspect, farmers experienced a windfall, how did they use it? They may have bought luxury consumer items or they may have tempered their desire to do this, preferring instead to invest their new-found wealth in more cocoa production. Like most cocoa farmers in the past, they may have decided to move to a new area to clear forests and start new plantings, rather than to replant old stands.

After the 1998 windfall, prices crashed in 1999. Did farmers change their minds about their investments in new plantings in response to this classic case of boom-and-bust? In less than 3 years, cocoa farmers faced three major crises: an ecological one in 1997, an economic one in 1998 and a market one in 1999. The first and third were real crises, hitting farmers severely, but the second one turned, as we shall see, into a triumph, creating a major windfall. Did the changing fortunes of the cocoa sector during these 3 years break the trend towards ever stronger performance seen previously?

Our analysis in this chapter has nine sections. After a brief historical perspective in the first section, we examine, in the second and the third sections, how the drought and the *krismon* interacted to affect yields and production and how these in turn affected world prices. In the fourth section we examine farmers' management responses to the drought, with special attention to the use of fertilisers. From the fifth to the nineth sections, we focus on prices and incomes and on what farmers did during and after their wonderful, but short-lived, transformation from rags to riches.

Historical Perspective

Indonesia and Sulawesi underwent their remarkable cocoa boom primarily because they possessed the two ingredients that other famous cocoa-producing areas have possessed in the past: large reserves of land, which is usually forested, and large reserves of labour, residing originally at some distance from the land. Information on a variety of factors, such as a new road that has been opened or a price increase in a neighbouring country, triggers massive migrations into the new cocoa growing areas (Figures 5.1 and 5.2). An ecological degradation or an economic change in neighbouring regions and countries may also trigger a migration decision. This is the way a national cocoa industry is born (Ruf, 1995). The migration is accelerated by the "copying" effect, as farmers hear about others' success and dream of making it happen for them (Pomp and Burger, 1995).

Over and above these two ingredients, Sulawesi had other advantages that made it ripe for a cocoa boom.

First, it had abundant rainfall and very fertile alluvial soils along the coast. These conditions favoured high yields of cocoa, as of other crops (Petithuguenin, 1998).

Second, the Darul Islam/Tentara Islam Indonesia (DI/TII)[1] uprising of the 1950s and 1960s sowed the seeds of rapid cocoa development in

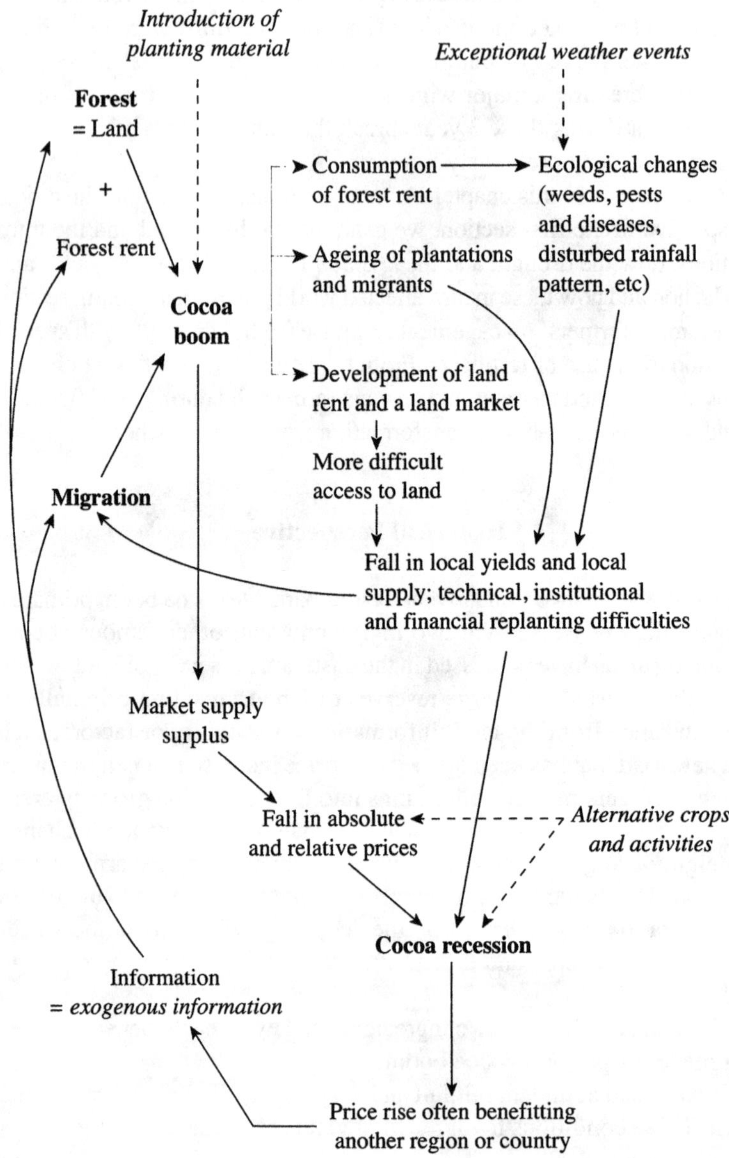

Figure 5.1 Factors affecting the cocoa production cycle

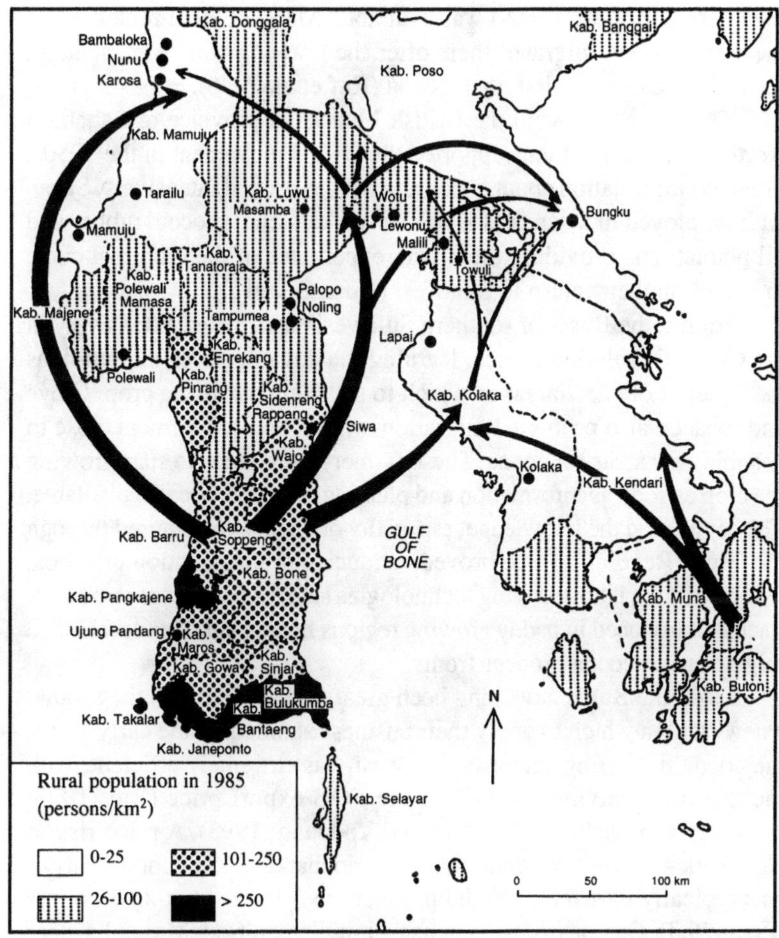

Figure 5.2 Southern Sulawesi and cocoa migrations in the 1970s and 1980s. The destinations to which migrants went in the 1970s and 1980s became the sources of new waves of migration in the 1990s.

the 1970s and 1980s by bringing relevant information and planting materials to Sulawesi. In 1958 two plantations were established around Pasangkayu, on the island's west coast. Both subsequently played a key role in the dissemination of planting materials. DI/TII campaigns, which made forays from base camps in remote forests, showed the movement's members where forest land was available. Many of them remembered these places and migrated there after the uprising was over, planting tobacco or cloves at first, then cocoa (Ruf et al, 1996).

Third, contacts with the British Malaysian province of Sabah, in Northern Borneo, which supported the DI/TII movement in the 1950s, provided information about cocoa and how to grow it intensively. Sabah later employed thousands of Bugis as workers on its cocoa, rubber and oil plantations, providing them with experience of the crop that came in useful on their return to Sulawesi (Durand, 1995).

Fourth, the Bugis of southern Sulawesi participated extensively in the Green Revolution in rice, learning the advantages of migration as they sought out new areas in which to settle and grow the crop. Clove and tobacco also prompted migrations which brought farmers close to suitable new areas for cocoa. These farmers were ready to start growing the crop as soon as information and planting materials became available. The capital and the knowledge, especially of fertilisers, acquired through the Green Revolution also proved conducive to the adoption of cocoa. On top of that, labour-saving technologies such as herbicides and hand-tractors introduced in paddy growing regions freed labor. This accelerated migrations to cocoa pioneer fronts.

Fifth, the Bugis have long been great traders. In cocoa they found a new field in which to apply their business acumen. In the early 1990s the cocoa marketing sector in Sulawesi was extremely efficient, with the grower receiving 80-90% of the FOB export price (Ruf, 1993; Akiyama and Nishio, 1997; Ruf and Yoddang, 1998). A price rise in New York—one of two centres of the world market for this commodity—was typically transferred to the producer in Sulawesi within 72 hours (Figure 5.3). On one occasion, when a middleman from Masamba, near Wotu at the head of the Gulf of Bone, tried to impose yesterday's lower price, he was forced to come up to the new price the next day or lose his market share. Competition was even more intense by 1996-97, when the time-lag for price changes was closer to 24 hours. This free market, together with a virtual absence of taxes, accounted for the attractive prices offered to producers. Bugis traders filled the niche between growers and exporters, promoting speed in the establishment of new plantations. The assumption of the middleman role by people from the same ethnic group as the growers partly explains why development happened rapidly even when the world price was low.

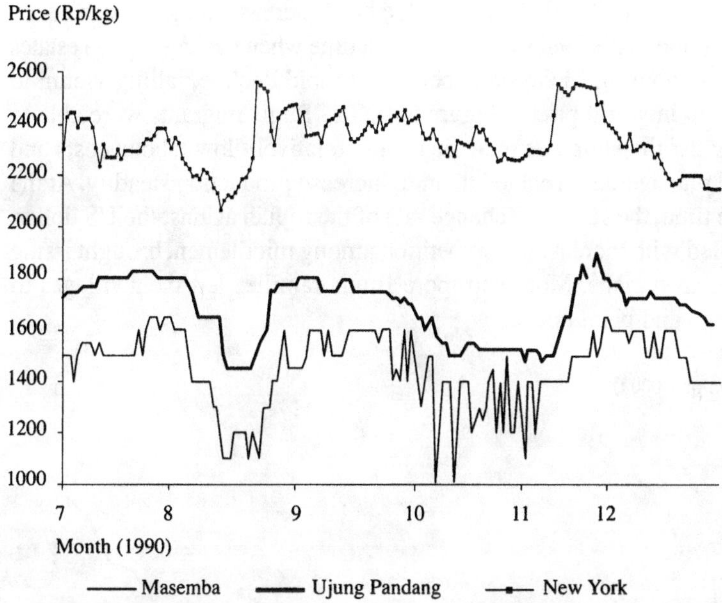

Figure 5.3 Daily cocoa prices in New York, Ujung Pandang and Masamba in 1990

Sixth, the Bugis have several traditional institutions that are highly effective multipliers of investment. Among these is the *gadai* or "pledging" system, under which a money lender (a farmer or a trader) takes over a plantation in exchange for extending a cash loan. The money lender retains the plantation and the income arising from it for up to 3 years, after which he or she returns it, receiving back the loan capital. Parents may help a son by pledging a plantation in *gadai*. The loan provides the capital needed by the son to migrate and buy more forest land on which further plantations can be established. The *gadai* system can also be used for other purposes, such as buying a car or going on a pilgrimage to Mecca. It is especially prevalent in Sulawesi, where it allowed many rice farmers to copy the first pioneer cocoa farmers, leaving their draught animals or their hand-tractors standing in the fields as they hurried to obtain the loan that would enable them to pursue their dream of riches.

All these factors help explain the huge increase in Indonesian cocoa production in the 1980s and 1990s, at a time when the large cocoa estates of neighbouring Malaysia experienced rapid decline, falling victim to a slump in world prices (Figure 5.4). The Bugis migrants were able to shrug off the slump as their rich soils, relatively low labour costs and good management enabled them to increase production steadily. At the same time, the sliding exchange rate of the rupiah against the US dollar, coupled with increasing competition among middlemen, brought rising prices in rupiahs. More and more Bugis families left their villages to migrate and plant cocoa.

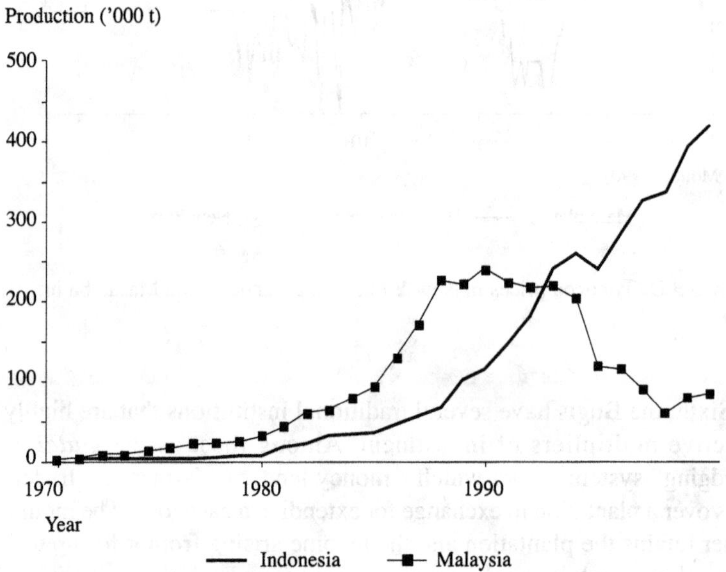

Figure 5.4 Production of cocoa beans in Indonesia and Malaysia, 1970-2000

Most frontier lands in Sulawesi experienced a typical pattern of development in which the plains were colonised first, followed by the hinterland in the hills. Where roads were not yet built, navigable rivers were followed upstream, as occurred in the Tarailu area near Mamuju on the west coast in the 1970s. Alternatively, the migrants followed the new roads built to service transmigration sites and estates, branching off these to make their own secondary tracks or paths. Thus, at any point on the map of Sulawesi, cocoa farms in the plains are usually somewhat older than in the neighbouring hills. For example, in the Lapai area of Southeast Sulawesi (Figure 5.5), which was one of the first to be developed, planting reached a peak in Watunohu, close to the sea, in 1981, whereas it peaked later in Lapai, an area still on the coastal plain but further inland, and later still, in 1987-90, in the hills behind Lapai.

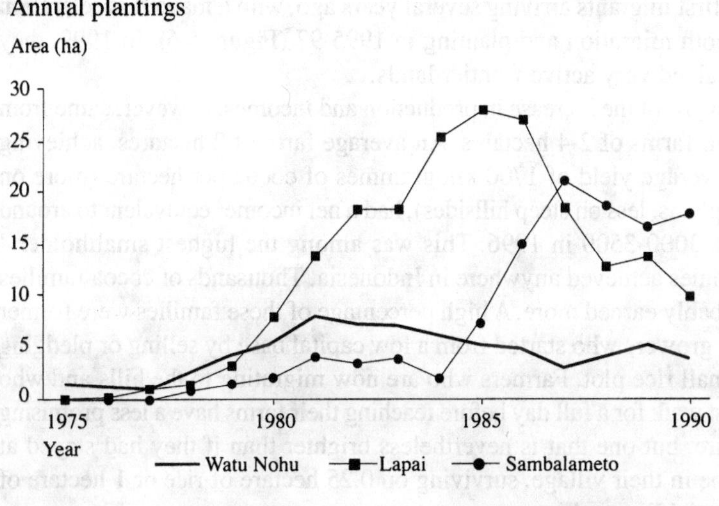

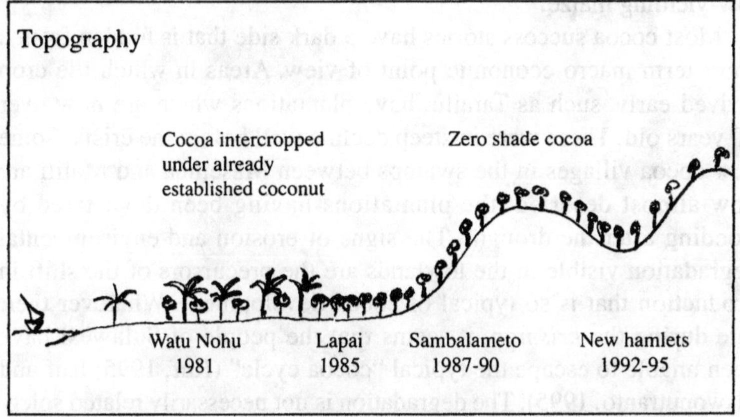

Figure 5.5 Annual planting rate sand topography in the Lapai area of Southeast Sulawesi (3-year moving averages)

Further into the hills, the wave of planting passed in 1992-94. Still further east, the process continues today.

In the mid-1990s, migrants were still able to find huge tracts of forest land for conversion to cocoa. These were situated on the alluvial plains of such areas as Malili and Towuti, which are on the frontier between the three provinces of South, Southeast and Central Sulawesi. These areas, together with Bungku and Poso areas in Central Sulawesi, saw the first migrants arriving several years ago, with a marked acceleration of both migration and planting in 1995-97 (Figure 5.6). In 1999, they remained very active frontier lands.

Most of the increase in production and incomes, however, came from small farms of 2-4 hectares. An average farm of 2 hectares, achieving an average yield of 1700 kilogrammes of cocoa per hectare (more on the plains, less on steep hillsides), had a net income[2] equivalent to around US$ 3000-3500 in 1996. This was among the highest smallholders' incomes achieved anywhere in Indonesia. Thousands of cocoa families probably earned more. A high percentage of these families were former rice growers who started from a low capital base by selling or pledging a small rice plot. Farmers who are now migrating to the hills and who must walk for a full day before reaching their farms have a less promising future, but one that is nevertheless brighter than if they had stayed at home in their village, surviving on 0.25 hectare of rice or 1 hectare of low-yielding maize.

Most cocoa success stories have a dark side that is hidden from a short-term macro-economic point of view. Areas in which the crop arrived early, such as Tarailu, have plantations which are now over 20 years old. These were in steep decline well before the crisis. Some new cocoa villages in the swamps between Masemba and Malili are now almost deserted, the plantations having been devastated by flooding after the drought. The signs of erosion and environmental degradation visible in the lowlands are the precursors of the shift in production that is so typical of cocoa development. Whatever their fate during the *krismon*, it seems that the people of Sulawesi have been unable to escape the typical "cocoa cycle" (Ruf, 1995; Ruf and Siswoputranto, 1995). The degradation is not necessarily related solely to cocoa, but also reflects the effects of aggressive forest clearing by logging companies. If they have not already done so, these factors will also cause problems in the deforested hills. Here, owing to the

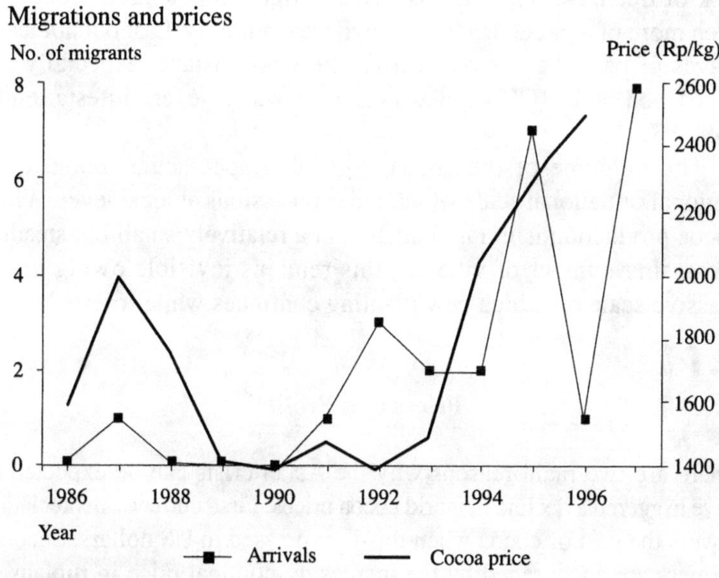

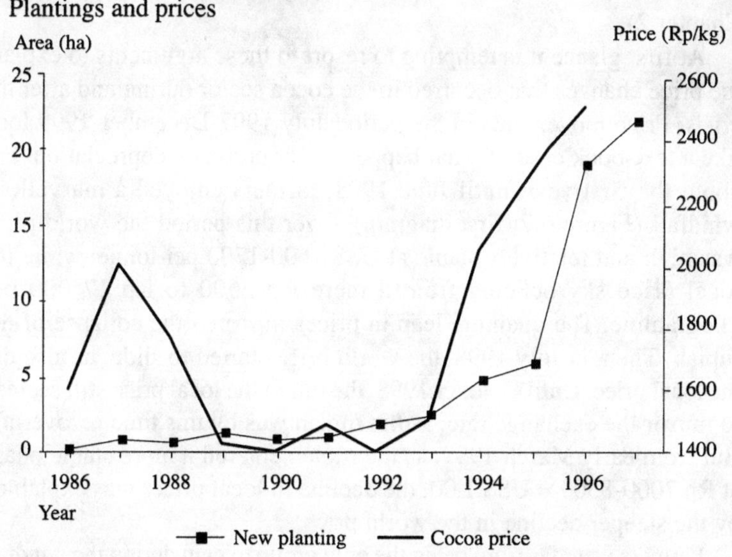

Figure 5.6 Cocoa migrations, plantings and prices in Bungku, Central Sulawesi, 1986-97

lack of tree cover and the absence of irrigation potential, drought is even more of a threat, leading to high tree mortality. Last but not least, waves of pests have swept across the whole island, especially the cocoa pod borer (CPB), of which there was a severe infestation in 1992-97.

The outcome of the cocoa cycle is a spectacular boom on a regional or national scale which hides recessions at local level. While cocoa production is in rapid decline in a relatively small but steadily increasing number of villages, this remains invisible owing to the massive scale on which new planting continues while forests last.

Prices and Profits

There are two main reasons why the Asian crisis can be expected to have triggered a decline in world cocoa prices. First, currency depreciation lowers the cost of cocoa when this is expressed in US dollars. Second, farmers are encouraged by the increasing nominal price in rupiahs to take better care of their farms, resulting in increased supplies (see Chapter 2).

At first glance it is tempting to resort to these arguments to explain the price changes that occurred in the cocoa sector during and after the crisis. Price movements in the period July 1997-December 1999 look like a text-book case of what happens after currency depreciation. For about the first year, until June 1998, farmers enjoyed a marvellous windfall (Figure 5.7, first diagram). Over this period the world price was high and relatively stable at US$ 1600-1700 per tonne, while the local price skyrocketed from a mere Rp 2500 to Rp 17 000 per kilogramme. The quantum leap in prices mirrored the collapse of the rupiah. Then, in July 1998, the world price started to slide, as also did the local price. Until October 1998, the fall in the local price still seemed to mirror the exchange rate, as the rupiah was by this time recovering. But from early March 1999, as the rupiah entered a more stable phase at Rp 7000-8500 = US$ 1.00, the decline in local prices was explained by the steeper decline in the world price.

Farmers were far from being the only group to gain during the windfall period. Middlemen, exporters and importers also got a big slice of the cake. This can be seen from Figure 5.7 (second diagram), which compares the international price converted into rupiah with the rupiah price actually paid to producers. Traders were able to play an exciting "money game" in which they gambled not so much on future prices but on future exchange rates. For instance, in July 1998, in the village of Noling, even a relatively small purchaser, buying less than 500 tonnes a year, told us that he decided on his buying strategy by watching the twice weekly TV broadcast on the stock exchange and exchange rates. If he thought the rupiah was going to weaken, he bought as much as possible. If he thought it might recover, he stopped buying.

The local price in rupiah for the most part follows the value of the US dollar in rupiahs. But not always: there are exceptions in January-February and June-July 1998 (Figure 5.7, third diagram). During these brief periods, the divergence between the local price converted into dollars and the international price shows that traders made even larger profits than at other times (Figure 5.7, fourth diagram). It seems likely that a small number of well informed American and European buyers acted together to influence prices in order to get a share of the windfall. Certainly, some share of the benefits created by the plunge in the rupiah will have accrued to international buyers. This, in turn, may have had some small impact on the world price, at least when it began to fall, in July 1998.

Nevertheless, this impact was probably very limited. There are other, much better explanations for the fall in world prices. These include an expected increase in supplies from West Africa (Côte d'Ivoire and Ghana) and a fall in global demand for cocoa beans, which boosted world stocks to more than 1.1 million tonnes. In early 1999, international buyers discovered that the Ivorian Caisse de Stabilisation (the national marketing board) had sold much less cocoa than expected. Suddenly, more than 150 000 tonnes of cocoa came back onto the world market. This was the decisive factor that triggered the fall. We conclude, tentatively, that Indonesia's monetary crisis probably had only a slight impact on the decline in world prices.

Turning to the second possible reason why prices fell—the supply response of producers—there are several important factors to consider:

- Even if smallholders responded to the 1998 price surge by increasing their investment in new land and new plantings, it will take at least 3-4 years before this is felt in terms of increased production. No

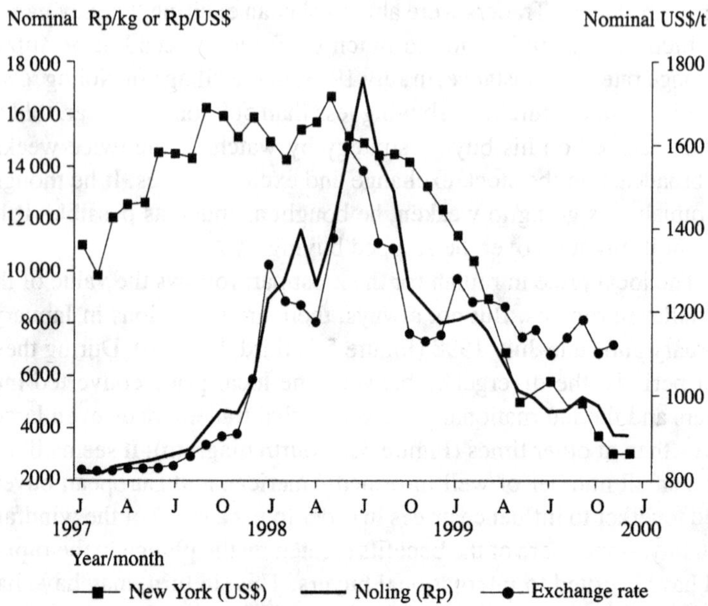

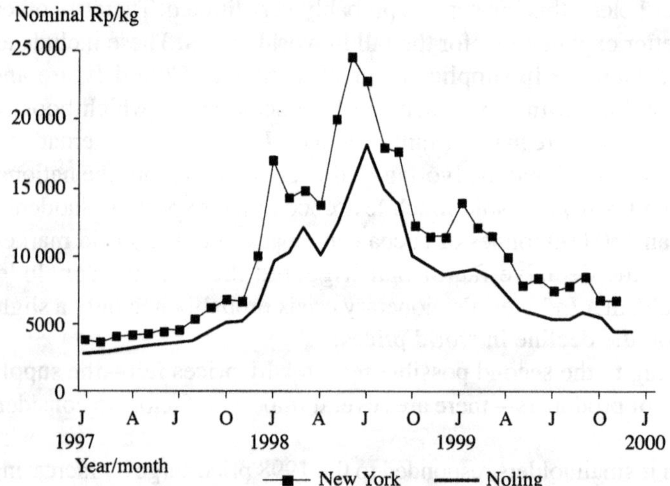

Figures 5.7 International and local prices of cocoa at rupiah-dollar exchange rates, 1997-99

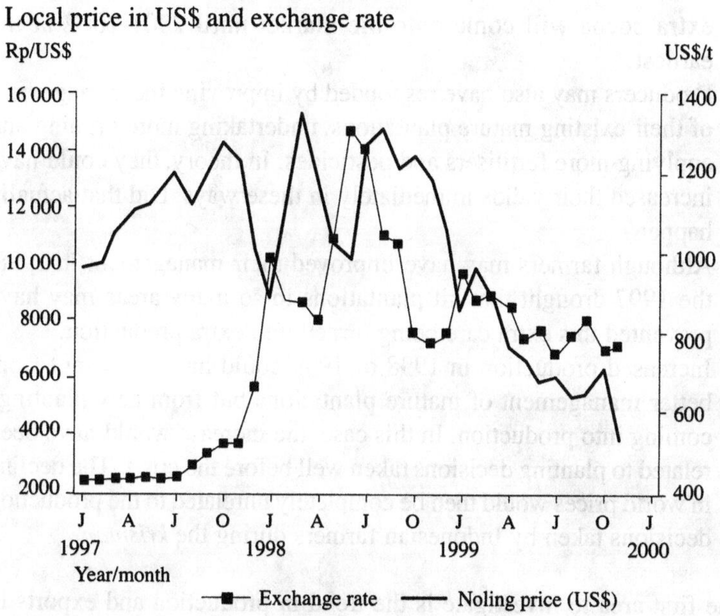

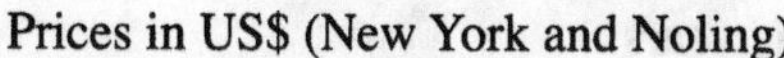

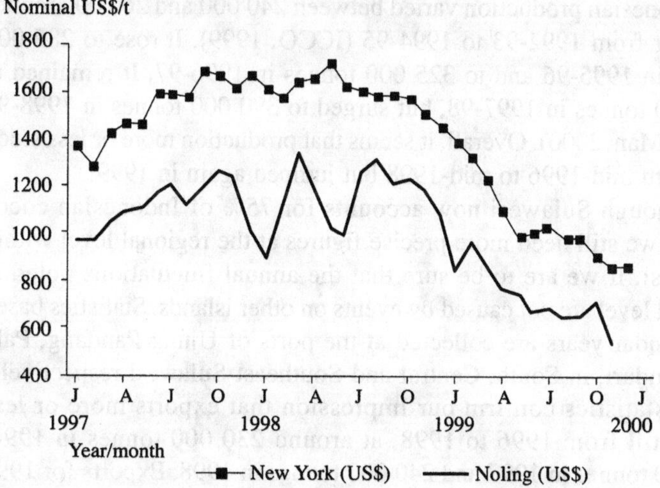

Figure 5.7 (continued)

extra cocoa will come onto the market until 2001-2002 at the earliest.

- Producers may also have responded by improving the management of their existing mature plantations, undertaking more pruning and applying more fertilisers and pesticides. In theory, they could have increased their yields immediately in these ways. Did that actually happen?
- Although farmers may have improved their management in 1998, the 1997 drought that hit plantations in so many areas may have prevented this extra care being turned into extra production.
- Increased production in 1998 or 1999 could have come not from better management of mature plantations but from new plantings coming into production. In this case, the increase would have been related to planting decisions taken well before the crisis. The decline in world prices would then be completely unrelated to the production decisions taken by Indonesian farmers during the *krismon*.

The first area to investigate is the trend in production and exports in 1998-99, at both national and provincial levels, and how this compares with performance in the pre-crisis years.

Indonesian production varied between 240 000 and 260 000 tonnes per year from 1992-93 to 1994-95 (ICCO, 1999). It rose to 285 000 tonnes in 1995-96 and to 325 000 tonnes in 1996-97. It remained at 330 000 tonnes in 1997-98, but surged to 390 000 tonnes in 1998-99 (Ed&F Man, 2000). Overall, it seems that production more or less stood still from mid-1996 to mid-1998 but jumped again in 1999.

Although Sulawesi now accounts for 75% of Indonesian cocoa supply, we still need more precise figures at the regional level within Sulawesi, if we are to be sure that the annual fluctuations noted at national level are not caused by events on other islands. Statistics based on calendar years are collected at the ports of Ujung Pandang, Palu and Kendari, in South, Central and Southeast Sulawesi respectively. These statistics confirm our impression that exports more or less stood still from 1996 to 1998, at around 230 000 tonnes in 1996, 245 000 tonnes in 1997 and 240 000 tonnes in 1998. Exports for 1999 can be estimated at somewhere between 300 000 and 310 000 tonnes, again confirming our impression of a net increase in that year.

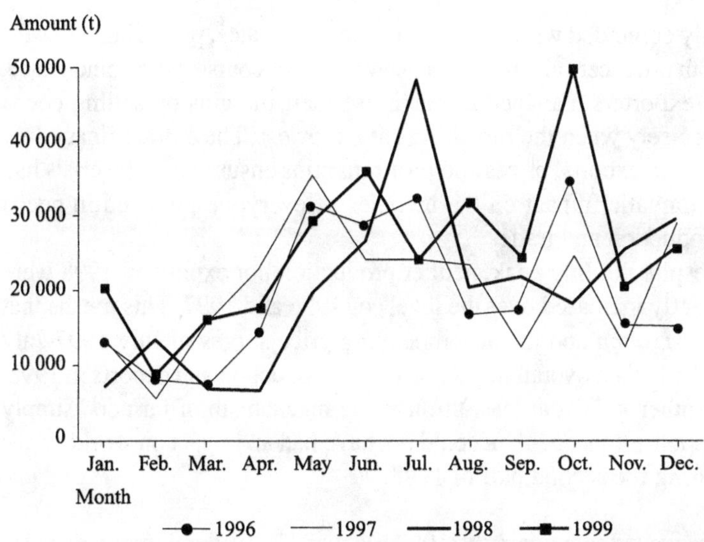

Figure 5.8 Monthly cocoa exports from Ujung Pandang, Sulawesi, 1996-99

The monthly record of exports from Ujung Pandang (Figure 5.8) shows that the volume of exports fell after July 1997, compared with 1996. This fall can be explained by the drought, which had been strongly in evidence almost everywhere in Indonesia since mid-1997. However, owing to a good start in the first half of the year, total exports over the year as a whole were maintained. In 1998, the low level of exports until April (except in February) again suggests that the 1997 drought was having a major impact. The spectacular peak in July 1998 can also be explained by the weather, with trees suddenly yielding after the return of rain in November-December 1997, following months of forced rest. After the July 1998 peak, even if farmers did try to increase productivity, there is no visible impact on exports. In 1999, after a good start in January, export performance was clearly stronger than in 1998.

Two preliminary conclusions can now be advanced:

- Everybody in the cocoa sector, from Indonesian farmers to international buyers, through middlemen and exporters, received a share of the 1998 windfall. The peaks in exports in February and

July coincided with the peaks in exchange rates, providing gains for both producers and traders. This was not, of course, pure coincidence, as exporters managed to maximise their margins by selling cocoa precisely when the rupiah was at its lowest. The extraordinary July peak in exports, prices and profit margins ensured that the crisis had a dramatic impact on the incomes of everyone involved in cocoa production and trade.

- Despite the July peak, neither production nor exports in 1998 were greatly increased over the levels of 1996 and 1997. This means that the *krismon* and the accompanying price surges of July 1997-July 1998 had no overall impact on cocoa production and exports in 1998. In other words, at least through the mechanism of farmers' supply responses, the *krismon* could not have had an impact on world prices during the second half of 1998.

Before we try to explain the 1999 recovery in production and exports, the standstill of 1998 needs to be fully understood. The main factor explaining it is the 1997 drought, which had an overwhelming impact on almost all agricultural production. We will now investigate the drought's impact on cocoa tree growth and production, and on the decisions taken by farmers.

The Drought and its Impact

No one who knows even a little about cocoa or who travelled in South Sulawesi in October 1997, as we did, needs scientific proof of the impact of the 1997 drought. Its effects were especially evident in the hills, where the golden canopies of the dying plantations resembled the autumn colours of trees in Europe. Farmers here prepared for the worst, although many did what they could, displaying a spirit of innovation and self-help by, for instance, buying water pumps and devising an irrigation system from a neighbouring river, where this was possible. In the alluvial plains, farmers and their trees fared somewhat better, also harnessing river water wherever this was available. New farms in frontier lands, enveloped by the humid atmosphere of the forest, did not suffer much, especially in Central Sulawesi, where the east wind had a positive influence.

We will first examine the effects of the drought in two neighbouring villages in South Sulawesi: Noling, on the alluvial plain, and Tampumea, in the foothills. The villages are representative of what is now a well established cocoa area. Planting started here in the late 1970s and peaked in the period 1983-90. Over the past decade, new migrants have kept on arriving and planting further and further up in the hills.

Cocoa production

Starting in March 1995, we counted the number of pods harvested by farmers each week in Noling and Tampumea on a fixed tree stock of 220 trees[3]. Our survey ended in late 1999.

The results (Figure 5.9) suggest that in many years there are two harvesting peaks, although the harvesting profile does show considerable variation from year to year. The years 1998 and 1999, however, were highly irregular, confirming the impact of the drought and its aftermath.

The profile for pod harvesting is fairly similar to the profile for exports, although the latter is less jagged. The high peak of 1998, from

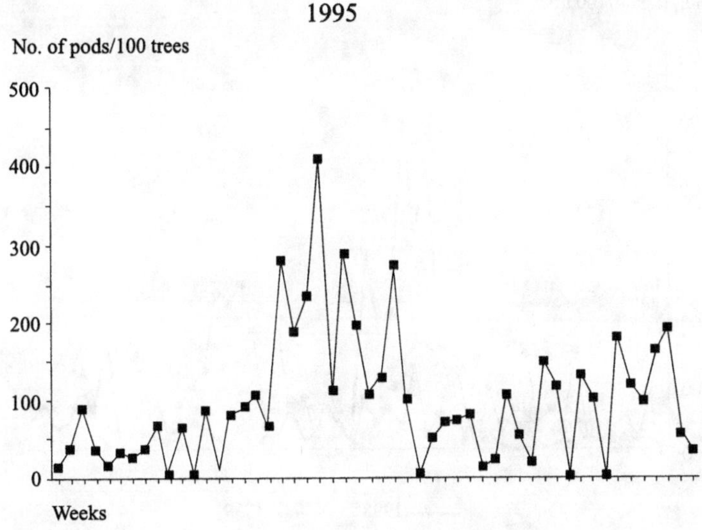

Figure 5.9 Cocoa pods harvested by farmers in Noling, South Sulawesi, 1995-99

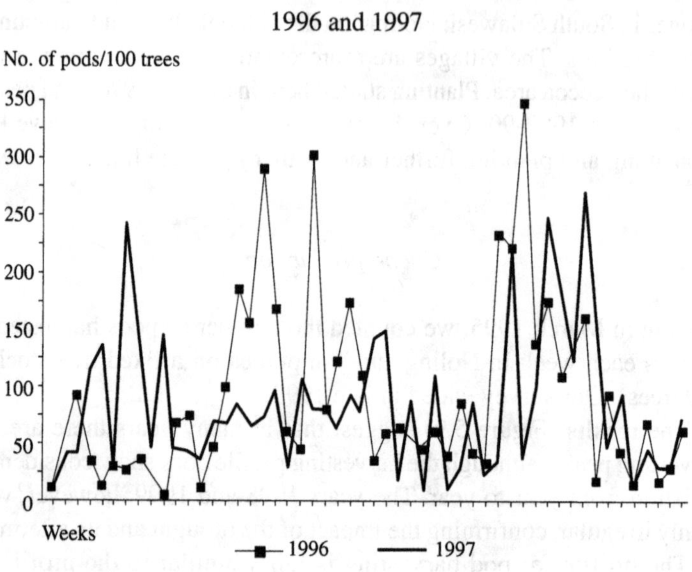

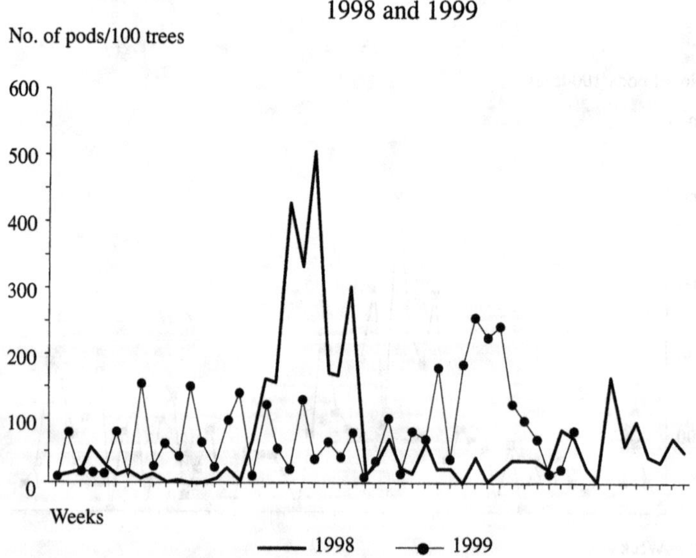

Figure 5.9 (continued)

the end of April to mid-June (weeks 17-25), occurs just 1 month before the peak in exports, suggesting that exporters benefitted more by luck than by design. Production was very low in the first 16 weeks of the year, then rose dramatically from April onwards. In June, thousands of trucks full of cocoa arrived in Ujung Pandang, to the benefit of everyone involved with cocoa.

According to the export data, the first half of 1997 was good, but this was followed by a low second peak. The disappointing second half of the year was due to the initial impact of the drought, which started mid-year. The pod harvesting data show an early peak but, surprisingly, a high second peak in September-October. There are two possible explanations for this.

First, in our survey, two of the farms were situated close to a river. On farms like this the drought proved harmless, even having a positive impact on the year's yield through its effect in keeping the soil well drained. In case of need, farmers improvised a home-made irrigation system, pumping river water to their trees. Several villages in the plains were in this privileged situation. Kaburi, near Noling, is an example. This village was the envy of its neighbours when, in January-February 1998, its producers were the only ones to bring cocoa to the middlemen's shops as prices rocketed above Rp 9000 per kilogramme.

Second, most cocoa trees exhibited a well-known physiological response to the drought. One of the first defenses of a drought-stressed tree in its fight for survival is to produce flowers and fruits. Many of the resulting cherelles and immature pods subsequently aborted, but a high number survived and reached maturity. These pods were harvested, but did not contain as many beans as normal.

In almost every part of the archipelago, the drought ended in heavy rains in November-December 1997. These rains, brought by the opposite winds and currents to those that cause El Niño, are known as La Niña.

The arrival of La Niña, combined with the abortion of cherelles and immature pods in late 1997, explains both the near total lack of harvested pods until mid-April 1998 and the sudden huge concentration of pods in June of that year. This peak in production took place both in the hills, where the trees were still recovering from the drought, and on the plain, where they were often affected by flooding. After this desperate spurt of production, the trees quite literally rested, again producing very little until the last 6 weeks of the year. During this resting period, we observed infestations of *Phytophthora* sp., a fungus favoured by abundant rainfall, leading to further tree mortality.

Finally, in 1999, after two promising weeks (8 and 12), the trees rested again until around September-October, when a new peak in production occurred. This came just in time to prevent mature cocoa areas from economic ruin.

Table 5.1 shows the total number of pods harvested over the period 1995-99, together with estimated yields and yield trends. Despite the small size of the tree sample, the effects of climate on production are obvious. Whatever farmers did on their farms, production in this well established cocoa area declined over the period as a whole. The decline can be estimated as at least 30% in the plains, even more in the hills, where the drought hit harder. Nineteen ninety-nine saw the beginnings of a recovery, or at least a return to greater stability, but the increasing losses caused by CPB[4] do not bode well for the future. Compared with 1995-96, yields in 1998-99 were low.

Table 5.1 Total number of pods harvested per tree, estimated yields and yield trends on farms around Noling, 1995-99

Year	*Pods/ tree*	*Pods/ kg**	*Cocoa/ tree (kg)**	*Trees/ ha**	*Yield (kg/ha)**	*Gain/loss over previous year (%)*
1995	44	25	1.76	1100	2017	
1996	46	25	1.84	1100	2108	+ 5
1997	41	26	1.58	1070	1687	– 20
1998	34	27	1.26	1040	1310	– 21
1999*	34	28	1.21	1040	1263	– 3.6

Note: 138 trees in the plains and 82 trees in the hills.
* Estimated.

Cocoa sales

On a weekly basis, we recorded cocoa sales by 10 farmers on 13 farm plots in Noling from 1995 to 1999. These farmers had plantations mainly in the plains around the village, but also in the neighbouring hills. Although our sample size was small, it generated a wealth of information. By mid-1997, we were able to differentiate two types of cocoa farm. On the alluvial plain were some farms with good management, where yields held up relatively well despite the drought. Farms in the foothills and the hills suffered terribly, as also did those in the plains that were badly managed, especially those under a share-cropping regime. Many of the trees on these farms died or nearly died, and it will take at least 3 years to even partially rehabilitate these areas, with little chance of a return to previous levels of production. In 1998, almost all farms suffered a further decline in yields, caused by the cumulative effects of the drought in the hills and the unexpectedly abundant rainfall in the plains (Table 5.2). A further limited decline took place in 1999 on well managed farms in the plains. Conversely, on poorly managed plains farms, yields started to recover slightly in 1999, wherever share-croppers' neglect could be rectified. Farms in the hills also began to recover in 1999.

The sales data provide a picture of yield levels and trends that is generally similar to that obtained from pod harvests. They confirm 1996 as a relatively good year compared with 1995. The exception is 1999, where the sales data show a 10% increase over 1998, compared with the continuing decline deduced from the pod harvest. This is explained by the low level of CPB infestation on the farms covered by the sales survey.

Of the two types of farm, the first one (Type A in the table) is fairly homogeneous, with yields closely bunched around the average. The second type (Type B), consisting of badly managed plain farms and farms in the hills, is homogeneous in terms of the trend from one year to the next but heterogeneous in terms of absolute yields. On the two worst farms in the hills, yields were around 1200 kilogrammes per hectare in 1996 but fell to 500 and to below 400 kilogrammes per hectare in 1997 and 1998 respectively, before recovering to 600 kilogrammes per hectare in 1999.

Table 5.2 Cocoa yields and yield gains or losses in Noling, Sulawesi, 1995-99

Farm location and management	*Yield and yield trend*								
	1995	*1996*		*1997*		*1998*		*1999*	
	(kg/ha)	*(kg/ha)*	*%*	*(kg/ha)*	*%*	*(kg/ha)*	*%*	*(kg/ha)*	*%*
Type A*	1758	2009	+ 14	1778	−11	1478	−17	1394	−6
Type B*	2182	2436	+ 12	1625	−33	1057	−35	1547	+46
Aggregate	1914	2166	+ 13	1722	−21	1323	−23	1450	+10

* Type A: Average farm on plain, well managed during the 1997 drought. Type B: (i) Good farm on plain but badly managed during the drought; (ii) farm in the foothills.

The data in the table may be interpreted as representative of the production loss in regions consisting entirely or mainly of mature cocoa farms. Despite the partial recovery in the hills in 1999, the global loss since 1996 is still around 30-35%. Other regions, where farms are newer, will have had better results. This explains the fact that overall production and exports appear stable from 1996 to 1998, before increasing in 1999.

From well established cocoa areas to frontier lands

A total of 101 farmers in three different areas were asked about tree production and mortality. The first area consisted of Noling, with 21 households, and of Tampumea, with 15 households. As already noted, this area was one of the first to be developed in South Sulawesi. The first trees were planted in the late 1970s and planting reached a peak in the mid-1980s. The second area was Lewonu, near Wotu, also in South Sulawesi, where cocoa migration and planting date from around the late 1980s to the early 1990s. Our sample here consisted of 24 households, mostly in the plains but some in the hills. Lewonu is thought to have been the first village in South Sulawesi to be attacked by CPB, in 1993. Many cocoa farms are still young, having come into production between 1996 and 1998[5]. The third area was Bungku, in Central Sulawesi, a recent frontier land where production began just before the crisis, in the mid-1990s. Here we covered 41 households. Our 101-farm sample can thus be considered representative of the different stages of cocoa production in Sulawesi.

Of the 101 families, almost all were Bugis migrants, the exceptions being some 7 or 8 families belonging to the indigenous forest-dwelling groups, the Luwu and the Bungku[6], and 14 Balinese families. Ten of the Balinese families live in Lewonu, while four live in Bungku. The low number of Balinese families is indicative of the relatively low involvement of transmigrants in cocoa development in South Sulawesi, at least until recently.

In these areas as a whole, the percentage of trees that died in 1997 due to drought was relatively small, around 6% (Table 5.3). It was almost zero on the plains and at the new front, but reached around 20% in the more deforested areas of the hills. In 1998, a few trees on the plains died due to flooding.

Table 5.3 Impact of the 1997 drought on tree mortality in cocoa producing areas of Sulawesi, 1997-98 (average per household)

Village	*Mature cocoa area (ha)*	*Cocoa trees before drought*	*Trees dying in 1997 (No.)*	*(%)*	*Trees replanted in 1998*
Tampumea (hills)	2.18	2859	646	23	301
Noling (plains)	2.68	2712	90	3	76
Lewonu (mostly plains)	1.75	1869	4	0.2	4
Bungku (mostly foothills)	0.58	1422	23	2	13
Average	1.52	2010	125	6	67

The total of dead trees over the 2-year period can thus be estimated at around 8%. Despite these deaths, the tree stock has grown. However, this was mainly because of the rapid increase in new plantings in frontier areas, not because of replanting in well established areas. Here, around 50% of dead trees were replanted, usually unsuccessfully[7].

Data on yields in 1996-98 were collected on the basis of discussions with each of the 101 farmers (Table 5.4). The 10 Balinese farmers in Lewonu occupy a special place, since they intercrop cocoa with coconut, a practice that reduces cocoa yields. Like the Bugis, their farms were among the first to suffer from CPB infestation.

Table 5.4 Trends in average yields in three cocoa producing areas of Sulawesi, 1996-98

Village	*Yield (kg/ha)*		
	1996	*1997*	*1998*
Noling (mostly plains)	2000	1808	1510
Tampumea (mostly foothills)	1400	1001	1021
Lewonu, Bugis (plains and foothills)*	1000	1296	1667
Lewonu, Balinese (mostly plains)*	788	816	933
Bungku (foothills)**		680	1004

* CPB outbreaks, especially in 1996; ** Young farms.

In Noling and Tampumea, average yields were similar to those obtained from the weekly survey described above. The 1997 yield data confirm that the drought had a relatively low impact on the plains and a much greater impact in the hills, while those for 1998 confirm the continuing decline in the plains and the slow recovery in the hills.

In Lewonu, where CPB struck early, yields were lowest in 1996 and improved in 1997 and 1998. The naturally increasing yield of young farms was at least partially responsible for this trend. Another factor was recovery from CPB as farmers learnt to control the pest. Farmers who experienced the pest early, before the *krismon* when prices were increasing, were in a better position than those who faced it in 1999, when the price collapsed.

In Bungku, the table shows the strong increase in production from one year to the next that is typical of frontier areas. Production rises regardless of external events. The yields are probably not accurate in absolute terms, since it is difficult to assess the productive area of young plantations.

If we accept as true the production levels given by the 101 farmers, we should obtain a profile of production over the 3 years that is close to the profile for exports. Sulawesi's exports stood still at around 230 000-240 000 tonnes annually between 1996 and 1998. A similar picture emerges from our sample (Table 5.5).

Table 5.5 Trends in cocoa production in three areas of Sulawesi, 1996-99

Village		*Production (kg)*			
	No of farms	*1996*	*1997*	*1998*	*1999**
Noling (mostly plains)	21	112 415	101 899	85 145	83 000
Tampumea (hills)	15	45 847	32 871	33 439	41 000
Lewonu (Bugis)	14	22 230	32 020	41 170	40 000
Lewonu (Balinese)	10	12 210	12 655	14 460	14 000
Bungku (foothills)**	41	4770	10 685	21 867	48 000
Total	101	197 472	190 040	196 081	226 000
Weighted total***	121	199 857	195 383	207 015	250 000

* Estimated; ** Young farms; *** Coefficient of 1.5 applied to the Bungku sub-sample.

In 1999, however, production increased only slightly in the 101-farm sample, moving from 196 tonnes to 226 tonnes (+15%), whereas exports jumped from 240 000 tonnes to 300 000 (+25%). The lower increase in production in our sample is explained by the under-representation of frontier lands. This demonstrates the key role of new migrations and plantings in maintaining cocoa supplies.

In sum, from our three data sets (pod harvests from 220 trees, weekly survey of cocoa sales from 13 farms and the questionnaire sent to 101 farmers in three locations), we draw the following conclusions:

- The 1998 windfall was real and large.
- In the mature cocoa areas of South and Southeast Sulawesi, the rise in prices did not lead to a positive supply response on the part of farmers because the 1997 drought and, to a lesser extent, the 1998 floods, reduced yields. In 1999, the rise of CPB again prevented a yield increase.
- As in most cocoa production situations, the apparent stability of production and exports at the whole-island level resulted from a combination of decline in established cocoa areas and increase in frontier lands.
- This means that Sulawesi's overall increase in production in 1999 is the result of investment decisions taken before the windfall, before the *krismon* and even before the drought.
- As a corollary, the monetary crisis clearly did not influence world market prices through the mechanism of price-elasticity of supply.

We now know that farmers in mature cocoa areas did not succeed in responding positively to price increases in the short term, but we do not yet know whether or not they tried to do so. This is the subject of the next section, in which we analyse fertiliser use.

Farmers' Management Responses

Fertiliser prices

Until the mid-1990s the price of fertiliser on the domestic market in Indonesia rose, but not as fast as the price of cocoa. By mid-July 1998, at the height of the *krismon*, urea and triple superphosphate (TSP) prices had risen by only 10-20% above their 1997 levels. However, in November-December 1998, when government subsidies were finally removed, these inputs suddenly became much more expensive

(Figure 5.10). Fertiliser was by now in very short supply, imports having run out not least because of the temptation to re-export them. By the end of 1998, the prices of all basic nitrogen (N), phosphate (P) and potassium (K) fertilisers were 100-200% higher than in mid-1997. Buying a single bag of potassium chloride (KCl) required three times more cocoa than 10 years earlier. In 1999, fertiliser prices scarcely dipped despite the partial recovery of the rupiah, while the price of cocoa nose-dived.

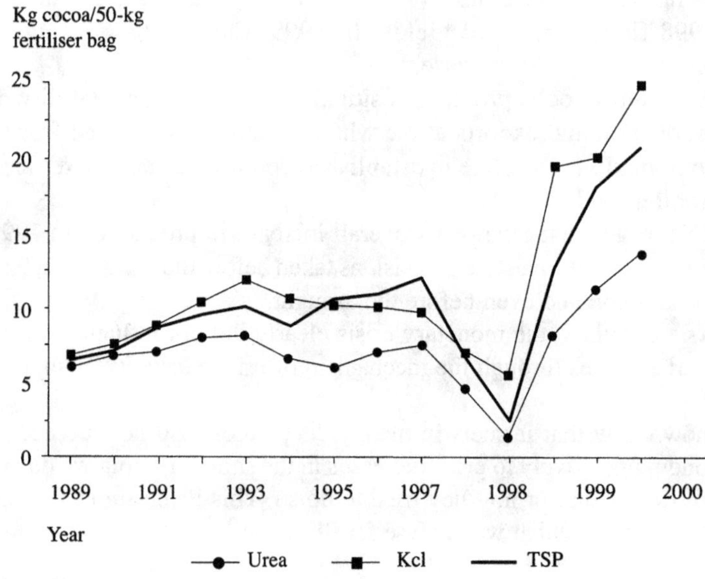

Figure 5.10 Cocoa: fertiliser price ratios in Noling, South Sulawesi, 1989-99

Fertiliser use

In Bungku, where most of the cocoa farms created from cleared forest are still young, virtually no fertiliser was used before the crisis and very little after. In Noling and Lewonu, where there are plenty of mature plantations, fertiliser use increased after a period of doubt in the first half of 1998 (Tables 5.6 and 5.7). If we consider the whole sample to be reasonably representative, then around 40% of cocoa smallholders in Sulawesi increased their fertiliser use in 1998 compared with 1997.

Table 5.6 Changes in fertiliser use in three cocoa producing areas, 1997-98

Use in 1998 compared with 1997	*Noling plain and Lewonu*	*Bungku**	*Total*
No. of farmers increasing	38	4	41
No. of farmers reducing	7	2	10
No. of farmers making no change	13	1	14
No. of farmers who never use	1	34	35
Total	59	41	100

* Pioneer front.

Table 5.7 Use of fertilisers in Noling, 1997-98

Village	*Use (kg/household)*		
	1997	*1998*	*% change*
Noling (mostly plains)	513	631	+ 23
Tampumea (mostly hills)	462	612	+ 32
Total	491	605	+ 23

This is an opportunity to stress the high level of fertiliser use on mature plantations in Sulawesi. In Noling, in 1993-94, a sample of 20 households and 48 farm plots showed an average use of 600 kilogrammes of NPK per hectare on the plain and some 500 kilogrammes in the hills (Ruf and Yoddang, 1996). In 1997, consumption was slightly lower, but in 1998 it increased again by some 20% on the plains and by up to 35% in the hills. In the hills, this increase may have helped to contain the fall in yields in 1998 and undoubtedly aided the slight recovery of yields in 1999.

Farmers were asked why they had increased or decreased their fertiliser use. Although the cocoa:fertiliser price ratio played a part in their decisions, the major determinant was tree condition after the drought (Table 5.8).

Table 5.8 Farmers' reasons for increasing fertiliser use in 1998

Reasons	*% of farmers*
Trees in poor condition after 1997 drought	59
Trees in poor condition after 1998 flooding	7
Good cocoa prices and high incomes made fertiliser purchase easy	17
Tree life-cycle: trees were just entering into production/ageing trees need more fertilisers	7
Tried a new fertiliser in 1997; not convinced, so returned to previous fertiliser type but in larger amounts	3
Copied from a succusful neighbour	7
Total	100

Most farmers who increased their use of fertilisers aimed not to maximise yields and returns but rather to save and rebuild their orchards. Of course, they were encouraged in this aim by the high incomes they obtained in 1998.

Income was a more important consideration among those who reduced their use of fertiliser. Because of the drought, the incomes of these farmers had not increased enough to enable them to buy large amounts of fertiliser. In some cases, too many trees had already died to make it worthwhile applying fertiliser. In others, the reason for reduced use was technical. In 1998, smallholders preferred to apply urea in an effort to help the trees rebuild a canopy. They waited until 1999 before applying other fertilisers. Only in one case was a decision in favour of some other investment (house building) mentioned as the reason for reducing fertiliser use.

At this stage, we could have continued by analysing the adoption of other inputs, such as herbicides. These were widely used both before the drought and the *krismon* and after them, when use may even have increased. However, we felt the fertiliser case study to be sufficient to demonstrate the issues regarding input use, which are as follows:

- On the back of rocketing prices and the resulting sudden increase in their incomes, most farmers owning mature cocoa farms did increase their use of fertilisers in 1998.
- However, this was done not to ensure optimum returns and profitability but rather to save trees at high risk from drought and, to a lesser extent, from flooding.

- Increased fertiliser use did not lead to increased production, but helped to offset losses.
- In frontier areas, fertiliser use remained marginal, for two reasons. First, the trees did not need fertiliser, as they were still benefitting from the fertility provided by forest clearance. Second, however much prices rose, production was just starting and incomes remained low.

It seems clear that farmers' short-term responses to the local cocoa price surge could not have influenced world prices. We can therefore turn our minds to the 1998 windfall. We will begin by examining the windfall in the context of trends in comparative prices since 1988-89.

Comparative Prices and Terms of Trade

In mid-1998, almost all cocoa farmers were smiling. The lifestyles of many testified to the excellent terms of trade they were enjoying for cocoa against most other goods and services. At the time of writing, in mid-1999, the smiles have become somewhat forced. Not all prices have increased as rapidly as those of P and K fertilisers, but farmers' purchasing power has undoubtedly fallen sharply.

For the analysis that follows we used our own data rather than official commodity prices, which are general for Indonesia and not necessarily relevant to Sulawesi. Our data include prices obtained in the rural market at Noling and prices quoted by farmers.

Motorcycles, cars and trips to Mecca

"With only one big cocoa sale, I got 9.5 million rupiah and I immediately bought three small Suzuki motorcycles, one for each of my sons," one farmer in Noling told us in July 1998. Another said: "Last year, you needed 2 tonnes of cocoa to buy one Yamaha bike. Now you need less than 1 tonne." There is not much to add to these farmers' comments, except to say that they were right to buy motorcycles in July 1998. By July 1999, for the same bike, they would have needed 3 tonnes of cocoa.

In 1991, a trip to Mecca cost Rp 6.5 million and could be paid for by selling 4 tonnes of cocoa. By 1994, the same trip cost Rp 7.5 million but required only 3 tonnes of cocoa. In February 1999, the cost of the trip jumped to around Rp 25 million rupiah but was easily covered by 2 tonnes of cocoa provided the trip had been paid for 6 months in advance. In the year 2000, to make the same trip, farmers may once again have to sell at least 4 tonnes of cocoa, possibly more.

Rice and cocoa

The price of rice was 200% higher by late 1998 than it had been in mid-1997. Impressive though it was, this rise did not lure farmers away from cocoa.

In every country where we have studied competition and complementarities between food crops and cocoa or coffee, we have always found that a rice: cocoa or rice:coffee price ratio below 0.5-0.7 is sufficient to keep farmers investing in the tree crop. Investment is endangered only when the ratio rises above 0.7 and approaches 1.0. This was the case in the coffee areas of Madagascar in the late 1980s (Blanc-Pamard and Ruf, 1992).

The behaviour of new cocoa farmers in Sulawesi in 1990 provided further confirmation of this finding. Prices in 1990 had slumped in comparison with those of 1987. Nevertheless, many farmers said they would continue to plant and maintain cocoa as long as its selling price remained higher than the purchase price of rice. Their main reason was the return to labour. Rice needs to be planted every year or twice a year, whereas cocoa is planted only once, "for ever", or at the most only every 25 years.

Figure 5.11 shows that the rice:cocoa price ratio in Sulawesi has long remained below 0.5. In 1987-88 and again in 1995-98, it was below 0.35, a level that stimulates new plantings. In mid-1998, it fell to 0.12, but it then rose sharply again in late 1998, when it reached a level close to 0.5. This price ratio, which was maintained in 1999, is the worst that Noling farmers have ever known. Surrounded by vast irrigated paddy fields, Noling is privileged with regard to rice supplies. In the more remote hill areas, the ratio may have risen still higher to 0.66, close to the danger threshold. If CPB tightens its hold, the future of cocoa in Sulawesi may become uncertain, especially for farmers who have given up food crops completely in order to concentrate on cocoa.

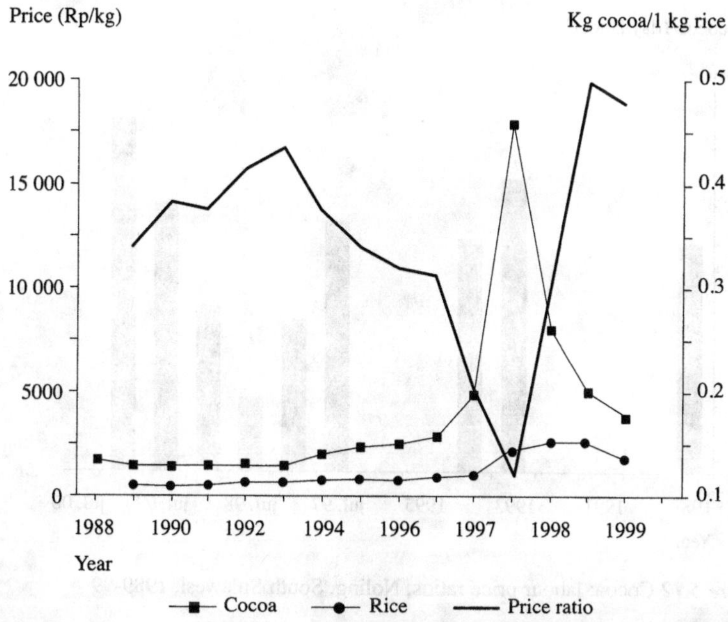

Figure 5.11 Prices of cocoa and rice at Noling market, 1988-99

Labour costs and participation

In 1989, smallholders needed to sell around 1.7 kilogrammes of cocoa to cover the cost of a day's hired labour (including one or two meals, coffee and cigarettes). In late 1993, as the price of cocoa recovered, this ratio started falling. In July 1998, due to the spectacular rise in the price of cocoa to Rp 18 000 per kilogramme, the ratio fell to an all-time low, around 0.5 kilogramme.

The increased profitability of cocoa triggered demands for increased pay from workers. The outcome was an 80% increase in the cash component of their daily wages, which rose from Rp 5500 to Rp 10 000. When meals and cigarettes were added, the daily labour cost doubled, from Rp 7500 to Rp 15 000. As a result, when the international price fell, the ratio returned first to 1.3 kilogrammes (Figure 5.12) then to 2 kilogrammes by June-July 1999, the same as the 1993 ratio.

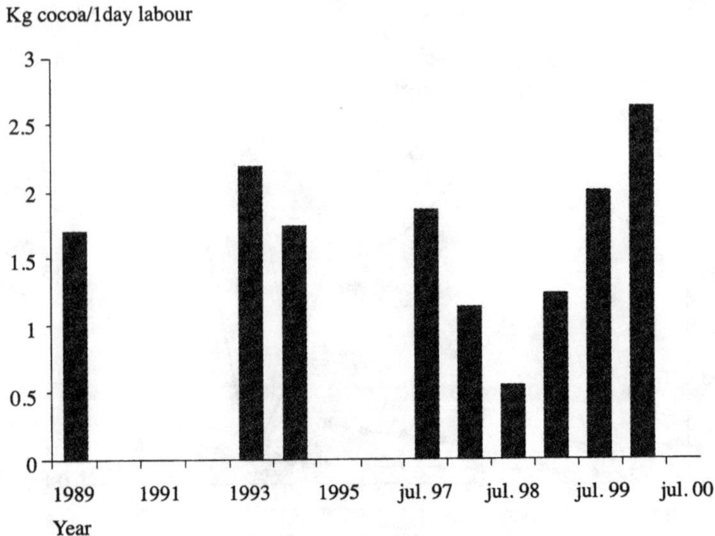

Figure 5.12 Cocoa: labour price ratios, Noling, South Sulawesi, 1989-99

That the wages of day labourers doubled suggests that there was a shortage of labour. At first sight, the increase in labour costs of 80-100% may seem modest compared with the increase of 150-200% in the prices of rice and fertilisers. In accordance with basic economic theory, the price of non-tradable or "less tradable" inputs such as labour seems to have risen more slowly than the prices of tradable ones in the wake of the crisis[8].

However, those willing to be hired as daily workers are either neighbours' sons and daughters or Balinese workers. For most of these workers, daily wages represent additional income, over and above what they earn from the family farm or from other activities, including other labouring contracts. The Balinese are in fact primarily share-croppers, known as *bagi hasil* workers. The effect of the windfall on these workers differed from that on day labourers.

From the point of view of the farm owner, share-cropping contracts have the advantage of being relatively stable, since labour costs are a known proportion of total income. The proportion of the crop accruing to the *bagi hasil* worker is low—at between one-sixth and one-quarter of the harvest—

mainly because fertilisers and pesticides must be bought by the owner. But if the price of cocoa increases, the cash income obtained by the share-cropper also rises, by a proportion close to, if not more than, that of the owner. That means that, in theory, *bagi hasil* incomes should have risen by around 400%.

Risk sharing covers not only fluctuations in prices but also those of the weather. Sulawesi in 1997-98 provided a perfect example of the latter. For share-croppers as for plantation owners, the fall in yields following the drought reduced the impact of the 400% increase in price. On average, the 1998 incomes of share-croppers increased by "only" 200-300%.

Many Balinese workers, who had previously accepted wages on a monthly basis, switched to *bagi hasil* contracts in 1997 (Table 5.9). This was a clever move, for it meant that their wages increased enormously when the 1998 windfall arrived.

Table 5.9 Trends in types of labour contract, Noling, 1993-98

	Trend					
	1993	*1994*	*1995*	*1996*	*1997*	*1998*
No. of workers paid on a monthly basis	7	6	9	9	0	1
No. of workers paid on a share-cropping basis	16	17	14	15	24	26
Total	23	23	23	24	24	27

Note: Sample size = 36 farms.

Land prices

In well established cocoa villages such as Noling and Lewonu, it is almost impossible to set a price on land in the plains. The area is full of cocoa and the few plots that are still unused are not for sale. In Lewonu and Tampumea, a few plots of fallow land can still be found in the foothills and hills. The prices of these almost doubled in 1998 (Table 5.10). In the more remote hills, forest plots are still sold at relatively low prices per hectare (Rp 400 000-500 000 in 1998 compared with Rp 300 000-400 000 in 1997), but these are more than a day's walk from the road and their ownership is subject to considerable uncertainty.

Table 5.10 Approximate prices of land and plantations in Noling and Lewonu, 1997-98

	Price (million Rp)		
	1997	*1998*	*Ratio 1998/97*
Fallow land in hills (Lewonu)	1.2	2	1.7-2
Mature cocoa farm in foothills (Tampumea)*	10-15	15-30	2
Mature cocoa farms in plains (Noling)	15-25	25-75	3

* Above Noling.

In Noling and Tampumea, the market for established farms was more active than the market for unused land in 1998. Several farmers decided to sell their small cocoa plots at a high price in order to get land at a low price on the new fronts at, for example, Towali and Bungku. This is nothing new—the Bugis are renowned for their acumen in cashing in at the right moment to fund a more ambitious venture in a new place—but the increased trade in used land was probably stimulated by the crisis. The price of land rose in proportion to the annual incomes anticipated by buyers, doubling in the hills, more than tripling in the plains.

Most purchases of land were thus made not in established cocoa villages but in the new frontier lands, often 300-500 kilometres away. Prices of forest plots in areas such as Bungku remained relatively low throughout the crisis, averaging only Rp 162 000 per hectare in 1998. The range, however, was very wide, from less than Rp 100 000 to Rp 1 million per hectare. There are so few indigenous people in the more remote hills that migrants could still get land there almost free of charge. They may have to pay something later to "administrative representatives" named by a local village chief or by sub-district and district heads.

Land thus remains extremely cheap for cocoa farmers who enjoyed the windfall in South Sulawesi. From the point of view of a farmer who sold his cocoa farm in Noling in 1998 and bought a few hectares in Bungku the same year, the price of land neither doubled nor tripled: it fell by 50-90%. As a basic, non-tradable factor of production, land will seem cheaper after a windfall than it did before, for as long as new frontiers exist.

In summary:

- Cocoa prices in 1998 rose by 300-400% over their levels in the first half of 1997, reaching their peak on 14 July 1998. As the prices of inputs and of most consumer goods rose by only 100-200% some 4-5 months later, most cocoa farmers enjoyed a wonderful windfall in real terms, despite the negative impact of drought on production.
- In 1999, cocoa smallholders found that comparative prices for some inputs had returned to pre-crisis levels and that the situation for some staple foods and fertilisers was even worse.
- Despite the upward pressure exerted by windfalls, the price of frontier land remains extremely low for those prepared to migrate.

We will now quantify the 1998 windfall.

The 1998 Windfall

After a slow recovery since 1993, the price of cocoa began rising rapidly in August-September 1997 (see Figure 5.7). Even at this early stage, the increase helped to make up for the yield losses incurred in the deforested hills, where mature but unshaded cocoa trees had suffered terribly from the drought. In all other ecosystems, 1997 was a better year than 1996. And in some areas, either because trees produced pods before dying or because proximity to a river made the drought harmless or even beneficial, farmers benefitted substantially from a conjunction of rising production and prices towards the end of the year (Table 5.11).

Then came the 1998 explosion in incomes. During the year, gross incomes from cocoa increased across the board, by 250-260% compared with 1997 and by around 330% compared with 1996. Since the price of most inputs and consumer goods rose by "only" 100-200% and these rises occurred only in the last few months of the year, most cocoa farmers undoubtedly enjoyed a marvellous windfall.

The additional gross income in 1998 compared with 1997 amounted to an average of Rp 19 million for a household in a hill village such as Tampumea and Rp 32 million for one in a plains village such as Noling.

Table 5.11 Average gross income per household from cocoa in three areas of Sulawesi, 1996-98

	No. of farms	*Gross income (Rp'000)*				
		1996	*1997*	*Change/ 1996 (%)*	*1998*	*Change/ 1997 (%)*
Noling (mostly plains)	21	13 827	17 211	+ 24	49 400	+ 187
Tampumea (hills)*	15	7894	7751	− 2	27 161	+ 250
Lewonu (Bugis)	14	6254	8005		35 288	+ 341
Lewonu (Balinese)	10	3460	4429		17 352	+ 292
Bungku (foothills)**	41	244	781		5600	+ 616
Total	101	31 680	38 179	+ 21	134 802	+ 253

* Above Noling. ** Young farms.

This came on top of incomes that had already enabled many farmers to buy motorcycles and build new houses in previous years. Putting it another way, in 1998 farmers in the hills earned a total gross income equivalent to around US$ 3200, while those on the plain grossed close to US$ 6000. These incomes had immense purchasing power when expressed in rupiah at June 1998 exchange rates (Figure 5.13). They represented extraordinary riches by rural Indonesian standards, especially at a time of poverty for almost everyone else.

The window of opportunity in which to maximise profits lasted only 4-6 months. It occurred between the simultaneous peaks in production and prices in May-July and the first significant increases in the prices of inputs, which came in late 1998. However, by this time most farmers had capitalised on their good fortune. What did they do with the money!

How the Windfall was Used

We will evaluate the *krismon's* effect on economic and social investments not by means of a static examination of expenditures in 1998 but rather by comparing what was bought in 1997-98 with purchases over the past 10 years. Besides the time dimension of our analysis, place will also be important. People in frontier areas spent money differently to those in well established cocoa villages.

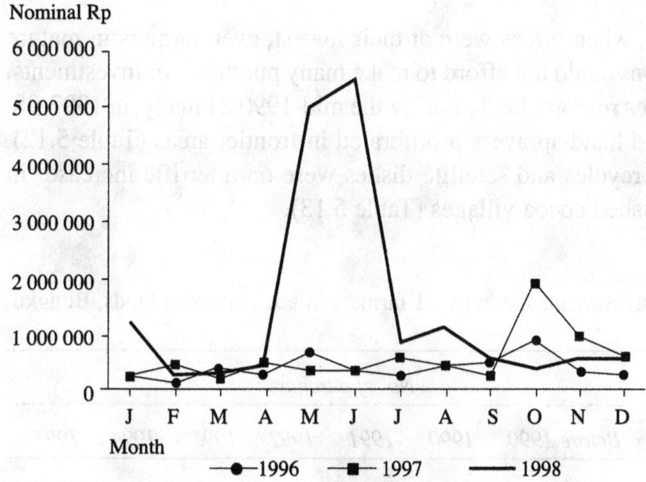

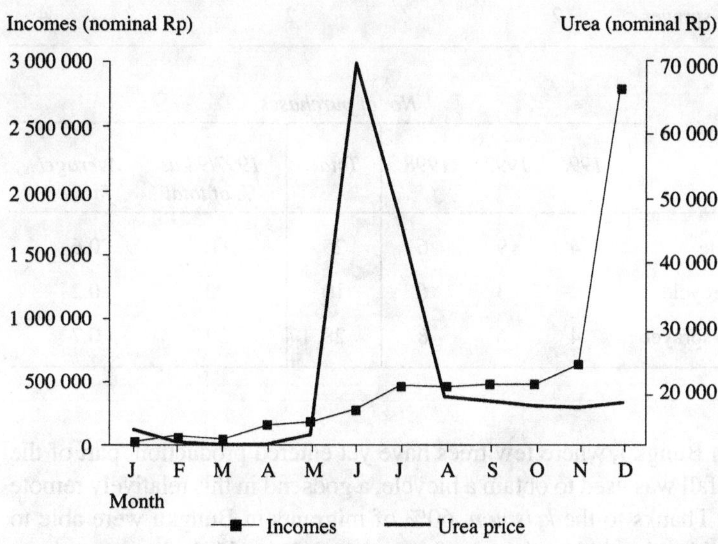

Figure 5.13 Cocoa incomes and input costs, Noling, South Sulawesi, 1996-98

Bicycles, motorcycles, cars and sprayers

In 1992-93, when prices were at their lowest, even farmers in mature cocoa regions could not afford to make many purchases or investments. Expenditures rose gradually during the mid-1990s. Finally, in 1997-98, bicycles and hand-sprayers proliferated in frontier areas (Table 5.12), while motorcycles and satellite dishes were on a terrific increase in well established cocoa villages (Table 5.13).

Table 5.12 Investments made by 41 farmers in cocoa frontier lands, Bungku, 1990-98

	No. of purchases												
Item	*Before 1990*	*1990*	*1991*	*1992*	*1993*	*1994*	*1995*	*1996*	*1997*	*1998*	*Total*	*1997/98 as % of total*	*Average/ farmer*
Bicycle	1			2			3	4	9	6	25	60	0.6
Motorcycle					1				3	6	10	90	0.2
Hand-sprayer	2			2		2	4	4	6	8	28	50	0.7

In Bungku, where few trees have yet entered production, part of the windfall was used to obtain a bicycle, a godsend in this relatively remote area. Thanks to the *krismon*, 60% of migrants in Bungku were able to buy a bicycle within 3-4 years of their arrival. In established cocoa regions, every family already owned one or two in the pre-crisis years.

Table 5.13 Investments made by 60 farmers in well developed cocoa areas, 1990-98

	No. of purchases						
Item	*Before 1990*	*1990*	*1991*	*1992*	*1993*	*1994*	*1995*
Bicycle	9	2	3	3	7	3	10
Motorcycle	1					1	6
Hand-sprayer	20	2	2			6	13
Motor-sprayer							
Water pump							
Television		1	1		2	1	2
Satellite dish + television			1			1	
Car/bus						1	1
Trip to Mecca	1		1			1	3

	No. of purchases					
Item	*1996*	*1997*	*1998*	*Total*	*1997/98 as % of total*	*Average/ farmer*
Bicycle	14	5	10	66	23	1.1
Motorcycle	2	8	13	31	68	0.5
Hand sprayer	10	6	8	67	21	1.1
Motor sprayer			5	5	100	0.1
Water pump		5		5	100	0.1
Television	1	3		11	27	0.2
Satellite dish + television	2	10	6	20	80	0.3
Car/bus	1	1	3	7	57	0.1
Trip to Mecca	4	4	11	25	43	0.5

Note: 45 farmers based in Noling and Lewonu in the alluvial plains, 15 in Tampumea, in the foothills.

Even before the crisis, cavalcades of motorcycles rather than bicycles paraded through the streets and paths of rich Sulawesi cocoa villages.

Their purchase was one of the most visible signs of the higher yields, prices and incomes achieved by Sulawesi farmers compared with most African farmers. With the crisis, the steady acquisition of motorcycles became a rush. In Palopo, 40 kilometres from Noling, dealers kept waiting lists of customers wanting the machines, new and second-hand. On average, roughly half of all families in well established cocoa areas now own a motorcycle. In some wealthy villages, almost every family has one, or even several. In frontier lands, the purchase of motorcycles is less advanced, but 20% of families now own one.

Perhaps the most impressive sign of Sulawesi's efficiency in producing and marketing cocoa is the purchase of cars and, more rarely, of trucks and buses. These purchases too were accelerated by the *krismon*. If their plantations had been spared by the drought, cocoa farmers were suddenly in a position to buy new and second-hand cars in 1998. Between May and July 1998, it was possible to buy new cars for the rupiah equivalent of US$ 5000 and second-hand cars for less than US$ 2000. The percentage of farmers who actually did so again varied according to location. In hill villages, where the drought hit hardest, it was low. On the plain, where some farmers harvested cocoa three to five times in May-June, it varied from 3% to 10%. In a plains village of 400 families, this meant the sudden arrival of between 12 and 40 extra cars. In villages such as Lapai, which was one of the earliest cocoa villages in Southeast Sulawesi, a few farmers were even able to buy four-wheel drives.

If our sample is representative, around 5% of farmers in mature cocoa areas on the plains owned a car before the *krismon*, whereas 10% did so afterwards. However, it is possible that our 60-farm sample has led to a slight overestimate, since it includes a few cocoa farmers in Lewonu who also own pepper and oil palm plantations.

Why did farmers buy cars? Besides prestige, they gave two reasons. They believed that they could save money on public transport, the cost of which has almost tripled. And, more significantly, they said that a car would enhance their efficiency in managing two cocoa farms situated at a distance of 200 or 300 kilometres from each other. Virtually all the farmers in our survey who bought cars also bought land in new frontier areas.

In frontier areas, the *krismon* provided an opportunity to accelerate the purchase of hand-sprayers. In mature cocoa areas, this effect was not observed, since the hand-sprayer is a relatively cheap and basic tool that families already owned before the crisis. Farmers in Sulawesi's frontier areas prefer hand-sprayers to motor-sprayers, which are more expensive. Because their farms are small (usually less than 3 hectares) and well maintained, they tend not to need the motor-sprayers that are typically used on the 10-hectare farms found in the frontier areas of Côte d'Ivoire.

In the plains, the situation is different. Suddenly, in 1998, motor-sprayers appeared in villages such as Noling, where there had previously been none. The *krismon* undoubtedly played a part in these purchases. But the switch from hand- to motor-sprayers is also a sign that trees are ageing and average farm size is increasing as people buy out their neighbours. Water pumps also appeared for the first time 0 0in 1997, bought by many farmers in rice growing areas to combat the drought.

Satellite dishes and trips to Mecca

Before the *krismon*, television sets were common in established cocoa villages, where 25% of families owned one. Satellite dishes were also a fairly common sight, often hung on a pole beside quite humble houses. However, the *krismon* greatly accelerated the rate at which families connected themselves up to CNN and other news services. By 1999, roughly half the families in plains villages owned a television set and one-third had a satellite dish.

Trips to Mecca were one of the main bonuses brought by the crisis to well established cocoa farmers. While thousands of others caught in the credit squeeze had to cancel their flight reservations, cocoa farmers filled the planes flying to Mecca in early 1999. Before the *krismon*, some 20% of cocoa families had sent one of their members to Mecca, usually the head of the family, sometimes his wife and ocasionally both. The percentage probably almost doubled in 1998-99.

Balinese farmers are usually Hindu and do not therefore wish to fly to Mecca. They proclaimed their faith by conducting Hindu ceremonies and by building and maintaining individual and communal temples. These activities flourished in the wake of the *krismon*.

Housing and building materials

One of the most visible signs of a farmer who has done well in any commodity is investment in a new house. However, the extent to which the economic surplus created by successful commodity development accrues to farmers depends greatly on whether or not the market is free. During the 1977-78 cocoa boom in Côte d'Ivoire, a marketing board appropriated most of the windfall, so farmers did not see much benefit from the spectacular peak in world prices, unless they cared to watch the growth of sky-scrapers in Abidjan. Brazilian planters, in contrast, bought flats and houses in cities over the same period, while lesser known cocoa smallholders in Mindanao in the Philippines and Flores in Eastern Indonesia were at least able to build themselves nice village houses. In 1994, the sudden hike in coffee prices combined with market liberalisation enabled farmers on the east coast of Madagascar to improve their housing enormously.

In Sulawesi, part of the 1998 cocoa windfall was also devoted to housing. Sand, stone and other building materials were visible in the backyards of many homes in 1998. However, as Sulawesi cocoa farmers had already benefitted for several years from a free market together with a relatively good price for their commodity, many of them, especially on the plains, had already built themselves a large and pleasant new house, made of either wood or bricks. The share of income devoted to housing in 1998 thus remained relatively modest, at around 15% among Bugis farmers in Noling and Lewonu.

Perhaps the most attractive visual impact of the *krismon* was the growth of individual Hindu temples in Balinese backyards. When these are included, the share of income devoted to building in 1998 rises to nearly 20% in Lewonu. The sum involved was around US$ 300-600 per family.

Savings and losses

Savings in cash (as opposed to assets) varied greatly between locations (Table 5.14). In frontier lands farmers still have little cash to save. Only a minority of pioneer farmers had some savings at the end of 1998. In established cocoa villages, however, savings were greater. In Noling and Lewonu, farmers declared average savings in rupiah equivalent to around US$ 500—a sum that is almost certainly underestimated. Farmers in different locations also varied in the mechanisms through which they saved. For instance, a relatively high proportion of farmers in established cocoa areas had opened bank accounts.

Table 5.14 Saving mechanisms of cocoa farmers at different locations, 1998

Saving mechanism	*Proportion of farmers (%)*	
	Established cocoa region	*Pioneer front*
Bank account	44	7
Middleman	8	0
Cash (at home)*	23	12
Subtotal	75	19
No savings declared	25	81

* At least temporarily.

The rate of savings would have been higher if it had not been for farmers' naïvety. Some farmers fell under the spell of crooks and were swindled through deposit schemes that promised fabulous rates of interest. Information on these scams is difficult to obtain, since farmers are often ashamed of their losses and unwilling to admit that they went in for usury, which is against the Muslim faith. In addition, losses are invisible, unlike the new prosperity resulting from high profits. In well developed villages such as Noling and Lewonu, something like 10% of potential savings are thought to have been stolen in this way, with around 5% of cocoa farmers having been victimised. A number of fairly rich farmers fell into the trap.

These cases of theft suggest that many farmers did not know how to save. In July 1999 they came to the middlemen with bags of cocoa and left, almost literally, with bags of bank notes. Small wonder that they were unsure how to handle their new-found wealth. This explains why some of them bought strange items such as washing machines or freezers, although there was no electricity supply to their houses. Farmers were painfully aware of the fragility of the windfall and of the need to buy something before prices rose. The range of goods on sale was not wide enough to allow sensible purchases.

The social cohesion of the Bugis, together with their strong Muslim faith, prevented the excesses that sometimes accompany windfalls in the rural areas of other developing regions. Smoking—a favourite foible—may have increased a little, but partying, drunkeness, brawling and wild women were nowhere in evidence.

Replantings versus new plantings

In October 1997, a few farmers with old farms in the plains were getting ready to replant by establishing nurseries. However, most farmers in this category preferred to look for better land elsewhere (Ruf, 1997). After the trough of 1992-93, new planting resumed in 1994 and began accelerating in 1996. By 1997-98, all the factors conducive to a new wave of migrations and plantations were in place. Much new planting in frontier areas can therefore be expected in the coming years.

In frontier areas such as Bungku, land is still abundant. However, migrants who came here some years ago enjoyed advantages in the search for land that are already no longer available to new arrivals. This first wave of migrants staked their claim to a few hectares of forest simply by slashing a small path round it, hoping to take ownership at virtually no cost, at least in the short term. Nowadays, migrants looking for new land must negotiate the price beforehand with the indigenous forest dwellers.

In developed areas like Noling, investing in land is now difficult, carrying high short-term costs. People seeking to expand their farms or to start new ones have to move to frontier areas in order to do so. When purchases associated with the *krismon* are ranked in terms of the amount spent, new land came in just below cars and motorcycles and above trips to Mecca. The average spent per farmer was the equivalent of US$ 800-1000 for those coming from Noling, US$ 700 for those from Lewonu and US$ 300 for people from the hills of Tampumea (see below).

The Rush for Land

For as long as forest land is available and there are no effective barriers to its acquisition, migration and deforestation will continue. The migrants will grow whatever crops enable them to survive and prosper.

This pattern is already well known in cocoa farming, having been seen in Ghana in the 1950s (Hill, 1956 and 1963) and in Côte d'Ivoire in the 1970s and 1980s (Ruf, 1995). In both these cases, development occurred under relatively low levels of management. In Sulawesi in the 1990s, management levels were generally higher, leading to much higher and occasionally spectacular yields. In particular, herbicides are available to help farmers reduce the labour costs of replanting cocoa on grass fallows. Despite these differences, the same relentless process of migration and deforestation is again evident (Ruf, 1995; Ruf et al, 1999).

Once "cocoa fever" has gripped migrants and raised their expectations, the prices anticipated by farmers keep increasing in their minds, even if in reality they are actually falling. As in a gold rush, the dream of riches may be enough to fuel continuing deforestation, despite periodic lulls.

Local shortages

From a long-term study of Noling and other villages along the road to Tampumea, we concluded that the rising price of cocoa has long had an influence on decisions to migrate and plant new areas. This was certainly the case in the 1980s, when land was still abundant and its purchase easy to negotiate (Figure 5.14).

Even when land is abundant, however, the price of cocoa is not the only factor stimulating new plantings. A "copying" effect is also evident, as around half of all farmers do not actually know the exact price of cocoa when they make the decision to plant (Pomp and Burger, 1995). From the success stories of people who planted before them and the evidence of their new purchasing power, farmers realise they can make much more money by planting cocoa than by growing maize or other food crops. If the price of cocoa rises, those who were first to plant buy more and more luxurious items, so the copying effect acts directly in turning price increases into new planting investments. After several years of cocoa farming, farmers tend to have more accurate information about prices than in the early stages of adoption. This is mainly because most potential investors are already cocoa farmers. The 1998 price hike may thus have a tremendous impact on land hunger for many years to come. It followed on the heels of steady price increases since 1994, which also provided farmers with a strong incentive to plant new areas.

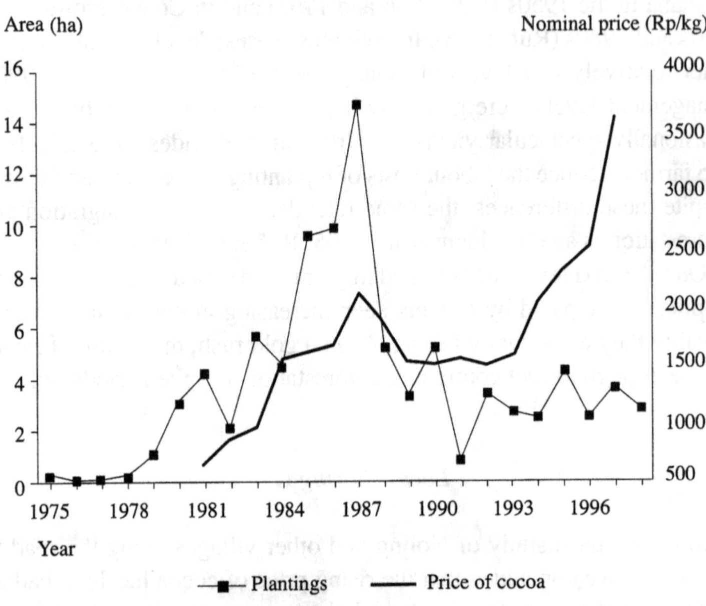

Figure 5.14 Cocoa plantings and prices in Noling and Tampumea, 1975-98

Land hunger is no longer evident around the villages of Noling and Tampumea, because the land here has been fully planted since around 1990. Expansion of planted areas into the adjoining forested hills is in theory forbidden, as this is classified as State Forest Land. However, in practice, enforcement by the Forestry Service is not very effective. Thus new plantings are still taking place in the steep hills behind Tampumea, where forest clearing has resumed in the 1990s, with pioneers building houses or shelters close to their new plantations. If this process continues as it has done on other fronts, it will lead to the creation of a new village. However, the pace of cocoa expansion into these remote hill areas is slowed down by difficulties of access.

The remoteness of these hills, and their steep slopes, mean that the only people who are willing to settle there are poor migrants who have no alternatives. These people lack experience in cocoa, as well as the capital to invest in more productive land. Those who have both these assets, such as the majority of established cocoa farmers in Noling and Tampumea, prefer to look for more accessible and fertile land in other areas, whether on the plain or in the foothills. Their accumulated experience and capital has a huge impact on deforestation and development in new frontier lands.

Land shortage reduced new plantings in villages like Noling, but it encouraged a relatively active market in existing plantations. The *krismon* triggered the concentration of land holdings, with the smallest farmers proving willing to sell their 0.5 or 1 hectare to richer farmers. With this money, they rushed to new frontier areas and got ten times this area. For instance, in June 1998, one farmer sold his 0.75-hectare plantation on good soils for Rp 35 million (US$ 2000-3500, according to the exchange rate assumed). With this money he bought 6 hectares of existing plantations and new land to the north of Palopo town, in a village just short of the pioneer front. However, the richest farmers, including the buyer of this 0.75 hectare, did not allow the small farmer to go alone in search of new land. In 1998, everybody, rich and poor, took part in the race, as is evident from the results of our survey in Noling and Tampumea (Table 5.15).

Table 5.15 Average investments (US$) made in new land and existing plantations by cocoa farmers in Noling, Lewonu and Tampumea, 1998

Investment type	*Investment**					
	Noling		*Lewonu*		*Tampumea*	
	US$	*%*	*US$*	*%*	*US$*	*%*
Local land and plantations**	481	56	520	68	69	22
Land and plantations elsewhere***	266	31	165	22	176	56
Repaying *gadai* plantations	12	1	10	1	21	7
Pledging *gadai* plantations	101	12	69	9	48	15
Total	860	100	764	100	313	100

* Exchange rate assumed: Rp 10 400 = US$ 1.00. ** Mostly plantations. *** Mostly land.

One farmer and a group of his friends had been negotiating for years with the local government and with indigenous farmers to acquire 7000 hectares in Central Sulawesi. Thanks to the 1998 windfall, he was able to buy 1000 hectares. He invested Rp 10 million (US$ 7000-10 000) in land in 1998, not with the idea of planting it all himself but rather in order to resell much of it at a higher price to neighbours and to new migrants arriving later on. He will also use *bagi tanah* contracts, sharing the plantations out later[9]. His case illustrates the speculative hunger for land that has gripped so many Indonesians since the crisis. It also shows how past profits from cocoa are reinvested in new areas where land is abundant and cheap.

If this case is included, the average investment in land made by farmers in Noling in 1998 was the rupiah equivalent of US$ 1300. Even if it is excluded, the figure is still US$ 813. For smallholder farmers, these are large sums of money.

Farmers in the two villages thus adopted two complementary strategies for acquiring more land. Smallholders sold a small plantation in order to buy a much larger area of unused land in a frontier area, while larger farmers bought mature plantations locally. The largest, wealthiest farmers used both strategies. As Noling and Lewonu farms are mostly on the plain, their owners are richer than those of Tampumea and other hill villages. Hence the difference between the two areas in terms not only of the amount of money spent but also of where land was purchased. The higher figure for the money spent locally is of course due to the higher prices of plantations in established cocoa areas. In terms of area the opposite is the case, with the bulk of investment falling in frontier lands.

In Noling and Tampumea, around 25% of farmers invested outside their villages, usually at quite a distance. They bought an average of 5 hectares each. While almost all purchases in the two villages consisted of plantations (there were a few pieces of fallow land), almost all investments made outside the village were in forest. Compared to other years, land purchases clearly accelerated, resulting in an equally clear acceleration in deforestation in frontier lands (Figure 5.15).

Cocoa drives deforestation

A major impact of the cocoa price hike in established cocoa villages is the organisation of cocoa farmers into groups that hire buses to go looking for forest land in remote areas. Many of these buses make for the borders between South Sulawesi and its neighbouring provinces.

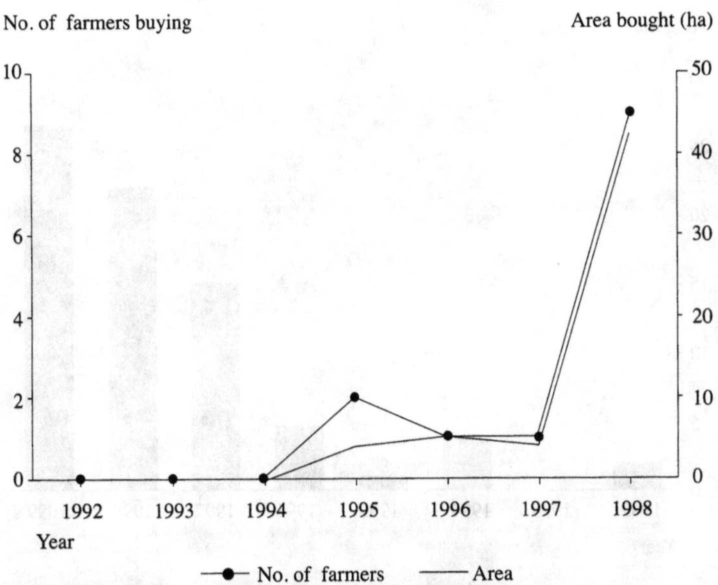

Figure 5.15 Land purchases made by Noling farmers outside their village, 1992-98

In a village such as Noling, this group activity was already evident in the mid-1990s, but it accelerated in 1998. At least three groups of 10-30 farmers in the village organised themselves in this way during the year.

Among the most active frontier areas in Sulawesi are Bungku in Central Sulawesi and Towuti, southeast of Malili, where the three provinces of Central Sulawesi, South Sulawesi and Southeast Sulawesi meet. In these areas, new planting started in earnest in 1992, when the price of cocoa was at its lowest. Planting accelerated in 1996-97 when the real price increased, but this was still before the crisis. In 1998 and 1999 the rate of growth seems to have slightly increased further (Figure 5.16). On the Bungku front, the average migrant farmer who had arrived earlier in the 1990s and who had already planted cocoa bought a further 0.9 hectare of forest in 1998—a very low figure compared to the average 5 hectares purchased in Towuti by the planters arriving from Noling.

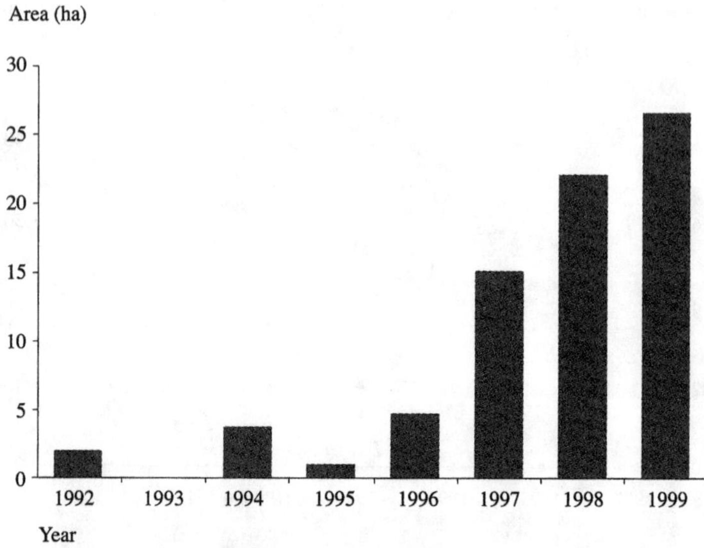

Figure 5.16 Annual cocoa plantings by 69 migrants around Malili and Mahalona Lake, 1992-99

This makes sense, because these new migrants tend to have less money compared to cocoa farmers coming from Noling. It is still difficult to predict the fate of farmers who encircled forest plots by slashing a path round them. If they managed to keep this land, then the figure goes up considerably, to 4.4 hectares per household, with a correspondingly greater effect on deforestation.

In summary, forest appropriation and clearing have risen enormously before and after the 1998 price hike. The rise is not due solely to the 1997 drought and 1998 *krismon*, since farmers often took the decision to plant some time earlier. The rate of planting does not seem likely to abate in the coming years.

If cocoa is indeed attracting new migrants in Sulawesi, it is fulfilling the role it has so often fulfilled in the past, that of creating new jobs. Lastly, then, we ask where migrants at the frontier come from and whether cocoa production is helping to reduce unemployment in Indonesia's cities.

Impact on Employment

Information about migrants' status and jobs before they came to Bungku and Towuti reveals the scale on which resources have been shifted from rice to cocoa (Table 5.16).

Table 5.16 Status and jobs of migrants before they came to Bungku and Towuti

Status/job	*Proportion of farmers (%)*	
	Bungku	*Towuti*
Rice		
Rice farmer	37	17
Rice farmer's son	13	10
Bagil hasil	0	12
Cocoa		
Cocoa farmer	13	13
Cocoa and rice farmer	8	13
Cocoa farmer's son	3	0
Cocoa worker in Malaysia*		10
Cloth trader, furniture trader, driver	10	10
Timber dealer	3	2
Agricultural worker	3	1
Fisherman	0	4
Resettled by army**	5	0
Inactive, still young, jobless	5	6
Retired or pensioner	0	2
Total	100	100

* Usually rice farmers' sons who moved to Malaysia for a few years.
** After suppression of the DTI/TII uprising in the 1960s.

The transfer of labour, capital and innovative skills through migration from rice-growing areas to frontier cocoa lands began in the early 1990s and continued in 1997-98 (Table 5.17). The factors behind the transfer include the availability of labour freed up by the Green Revolution, the capital accumulated by rice farmers, the shortage of draught animals and the need to invest in new tools for rice farming.

In Towuti, 10% of the migrants are former workers in Malaysian cocoa plantations but they are usually paddy farmers' sons as well. They even often spend one or two years in the father's rice farm between their return from Malaysia and their recent migration to Towuti.

Table 5.17 Employment sectors of migrants before their arrival in Bungku and Towuti, 1997-98

Sector	*Proportion (%)*			
	Bungku		*Towuti*	
	All migrants	*Migrants arriving in 1997-98*	*All migrants*	*Migrants arriving in 1997-98*
Rice	50	47	39	36
Cocoa*	24	35	36	39
Other rural	16	0	6	6
Urban activities	10	18	19	19
Total	100	100	100	100

* Including workers formerly in Malasysia cocoa plantations.
Note: Survey conducted in September 1999 in Bungku and June 1999 in Towuti.

Although the rice lands are the origin of the largest battalions of migrants, those who display the most entrepreneurship are the migrants who already own a cocoa farm somewhere else. These people know more about cocoa and also have the necessary planting material. Their past experience helps them anticipate problems and assess realistically what they will be able to achieve. They can afford to be, and often are, much more ambitious than on their former cocoa farms, clearing and planting much larger areas. The same characteristics were observed in Côte d'Ivoire in the 1970s and 1980s.

Our surveys in Bungku and Towuti also revealed that a few people formerly employed in the services sector of the economy, particularly in urban-based activities such as cloth trading and driving, had also come to the frontier to plant cocoa. These people had benefitted from the contacts made with the rural and cocoa sectors through their earlier jobs, which had enabled them to get information about cocoa.

Many unemployed urban carpenters and construction workers came to established cocoa villages such as Noling to build houses in 1998. Some of them stayed and are now among the few pioneers in the remote hills behind Tampumea. These people have accepted extremely difficult and risky conditions in which to start their new "cocoa" lives. A few "pedicab" drivers, ostensibly from Ujung Pandang, also came to work on cocoa farms and, more often, in the local logging businesses launched by wealthier cocoa farmers. However several of these people also turned out to be maize farmers from the south and can therefore be considered as coming from villages rather than from the city.

It is clear that the opportunities provided by cocoa in 1998 attracted a few artisans and workers to grow the crop. However, the cocoa sector did not become an employment magnet, drawing thousands of unemployed people from the cities. Most jobs were created by and for people from rural areas. There were two main reasons for this. First, migrations from cities were mostly short-term. Few city dwellers wished to install themselves permanently in the countryside, and the poorer ones could not afford to buy land, even in remote locations. Most worked as labourers on plantations. Second, although the windfall helped spread information about cocoa growing in the cities, farmers and villagers in established cocoa villages and even in paddy rice villages were better informed. If new opportunities to acquire suitable land opened up, they heard about it first, as they already had neighbours and cousins everywhere on the pioneer fronts. Hesitating have-nots in the cities were left on the starting line.

Conclusions

Our research on the cocoa systems of Sulawesi during the 1990s enables us to draw the following conclusions:

- The year 1997 will be remembered for a disastrous El Niño-related drought which decimated yields. As has so often occurred elsewhere in the past, the fall in yields became a driving force behind migration and new planting. With tree mortality around 20% in the deforested hills, the drought revealed the limits to the sustainability of cocoa farming systems in these areas. Increasing CPB infestation was another sign of decline. Conversely, the drought helped to launch innovations such as water pumps and to increase the adoption of fertilisers and pesticides.
- The weather also intervened in 1998, when La Niña-related flooding caused problems in the cocoa farming systems of the alluvial plains.
- However, 1998 will chiefly be remembered as simultaneously the terrible "krismon year" in most of Java and the fabulous "cocoa year" in Sulawesi. Throughout Sulawesi, 1998 brought a spectacular

windfall to most cocoa farmers, as high prices and high yields coincided. Farmers enjoyed their new-found wealth by buying motorcycles and cars and flying to Mecca. Possession of the means to enjoy these luxuries was not new but was accelerated by the crisis.

- Middlemen and exporters also benefitted greatly from the 1998 windfall. Some of them made huge profits.
- There was a headlong rush for land in 1998-99. This was accelerated partly by the drought but much more by the windfall, which created marvellous opportunities to invest.
- The behaviour of existing and new cocoa farmers in response to the simultaneous economic and ecological crises confirms the pattern of production observed in the past and the image of cocoa as an unsustainable crop dependent on massive migration and deforestation for its development. The windfall encouraged ten times more new planting than replanting, which was largely unsuccessful.
- What will happen in years to come remains to be seen, but new planting can be expected to continue. Farmers may develop further technical innovations, such as home-made irrigation systems and the use of new types of fertilisers and pesticides, but these are unlikely to win the sustainability battle.
- Fortunately, Sulawesi smallholders benefit from a free market. The existence of a marketing board, such as that of Côte d'Ivoire in the 1970s and 1980s or that established at the expense of Sulawesi's clove farmers, could have led to disaster.
- There was no real impact on world prices in 1998-99 as a result of farmers' short-term supply responses. The overwhelming effect of the drought prevented farmers from making such responses. The increased use of fertilisers and other inputs in 1998 was a response to drought more than to rising cocoa prices. The overall increase in production in 1999 and 2000 is the result of new plantings done before the windfall.
- Without the drought of 1997 (and to a lesser extent the excessive rainfall of 1998), Sulawesi's ports would have exported even more cocoa in 1998-99. Despite these setbacks, Indonesia is close to fulfilling the predictions made in the early 1990s that it would become the second-largest cocoa producer in the world by the turn of the century.

- This status, which should materialise within the next few years, is being achieved without any investment from the state or from large private companies. The investments are being financed entirely by smallholders.
- By stimulating increased consumption, the windfall had a knock-on effect on the rest of the economy, both on other islands and in Sulawesi. While shops were unable to sell anything in Java, Sulawesi's cocoa farmers and traders aided the survival of commercial activity throughout the country by providing a ready outlet for goods and services.
- The impact of the windfall on jobs is less certain. Through migration, forest clearance and new planting, the windfall triggered the creation of thousands of jobs in the cocoa sector. Most of these job opportunities were grasped by people from families who either came from rice growing regions or were already involved in cocoa. Migrations from cities remained relatively insignificant.
- The local price of cocoa plunged after the spectacular 1998 windfall. This was a major disappointment for farmers in Sulawesi. In late 1999, cocoa: input price ratio are even lower than before the *krismon* and it seems that relatively low prices can be expected for some time to come. As proven by most cocoa stories in the past, the combination of pest damages—here the CPB infestation probably enhanced by the 1997 drought—, increasing input prices and persisting low cocoa prices is dangerous. Along with land conflicts related to too rapid migrations—an equally typical component of cocoa stories—this is one of the two main dangers for the future of cocoa in Sulawesi. Nevertheless, we believe that the trade-off will remain positive in the years to come.
- The main policy pitfall to avoid in the short term is the introduction of a tax on cocoa incomes. Because of the 1999 downturn, this would not be the right time to impose it. Taxation can be kept in mind in case there is another price surge a few years from now.

References

Akiyama, T. and Nishio, A. 1997. Sulawesi's cocoa boom: Lessons of smallholder dynamism and a hands-off policy. *Bulletin of Indonesian Economic Studies* 33 (2): 97-121.

Berry, S. 1976. Supply response reconsidered: Cocoa in Western Nigeria, 1909-44, *Journal of Development Studies* 13 (1): 4-17.

Blanc-Pamard, C. and Ruf, F. 1992. Reflections on peasant coffee production. In: Blanc-Pamard, C. and Ruf, F. (eds), *La transition caféière. CIRAD-SAR, Collection systèmes agraires* (16): 217-237. Montpellier, France.

Durand, F. 1995. Farmers' strategies and agricultural development: The choice of cocoa in Eastern Indonesia. In: Ruf, F. and Siswoputranto, P.S. (eds), *Cocoa Cycles: The Economics of Cocoa Supply*. Woodhead, Cambridge, UK.

Ed&F Man. 2000. Cocoa Market, Interim Report.

Hill, P. 1956. *The Gold Coast Farmer*. Oxford University Press, UK.

Hill, P. 1963. *Migrant Cocoa Farmers of Southern Ghana: A Study in Rural Capitalism*. Cambridge University Press, UK.

ICCO (International Cocoa Organisation). 1999. Quarterly Bulletin of Cocoa Statistics 24 (4). London, UK.

Jamal, S. and Pomp, M. 1993. Smallholder adoption of tree crops: A case study of cocoa in Sulawesi. *Bulletin of Indonesian Economic Studies* 29 (3): 69-94.

Lineton, J. 1975. Pasompe' ugi': Bugis migrants and wanderers. *Archipel* 10: 173-201.

Pelras, C. 1982. La mer et la forêt, lieux de quête, d'exil et d'errances: Quelques aspects de l'univers légendaire Bugis (Célèbes, Indonésie). *Le monde alpin et rhodanien* 1 (4): 313-331.

Pelras, C. 1996. *The Bugis*. Blackwell, Oxford, UK and Cambridge, USA.

Petithuguenin, P. 1998. Les conditions naturelles de production du cacao en Côte d'Ivoire, au Ghana, et en Indonésie. *Plantations, recherche, développement* 5 (6): 393-405.

Pomp, M. and Burger, K. 1995. Innovation and imitation: Adoption of cocoa by Indonesian smallholders. *World Development* 23 (3): 423-431.

Ruf, F. 1993. Indonesia's position amongst cocoa-producing countries. *Indonesian Circle* (61): 21-37.

Ruf, F. 1995. *Booms et crises du cacao: Les vertiges de l'or brun*. Karthala, Paris, France.

Ruf, F. 1997. From tree-crop planting to replanting: 1997, a new turning point in the Sulawesi cocoa boom? In: Proceedings of a Workshop on the Future of Indonesian Cocoa Through Planting, Replanting and Pest and Disease Control, 4 November 1997, CIRAD and ASKINDO, Jakarta, Indonesia, pp. 13-46.

Ruf, F. and Ehret, P. 1993. Compétitivité et cycles du cacao: Vrais et faux problèmes sous l'éclairage Indonésien. (Competitiveness and cocoa cycles: Real and false problems from an Indonesian angle). In: Etienne, G., Griffon, M. and Guillaumont, P. (eds), Afrique-Asie: Performances agricoles comparées. *Revue française d'économie*, pp. 255-301.

Ruf, F. and Siswoputranto, P.S. (eds) 1995. *Cocoa Cycles: The Economics of Cocoa Supply*. Woodhead, Cambridge, UK.

Ruf, F. and Yoddang. 1996. How do Sulawesi cocoa smallholders achieve 2000 kg/ha? Why 2-day fermented beans? Paper presented at the Twelfth International Conference on Cocoa Research, 17-23 November 1996, CPA Salvador-da-Bahia, Brazil.

Ruf, F., Ehret, P. and Yoddang. 1996. Smallholder cocoa in Indonesia: Why a cocoa boom in Sulawesi? In: Clarence-Smith, W.G. (ed.), *Cocoa Pioneer Fronts since 1800: The Role of Smallholders, Planters and Merchants*. Macmillan, London, UK, pp. 212-231.

Ruf, F. and Yoddang. 1998. The cocoa marketing sector in Sulawesi: A free market and "almost perfect" competition. *Plantations, recherche, développement* 5 (3): 161-175.

Ruf, F., Penot, E. and Yoddang. 1999. After tropical forest, replantation of rubber and cocoa trees: Garden of Eden or chemical inputs? Paper presented at Planetary Garden: The First International Symposium on Sustainable Ecosystem Management, 14-18 March 1999, Chambéry, France, pp. 318-324.

Notes

1 The stated aim of the DI/TII movement was to build an independent Muslim state in Sulawesi. The movement's chief was Kahar Muzakar, who was close to President Sukarno until 1945 and played a leading part in booting the Dutch out of the island. He and his men were dissatisfied with the poor thanks they got from Sukarno and his army (Pelras, 1996). In 1958, in the search for ways to finance their rebellion, Kahar Muzakar and his second-in-command, Kaso Gani, sent four people to *Sabah*, Malaysia as migrant workers to learn about cocoa and to smuggle back some pods.

2 In this case, net of material input costs but not of labour, since this is mainly provided by the family.

3 The 220 trees were on 16 farms belonging to 12 farmers, with 138 trees in the rich alluvial plains and 82 in the foothills or the hills.

4 The CPB lays its eggs on the pod. The hatched larvae penetrate the pod, where they consume the pulp and placenta. The beans turn flat, wither and

become clustered in a compact placenta. In most cases, at least some pods can be harvested before infestation and some beans can be saved from infested pods. In exceptionally heavy infestations, all beans may be lost. Around Noling in 1999, infestation was low but rapidly increasing, especially in the hills.

5 In 1995-96, farms in Lewonu were severely hit not only by CPB but also by a government programme in which all pods and cherelles in infested areas were simply removed from trees. Although both the pest and this somewhat debatable control method may have played a part in local diversification into pepper, they did not dissuade farmers from planting new cocoa areas further up in the foothills.

6 As has happened in almost all cocoa areas worldwide, indigenous people in Sulawesi tend to be ousted by the migrants. Noling, where there is a larger number of them, is the exception. The indigenous population is probably stronger here because it hosted one of the DI/TII uprising's main base camps in the 1950s.

7 It is extremely difficult to replant successfully in deforested hills, especially if dead trees are randomly scattered. In these situations, replanted seedlings have to compete with surviving mature trees.

8 Tradable/non-tradable: a good is called tradable if it can be easily exported or imported. Cocoa beans, rice and fertilisers are typical tradable goods. Symetrically, a non-tradable good can be bought and sold but not easily imported or exported. Houses, land and plantations are typically non-tradable assets. Labour is often considered as a non-tradable factor but this may often be a mistake, especially in cocoa stories since they rely on migrations. That is the case in Sulawesi. Bugis farmers and their sons do have an alternative to local employment. They may opt for migration to Malaysia (and thus help Malaysia to save part of its cocoa sector). Bugis labor is quite tradable between Indonesia and Malaysia.

9 *Bagi tanah* means "land sharing". A piece of land is acquired by somebody who plants cocoa on it without being paid a wage. Payment is made when the plantation is shared out (usually equally) 3 or more years later, once it has entered production.

Chapter 6

Transmigrants and the Cocoa Windfall: "Paradise is Here, not in Bali"

François Ruf, Yoddang and Waris Ardhy

"Are you originally from Bali, the 'paradise island'?"
"Bali may be a paradise for rich people. For us, paradise is here, in Central Sulawesi, not in Bali."
"Have you ever returned to Bali?"
"Yes, at least 10 times since 1983."
"How? It must be a very long trip by bus and sea."
"Not at all, I fly. A return air-fare to Bali from Palu is Rp 700 000. That's less than a month's profit from the harvest of cocoa."

This is an excerpt from a conversation with a Balinese farmer at Kasimbar, Central Sulawesi, in March 1997, just before the *krismon*. As we have seen, Bugis migrants were the major beneficiaries of Sulawesi's 1998 cocoa windfall. We also know that, around the Bone Gulf in South Sulawesi, Balinese transmigrants' sons often provide labour for Bugis farmers and have themselves adopted cocoa as a means of climbing the ladder towards middle-range incomes. However, both as labourers and as medium-sized cocoa farmers, the Balinese in this area seem to have benefitted less from the windfall than did the Bugis.

In this chapter we will first identify and examine some of the extraordinary successes achieved by the more efficient Balinese cocoa farmers. Although some of these farmers live in South Sulawesi, the most impressive case histories are to be found in Central Sulawesi, specifically in the isthmus of the province between Palu and Toli Toli (Figure 6.1). That is where the above conversation was recorded.

Balinese are expert rice growers, both in their original "paradise island" home and also around Parigi in Central Sulawesi, one of the main areas in which they settled in the late 1960s and 1970s, either under government transmigration schemes or as spontaneous migrants. Their expertise, together with their strong sense of community, explains why at least some transmigration sites have proved relatively successful. At any rate, this success owes little to transmigration policies and their implementation (Charras, 1982; Levang, 1995). Often, the Balinese faced delays in getting access to the land they had been promised, followed by high costs in clearing land. These and other problems prompted a few of them to migrate locally and to take up cocoa growing. When this proved a success, other transmigrants—even those with relatively good land on the schemes—soon followed.

Our first objective in this chapter is to illustrate the success of the Balinese as cocoa growers, both before and during the 1998 windfall. We will use the Kasimbar area as a show-case. Here, several Balinese transmigrants benefitted enormously in 1998 because they had adopted cocoa in the early 1980s, soon after their arrival in the village.

These cases are, however unusual. Most transmigrants switched from rice to cocoa rather later. The Balinese, like the Javanese who also arrived under transmigration schemes, were impressed by the Bugis' success and began to copy them. Our second objective in this chapter is therefore to evaluate the impact of Balinese and Javanese transmigrants on cocoa production in Sulawesi. In so doing we will try to answer two major questions. First, has the late adoption of cocoa by most transmigrants played a role in the recent growth of the sector and will it do so in the years to come? Second, was late adoption the direct result of government policies? Indonesian policy makers were, until recently, so obsessed with making the country self-sufficient in rice that they tried to prevent the adoption of non-food crops by transmigrants. If the answer to our second question is "yes", then the actions of these policy makers may have considerably reduced the positive impact of the *krismon* on the livelihoods of most transmigrants.

Migration is, as we have seen, a central feature of the typical cocoa boom. Our third objective is to explore the issues raised by Sulawesi's cocoa migrations for the island's indigenous forest dwellers. How did the krismon and the windfall affect the fate of these original inhabitants of the frontier lands? And how did the migrants and transmigrants react to conflicts over access to land with this and other groups?

This chapter has nine sections. The first section examines how the age structure of cocoa orchards in Central Sulawesi affected the impact of the *krismon*. In the second section we visit Kasimbar, to look in detail at the success stories told by Balinese transmigrants. The third section examines the effects of the 1997 drought and the 1998 windfall in this part of Sulawesi, while the fourth section describes how the Balinese used their windfall. The downturn of 1999 is examined in the fifth section, while the sixth section deals with the involvement of transmigrants in new plantings. The last three sections investigate the impact of the *krismon* on the lives of indigenous forest dwellers, the rush for land and how this accentuated social and economic differences between the various ethnic groups, and the effect of the cocoa boom on deforestation.

Our analysis is mainly based on a July 1999 survey of 72 cocoa smallholders who owned some 200 cocoa farm plots. The survey focussed chiefly on the east coast of the Central Sulawesi isthmus, specifically on the Balinese village of Kasimbar and on the Tinombala transmigration scheme north of the isthmus near Toli Toli, where Javanese farmers have become attracted to cocoa. The survey also covered the village of Oyom, also near Toli Toli. Oyom is an indigenous village that is becoming a Bugis village: the Bugis have migrated there in large numbers and the indigenous people have retreated into the hinterland. We also use the results of a preliminary survey undertaken on the west coast in March 1997, covering 27 households (from all ethnic origins) who owned some 75 farm plots. Unfortunately, we had no time to update this survey in 1999, but the data we already had on the age structure of cocoa farms in 1996 provides a useful benchmark. A third brief survey was undertaken in March 1999. It involved 27 Bugis farmers around Lake Poso and in the sub-districts of Mori Atas, Petasia and West Bungku, southeast of the lake (Figure 6.1)[1].

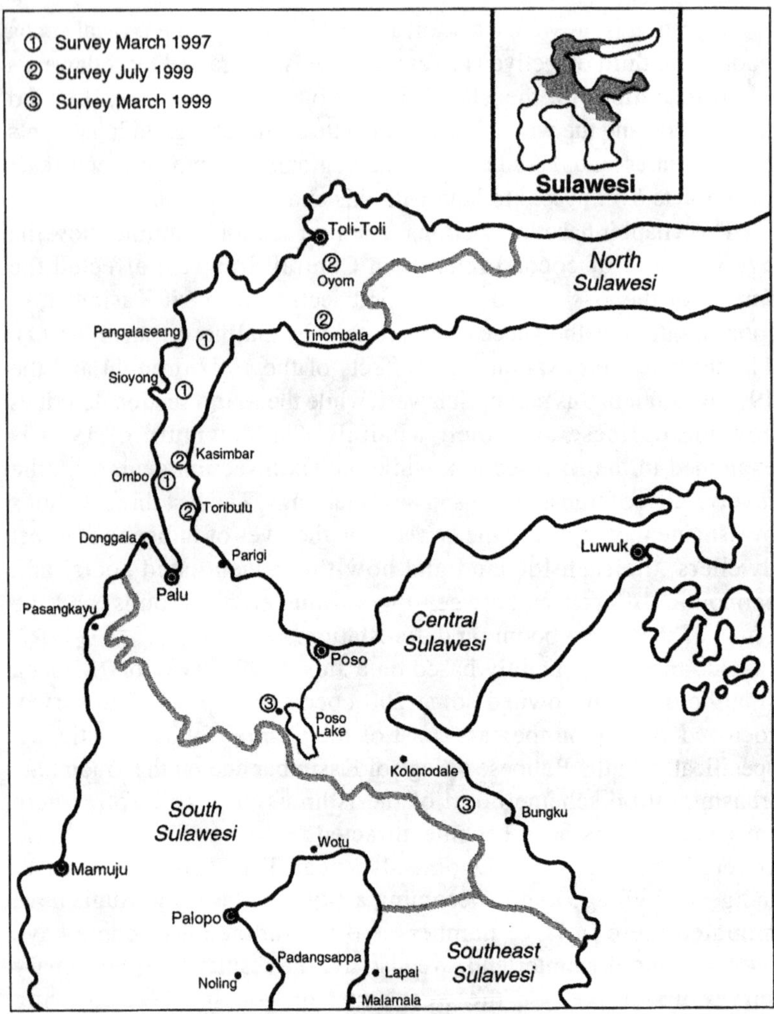

Figure 6.1 Central Sulawesi

Farm Age and the *Krismon*

The age structure of cocoa farms provides insights into farmers' investment decisions. What point in the cocoa cycle had been reached in Central Sulawesi when the *krismon* struck?

The cocoa cycle

Cocoa arrived only recently in Central Sulawesi. Despite CPB and climatic hazards, the crop quickly turned the province into a "paradise" for migrants. In 1995, cocoa exports from Palu, the region's main port, amounted to only 2000 tonnes per year. By 1998, they had reached 65 000 tonnes[2]. Although development is recent, the classic cocoa cycle can already be observed. Each of the three small areas we studied has experienced its own cycle, with its own waves of migration and plantings. The shift from the west to the east coast and the push southwards first to Lake Poso and then to Bungku are clearly visible (Figure 6.2).

The west coast—specifically the areas 50-200 kilometres south of Toli Toli—hosted the first cocoa villages of Central Sulawesi, with plantings starting in the late 1970s. In several villages here, Bugis families are the descendants of migrants who arrived two or three generations ago. Many of the older farmers are refugees from South Sulawesi who escaped the army repression of the DI/TII uprising in the 1960s. In some cases they went to Malaysia first, then returned to the west coast of Central Sulawesi in the 1970s, as this was the closest point to Malaysia. Others came back from Sabah or East Kalimantan, where they had worked as labourers in agriculture, construction, oil or mining. Many migrants participated in the tobacco expansion and the clove boom of the 1970s. Some originally came on a short visit to trade in tobacco, clothes and other goods, but stayed to plant cloves or coconuts.

Most migrants arriving on the west coast before 1978-79 did not originally plant cocoa. However, on the strength of information about the crop from Malaysia, Sebatic[3] and former DI/TII activists, they adopted the crop when planting materials became available early in the 1980s, with a peak in planting around 1986. A second wave of planting occurred in 1990-91 and a third in 1995-96, continuing into 1998-99.

On the east coast there were fewer Bugis before the cocoa migrations began. In the late 1970s a few came to the east coast to grow tobacco, but they arrived in much smaller numbers than on the west coast. However, in the late 1960s and 1970s, the east coast became host to a number of government transmigration projects (Charras, 1982). Balinese and Javanese transmigrants arrived in their thousands to plant rice. Alongside the official transmigrants were the squatters—spontaneous migrants from Bali who followed the transmigrants and moved onto their land when they left the schemes to find more land elsewhere. The squatters were still willing to grow rice at this stage. This is how the village of Kasimbar was founded. The villagers continued to grow rice until they heard about cocoa from a neighbouring estate. Cocoa arrived relatively early on the east coast, in 1980-81, but caught on only slowly. There was a small peak in plantings in 1986, but a second, much higher peak occurred in 1992-93, for which the village of Kasimbar was largely responsible.

Further south, between Lake Poso and Bungku, spontaneous migrations occurred later and were almost entirely motivated by cocoa. There was a sharp increase in both migrations and plantings in 1993, which turned into exponential growth in 1996-97. Planting had reached a peak by the time the *krismon* struck. Besides the spontaneous migrations, there were also official transmigration schemes, again growing rice.

The krismon *and other influences*

As in South Sulawesi, the pattern of plantings on the west coast and in Bungku reflects considerable activity in the 2 years before 1997-98. Several new areas were gearing themselves up for a new cocoa boom. This is explained partly by the trend in cocoa prices, which had risen steadily since late 1993 in nominal rupiah terms. But a more convincing explanation is the accumulation of information, experience and capital by rice farmers, more and more of whom decided to move into cocoa. They bought the small farms of already established cocoa farmers in South Sulawesi, enabling these farmers to acquire larger plots in Central Sulawesi.

In Central as in South Sulawesi, the rising prices of 1998 were not the only factor influencing farmers' decisions to increase their plantings that year and the next. The drought of 1997 and the floods of 1998 also triggered new migrations and plantings. Nevertheless, the *krismon* strongly affected planting decisions in 1998-99, especially on the east coast, where preparation for a new wave in 1996-97 was less obvious and the 1998 leap in prices took farmers by surprise. It was as if they were woken up by it.

Arrivals

West coast (24 migrants)

No. of migrants

3
2.5
2
1.5
1
0.5
0

1971 1974 1977 1980 1983 1986 1989 1992 1995 1998

Year

East coast (63 migrants)

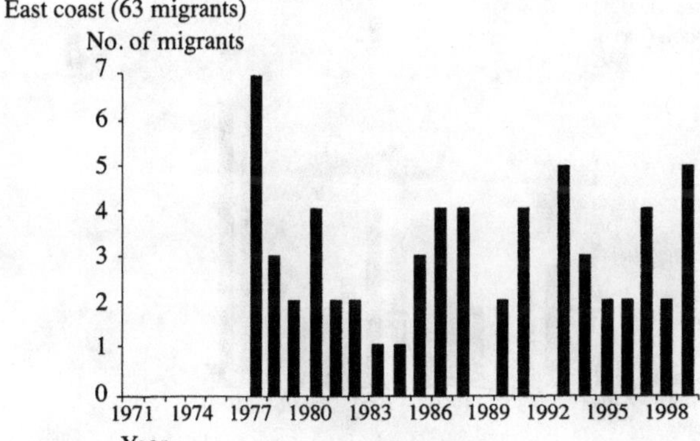

Bungku and Poso Lake (25 migrants)

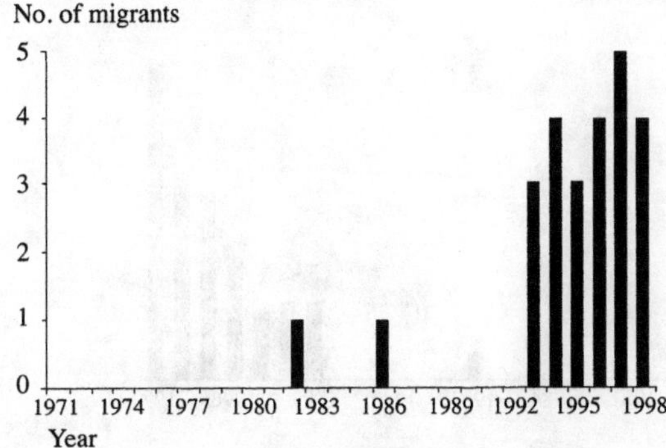

Figure 6.2 Migration and planting patterns in three areas of Central Sulawesi

Plantings

West coast (27 farmers)

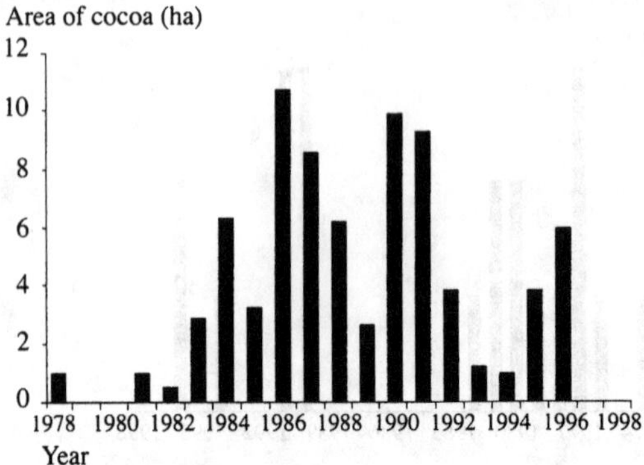

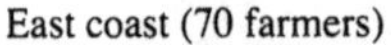

East coast (70 farmers)

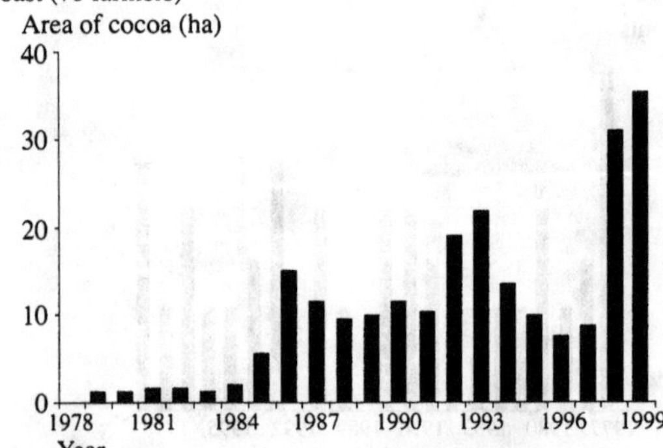

Bungku and Poso Lake (25 farmers)

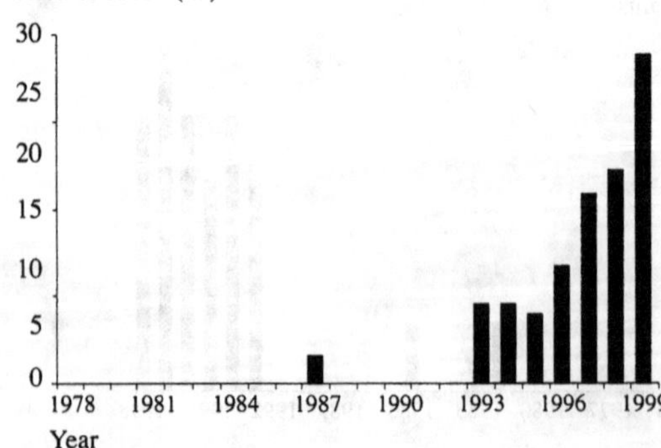

Figure 6.2 (continued)

This is what happened in Kasimbar, where we will now describe the course of events in more detail. Although our description is specific to Kasimbar, this is not the only Balinese village to have jumped onto the cocoa bandwagon just in time for the windfall. In 1998, neighbouring Balinese villages such as Burange also enjoyed high incomes, often over Rp 30-40 million per household.

The Kasimbar Success Story

The first Balinese arrived in Kasimbar in 1977 and the influx continued until 1983 (Figure 6.3). They came originally to grow rice, many of them having already migrated once before for this purpose, between 1965 and 1972. Those deciding to migrate from Bali were mostly landless (Charras, 1982). Many had been day labourers, *bagi hasil* share-croppers or boys who climbed coconut trees; some had also been drivers or construction workers. Most left Bali for the unknown because they wanted to escape these conditions and begin again on a piece of land they could call their own, where they could work for themselves and be independent.

The first arrivals consisted of both official transmigrants and spontaneous migrants. Official transmigrants were, in theory, assisted by the government, which was supposed to provide them with a house, some food and some partially cleared forest land. Spontaneous migrants came mainly because they had heard along the grape-vine that land was available. One farmer's story illustrates the mix of factors at work in decisions to migrate. He had registered for transmigration to Sumatra in 1963. In 1969 he was still waiting when the Gunung Agung volcano that overshadowed his home erupted, forcing him, along with many others, to find somewhere new immediately. A former transmigrant to Sulawesi, who had temporarily returned to Bali, told him that he did not need to wait for a place on a transmigration scheme. Land could easily be found in Central Sulawesi, and the move would not cost him much. He was persuaded and went there instead.

Transmigrants were "programmed" by government officials to participate in the national drive for rice self-sufficiency. But many spontaneous migrants in Central Sulawesi also arrived intending to grow rice with, possibly, some coconut and fruit trees. Again, what mattered to them was possessing their own land.

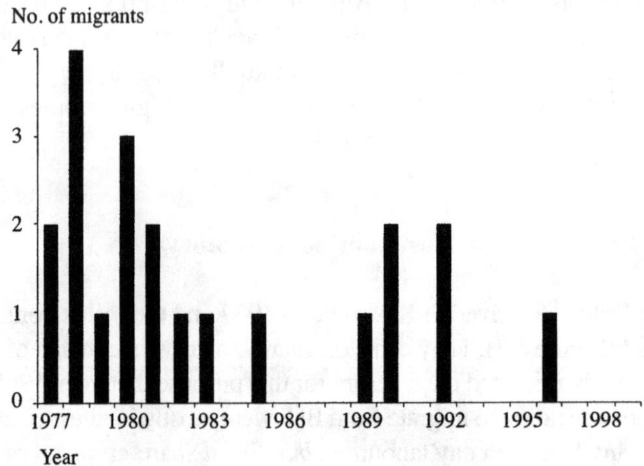

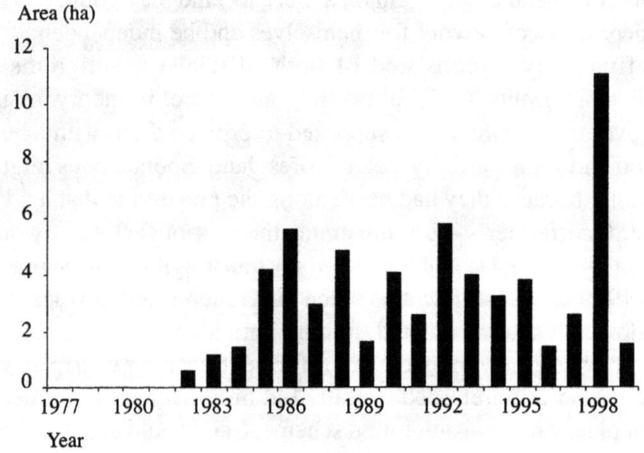

Figure 6.3 Balinese migrations and plantings in Kasimbar

Some rice transmigration sites in Central Sulawesi were highly successful. This cannot, however, be attributed to efficient administration but rather to the expertise of the Balinese as rice farmers and to their great sense of community. These two factors enabled them, with only

2 days of collective work per week, to build an irrigation network from scratch and to manage and maintain it equitably in such a way as to maximise and sustain rice yields (Charras, 1982; Levang, 1995). Nevertheless, according to farmers interviewed in 1999, the early years were difficult. Even on official transmigration sites, many transmigrants were allocated plots that were still forested and did not receive any help with clearance, probably because the money for this had somehow "evaporated". In many cases, the first rice crops failed.

The Balinese were experts in rice cropping but not in clearing forest. This is why a few of them soon moved away from the schemes in search of fallow land that had already been cleared by indigenous people for shifting cultivation. It was not difficult to acquire such land, which in the eyes of the indigenous farmers was no longer fertile and so had almost no value.

Spontaneous migrants began arriving in Kasimbar directly from Bali. They bought land mainly from indigenous people but sometimes from Balinese pioneers—those who wished to return home to Bali or who needed capital for other reasons.

Rice remained the villagers' priority. The spontaneous migrants began building their own irrigation system, digging the canals by hand. Despite rich soils, yields were again disappointing, mainly because the water supply could not be properly controlled owing to poor drainage and the steep and irregular slopes of the watershed. From 1977 to 1980, the villagers lost most of their four harvests. Some farmers decided to switch to growing cloves and rambutans instead.

Kasimbar heard about cocoa in 1980. Some Balinese farmers say that a few cocoa trees had existed before that in a neighbouring village, but they had not paid them any attention. The villagers' contacts with the labourers of a nearby logging company, PT Iradap Puri, were the crucial influence. The labourers told them that the company was going to plant cocoa. One of the Balinese transmigrants in the village managed to convince a small group of farmers to try the crop too. "If a big company adopts a new crop, it may be good for smallholders too," he argued. "What's more, we are almost sure to have a market by selling our cocoa to that company."

The group followed his advice in 1980-81. The other farmers in the village watched, not so sure that a market existed. Then, in 1983, they received proof, seeing with their own eyes the first middleman coming to Kasimbar to buy the first beans. They started planting cocoa too, and neighbouring villages followed.

This first wave of cocoa plantings took place on rice land converted for the purpose. The few plots that had been planted to cloves also soon gave way to cocoa. On these rich soils, the crop did not need much fertiliser. Shade trees were used to establish the young cocoa seedlings and to reduce the need for weeding. Once the cocoa trees started producing and shading the soil with their own canopy, farmers removed the shade trees in order to maximise cocoa yields. They also learned how to prune the trees, passing the knowledge on from farmer to farmer. Following these time-honoured practices, the first cocoa innovators soon achieved excellent yields, around 2 tonnes of dry beans per hectare in 1986. In the competitive and tax-free market from which cocoa benefitted, these yields started generating unexpectedly high incomes, especially in 1987. when the devaluation of the rupiah (in September of the previous year) increased the nominal price by at least 30%. The impact on incomes was reflected in the increasing frequency with which Balinese farmers flew back to Bali to visit their families and friends. Local friends in transmigration sites admired the motorcycles or even cars in which the farmers arrived to visit them. From 1987 onwards, impressed by these pioneers' success, more and more Balinese arrived in the village from other transmigration sites and from Bali.

By 1993, fertile land in the plain around Kasimbar had become scarce and expensive. Arrivals slowed to a trickle and new plantings petered out in about 1996. The only exceptions were a few latecomers invited from Bali by brothers or other family members.

By 1995-96, Balinese migrants were enjoying what was already a spectacular cocoa boom. In March 1995, we visited Kasimbar and Burange and found visible signs of their success: attractive new houses, charming Balinese temples in every backyard and small buses parked beside some houses. In March 1997, we returned and interviewed a few farmers. We saw more temples, of even finer quality. The cemented surfaces in front of houses had increased in area, as also had the amount of cocoa beans drying on them. Cocoa plantings had slowed, but the dynamism and innovation of the villagers had not. The wealthiest farmers were buying plantations from others who needed cash.

Other successful farmers began thinking in terms of diversifying their enterprises. As they had first learned about cocoa from an estate, they kept an eye on what the estates were doing. In 1996, one of the wealthiest farmers, who owned 9 hectares of cocoa, heard that an estate belonging to Suharto's son was starting a pulp tree plantation on the west coast. The farmer bought 3 more hectares of land in the hills and planted pulp trees, managing to get the expensive tree seedlings through family channels. He invested a total equivalent to around US$ 2000 in this enterprise. A small group of farmers followed suit while, as usual, others watched. Beyond the fact that the former president's family did, sometimes, give farmers good ideas, this anecdote illustrates the kind of diversification of which larger farmers were capable once opportunities on the plain became scarce.

Most farms were small. In 1996, while one or two cocoa farmers owned 9-10 hectares, a few more owned around 4.5-6 hectares and the majority around 2 hectares. There were, of course, some "losers", who owned less than 1 hectare, having sold part of their farm to meet a family emergency or other unforeseen needs. With average yields of 2-2.5 tonnes per hectare and prices fluctuating at around Rp 2300-2600 per kilogramme between 1995 and July 1997, even an average 2-hectare farm had an annual gross income of about Rp 10 million (US$ 4000-5000). As the soils were rich and had been forested only a few years ago, they did not require much fertiliser. The use of less than 200 kilogrammes of fertiliser per hectare and of almost no pesticides resulted in an annual net income of around US$ 4000. This was an extraordinary amount compared to the income from rice. Farmers who had managed to get 5 hectares of land and who hired labourers had a net income from cocoa equivalent to around US$ 8000-9000 in 1996.

The Drought and the Windfall

In 1997, while drought ravaged the hill farms of South Sulawesi, farmers in the plains of Central Sulawesi registered little more than mild discomfort. Most of their farms were still young and yields were on a naturally rising trend. Despite minor stress to the trees and a slight dip in production at the end of the year, rainfall remained sufficient to keep the trees alive and make 1997 a good year in terms of yields. The only real problem was CPB, which began hitting farms in Central Sulawesi earlier than in South Sulawesi[4]. In some areas, especially on the west coast, yields were halved, falling to 1000 kilogrammes per hectare. Elsewhere, however, yields in 1997 were higher than in 1996.

In 1998, rainfall was excellent and yields were maintained or even increased, except where CPB struck. For example, on the west coast and around Tinombala on the east coast, 1998 yields were just about equal to those of 1997 (Figure 6.4). Around Kasimbar and along the southern reaches of the east coast, which were spared from CPB until late in the year, 1998 appears as easily the best year in terms of yields and production.

Against this background the *krismon* had a variable though universally beneficial effect. In villages that are relatively far from markets, such as Oyom on the west coast, which has a poor road to the regional capital Toli Toli, the windfall was somewhat reduced. The highest daily price recorded here was Rp 16 000 per kilogramme, in July 1997. Kasimbar, in contrast, is only an hour by asphalt road from Parigi, with the result that prices here were as high as in the main cocoa areas of South Sulawesi, reaching an all-time high of Rp 20 000 per kilogramme for 1-2 days in July 1998. In consequence, the windfall in Kasimbar reached stupendous levels compared both to those of other Central Sulawesi villages and even to those of South Sulawesi.

The Balinese farmers of Kasimbar, who had started with nothing 10 years ago, had worked hard to achieve their success by the time the *krismon* arrived. During the *krismon* itself, however, they struck extremely lucky, in three senses. First, by 1997-98 their farms were more or less at the high point of their natural production cycle. Second, they enjoyed optimum ecological conditions in 1998, experiencing perfect rainfall and no CPB until late in the year. Third, the village was ideally placed to gain from the high prices, since it was close to a major market and port.

In the right place at the right time, Kasimbar farmers who owned 5 hectares earned gross incomes of Rp 150 million or more in 1998. Compared with the Bugis people, how did these highly successful farmers spend their windfall?

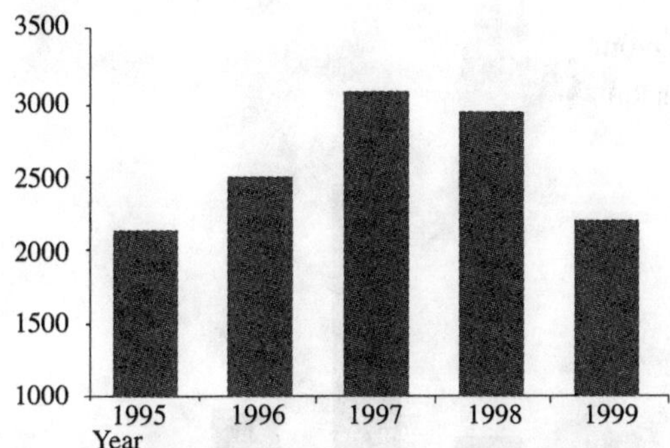

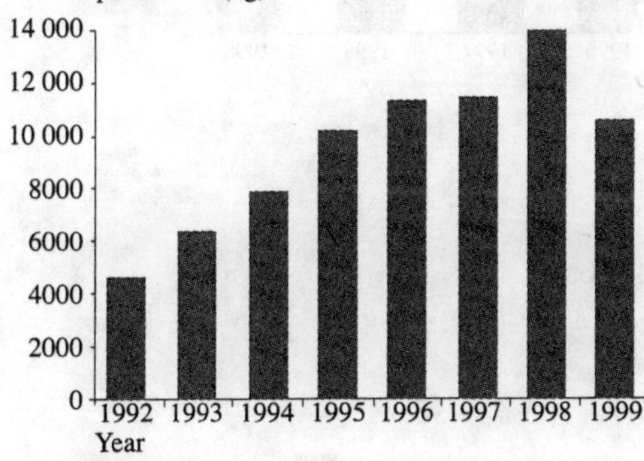

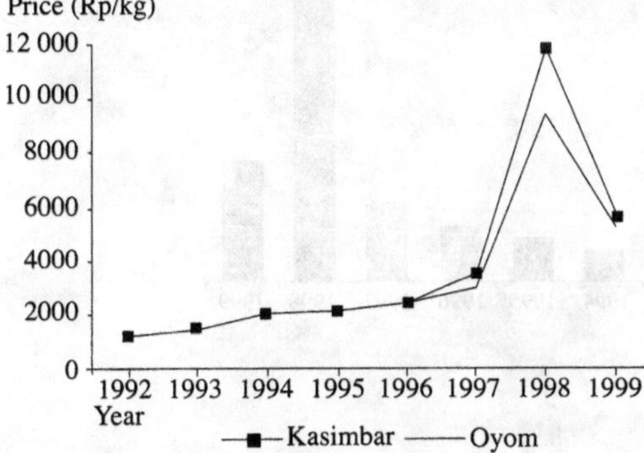

Figure 6.4 Trends in cocoa production and prices and gross incomes on two 5-hectare farms at Oyom and Kasimbar, 1992-99

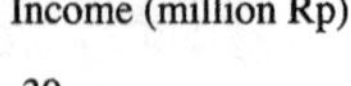
Gross income at Oyom

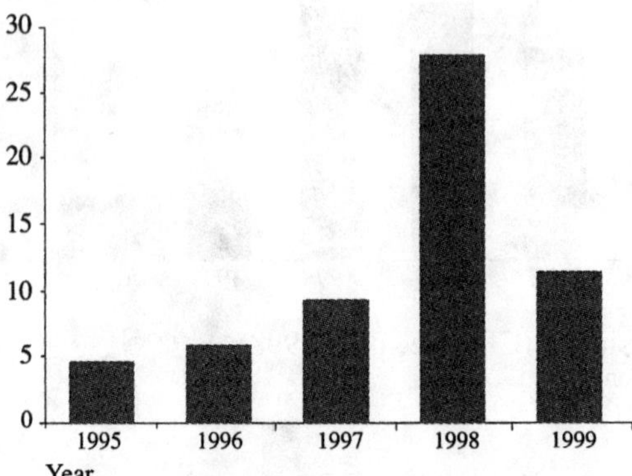

Gross income at Kasimbar

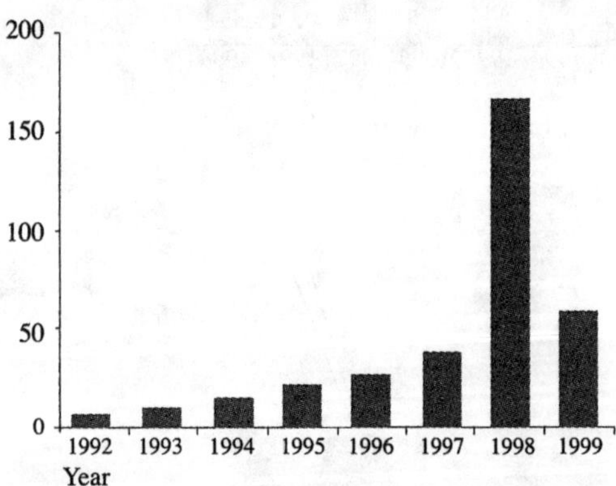

Figure 6.4 (continued)

Use of the Windfall

To obtain a picture of the use farmers made of their windfall, we studied a small sample consisting of 12 medium-sized or large farms owned by Balinese in Kasimbar, 5 medium-sized farms owned by Bugis in Toribulu (south of Kasimbar) and Tinombala and 4 small farms owned by Javanese in Tinombala. The Javanese farmers had begun planting cocoa only 2-3 years previously. Although the small size of this sample means that the figures are not significant, the sample is sufficient to draw out the main trends among the migrants and transmigrants of different ethnic groups (Tables 6.1 and 6.2).

Table 6.1 Approximate incomes from cocoa and other sources and major expenditures in three types of cocoa farm, Central Sulawesi, 1998

	Income and expenditure (million Rp)		
Ethnic group:	*Balinese*	*Bugis and other*	*Javanese*
Average production (t)	*4-13*	*4-6*	*0.2-0.4*
Cocoa gross income in 1998	87 811	45 120	2033
Cocoa gross income in 1997	23 565	12 312	0.533
Increase in 1998 (%)	+ 273	+ 266	+ 281
Cocoa gross income in 1998	87 811	45 120	2033
Main expenditures in 1998	81 533	50 277	9917
Balance	+ 6278	- 5157	- 7884
Cocoa gross income in 1998	87 811	45 120	2033
Other agricultural income	109	6434	1233
Agricultural wages	0	0	333
Sale of asset (house)	0	2500	5000
Trade incomes	218	0	0
Civil servant salary (teacher)	1309	1368	0
Credit (buying vehicle)	2727	0	0
Savings from previous years	5181	8000	666
Total gross income in 1998	97 355	63 422	9 267
Balance	15 823	13 144	- 651

Note: Balinese farmers lived at Kasimbar, were early adopters of cocoa and had large farms producing 4-13 tonnes of cocoa annually. The Bugis group, whose members came from various districts of South Sulawesi, lived at Tinombala or Toribulu, were intermediate adopters and had medium-sized farms producing 4-6 tonnes of cocoa annually. The Javanese farmers of Tinombala were late adopters and had small farms producing 0.2-0.4 tonnes of cocoa annually.

Table 6.2 Approximate costs and major investments in three types of cocoa farm, Central Sulawesi, 1998

	Breakdown of costs (%)		
Ethnic group	*Balinese*	*Bugis and other*	*Javanese*
Total costs (million Rp)	81 533	50 277	9917
Cost items			
Labour:			
Share-croppers	0.0	0.0	0.0
Monthly labourers	1.3	1.1	0.0
Daily labourers and piece work	2.9	2.7	0.0
Sub-total	4.1	3.8	0.0
Tools/inputs:			
Hand-sprayer	0.3	0.1	0.3
Fertilisers	0.8	2.0	1.1
Pesticides	0.3	0.8	0.2
Herbicides	0.2	0.2	0.3
Planting materials	0.2	0.0	0.0
Sub-total	1.8	3.0	1.9
Land:			
Purchase	11.1	2.6	0.0
Pledging and renting	0.0	0.8	0.0
Sub-total	11.1	3.4	0.0
Transport/Communications:			
TV, satellite-dish, radio	1.8	6.9	0.0
Motocycles	8.0	3.9	33.6
Cars	31.7	21.1	0.0
Trucks	5.6	0.0	0.0
Sub-total	47.1	31.9	33.6
Workship:			
Pilgrimage to Mecca	0.0	18.3	0.0
Individual Hindu temple	4.1	0.0	0.0
Sub-total	4.1	18.3	0.0
Other:			
Building material and houses	22.1	33.8	60.5
Trip back to Bali or Java	1.8	0.0	0.0
School, wedding and ceremonies	5.5	5.8	4.0
Investment in trade, shops, etc	0.3	0.0	0.0
Losses to gambling and theft	2.0	0.0	0.0
Total	100	100	100

Note: See Table 6.1.

Labour and other inputs

The costs of labour and other inputs to cocoa farming were low. Large and medium-sized farms devoted around 4% of their total costs to labour, while small farms supplied all their own labour and so spent nothing. All three groups spent 2-3% of total costs on inputs such as fertilisers and pesticides. These figures are lower than the 10-12% devoted to labour and the 4% devoted to other inputs by farmers in South Sulawesi. Three factors explain this difference:

- In the first few years of production, frontier lands benefit from a "rent" derived from clearing and burning forest. Soils are fertile, requiring little fertiliser, and weeds and insect pests are not yet a problem
- The comparative lack of impact of the drought on the east coast of Central Sulawesi and the relatively fertile soils meant that inputs were efficiently used and could therefore be applied in smaller quantities
- Fewer farmers in Central Sulawesi have to resort to share-cropping contracts. Employing day labourers is advantageous to farmers when cocoa yields and prices are high.

In addition, as in South Sulawesi, one of the reasons why 1998 brought such large profits is that there was a time-lag of several months before labour and other input costs rose in response to currency depreciation. Eventually, as we know, they did rise considerably.

Temples, cars and homes

Not surprisingly, as in South Sulawesi, farmers spent a lot. In Kasimbar, for example, most of the medium-sized and large farmers spent almost all their income from cocoa. Some of them even borrowed in order to buy cars. The Bugis and the Javanese tended to spend more than the Balinese, resorting to non-cocoa sources of income to help fund their purchases. Among the Bugis, these additional sources consisted mainly of other cash crops, for example coconut and pepper. The Javanese managed to raise some cash from the sale of rice, from their wages as agricultural labourers and as minor harvesters of rice and fresh coconut. The sale of assets, such as a house in a transmigration scheme, was another option that could be used to consolidate a new beginning in cocoa farming, enabling, for instance, a new house to be built on the new plot.

A wander through one of Central Sulawesi's delightful Balinese villages, punctuated with colourful sculptures and temples in the shade of cocoa and coconut trees, engenders first a feeling of peace and perfection and second the thought that worship must be expensive, requiring as it does the hiring of master craftsmen and the purchase of building materials[5]. This turned out not to be so, however. For the Balinese, building a private Hindu temple is a priority, but such temples accounted for a mere 4% of annual expenditures. The Balinese of Kalimbar did not forget their earthly well-being. They invested 22% of outgoings in improving their houses and 45% on motorcycles, cars and trucks. Two or three of the richest Balinese farmers now own two cars, or one private car and a commercial vehicle. In our sample, 50% of families bought a car in 1998 and 50% bought one or two motorcycles. Large farmers are slightly over-represented in our sample, but villagers say that 20-25% of Balinese farmers in Kasimbar bought a car in 1998 and that 80-90% bought one or more motorcycles.

These figures are borne out by the constant procession of motorcycles along the village lanes and the frequent trips away from the village made by cocoa farmers, their cars bulging with cocoa bags for delivery to the middlemen in Parigi. Some farmers have invested in trucks or buses, which they run as a transport service for others, taking cocoa to town or running other errands. Vehicles are not merely status symbols. As farmers noted, they are true investments, contributing to economic development by saving journey time to the fields and to market and by reducing transaction costs, so that their terms of trade for cocoa, inputs and other goods are greatly improved.

Investment in land

After vehicles and housing, the third major item on which farmers spent money was land. At least 50% of Kasimbar farmers bought land in 1998.

They were forced to purchase it mainly in the hills, because of a shortage in the plains.

Although their incomes had been rising for years, Balinese farmers bought little land in the hills before the *krismon*. That they have since done so represents an interesting change of attitude. Once they had colonised the best land around them on the plains, they sought to improve their life-styles. Cocoa farms in the hills were considered to be too far from the house and to offer lower returns. The Balinese have no forest clearing skills, so the secondary forest or old shifting cultivation plots offered for sale by indigenous people had little appeal. In addition, unlike that of the Bugis, Balinese culture places a high value on community life around the temple, discouraging moves away from the village. The villagers therefore used to let the hills be colonised by new migrants who were happy to settle there, while they themselves concentrated their energies in the plains. Consequently, land in the plains around the village became scarce and expensive before the *krismon*, limiting further expansion.

When the price of cocoa peaked in 1998, the Balinese of the plains "woke up". Many started looking for additional land in the remote hills. In our sample, 8 out of 17 Balinese farmers bought land in 1998. Their purchases ranged from 1 hectare relatively close to the village to 27 hectares an hour or so's journey away by car.

The 10-11% of 1998 expenditures devoted to land means that each farmer spent several million rupiahs. Although land prices have risen, an outlay of Rp 8-10 million still allows the purchase of 2 hectares of land not too far from the main road. In the remote hills the figure is nearer 10-20 hectares. The huge incomes derived from cocoa in 1998 are the driving force behind the newly awakened hunger for land and are therefore behind the sharp increase in land prices.

The change of attitude with regard to expansion in the hills is not solely explained by incomes, however. An indirect impact of the *krismon*, through the purchase of cars and motorcycles, was to "shorten" the distances travelled to new hill farms. Instead of being 5 hours walk from the house, a forest plot in the hills is suddenly only half an hour away by car or motorcycle, plus half an hour's walk. The usefulness of the car in allowing two widely separated cocoa farms to be more easily managed was also stressed by farmers in South Sulawesi.

Changing lives

Most Balinese farmers in the plains had already improved their lifestyles enormously before the *krismon*. In 1998, it was only 10 years since all a farmer got for 20 pods of cocoa was 2 kilogrammes of sugar. For the farmers of Kasimbar, that time seems an age ago. In the space of a few years, their lives have changed out of all recognition. Kasimbar is one of the most successful examples of cocoa development we have ever seen.

Sulawesi's free cocoa market is one of the major factors accounting for this success. Sulawesi forms a marked contrast with Africa, where so much of the wealth generated through cocoa is creamed off by government through fixed prices and taxes.

The new ownership of vehicles among the Balinese of Kasimbar has increased their bargaining power. If farmers do not like the price offered by one middleman, they simply drive on to the next one. Farmers can go to town with a bag of cocoa whenever the price seems right.

One of the "farmers" we interviewed we ended up excluding from our sample because he was too rich. In addition to growing cocoa on a farm employing 10 day labourers, he was a cocoa middleman in his own right, had a business buying and selling cars, traded in agricultural inputs and owned a grocery shop. He has more than Rp 300 million in his bank account. Only 20 years ago, in 1980, he had arrived in Kasimbar with nothing, following a move made a few years earlier by his father. He borrowed land from his father, grew onions on it to earn cash and saved up to buy his first plot of land. At that time he walked everywhere; now he boasts a four-wheel drive.

The 1999 Downturn

"One kilogramme of cocoa could buy 10 kilogrammes of rice. Now, it is one for one," a farmer told us. He was describing the disappointing slump in cocoa prices that followed the 1998 windfall.

By July 1999, the price of cocoa in Kasimbar had fallen to Rp 4000 per kilogramme from its historic peak of Rp 20 000 a year earlier. At the same time, the prices of staple foods, inputs and other goods had risen by a factor of 1.5-4 over their 1997 levels (Table 6.3). Understandably, the villagers today are pessimistic.

Table 6.3 Average prices of foods and agricultural inputs in Kasimbar, 1997-99

	Prices (Rp)			
Item	*July 1997*	*July 1998*	*July 1999*	*Increase 1999/97*
Cocoa (1 kg 7% moisture content)	2600	17 000	5000	x 2
			4000	x 1.5
Rice (1 kg)	1200	2000	2500	x 2
Sugar (1 kg)	2500	5000	2500	x 1
Fish (4-5 small fishes)	600	-	3000	x 5
Herbicide: Round-up (1 litre)	18 000	18 000	50 000	x 3
Fertiliser: urea (50 kg bag)	15 000	25 000	60 000	x 4
Pesticides: Decis (0.5 litre)	21 000	35 000	57 000	x 2.7
Labour: 1 day (harvesting cocoa)	7500	15 000	15 000	x 2
Land: 1 ha (in foothills)	2 000 000	5 000 000	5 000 000	x 2.5

Two factors make the 1999 downturn especially difficult for Kasimbar farmers to cope with. First, unlike the villagers of Noling, which has its own dam and irrigation system, they have stopped growing any rice. For the past 5-6 years, Kasimbar's cocoa farmers have been buying almost all their rice and other food items. The only exception is cooking oil, which is partly provided by coconuts. In 1999, they suddenly realised how dangerously exposed this strategy left them. Second, they suffered increasing infestations of CPB. Farmers had to absorb a five-fold increase in their annual purchases of pesticides at a time when input prices had tripled. "Cocoa is becoming like paddy: too many costly chemicals," said one farmer.

Kasimbar's farmers have complained vociferously about high input prices. They understand perfectly that the domestic cocoa market is free and competitive, but blame the government for the fact they can no longer afford pesticides and fertilisers. Locally, this has become a major political issue.

A much talked about reaction to the downturn is diversification. Farmers are looking once again at pepper and rambutan, with a view to investing in planting materials. They also keep an eye on the innovator who planted 3 hectares of pulp trees in the hills in 1996. If they were sure that a market for these exists, many would be willing to copy him. A further factor discouraging cocoa planting in the hills is that CPB attacks appear to be more severe there, while infestations are more difficult to control on steep slopes.

If pulp trees are one day widely adopted, this could be seen as one more positive outcome of the *krismon*. It would be more accurate, however, to view such an occurrence as due to a combination of factors. These include the innovative spirit of a few entrepreneurial farmers with enough capital and income to take risks, the copying effect we have already seen in cocoa, and what may be termed information free riding, in other words the pragmatism of those who allow a few others to take risks and then profit from their experience. CPB infestation and the down-side of the price cycle would also have played an important part.

Despite the decisions of a few farmers to invest in pepper, pulp trees and rambutan, cocoa is likely to remain the area's principal industry for many years to come. An orchard with an annual yield of 2 tonnes per hectare and an income potential of several thousand US dollars will not be given up easily.

The Transmigrants

As one of the first villages on the east coast to adopt cocoa, Kasimbar had many followers. The village served as a cocoa information centre for thousands of rice-growing Balinese settled on transmigration schemes.

These people were late adopters of cocoa (Figure 6.5). On the west coast, spontaneous Bugis migrations and cocoa adoption occurred much earlier and may even have fallen off somewhat in the early 1990s, partly because of the decline in prices but more probably because the Bugis from South Sulawesi found other places to migrate to. One of these places was Mamuju district, where transmigration and estate projects

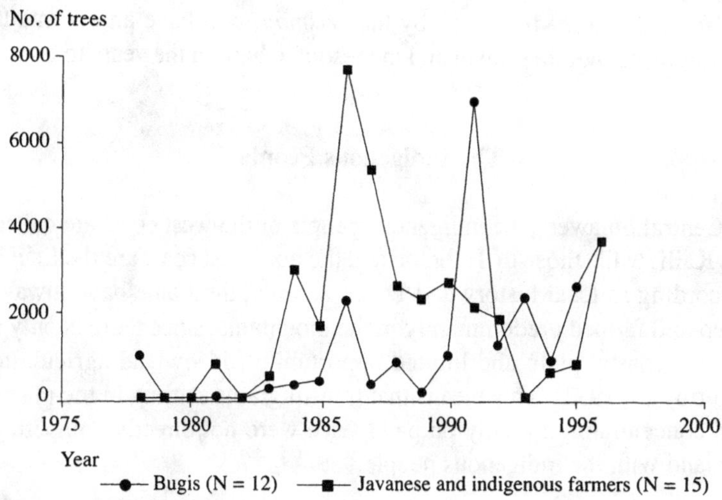

Figure 6.5 Cocoa plantings according to farmer origin, west coast, Central Sulawesi, 1975-2000

led to the building of new roads and bridges, paving the way for thousands of spontaneous Bugis migrants[6]. Whatever the reason, Bugis migrations to the west coast slowed down in several areas in the mid-1990s, just as Balinese and Javanese transmigration was increasing. The latter started planting when international and domestic prices were low.

On the east coast trends appear slightly less clear, but a trip from Parigi to Poso and then around Lake Poso leaves no doubt about the intensity of new plantings by Balinese transmigrants. For the past 3-4 years—and this seems to have accelerated in 1998—transmigrants have planted thousands of hectares of cocoa. To these should be added the thousands of plots belonging to transmigrants in the Tinombala area. One hectare of CPB-free cocoa trees in the plains can easily produce 250 kilogrammes of pods at 2 years old, rising to 1000 kilogrammes at 4 and 2000 kilogrammes at 6. These new plantings are thus playing a crucial role in Sulawesi's growing cocoa exports.

We conclude that the government's transmigration policy, intended to promote rice self-sufficiency and provide a reservoir of labour for estates, in fact had an entirely different effect, serving instead to accelerate the cocoa boom initiated by the Bugis. This "accelerating effect", when added to that already caused by the *krismon*, will have an enormous impact on economic growth and the resource base in the years to come.

The Indigenous People

In Central Sulawesi, the indigenous people of the west coast are called the Kaili, while those of Tinombo and the northeast coast are the Lauje. According to local history and Dutch records, the Lauje have always lived and farmed predominantly in the mountains, since there is only a narrow coastal plain and limited opportunity for lowland agriculture (Murray Li, 1993). This means that transmigrants settling in the plains and concentrating initially on paddy rice were not directly competing for land with the indigenous people.

Land users and sellers

What is meant by indigenous people? In very few cases can they be defined as those who have "always" (i.e. since the dawn of history) lived somewhere. More often, "indigenous people" are simply those who got to a place first, before the more recent arrivals who are labelled "immigrants". On a regional or national scale, indigenous people may arrive a long time, perhaps 100 or 1000 years, before the immigrants. For example, the Maori migrated from Polynesia to New Zealand by canoe about 1000 years before the massive influx of white people in the nineteenth century. On a smaller scale, these figures are usually reduced to only a few years, depending on the geographical unit considered. For instance, a few Lauje people native to the northern east coast of Sulawesi took advantage of the new road built to service transmigration sites in the 1980s to move into forest areas which they could hardly have penetrated before. They bypassed the transmigration site and settled in the hills behind it. From an ethnic and provincial point of view, they remain "indigenous". At the micro-geographic level, they are just the first migrants, the true pioneers, having come a few years before the transmigrants and other migrants began to be interested in this area. The time-lag was long enough to enable them to claim rights to the land adjoining the transmigration site. They are in a position to exchange these rights, either all or in part, for small amounts of money. This is their way into the market economy.

Of course, migrants and transmigrants also sell land and plantations, for various reasons. Some transmigrants find their new life too difficult and decide to sell up and return to Java or one of the other islands. In a few cases, this may have been their intention from day one, when they registered for the transmigration scheme[7]. Others face financial problems and decide to reduce their holdings. More frequently, among the Bugis at least, migrants develop the strategy of selling 1-2 hectares of land at a high price in an already developed area, in order to buy a larger area at the frontier. Still others sell part of their plantation to fund a pilgrimage to Mecca.

However, indigenous people remain the major group that sells land in Central Sulawesi. An indigenous person has a right to land acquired by early occupation of an area, usually because the forest was cleared either by him or by his father or grandfather. Of course, a grand-father may have several grandsons, leading to conflicts between them that intensify when the value of land rises. The forest used to be a habitat and a source of food in its own right, as well as a key production factor in the slash-and-burn farming system. Low population density enabled the forest to regenerate once plots had been abandoned. Indigenous people often grow tree crops, such as coffee and fruits, on a small scale, before migrants come and grow the same crops on a larger scale as sources of cash. The first migrants are usually made welcome and given land for a very low price, almost free. When these migrants start earning an income from their labour, others follow them into the new area. They also invite relatives and others from their home villages to join them. Demand for land rapidly increases, weaving a complex web of conflicting and mutual interests between the different groups. When the numbers of migrants rise beyond a certain level, the indigenous people begin seeing the forest in a different light, as a potential source of cash through conversion to plantations.

The ambiguous transactions that often take place in frontier areas can be understood as an interaction between land and labour. On the one hand are the indigenous people, who try to use their right to the land but do not have enough labour to exploit it fully. On the other are the immigrants, who bring their labour in search of new land to work. In most cases, the migrants gain most by the transactions.

Step by step, they acquire all the land—or at least all the best agricultural land—without having to expend much labour in the service of others. However, if they go too far, and the indigenous people retain some strength of numbers, over-rapid migration may backfire, leading to violence, including the torching of homesteads and growing crops.

In Central Sulawesi it seems likely that, over the next decade at least, indigenous people will continue to be willing to sell land. After all, they themselves had acquired the land free, clearing the forest by slash-and-burn to grow upland rice or maize for a year or two before moving on, allowing the forest to regenerate. Selling the land instead of merely abandoning it offers a good opportunity to raise additional cash. "If I don't sell it, somebody else will," runs the argument, especially when migrants start to arrive in large numbers and competition for land hots up. Another reason for selling is that indigenous people run the risk of having their land confiscated by a private company or a government project preparing for a new estate or a transmigration scheme.

For growing numbers of indigenous people, a better option than selling forest is to copy the immigrants by clearing the land and planting it to coffee and cocoa before selling 3 years later, when the plantation comes into production. Selling "ready-to-harvest" plantations is an excellent way of turning labour into capital and then cash. When cash is needed, land can be sold and assets rebuilt from scratch, using free access to forest. In this way, some indigenous people become experts at forest clearing.

In one case we encountered (Table 6.4), an indigenous forest dweller moved in 1980 from his home village, Tinombo, some 80 kilometres southwards onto a heavily forested hill at Ongka, close to what is now the Tinombala transmigration project. He explored it, then decided to base himself close to a river. He started slashing and burning, opening new land every year and from time to time selling part of it to migrants. He grew food crops but also planted a few cloves, coffee (in 1988) and cocoa (in 1993). In 1996, he sold most of the land to fund a divorce from his third wife and to marry a fourth.

Many migrants are happy to buy ready-to-harvest plantations. In so doing they bypass the onerous task of clearing forest, at which they are often not skilled. They also avoid the risk of being accused by a government official of having cleared forest, which in many areas is theoretically illegal. They get immediate returns to their labour and are often able to improve the plantation still further in the short term.

Against this background, given that one of the effects of the *krismon* was to increase the price of land, indigenous people may be thought to have benefitted. However, this does not seem to be so in the hills near Tinombala, where Javanese transmigrants remain slow to move off the official site and into the hills. They are reluctant to do so for fear of problems with indigenous people and with local government officials. In the mid-1990s, one Bugis migrant to this area summoned 17 other newcomers from his original village to join him. He negotiated land for them with indigenous people in Tinombala, but then found himself the subject of complaints from indigenous people in the neighbouring village of Ongka, who also claimed rights to the land. It took him several years to solve this problem. This type of conflict slows down the demand for land by migrants, attenuating the impact of the *krismon* on land prices. The influx of migrants seems likely to continue almost everywhere, but more slowly in areas where such problems arise.

In and around villages such as Kasimbar, several indigenous people took advantage of the *krismon* by selling land that was in high demand from the Bugis and Balinese farmers. To some extent, indigenous people benefitted from the influence that the Bugis had on the Balinese. The latter saw the Bugis buying forest on steep slopes—areas which they would not previously have considered viable—and copied them by also buying this kind of land.

Table 6.4 Land sales by an indigenous forest dweller in Ongka, Central Sulawesi

Year	*Area sold (ha)*	*Type of sale*	*Buyer's origin*	*Amount (Rp)*
1983	1	Cleared forest (slash-and-burn)	Tiolo, Central Sulawesi	150 000
1994	2	Cleared forest (slash-and-burn)	Balinese	300 000
1996	2	Coffee farm (8 years old)	Javanese*	3 500 000
1996	2	Cocoa farm (3 years old)	Bugis, South Sulawesi	7 500 000
1996	2	Cleared forest + a few coconut trees	Bugis, South Sulawesi	3 500 000
1997	4	Cleared forest (slash-and-burn)	Nephew, other relatives	0

* This buyer subsequently converted the plot to cocoa.

Cocoa farmers

Indigenous people too are jumping onto the cocoa bandwagon. Increasing numbers of them are interested in planting the crop and are searching for land. Like the Bugis, they are adopting the strategy of planting land in order to resell it and so advance further into the hills. In their search for new land they find themselves in the position of a "migrant". If they are willing to settle in remote hills, they can still obtain forest land free of charge. If not, they must buy fallow or forest land, competing with others in the rush to become an owner.

The Kaile and Lauje of Central Sulawesi form a marked contrast to the indigenous Luwunese of South Sulawesi. Around Noling at least, the latter have long participated in the land rush, becoming relatively large cocoa farmers themselves and even collaborating with Bugis in organising buses for groups wishing to acquire land in the pioneer areas of the province, particularly the forests beyond Malili. Unlike the indigenous people of Southeast Sulawesi, for example the Tolaki, who were literally swept away by the Bugis migrations, the Luwunese took to cocoa development right from the beginning. Here again, the DI/TII uprising of the 1950s seems to have been an influence. Many Luwunese who took part in the uprising were trained and influenced by its leader, Kahar Muzakar. The movement triggered a mingling of peoples, cultures and experiences, disseminating information on land, agriculture, cocoa, pepper and other profitable commodities. In addition, the uprising's principal base camp was in the hills behind Noling. All these factors, inherited from the 1950s, moderated the outcome of the 1998 *krismon* to the benefit of this indigenous group. In contrast, the Lauje and Kaili of the relatively remote northern hilly spine of Central Sulawesi were untouched by these influences and have, even now, only just begun to join the rush for land and the investment in cash cropping.

The Rush for Land

The indigenous people of Central Sulawesi are, as we have seen, still timid about the land rush, participating in it to only a limited extent. They are out-distanced economically by most migrants and especially by the Bugis. Even the arrival of newcomers does not prevent the average migrant from adding 0.5-1 hectare to his cocoa farm every year. This means that, between them, the migrants have bought a great deal of land in the past few years (Table 6.5).

Table 6.5 Area of mature and immature cocoa per farmer before and after the *krismon*, east coast of Central Sulawesi, 1999

Farmers' origin	*No. of farms**	*Area (ha)*			
		Before 1998		*1999*	
		Average	*SD±*	*Average*	*SD±*
Bugis (Tinombala/Oyom)	28	3.24	2.05	4.48	3.99
Balinese (Kasimbar)	17	2.97	1.31	3.64	1.98
Javanese/Balinese (Tinombala)	11	1.14	0.67	1.31	0.46
Indigenous	11	1.18	0.55	1.40	0.70

Note: SD = Standard deviation.
*The six migrants and one indigenous farmer entering the cocoa sector in 1998 have been excluded from the average in the "before 1998" column.

The Bugis and the Balinese were by far the most dynamic groups of cocoa farmers before 1998. Not surprisingly, given their larger planted areas, they benefitted most from the *krismon*. In terms of area planted, the Balinese in Kasimbar lag slightly behind the Bugis, despite their evident wealth. This is because they tend to hesitate to plant cocoa in remote hills. Some have started planting a few pepper and fruit trees in these areas, but others wait, giving themselves time to think about what to do. If this non-cocoa land is included in our figures, then the Balinese in Kasimbar emerge as the largest land owners (Table 6.6).

Table 6.6 Total land area owned by farmers of different groups, east coast of Central Sulawesi, 1999

Farmers' origin	*No. of farms*	*Area (ha)*	
		1999	
		Average	*SD±*
Bugis (Tinombala/Oyom)	28	5.98	4.34
Balinese (Kasimbar)	17	7.95	7.40
Javanese/Balinese (Tinombala)	11	1.85	0.58
Indigenous	11	1.95	0.95

Note: Including land not yet planted and a few pepper and rambutan plantations.

Social differentiation within each group follows the same basic principle. The better established and richer a farmer before the *krismon*, the more land he acquired during it. The *krismon* has, then, widened the gap between rich and poor in this most basic determinant of present and future wealth.

There is no need for a large sample to demonstrate the extent to which the richest farmers have accumulated land. In Kasimbar, among the 17 Balinese farmers sampled, the 5 who already owned 4 hectares or more of cocoa before 1998 accounted then for 50% of the total area owned by all 17 farmers. The other 50% was owned by the remaining 12 Balinese. By 1999, the same 5 biggest land owners were in possession of 70% of the total, leaving only 30% owned by the 12 others.

In Tinombala, a mixed group of Bugis, Javanese, indigenous farmers and others displayed the same trend. Those who bought several hectares of land already owned either a large farm or a medium-sized one, supplementing the income from this with off-farm earnings. Following a well-trodden path in cocoa development everywhere, small-scale farmers first seek to acquire land far from their existing base, because it commands a lower price. At Tinomobala it is still possible to buy cheap land, but only in the hills and far from the road. The richer farmers tend to avoid this. They leave that kind of land to the newcomers, who carve small farms out of the forest. Those in between these two groups, who own medium-sized farms, tended to plant land they had acquired before the crisis (Table 6.7).

A significant number of relatively wealthy Bugis and Balinese farmers now own cocoa farms of more than 20 hectares. The trend towards inequity in land holdings is, as we have already seen, almost universal in cocoa development and to some extent would have happened anyway. Nevertheless, by greatly increasing the incomes of the largest farmers, the *krismon* accelerated the trend.

Deforestation

By taking a 300-kilometre bus-ride and then a trip in a small boat, farmers from Noling, in South Sulawesi, are able to acquire forest plots in the new frontier land around Towuti, in Central Sulawesi. Around 25% of Noling farmers did this in 1998, each buying some 5 hectares on average. That makes an estimated area of forest cleared in 1999-2000 of some 500 hectares, just by migrants from a single village.

As we have already seen, at Bungku, on the southeast coast of Central Sulawesi, the average area of forest actually cleared by each farmer in 1998 was 0.9 hectares. However, the amount of forest appropriated by slashing a path round a plot was around 3.6 hectares. These larger areas are now being cleared and, together with the 4.5 hectares acquired before 1998, will eventually make cocoa farms of around 9 hectares in size—much larger than the average 2-3 hectares found in South Sulawesi.

Table 6.7 Accentuation of equity differences by the *krismon*, Tinombola, 1999

Cocoa area (ha)			*Impact of capital and income*
Before 98	*In 1999*	*Gain/loss*	*on the change*
*Large or middle sized farms**			
9.75	29.75	+ 20	Former low-ranking bank employee helped on his arrival in 1986 by indemnity when he left the bank. The 20 ha bought in 1998 are in Mamuju, 400 km from Tinombala
7.5	17.75	+ 10	Married an indigenous girl, making access to local land easier**
2.75	7.75	+ 5	Helped by a clothing business that did quite well during the *krismon*
Average farmers			
2.25	2.25	0	
2.5	3.5	1	Planted 1 ha on land bought in 1997
1.75	3	1.25	Indigenous farmer: free access to forest land
4	4	0	
*Newcomers****			
0	1	+ 1	Sold some cocoa and rice from his first small farm in Tolai
0.45	0.45	House	Sold an irrigated rice field
0	1.5	+ 1.5	Sold a house inherited from his parents in the rice area
Loser			
1	0.5	– 0.5	50% of farm area entirely flooded

* With off-farm income. ** However, the land he bought in 1999 was 200 km away, in Bungku. *** These farmers create or add to their small cocoa farms by investing cash earned from rice farming.

On the isthmus of Central Sulawesi, investment in land, and hence deforestation, also varies greatly. In all three of our survey villages—Kasimbar, Tinombala and Oyom—the windfall of 1998 accelerated land purchases, but, as we have seen, these were much larger among the previously successful Balinese farmers of Kasimbar. Around 50% of Kasimbar farmers bought an average of 8.6 hectares in the hills in 1998, leading to an average holding of 4.3 hectares for all farmers in the village, compared to a mere 0.2 hectare in 1996-97. In other villages, such as Tinombala and Oyom, holdings merely doubled, from 0.25 to 0.5 hectare.

Altogether, land acquisition in the three villages amounted to 0.25 hectare per farmer in 1996 and 0.22 hectare in 1997, but jumped to 1.5 hectares in 1998. It then fell back to 0.53 hectare in 1999. However, of the 1.5 hectare acquired in 1998, only 0.8 hectare was forest. The other 0.7 hectare was either fallow (with forest re-growth of less than 10 years) or grassland, which was stocked with a variety of tree crops besides cocoa, including pepper, fruit species and eucalyptus. The *krismon* did, then, lead to reforestation of a kind, which will at least have contributed to carbon storage even if it did nothing much for biodiversity. The practice of rehabilitating degraded grassland with leguminous shade trees was brought to Central Sulawesi mainly by the Balinese, who may be able to pass it on to the indigenous people. By using herbicides, even an *Imperata cylindrica* fallow can be planted to cocoa, provided soils are fertile and shade trees are also planted (Ruf and Yoddang, 1997).

Overall, however, it is clear that deforestation in the isthmus of Central Sulawesi and on the southern reaches of its east coast, already well advanced before the *krismon*, was greatly accelerated by it. Forest conversion remains the prime factor behind the boom in Sulawesi's cocoa exports. Unless there is a radical change of government policy, it looks virtually unstoppable.

Conclusions

Our research in Central Sulawesi confirmed that here, as in South Sulawesi, most cocoa farmers experienced a windfall in 1998. Like the Bugis, successful Balinese migrants spent a great deal of the money, mainly on family and social investments such as motorcycles, cars, housing and so on. They shared with the Bugis considerable scepticism about the future of Indonesia's currency, buying assets as a means of storing their wealth.

However, there were some differences between the way the Bugis and the Balinese used the windfall. Except for a few wealthy farmers, the Balinese did not save much in bank accounts. In addition, they did not waste or lose money, nor did they borrow very much to finance new purchases.

The *krismon* accelerated land purchases and cocoa planting among the Balinese, as it did among the Bugis. After vehicles and houses, investment in land was the third largest item of expenditure, preparing the way for substantial expansion of the cocoa area and the accumulation of considerable wealth in the future.

The 1999 downturn caused difficulties for established cocoa farmers, but did not halt migration and land purchases. Coupled with CPB infestation, the downturn may encourage some further diversification into such crops as pepper, rambutan, coffee and, possibly, pulp trees. However, cocoa is still likely to account for the bulk of new plantings, at least for the next few years.

Local increases in production in 1997-98—statistically hidden by the decrease in the mature cocoa farms of South Sulawesi—and the more general increase in production in 1999 had little to do with farmers' short-term supply responses. They were related to planting decisions taken before the crisis. In Central Sulawesi, these new plantings partly reflect the past experience of the Bugis and their accumulation of capital and knowledge. Since 1994-95, Bugis farmers have begun clearing more land and planting more cocoa per family.

Transmigrants from Bali and, to some extent, Java, who used to grow rice, are playing an increasing part in the growth of cocoa production and exports. Their relatively late adoption of cocoa meant that some of them were exceptionally well placed to profit from the windfall. Without the Balinese, Sulawesi production would probably have fallen in 1998 and risen much less in 1999.

At least in Kasimbar, Bugis and well established Balinese farmers had different responses to the *krismon*. Among the Bugis, the *krismon* merely accelerated an existing trend to acquire land wherever possible. Among the Balinese, the *krismon* triggered a shift into the hills that was entirely new. Having acquired a few hectares in the plains and planted enough cocoa to bring in a few thousand dollars every year, the Balinese were not on the look-out for more land in different areas. They tried to buy only the land around them, in the plains and close to the village. That is one of the reasons why land prices had peaked in Kasimbar.

The reasons why the Balinese did not buy much land in the hills were social, as well as economic. The Balinese have strong community ties and like to live around the village temple. This did not hold them back economically. On the contrary, Balinese culture and social organisation, although less well adapted to migration than those of the Bugis, can clearly be highly successful. The Hindu temple and the Bugis mosque have similar functions, serving to maintain social cohesion in an otherwise adventurous and migratory life-style. However, this form of social control has until now had more influence on the investments in land made by the Balinese. The *krismon* seems to have changed that, at least in Kasimbar. The windfall proved too large to resist the temptation to invest in the hills any longer. The Balinese were probably influenced by the Bugis in this change. "If Bugis buy this kind of land, on steep slopes, there must be something to be gained from it. So why not us too?"

As regards land prices, responses to the windfall remind us that the determining factors are not only the price of cocoa and the income that can be expected from it. Other factors are also at work, including:

- The wealth accumulated in previous years
- The experiences of others who buy apparently marginal land (the copying effect)
- Conflict over land between indigenous people and estates or other migrants
- Government control over forests, which clearly relaxed during the crisis.

The success story told by Kasimbar's cocoa farmers epitomizes a development episode that would have been extremely difficult to forecast when the Balinese left their island homes to take up a new life in the unknown land of Sulawesi in the late 1960s and 1970s. It also reveals the contradictions inherent in the transmigration policies of the Suharto government. The officials in charge of transmigration, like the farmers themselves, had thought only of rice production.

In the early years, many Balinese immigrants achieved spectacular successes with rice, because of their existing expertise in the crop and their ability to organise irrigation and cultivation. These qualities served them well, especially since the promises of assistance in these areas made by the government were seldom met. The Balinese transmigrants had to start from scratch.

These problems prompted some transmigrants to move off the schemes and do deals with indigenous farmers who were willing to sell land that had been cleared, cultivated for a year, then abandoned, following the typical cycle of shifting cultivation. This was the first step on the road to success: a straightforward transaction between those who had mastered the art of forest clearance and those who could apply to the land a larger supply of labour and new areas of expertise, such as irrigation. Despite this expertise in irrigation, the second step was a failure: in Kasimbar, the Balinese found they could not cultivate irrigated rice because the agro-ecological conditions for it were not right.

The third step was the contact between the transmigrants and workers from a neighbouring estate that had planted cocoa. Once a few farmers had successfully adopted the crop, the close social network of Balinese transmigrants in the province became the perfect vehicle for disseminating information and planting materials. Before 1980, Kasimbar was nothing but a peripheral rice transmigration project. In the decade to 1990, it became a centre of innovation in cocoa production. And from 1990 to 2000, the village continued to serve as a resource for a widening circle of Balinese from the east coast and elsewhere.

Partly, the move of the Balinese into cocoa production can be seen as a reaction to the corruption and dishonesty of the government. Had the Balinese transmigrants received the help they had been promised when they accepted a place on the transmigration scheme, they might never have set foot on the road that led to their prosperity today.

What final conclusion should we draw from all this? Although the *krismon* benefitted individual cocoa farmers in the short term, it also accelerated the "forest clearing machine" that is cocoa migration. As late as 1999, most of the forest along the hilly spine of Central Sulawesi had been spared. But how long can that last? The sound of chain-saws can now be heard everywhere, at any point on any road or track in the hills. Once again, we ask the recurrent and universal question: is this wise? Especially in such a narrow corridor of land, the consequences of deforestation on the natural resource base could be disastrous. The best we can hope for is probably some sort of compromise—perhaps the retention of belts of forest between the cocoa farms. Achieving this would require strong participation by farmers' organisations in planning and implementing effective management of the land on a watershed basis. Can this be instituted before the last forest has gone?

References

Charras, M. 1982. *De la forêt maléfique à l'herbe divine: La transmigration en Indonésie: les Balinais à Sulawesi.* Maison des Sciences de l'Homme, Paris, France.

Durand, F. 1995. Farmers' strategies and agricultural development: The choice of cocoa in eastern Indonesia. In: Ruf, F. and Siswoputranto, P.S. (eds), Cocoa Cycles: *The Economics of Cocoa Supply.* Woodhead, Cambridge, UK.

Eisemann, F.B. 1992. *Bali. Sekala and Niskala. Vol. II: Essays on Society, Tradition, and Craft.* Periplus Editions, Hong Kong.

Levang, P. 1995. Tanah sabrang (la terre d'en face): La transmigration en Indonésie: Permanence d'une politique agraire contrainte. PhD thesis, Ecole nationale supérieure d'agriculture (ENSA), Montpellier, France.

Murray Li, T. 1993. Tenure Issues in Rural Development Planning: A Case Study from Central Sulawesi. Sulawesi Regional Development Project, Discussion Paper No 3. University of Guelph, Canada.

Ruf, F. and Yoddang. 1997. Pest outbreaks, adoption or non-adoption of pesticides: The pod borer case in four provinces. In: Ruf, F. and Lançon, F. (eds), Indonesia Upland Agricultural Technology Study. Report prepared for the World Bank. CIRAD, Montpellier, France.

Ruf, F. and Yoddang, 1999. Smuggling and cocoa adoption by migrants: The fascinating case of Sebatic Island, Indonesia. Paper presented at the International Conference on Migration and Countries of the South, 18-20 March 1999, University of Avignon, France.

Notes

1 Our sampling in each of these areas was far from perfect. For instance, between Poso and Bungku a huge number of Balinese transmigrants have started planting cocoa but were not included in the survey. However, we believe our sample to have been reasonably representative of the social and geographical diversity of Central Sulawesi. Beyond our surveys, our team also made the occasional swift field visit to gather data informally. For instance, in Burange and Kasimbar, we held short talks and plantation visits with farmers in October 1992, March 1995 and March 1997, which provided helpful information to back up our survey on the impact of the *krismon* in July 1999.

2 Although partly explained by a switch of deliveries to Palu from Ujung Pandang and the fact that some 3000 tonnes may have come from the neighbouring Moluccas Islands, these export figures reflect a spectacular rise in production in Central Sulawesi.

3 Sebatic is a small island dissected by the border between Malaysian Sabah and Indonesian Kalimantan. Approximately two-fifths of Sebatic are Malaysian while three-fifths belong to Indonesia. A substantial cocoa boom occured in Sabah in the 1980s and spilled over to Sebatic. Former DI/TII members also played a part in cocoa adoption on the island (Ruf and Yoddang, 1999).

4 Many farmers suggested that CPB infestation was associated with the introduction of hybrid planting materials by the extension service. This hypothesis is supported by our own observations in several areas and by observations in the Moluccas by our team's geographer (Durand, 1995). The cotyledon of most recent hybrids is relatively soft, allowing penetration of the pod by CPB larvae. The pods' wrinkled surface may also provide a better habitat for the insects than the smoother pods of traditional varieties. Our hypotheses on this point are not proven, however.

5 This phenemenon is so impressive that it deserves a fuller description: "The stone walks of many of Bali's temples are a riot of decoration. A bewildering variety of toothy stone faces with bulging eyes and long fangs peer, leer, grimace, and smirk from a veritable stone jungle of vegetation. Some walls show battle scenes, with refined men in elegant costume. Some murals are downright dreadful, with grotesque and gory scenes of torture. Still others are plain, everyday events—men drinking *tuak*, children riding bicycles. Statues, large and small, guard every gate and shrine. The profusion is such it would seem that Balinese stone carvers can't abide a blank space... Music, carving and the construction of offerings are all forms of celebration of the Hindu-Balinese faith." This fine description, given in Eisemann (1992), is of Bali itself. Equally impressive is the fact that, when the Balinese migrate, they bring this creativity with them, especially when they are economically successful, as they are in Sulawesi.

6 Even before 1980, there were hundreds of Bugis migrants in Tarailu and villages upstream, but they had to follow the old ways and colonise the forest by river. By 1990, it was fascinating to see how the area had filled up, with Bugis migrants along the river and transmigrants along the roads. Even more fascinating was how the area had been organised politically. Javanese or Balinese transmigrant schemes were always located near a Bugis village. The "Camat" (the head of the sub-district) was usually Javanese or Balinese.

7 Some even became professional players of the "game", registering themselves as transmigrants, settling in their new area, then selling everything when the food subsidies stopped. They would then return to Java and register for a new transmigration site. In northern Mamuju, we met several people who were undertaking their second or third transmigration adventure. Some said they "saw Indonesia" that way.

Chapter 7

From Migration to Motorisation: How Market Liberalisation Has Benefitted Coffee Farmers

François Ruf and Yoddang

"If I have something to recommend to other farmers, it is as follows: plant whatever you want on half your farm plots, but keep coffee on the other half. Coffee has to remain the linchpin of your farm."

This is what an Indonesian coffee farmer told us in 1990. Events before that year had shown his advice to be sound. But considering what has since happened to coffee prices, which fell very low in 1992 before rocketing in 1994 and 1998, his statement may be seen as prophetic.

The main objective of this chapter is to analyse the impact of the 1998 crisis and the accompanying peak in coffee prices on farmers' production, income and investment strategies. As in the case of cocoa, if the marketing chain is efficient, coffee farmers should have benefitted from a sizeable windfall. Did they in fact do so? And if so, how did they spend it? How did the 1997 drought affect matters? In short, what happens to coffee farmers when a country is undergoing a severe economic, social and political crisis but prices for the crop are high?

To answer these questions, we chose to investigate a small area of Bengkulu Province. Lying along the west coast of southern Sumatra, Bengkulu is one of Indonesia's main coffee producing regions. Our area lay mostly in the sub-district of Kepahiang, which lies in the hills inland from Bengkulu City (Figure 7.1). Questionnaire surveys were conducted in mid-September 1998, covering 40 households which draw their main income from coffee.

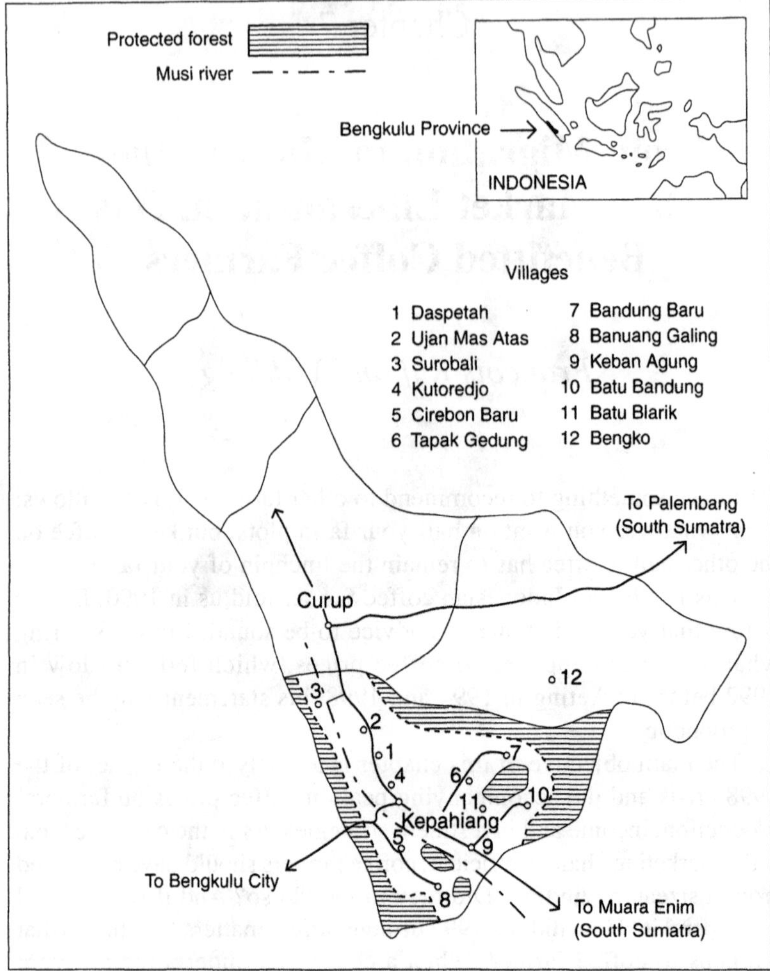

Figure 7.1 Kepahiang sub-district of Bengkulu Province, Sumatra, Indonesia

The development of frontier lands to coffee in Asia, including Indonesia, got off to a late start compared with South America and Africa. In several areas the pace of development is still slow (Daviron and Fousse, 1994). Indonesia's share of the world coffee market remains very low. Although the country's smallholders are planting coffee, Vietnam is expanding its coffee sector much faster. The potential influence of the Indonesian crisis on the world coffee market is therefore limited. That is why we concentrate instead on what happened within the country.

Several features of the coffee sector are likely to make its performance in response to the *krismon* differ from that of cocoa. One of coffee's most attractive characteristics for farmers is that it can be stored more easily than cocoa. In addition, Indonesians themselves consume around 100 000 tonnes of coffee annually, heightening the competition between domestic and international consumers when supplies are short. These two characteristics make farmers' deliveries of coffee to traders relatively sensitive to price changes. Lastly, coffee yields respond even more than cocoa to the "forest rent" effect. Despite this fact, replanting is more common in coffee- than in cocoa-growing areas, because of the greater shortage of suitable unused land. This means that increases in production imply less deforestation than they do in cocoa.

Our analysis is in six sections. The first section deals with the historical background necessary for an understanding of Indonesia's smallholder coffee sector and why it has remained so dynamic despite its long history. We then focus, in the second, the third and the fourth sections, on Kepahiang sub-district and the impact of the ecological and economic crisis on coffee farmers there. The fifth section describes how farmers spent the windfall they received. We draw some conclusions from our findings in the last section.

The Ingredients of Indonesia's Coffee Boom

Boom-to-bust cycles in cocoa are, as we have seen, based largely on the consumption of "forest rent" by migrating smallholders (Ruf, 1995). Are the same factors at work in Indonesia's coffee sector? The question is especially relevant for southern Sumatra, where 50% of the country's coffee is produced.

From estates to smallholdings

Indonesia was the world's leading coffee producer in the eighteenth century. Production was concentrated in Java, where the arabica type was widely grown. By the early 1880s, when exports began declining,

Indonesia was still the second largest coffee exporter in the world, after Brazil. The gap between the two producers was by this time considerable, however. While Indonesia produced some 80 000-100 000 tonnes per year, Brazil managed 220 000 tonnes. Indonesia's exports nose-dived in the 1880s, when estate crops were hit by a combination of diseases and poor management, after which the country took some 40 years to recover. The recovery was based largely on robusta coffee, which was less vulnerable to pests and diseases and cheaper and easier to process. Eventually, in the early 1920s, Indonesia once again reached annual exports of 100 000 tonnes (Figure 7.2).

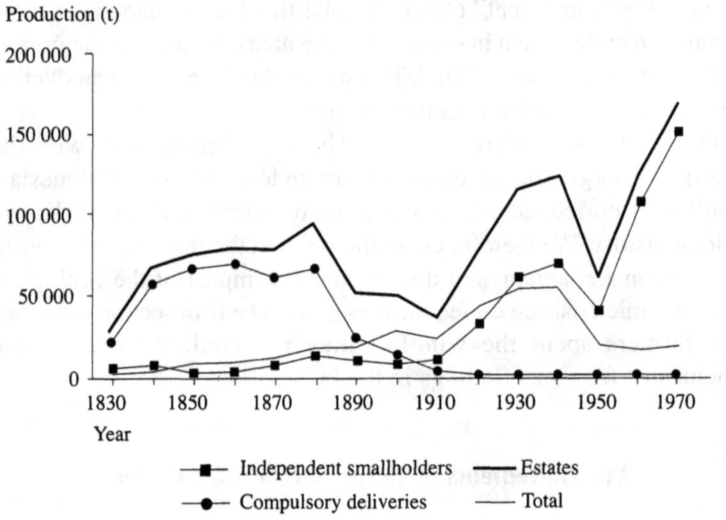

Figure 7.2 Coffee production in Indonesia, 1830-34 to 1970-74
Sources: McStocker (1987), BPS (1961, 1963, 1971).

Large estates predominated from 1895 until about 1920, but by the early 1930s most of the coffee area consisted of smallholdings, which virtually replaced the estates altogether in the 1950s. Despite the price recovery of the 1920s, production on estates stood still throughout the decade, before declining sharply when prices fell by more than half between 1929 and 1932. The true Indonesian coffee boom of the twentieth century had its origins in the 1950s and began in earnest in the 1960s. Its engine of growth was the Sumatran smallholder (McStocker, 1987).

The boom occurred because of the low overhead costs of smallholders and their greater efficiency compared to estates. When smallholders have easy access to land, planting materials and information, they are more efficient than estates at mobilising labour and converting both land and labour into tree-crop capital. The history of Indonesian coffee production gives much credence to this view (Clarence-Smith, 1998). The era of the coffee estates was brief, barely more than a few decades around the turn of the twentieth century, sandwiched between two periods in which smallholders accounted for the bulk of supplies. The first period, 1830-90, was that of compulsory deliveries, when smallholders were forced to grow the crop by Sumatra's Dutch colonial masters. The second period began in the 1920s, when the regime was liberalised and a free smallholder sector emerged, with the skills and resources needed to grow the crop.

Forest rent

We know little of what production on small farms was like in the frontier lands of the 1920s. But what we do know is that the conquest of new land and the clearance of forest must have generated an "economic rent"[1].

In the humid tropics, surplus land is a major, but not the only, component of economic rent. This land is forested, so "forest rent" is also involved (Ruf, 1994; Clarence-Smith, 1994). By planting tree crops on cleared forest rather than cultivated land, farmers achieve higher yields and incomes. In Kepahiang, as in nearby Lahat, in South Sumatra, farmers believe a farm planted after dense forest has been cut down will produce up to 2-4 tonnes of coffee per hectare per year. This compares with only 1.5-2.00 tonnes during the best year (called "*agung*" or "royal") when the farm is replanted after grass fallow or a previous coffee farm (Table 7.1).

The yields expected by individual farmers may vary, but all farmers agree on two points:

- Forest rent is highly significant in coffee farming. It largely explains both the hunger for forest land and the "shifting cultivation" system used to grow coffee.

- The coffee production cycle is characterised by high yields in the early productive years of a plantation. Sensibly, farmers seek to optimise these yields, achieving maximum returns to their investment during this period (Godoy and Bennet, 1989; Taher, 1991). After years 6 or 7, yields rapidly decline. However, the continuing quest for the "*agung* effect" encourages farmers to rejuvenate their plantations in order to keep their yields as close as possible to the maximum achievable (Ruf, 1997).

In South Sumatra, an old coffee farm that still has its original shade trees will, if left for 10-20 years, regenerate bush and additional wild trees, restoring part of the forest rent. By the 1950s Indonesian smallholders had already noticed this and were practising shifting cultivation. Cramer (1957) describes their system as follows: "It [the coffee plantation] is kept for only 5 to 7 years and then abandoned. Every year a new field is opened but if the new fields have been planted with coffee, the soil needs to be rested for 7 to 10 years, and for an even longer period for poor soils. From an economic point of view, the system of maintaining the coffee plantation for only a few years and opening new land every year has proved to be a defensible system. In southern Sumatra, with its very wet climate, robusta gives the heaviest yields in the first cropping years."

Table 7.1 Typical robusta coffee yields over the life-cycle of a farm in Lahat, South Sumatra

Years after planting	*Yield (kg/ha)*	
	If replanting	*If planting after forest*
3	100	
4	500-700	
5	1000	
5-6 *(agung)*	1500-2000	2000-4000
6-7	1000	
7-8	700	
8-9	500	
9-10	400	

The highland environment of southwest Sumatra, with its fertile volcanic soils and cool, wet climate, promotes exceptionally high yields during the years immediately following maturity. This is one of the reasons why farmers here like to make sure they have a stock of young trees. As long as forest is available, the best way to achieve this is to keep clearing and planting new forest areas.Farmers return to abandoned farms when the bush regrowth is considered sufficient to have regenerated at least some forest rent. After a few decades of this system, families with insufficient land start returning to abandoned farms more frequently. A market in old coffee groves gradually establishes. Migrants enter the market either by buying farms or through the *bagi tanah* system of exchange of land for labour. In this system the newcomer clears land and plants it, and is paid 3 years later in the form of part of the land just as the trees come into production. The last of the migrants to arrive in an area, and the next generation, find it more difficult to acquire land. Share-cropping contracts become more common. In the traditional forms of such contracts, labourers work on an owner's existing plantation, tending and harvesting the crop in return for a share of the harvest. Since the 1980s, farmers have come up with complex new institutional arrangements such as the *sorongan*, whereby a plantation is maintained and harvested for 6-8 years under a rental agreement. This system is modelled on the economic life of a coffee grove.

As the pressure on land mounts and landless families become more numerous, some try to clear state forest land or land held under private concessions. Coffee farmers on such land face the risk of expulsion. Pressure is now apparent in the Kepahiang sub-district, where the replanting of coffee groves and the clearing of new forest areas are occurring simultaneously. The fallow period allowed for abandoned plantations is becoming shorter. These changes have been accompanied by the creation of ingenious new institutional arrangements for sharing labour, land and the resulting tree capital.

Important though it is, forest rent is only one component of a coffee boom. To optimise economic rent, labour is needed. In most cases, labour arrives with the migrants; indigenous forest dwellers seldom have enough.

Migration

Originally in Java, Indonesia's coffee heartland shifted to southern Sumatra in the second half of the twentieth century. Currently, three provinces—Lampung, South Sumatra and Bengkulu—produce more than 50% of the country's coffee. This shift in production was mainly associated with migration.

It is difficult to specify the percentage of migrants in the region's total population. The figures given by different authors vary according to definitions of migrants and indigenous people and according to the district or sub-district. The range is wide: roughly 20-80% (Ruf, 1994).

Migration was broadly of two kinds: spontaneous migration, mainly for the purpose of growing tree crops, and transmigration organised by the government, which focussed mainly on food crop production. Land availability and the growing demand for coffee worked together to fuel the process of spontaneous migration, which was also driven by the inherently unsustainable nature of much tree-crop production. Spontaneous migrants established their own farms, planting coffee in the Barisian mountains, rubber in the northern plains of Palembang and pepper in Lampung.

Charras and Pain (1993) describe how, on the plateau of Kotaway, in South Sumatra, large-scale migration set in during the 1950s, a period which coincided, as we have seen, with the resurgence of demand for Indonesian coffee. According to these authors, the "massive invasion and conquest" began with the arrival of Semendo and Ogan Ulu people from neighbouring districts to the west. They were closely followed by people from Java, mainly the Sundanese. The process of colonisation began to speed up in the 1970s, when tracks made by a forest concession opened up new forest areas. During this period a large influx of migrants arrived from Lampung. By 1982, no more land was available outside protected areas, which had also undergone major encroachment. The population of the plateau in 1989 was estimated at about 2675 families, consisting of 40% Javanese, 25% Sundanese, 1.5% Balinese, 30% Semendo-Kisam and 3.5% Ogan.

Smith and Bouvier (1993) examine the factors that determine the sites chosen for spontaneous settlement by migrants. These include the migration history of the pioneer group, information networks among families and friends, the fertility of the site, its access to market, and the chances of obtaining authorisation to clear it. New settlements are often an extension of existing ones that have reached saturation point. New land is needed as immigration continues and the children of first-generation settlers grow up. It is also needed to offset the diminishing soil fertility and falling yields of existing plantations. Much migration of this kind takes place locally.

According to Sevin (1989), Lampung Province had a very low population until the end of the nineteenth century. The mass exodus from Java, whether officially prompted or spontaneous[2], coincided with the coffee boom of the 1960s, 1970s and 1980s, again demonstrating the key role played by migration in the exponential growth of Indonesia's coffee sector.

In Bengkulu, from the 1950s onwards, an increasing number of families arrived from the neighbouring province of South Sumatra, migrating into the Barisian mountains to take advantage of their rich, volcanic soils. Spontaneous migrants often created their own villages at some distance from the main road and from the villages of indigenous people. They also had Javanese and Balinese "transmigrants" as neighbours, some of whom were official settlers while others were more spontaneous, since they had left or "escaped" from the unsuccessful transmigration schemes established further north, on the poor podzolic soils of the plains. Although Sumatra was the major destination of the government's transmigration programme, very little transmigration was inspired by coffee[3]. Theoretically, transmigrants were free to choose what to grow. In practice, especially from the 1970s onwards, the government obsession with rice self-sufficiency put strong pressure on most transmigrants to grow rice and other food crops, even when soils were poor and irrigation infrastructure was lacking. As a result, many transmigration schemes failed, prompting their inhabitants to look for better conditions elsewhere and to switch from food crops to tree crops, including coffee, which they began growing in remote hill areas.

In short, the government's transmigration programme can be seen as having had the unintended consequence of contributing to the growth of southern Sumatra's coffee sector. However, the programme played a much less important part in this than spontaneous migration.

Despite the barriers erected by the government, migrants have proved to be efficient producers of coffee. We must ask ourselves why this is so.

Smallholders' efficiency

Migrant smallholders are more efficient than estate owners at converting land and labour into capital. Since the land they occupy is usually free or at least very cheap, migrants do not need much capital. In addition, they arrive in huge numbers, bringing a vast additional labour force into the frontier area.

For example, over the 5-year period 1975-80, nearly 450 000 migrants are thought to have arrived in southern Sumatra, triggering change on a massive scale (Charras and Pain, 1993). Even if only 10% of them became engaged in coffee production in the Barisian mountains, that still means 45 000 new coffee farms. Capitalising on the area's rich forests and soils, these 45 000 farms will easily have produced 2-3 tonnes of green coffee each per year in the mid-1980s. That makes 90 000-130 000 additional tonnes of Indonesian coffee available for export or domestic consumption. This simple calculation is borne out by the official statistics, according to which southern Sumatra produced some 100 000 tonnes of coffee in 1975, rising to over 200 000 tonnes by the late 1980s. That compares with figures for Indonesia as a whole of 175 000 tonnes in 1975 and 325 000 tonnes in the mid- to late 1980s.

Besides being more numerous, migrants are intrinsically more efficient than indigenous forest dwellers at creating a coffee farm. Most Sumatran coffee migrants know how to cut down forests at low cost, using good axes and, more recently, chain-saws. They are prepared to accept a difficult life during the early years, working hard in order to cash in on the high income they can expect from coffee in the medium term. In some cases, though not always, they bring some capital with them, which helps them acquire land and planting materials. And they respond quickly to price signals, increasing the rate at which they plant whenever prices rise.

Success breeds success. Nothing is more persuasive to the would-be coffee grower than the sight of a migrant returning to his village of origin with a motorcycle and smart new clothes after 5 years' absence. Sights such as these have regularly triggered new waves of migrants in southern Sumatra. And if the price of a commodity shoots up while suitable land is still available, migrations can only accelerate even further. The international price of coffee rose continually from the 1940s until 1955, then fell, before rising once again in the mid-1970s. While the

Barisian mountains were filling up with coffee migrants, the price jumped from US$ 0.76 per pound in 1975 to US$ 2.24 in 1977. The nominal price in rupiahs followed a similar trend, providing a strong incentive to migrate and to choose to grow coffee rather than other crops. Since then, even during low-price periods, migration and new plantings have continued and production has risen steadily. Each price hike enormously accelerates migrations, fresh plantings, production and exports. Despite the "bad" years of 1992 and 1995, exports in the 1990s were still well above those of the early 1980s (Figure 7.3).

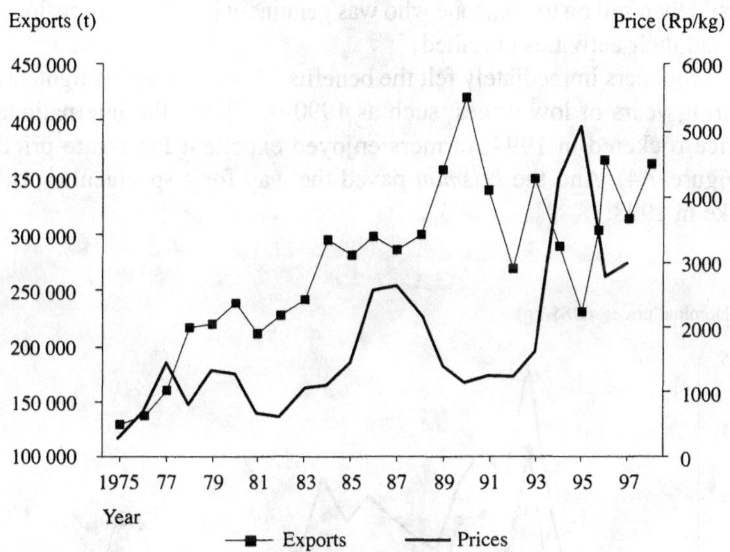

Figure 7.3 Indonesian coffee exports and traders' prices, 1975-98. Source: BPS.

Market liberalisation

The history of Indonesian coffee production is one of recurrent bouts of tight government control over the market, interspersed with periods of liberalisation. Government policy over the past 20 years has in part reflected the international export quota system agreed among producer countries under various International Coffee Agreements. Ruf (1994) identifies four key periods, as follows:

- October 1980-February 1986: quota system imposed on all producer countries
- March 1986-September 1987: system abandoned
- September 1987-June 1989: system reimposed
- July 1989 and thereafter: system definitively abandoned.

In 1989, under pressure from the World Bank, Indonesia bowed to changing international circumstances by dropping its own system of allocating export quotas within the country. Those whose political connections had enabled them to gain possession of a quota, which they could then sell on to someone who was genuinely in the export business, found their activities curtailed.

Producers immediately felt the benefits. Traders' margins tightened during years of low prices, such as 1990-91. When the international price rocketed in 1994, farmers enjoyed excellent farm-gate prices (Figure 7.4). And the *krismon* paved the way for a spectacular price hike in 1998.

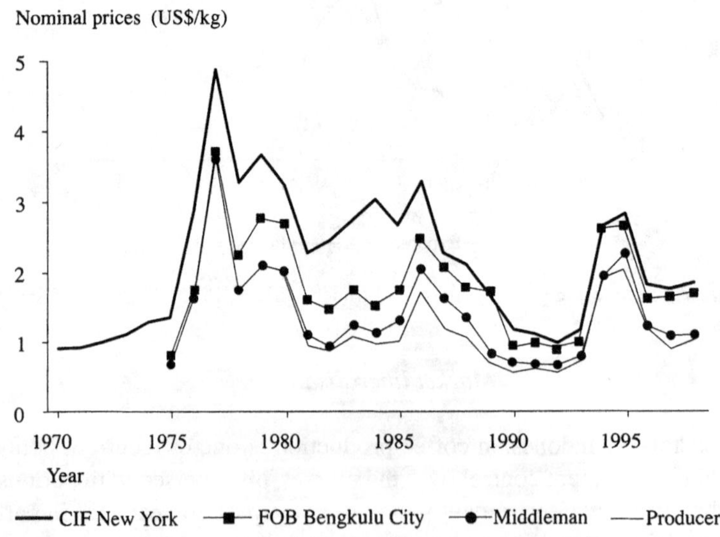

Figure 7.4 Coffee prices for producers and middlemen, 1970-98. Sources: BPS/USDA/ICO/AIKE.

Exports and domestic production

Indonesia's coffee exports were worth nearly US$ 600 million in 1997-98, giving this commodity third place in the ranking of agricultural exports. Coffee lagged far behind palm oil and rubber, which were valued at around US$ 1500 million each, but came in ahead of cocoa, which brought around US$ 400 million into the country.

However, coffee in Indonesia is not solely an export crop. Indonesians consume some 100 000 tonnes of it every year, in amounts that vary according to price and income. Domestic consumption was estimated at around 60 000 tonnes in 1981. This rose to 120 000 tonnes in 1997, just before the crisis.

Table 7.2 shows the recent performance of coffee production and exports compared with cocoa. Cocoa appears to have moved ahead steadily in the second half of the 1990s, while the trend for coffee looks more erratic. This mainly reflects the impact of the 1997 drought.

Table 7.2 Annual production and exports, coffee and cocoa, 1995-99

	Volume (t)				
Years	*1995*	*1996*	*1997*	*1998*	*1999*
Cocoa production	238 000	284 000	327 000	331 000	390 000
Coffee production	348 000	474 000	420 000	420 000	432 000
Coffee exports	257 340	384 060	327 000	360 000	336 000

Note: The data are indicative only. The comparison is not exact because the years are not divided up in the same way by the two statistical sources. For coffee, the year 1997 means April 1997-March 1998, so production is mainly that of the 1997 calendar year. For cocoa, 1997 means October 1997-September 1998 and so refers mainly to the 1998 supply. To make the data more comparable, we have changed the figures, taking those for the previous year in the case of cocoa.
Sources: ED&F Man (1999), USDA (1999).

We showed in Chapter 5 how the new cocoa plantations entering production in 1997-98 masked the severe impact of the 1997 drought on production from mature farms. In the case of coffee, the relative maturity of plantations, a lower proportion of which are on pioneer fronts, allows the yield losses sustained in 1997 to stand out more clearly. Nonetheless, production in 1997 fell by only around 11%, and appeared to stabilise in 1998 before rising again in 1999-2000.

Domestic coffee consumption fell heavily in response to the crisis. It was only 95 000 tonnes in 1998 and seems unlikely to rise above this level in 1999-2000 (USDA, 1999). There were two reasons for the fall. First, faced with a threefold rise in the price of coffee, many poor domestic consumers had to give up buying it. Second, not surprisingly, traders diverted supplies away from the domestic market towards exports, in an attempt to extract as much profit as they could from the collapse of the country's currency.

Kepahiang before the Crisis

Land use in Kepahiang is a classical outcome of Indonesia's coffee boom. Most middlemen and local exporters in the nearby town of Curup say that, as long as land is available, farmers plant more coffee when prices are high. But they do not stop planting when prices fall again. In other words, the view expressed by the farmer quoted at the beginning of this chapter is universally shared. Even during price troughs, coffee remains the major, and the safest, source of income for everyone in the area. Diversification into alternative crops such as ginger or chilli is limited to few farmers and to only part of their farms.

Planting, replanting and prices

Let us begin our case study of Kepahiang by taking a closer look at planting rates. A combination of factors, including price fluctuations, land saturation, creative arrangements for attracting labour and the growing weakness of government appear to have encouraged investments in both planting and replanting.

Three periods of rising producer prices can be expected to have influenced planting rates: 1977, 1983-87 and 1994-95. The effects of the 1977 price hike cannot be assessed through field surveys done in 1998, because a high percentage of the farms created in the late 1970s and early 1980s will doubtless have been cut down and replanted in the meantime. However, the impact of the price rises of 1983-87 and 1994-95 can be examined. The first of these rises was associated partly with the rupiah devaluations of 1983 and 1986 and partly with the international price rise of 1984-85, itself explained by the impact of the 1983 drought in West Africa. The second rise was associated with a recovery in the international price after a long period of decline.

In our 40-household sample, the price rise of 1986-87 triggered accelerated planting in 1988. During 1989-93, planting remained at a high level despite 5 years of relatively low prices (Figure 7.5).

To some extent, this pattern can be explained by comparative and anticipated prices. Established coffee farmers regard the price of coffee as more attractive and more stable than the prices of other commodities, even when it is relatively low. They also believe that the price will bounce back to a higher level later on.

But established farmers' faith in coffee was not the only factor at work. Most of the farmers who planted coffee in 1989-93 were Javanese migrants, who had arrived relatively recently. At this late stage of migration, their greatest need on arrival was to save money in order to buy land, which was no longer plentiful. To this end they worked as share-croppers (*bagi hasil*) for 2 years, saving just enough to buy cheap land in remote or risky locations with uncertain rights, for example on the edge of state forest and estate concessions. The relatively low price of coffee in the mid-1990s doubtless also helped keep land prices low. Lower coffee prices mean lower anticipated incomes, leading to deflated land prices, but indigenous people are still willing to sell land because they need the cash.

This is an important point because, if new migrants buy land at low prices when the commodity price is low, production may be expected to increase a few years later when the price is high. This increased production could be interpreted as a short-term supply response to rising prices, but in fact it has more to do with the previous fall in the commodity price than with the current rise. As we have seen, a similar price mechanism is also at work in the cocoa sector[4].

The trend for replanting looks similar to that for planting. The decision to replant is most frequently taken while the price of coffee is low. This makes sense because, although yields have declined as the trees have aged, replanting still entails the sacrifice of income in the short term—an easier decision to take when the price is low.

Thus, in our sample, while coffee prices rocketed in 1994-95, the aggregated annual planting and replanting rate fell. A further partial explanation of the decline of new plantings in 1994-95 was the pressure

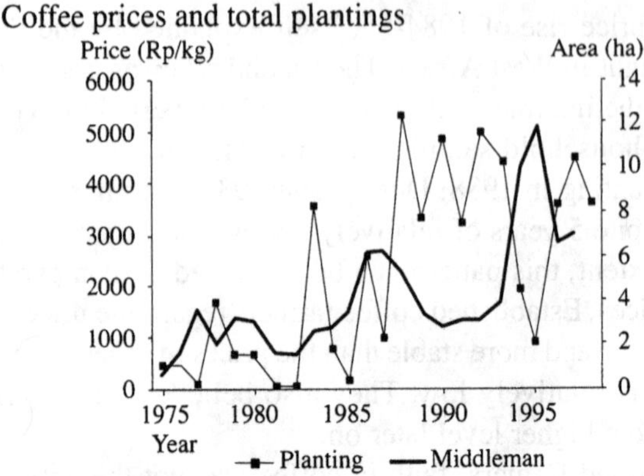

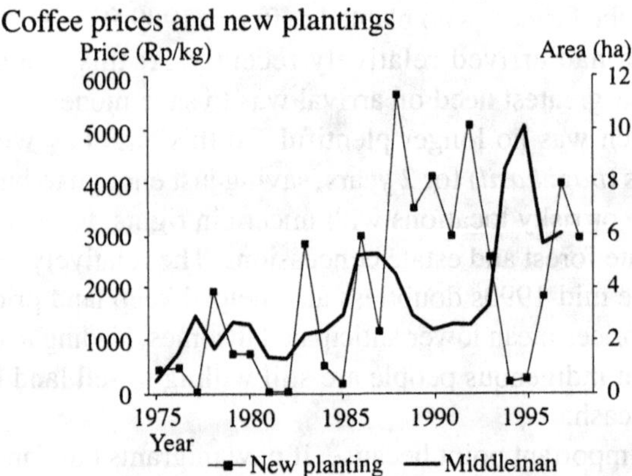

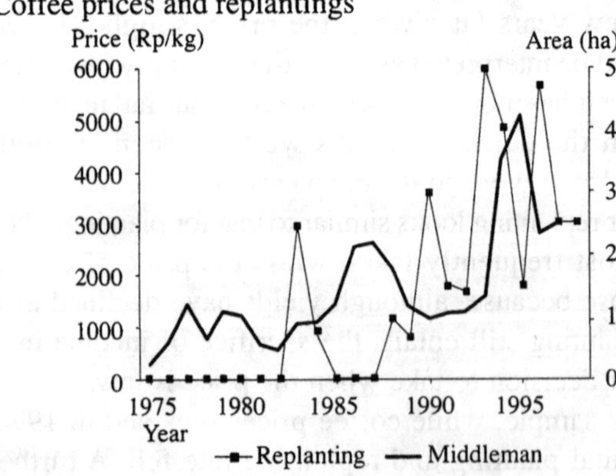

Figure 7.5 Coffee prices and annual plantings and replantings in Kepahiang, 1975-98

from government to protect state forest. This may explain farmers' relatively greater reliance on replanting around this period. Replanting again surged forward in 1997. As there is little forest left to satisfy farmers' appetite for land, it is now the most frequent method of investing in coffee.

Of the 108 plots surveyed in our 40-household sample, 37 had been acquired as existing coffee farms rather than as forest land. Some 24 of these 37 had been replanted immediately or a few years after acquisition. Replanting thus accounted for 22% of all plots and had been adopted by 50% of farmers. This high level of replanting is the single biggest difference between the coffee systems of southern Sumatra and the cocoa systems of Sulawesi. It reflects the relative land saturation in Sumatra, the high yields of coffee obtainable in the early years of production, and the fact that replanting is easier for robusta coffee than for cocoa.

New plantings recovered again in 1997-98, rivalling the high rates for replanting. This reading of events is borne out by the fact that our 1998 data were probably under-estimated, since the survey was conducted in September and did not capture any planting between then and December. The renewed strength of new planting in 1997-98 suggests that farmers decided to risk planting in protected forest areas while the regime was in trouble and prices were high.

This brief account of farmers' planting strategies reveals the relentless pressure placed on all forest areas in Indonesia, especially protected forests. It is as if the process of deforestation is unstoppable, whatever the signals sent to migrants by government and market forces.

Land saturation

Some of Kepahiang's coffee villages are surrounded by protected forests. As the pressure on land rises, the temptation to risk planting in these areas becomes irresistible.

The area has a long history of squatting on protected land. Under the *ancien régime*, these incursions occasionally backfired. In Tapak Gedung, some 500 hectares of coffee farms were even converted back to *forest konservasi*. This was done forcibly, by evicting the farmers. Now that the authoritarian regime of Suharto has given way to a more liberal one, people think they are less likely to be evicted in this way.

In the east of the sub-district, near Bandung Baru and Batu Bandung, and around Bengko in the neighbouring sub-district of Perwakilan Blitar, thousands of hectares of forest and cleared land had been taken over by a private estate. The estate intended to plant tea and arabica coffee, but failed several years ago for reasons unrelated to the *krismon*. As a result, the villagers have a large area of unused land "on their doorsteps". Villagers began planting on this land in 1998. In some cases, they grew only food crops but some planted coffee groves as well, especially on previously forested land.

Whatever else it may demonstrate, the Kepahiang area is certainly a show-case of one major social dimension of the Indonesian crisis: the government's loss of control over land, which is now under redoubled pressure from farmers.

Farm size, production and incomes

Our 1998 survey of 40 farmers, which included 18 migrants (44%) from other provinces of southern Sumatra and from Java and Bali, showed an average farm size of 3.42 hectares per household, including 2.21 hectares planted to coffee. A similar but larger survey in 1990, which had included the same percentage of migrants, showed average farm size to be 3.5 hectares, including 2 hectares of coffee.

Until the 1980s, the Kepahiang area still had forest and was able to satisfy the migrants' appetite for land. Under these circumstances, some farmers were able to create larger coffee farms than was possible in neighbouring and more densely populated regions of southern Sumatra. For instance, the areas of Lahat and Pagar Alam, southeast from Kepahiang in South Sumatra, have much higher populations, with the result that the average coffee farm is much smaller.

The 1998 survey indicated that average farm production in 1996 was around 3.212 tonnes of "Asalan" coffee (i.e. having a 20% moisture content). This generated a gross income of roughly Rp 8.6 million, equivalent to US$ 3660. This compares with gross incomes of Rp 8 million and Rp 14 million for cocoa farmers in the hills and plains of Sulawesi.

These figures do not, of course, tell the whole story, since some 5-10% of coffee farmers in Kepahiang are landless share-croppers, who have much lower incomes. Nevertheless, these relatively high incomes remind us that, although prices fluctuate, coffee is almost always a valuable export crop for Indonesian farmers, including share-croppers. This is in large part because the market is a competitive one.

The Drought and its Impact

Figure 7.6 shows monthly exports at the national level for 1996-98. The peak in exports normally occurs in July-August, lagging behind the peak in harvesting by around 1-2 months. The lower than usual peak in 1997, which is followed by a steeper than usual decline in the second half of the year, reflects the early impact of the 1997 drought.

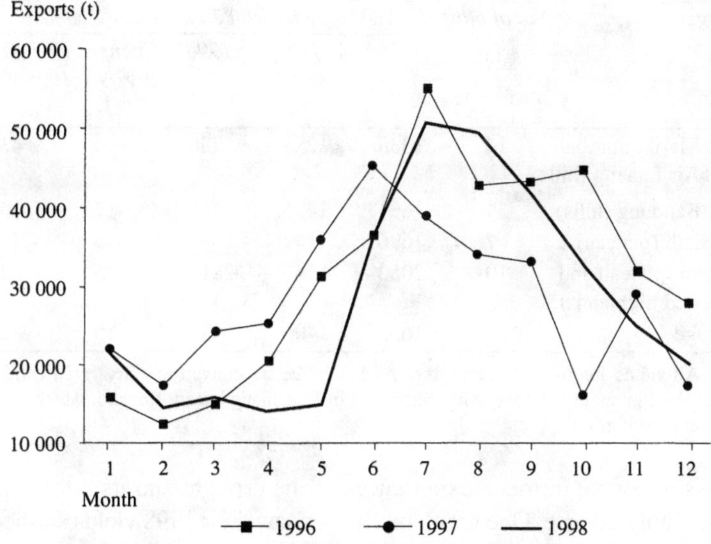

Figure 7.6 Indonesian coffee exports, 1996-98. Source: USDA (1998, 1999).

At farm level the impact appeared moderate, at least compared to the devastation of Sulawesi's cocoa orchards. In Kepahiang the average number of trees reported to have died in 1997-98 was no more than 100 per farm, representing less than 1.5% of the total tree stock. Around 50% of these dead trees were immediately replaced with new plantings.

The data for yields tell a more complex story (Table 7.3). The drought was most keenly felt in the second half of 1997, so had limited impact on the production figures for that year since the harvesting season peaks in April-May. In 1998, the delayed impact of the drought, together with the high winds and heavy rains that marked its end, showed up in the figures, although the effect varied greatly from location to location. Overall, yields fell by 15% in 1997 and by 13% in 1998, compared with 1996. Production averaged 3.212 tonnes per household in 1996, compared with just over 3.000 tonnes in 1997-98. The corresponding decline in production is thus only 6.5%. This figure is similar to the 11% decline recorded in the official statistics for national production.

Table 7.3 Coffee yields in four types of village, Kepahiang and Rejang Lebong sub-districts, 1996-98

Villages	*No. of plots*	*Yields (kg/ha with 20% moisture content)*				
		1996	*1997*	*1998*	*Change 1997/96 (%)*	*Change 1998/97 (%)*
Batu Blarik, Surobali and Air Lanang (hills)	14	1338	1285	730	- 4	- 43
Batu Bandung (hills)	34	1661	1406	1262	-15	- 10
Daspetah (plateau)	7	1696	1449	1691	-15	+ 17
Bengko (plateau and forested highlands)	10	2050	1547	2815	-25	+ 37
Average		1655	1406	1432	-15	+ 2

Note: All yields are given in the form of Asalan coffee. To convert into dry green coffee, reduce the figures by 10-15%. All villages are in Kepahiang except Bengko, which is in Perwakilan Blitar.

As in cocoa, farmers' experiences of the drought and its aftermath were highly diverse. One group of villages saw their 1998 yields slashed by 40% compared to those of 1997. At household level, 3 of the 40 farms in our survey were devastated, with 80-90% of production wiped out. One village was affected much more lightly, with losses averaging around 10%. And two villages seem to have actually benefitted from the drought, one by bouncing back to its 1996 level of production and the other taking a quantum leap forward to a record new high, with yields 30-40% up on 1996. How can these different experiences be explained?

New plantings and tree age

Since annual yields vary greatly over the tree's life-cycle, great care must be taken in interpreting "average" yields. As we have seen, in the early 1990s many farmers planted coffee because they anticipated higher prices, while many others bought cheap land and prepared to do so. Their investments began to pay off in 1994-95, when the first of these plantings came into production just as the price of coffee started to rise. Yields on our survey farms bore up well in 1998, with the relatively young age of a number of plots helping to contain and compensate for the negative effects of the drought. Overall, however, this compensation effect was much less visible in coffee than in cocoa. In only 2 of the 40 farms in our sample was there a clear effect of tree age, with an increase in production in 1997-98 clearly linked to new plantings. Of the 38 remaining farms, some may have had at least one plot entering into production, but the effect was not yet significant even at the household level.

The "royal year" effect, which we also looked for in our study, seemed relatively well distributed over the years. For instance, in the village of Daspetah, several farmers had plots that had allegedly had their royal year in 1997. Normally, the yield declines sharply after this, but in 1998 these plots still produced a yield close to that of a royal year. This effect can be attributed to the drought, which had a beneficial effect on yields in this plateau location (see below).

Plateaux, hills and forests

Farmers confirmed that, as our data suggested, the 1997 drought had reduced coffee yields in the hills and foothills. These effects were evident in Batu Blarik, Air Lanang, Benuang Galing, part of Batu Bandung and several other villages of the Kepahiang sub-district. In the uplands, high winds also affected yields, in some cases stripping trees bare of their leaves. In the valleys, in contrast, the winds had almost no impact. Frost may have been an additional yield-reducing factor in some villages in the mountains.

In the upland village of Batu Blarik, at about 350 metres above sea level, yields fell by half. Other villages in similar situations experienced losses of 50-75%. However, Daspetah and the surrounding villages were protected by their topography. They are on a plateau, which remained somewhat cooler than other areas. Here the drought seems to have had a beneficial effect.

The 17 farmers we interviewed in Batu Bandung gave a perfect illustration of the diverse effects of the drought. They said that the drought had increased yields in remote mountain areas which had preserved a forest atmosphere. Plots close to the forest, about 4-5 kilometres from the village, had given particularly good yields in 1998. For instance, one farmer claimed yields of 5-6 tonnes per hectare. In contrast, farms at lower altitude, close to the main village, had experienced lower yields.

The village of Bengko, at about 1500 metres in the hills, is one of the best coffee producing centres in the region and another good example of how the highland climate moderated the effects of the drought. Farmers here said that yields in 1997 suffered more from the wind than from the drought. In 1998 the village had greatly benefitted from its humid atmosphere, which was the result of its proximity to the forest. The village's coffee trees had shown the classic physiological response to a slight drop in output in the previous year by greatly increasing production in 1998.

Shade trees

Farmers in Batu Blarik and Batu Bandung said that coffee plots with good shade-tree cover were less affected by the drought. The absence of shade, on the other hand, led to dying trees and falling yields. Other farmers said that trees located in the valley and on slopes facing east or west are less exposed to sunshine and bear more berries than trees on hilltops, where the sun shines the whole day. Shade not only enhances yields during a drought year but also appears to stabilise yields over time, prolonging the life-cycle of the coffee trees. Without shade, coffee trees remain productive for only 5-6 years under southern Sumatran conditions. With it, the cycle extends to 8-9 years.

Too much shade, on the other hand, reduces yields. The price peak of 1998 encouraged some farmers to reduce the amount of shade over their plots, but they took out only what they called "extra" shade. For instance, in the village of Surobali, where Balinese migrants were intercropping coffee and vanilla with shade-trees, most farmers gave up trying to grow vanilla, which was suffering from a disease, and eliminated the shade-providing trees used to support the vanilla creepers. In so doing they hoped to maximise their coffee yields.

Labour and expertise

The high yields achieved in Bengko in 1998 were not due solely to the village's proximity to forest and the new farms coming into production there. Around 70% of the village's population, some 510 families, consists of spontaneous migrants from East Java. These Javanese migrants have better access to labour than other migrants or indigenous people, finding it easier to recruit day labourers. This is because of the steady influx into the village of new arrivals, who need to sell their labour on a daily basis.

Large areas of East Java are famous for their coffee and for the expertise of their coffee growers. The migrants appear to have brought that expertise with them. An interesting feature of farms in Bengko is the *tipung* or "umbrella pruning" system practised by farmers. The main stem of the coffee tree is cut at 2 years, after which the tree grows in an umbrella shape, facilitating harvesting. When the whole grove is managed in this way, harvesting time is greatly reduced. Farmers can maintain the umbrella easily by pruning.

Farmers also use the technique of side-grafting to prolong the life-cycle of coffee groves and produce trees with stable and high yields over a longer period than ungrafted trees. One farmer we interviewed had practised side-grafting in 1995. In 1998 his plot of 400 productive trees yielded about 1 tonne of coffee, equivalent to around 3.35 tonnes per hectare. The original trees had been planted in 1986 and he had introduced the *tipung* system 2 years later. In our 40-farmer sample, the 7 farmers who had adopted side-grafting between 1994 and 1998 had an average yield of 2.37 tonnes per hectare in 1998, compared with only 1.43 tonnes for the whole group.

In summary, the most important variables accounting for the different impact of the drought on production were location (whether plateau or hills), proximity to forest (forest rent), access to labour and management techniques. Each village was thus differently placed when the 1998 windfall occurred. Farmers who lost 50% of their yields in 1998 benefitted much less from the windfall. Those in Bengko had what they called "the year of their life".

The Windfall

The prices paid by coffee farmers for other commodities and inputs rose considerably less than the price of coffee in 1998. Despite depleted forest reserves, the price of land also rose less rapidly than that of coffee. Luckily for farmers, the peak in the price of coffee coincided with that of harvesting in a year in which many plantations showed good yields. All these factors combined to provide farmers with a spectacular windfall in their income from coffee in 1998.

International and local prices

As in the case of cocoa, the prices received by Indonesian coffee producers in 1997-98 reflected movements in exchange rates. These movements were the major source of the windfall (Figure 7.7).

Beginning in late 1997, the rupiah price of Asalan coffee rose four- or fivefold over a period of a few months. The price per kilogramme to producers in 1996-97 fluctuated around Rp 2000-3500. During the first week of January 1998, it rocketed to Rp 7500. From then until May it was around Rp 8000-11 000, finally reaching its peak of Rp 16 500 per kilogramme during the first week of July. After that it fell to Rp 13 000 in August and September 1998.

Unlike the price of cocoa, that of coffee did not slump in 1999, but merely fell back towards its January 1997 level. Prices fell first to Rp 9000-10 000, then to Rp 8000 during the main harvesting months of June-July. The higher international prices maintained enabled coffee farmers to withstand the partial recovery of the rupiah, with its depressive effect on local prices, better than cocoa farmers.

Better margins for farmers were an added factor boosting the windfall. Trends in monthly prices expressed in US dollars show how the falling rupiah exchange rate took its toll on exporters and middlemen. Traders

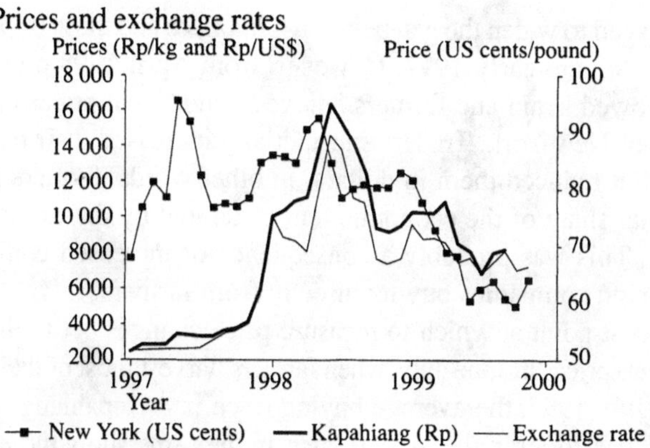

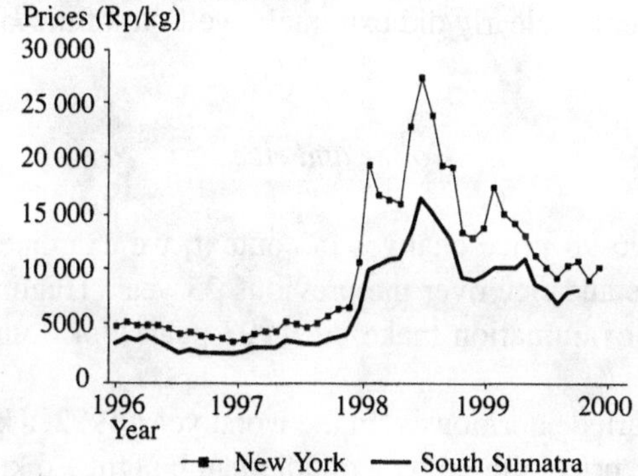

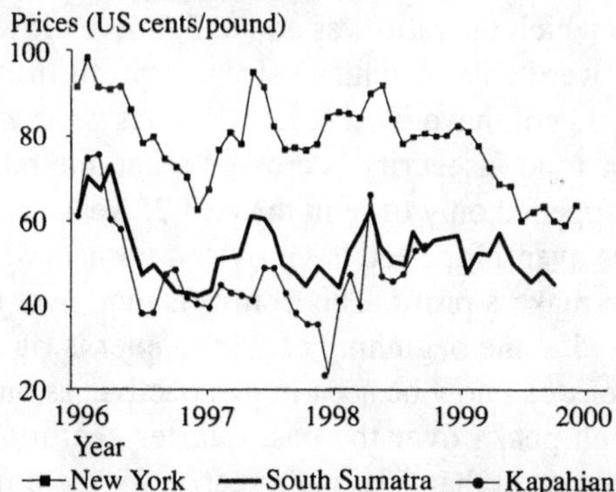

Figure 7.7 Monthly coffee prices and exchange rates, 1996-99. Sources: USDA/AIKE.

had managed to widen the gap between CIF prices and those of producers in late 1996 and early 1997. However, from April 1998 onwards the gap narrowed again and farmers enjoyed better local prices compared to those of New York. Traders substantially increased their margins in rupiahs but reduced them in dollars. In other words, farmers gained a substantial share of the economic rent generated by the exchange rate collapse. This was probably a consequence of increased competition, with foreign companies buying directly from farmers.

The best point at which to measure price changes between years is to compare prices in June-July, when farmers harvest most of their berries. In June-July 1997, the average buying price in a Kepahiang shop was Rp 3045 per kilogramme. A year later, in the same shop, the price was Rp 13 640 per kilogramme—350% higher. Despite losing ground to farmers, middlemen clearly did extremely well out of the *krismon*.

Coffee and rice

To put the 1996-98 price changes in context, we examined the price ratios of coffee and rice over the previous 25 years (Figure 7.8). The results of this examination make the 1998 peak look somewhat less impressive.

The ratio varied enormously. In the worst year, 1992, a kilogramme of coffee at the price offered by a middleman bought 1.6 kilogrammes of rice, whereas in the best year, 1997, it bought 9.5 kilogrammes. There were 9 years in which the ratio was above 5.0. Even if we assume that the middlemen were able to achieve sizeable profit margins, the ratio for farmers would still have been at least 4.0. As we saw in Chapter 5, the threshold of food insecurity is crossed when the ratio falls below 2.0. This has happened only once in the past 25 years, whereas at least one year in three over this period has provided farmers with outstanding opportunities to make a profit. This confirms that, over the long term, the farmer quoted at the beginning of this chapter is right.

The 1998 peak can now be seen in perspective, as only one among four or five such peaks over the past quarter century—and not the most impressive one at that. The main reason for the difference is that the price of rice also rose sharply in 1998.

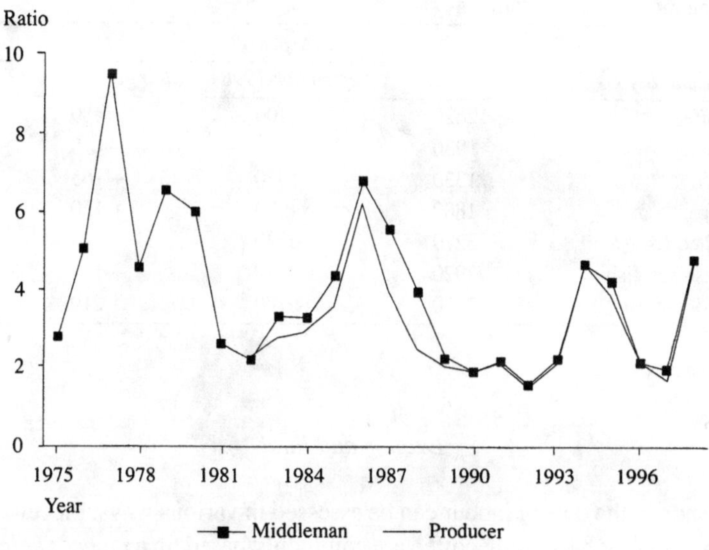

Figure 7.8 Coffee: rice price ratios, Kepahiang, Bengkulu, 1975-98. Source: BPS data.

Farmers' perceptions

Merely asking farmers about the prices they obtained in 1997 and how these compared with the prices of 1998 does not, of course, provide rigorous data. Nevertheless, it is enough to gauge farmers' perceptions of the price environment.

Almost all the farmers we interviewed immediately referred to the record prices of June-July 1998. They expressed great satisfaction over the high prices obtained throughout the year, describing 1998 as "the year of their lives". Despite the considerable increase in food prices, farmers felt that coffee had no competitor in 1998. They expressed little interest in diversifying into other crops, pointing to the price of ginger, which stood still throughout the year, as the reason why (Table 7.4).

Table 7.4 Prices of coffee and other commodities quoted by coffee farmers in September 1998, Kepahiang

	Price (Rp/kg)		
Commodity	*1997*	*September 1998*	*Change 1998/97 (%)*
Coffee	2620	15 100	+ 480
Ginger	930	930	0
Rice	1330	3530	+ 165
Sugar	1800	4500	+ 150
Salted fish *(teri)*	3270	6330	+ 94
Fresh sea fish	3920	11 170	+ 185
Cooking oil	2120	6780	+ 219

Labour and land

Trends in the cost of labour can be assessed in various ways. Piecework contracts for harvesting coffee are commonly based on a rate per *kaleng* of coffee harvested, a *kaleng* being a basket of 12-15 kilogrammes of fresh berries (equivalent to 3-4 kilogrammes of green coffee). A man is generally able to harvest eight *kalengs* a day. On this basis, labour costs in 1998 were double those of 1997 (Table 7.5).

Table 7.5 Trends in labour costs assessed through piecework contracts for coffee harvesting, Kepahiang, 1982-98

	Cost (Rp)			
	1982	*1991*	*1997*	*1998*
Per *kaleng*	200	500	1500	3000
Per day	1600	4000	12 000	24 000
Coffee	650	1200	2700-3000	12 000-13 000
Ratio*	3.3	2.4	1.8-2	4-4.3

* Of price of coffee to labour cost per *kaleng*.

If the assessment is instead based on share-cropping contracts, the changes in labour costs look more favourable for labourers. In cases where yields fell greatly, labour costs merely doubled. However, on average yields fell by only 10-15%, so the average increase in wages was probably more like 340%. Farmers hiring labour under share-cropping arrangements could not therefore rely on reducing labour costs as a means of increasing their net incomes.

Land prices in Kepahiang are difficult to estimate as there are relatively few sales of any type of land. Forest land, grassland, fallows and productive, ageing or old plantations may all be sold, each fetching a different price. Old coffee plantations apparently doubled in price in 1997-98, from approximately Rp 3 million to Rp 6 million per hectare.

Like cocoa farmers, those who dare to farm in protected forests and private concessions could get land at much lower prices than in their own village. Compared to the cocoa migrants of Sulawesi, the coffee farmers of southern Sumatra have fewer opportunities to buy cheap land by moving to new pioneer fronts, although a few tried to do so in 1998. Nevertheless, as we might expect of a non-tradable factor, land, including mature coffee plantations, increased in price much less than coffee in 1998.

Coffee and chemical inputs

As coffee farmers use little fertiliser, they were not greatly affected by the fertiliser price hikes. They were more concerned about herbicide prices. These did increase, but relatively slowly. By September 1998, 1 litre of Round-up was around Rp 45 000, twice its price in previous years. A further substantial price increase occurred at the end of the year.

Net incomes

Having fallen by 13% in 1997, the average incomes of coffee farmers rose by 340% in 1998 (Table 7.6). A case by case analysis revealed broadly similar results across farms. As in cocoa, coffee farmers who suffered a slight yield loss in 1998 as a result of the drought still benefitted greatly from the price rise. Even the 5-10% of farms that suffered an 80% collapse in yields earned some additional income.

Table 7.6 Estimated annual incomes on coffee farms in Kepahiang sub-district, Bengkulu, Sumatra, 1996-98

	Amount (Rp)		
	1996	*1997*	*1998*
Gross income	8 672 806	7 514 000	33 089 650
Share-cropping costs*	1 372 410	1 538 500	6 395 400
Net income	7 300 395	5 975 500	26 694 250

* = share-croppers' incomes.

Once coffee is harvested and partially dried, the first cost faced by some 20% of coffee farmers is that of sharing either the beans or their proceeds with one or two share-croppers, known as *bagi hasil* workers. What is a labour cost to some is, of course, an income for others—namely the low but growing numbers of families who hold no land.

In Kepahiang, the windfall brought substantial benefits to share-croppers. For example, the proportion of share-croppers able to buy motorcycles in Bengkulu was considerably higher than among cocoa share-croppers in Sulawesi. There are several reasons why these labourers did so well.

The proportions of the harvest taken by the landowner and the *bagi hasil* worker have changed over the years. In the 1980s, one-third of the harvest went to the share-cropper. By the late 1990s, this proportion had risen to two-fifths, at least in Kepahiang. This is the sign of a tight labour market in which labourers are, to some extent, able to call the tune. Compared with the proportions taken by cocoa share-croppers in Sulawesi, who receive only a quarter of the harvest, the proportions in coffee share-cropping also testify to the larger amount of work involved in harvesting coffee and the lower amounts of chemicals used in its production. Coffee farmers in Bengkulu use little fertiliser or pesticide. They do use herbicides, but share-croppers contribute to the cost of these as they are in charge of weeding.

Another reason why *bagi hasil* incomes are relatively high is a second change in contractual arrangements that occurred during the 1990s. Nowadays, *bagi hasil* labourers are often hired not only to maintain and harvest an established plantation but also to clear new land and establish a coffee farm. In these cases their share of the harvest rises to 50%.

These changes in contractual arrangements, which occurred before the *krismon*, ensured that the benefits of the 1998 windfall were more equitably shared than they might otherwise have been.

How Farmers Spent the Money

The most important conclusion from our survey is that 100% of coffee farmers, whether landowners or share-croppers, benefitted from the 1998 windfall. How did they use their new-found wealth?

Savings in kind

Once share-croppers and other creditors have been paid, smallholders need feel no urgency with regard to selling their coffee crop, which can easily be stored. Coffee beans are used as a sort of deposit account or insurance policy, kept as a hedge against inflation, currency fluctuations and other hazards. Especially at a time of inflation, farmers feel it is better to store coffee than to keep money in the bank.

The first priority of the average farmer in Kepahiang in late September 1998, after he had paid his share-croppers, was thus to save about Rp 10 million in the form of some 900 kilogrammes of coffee. This was usually stored at home (Table 7.7).

Table 7.7 Share of incomes allocated for saving and spending, Kepahiang sub-district, September 1998

	Amount in:	
Income	*Rp*	*US$*
Saved as coffee beans	9 967 100	960
Cash for spending	16 727 150	1610

The balance of farmers' earnings was available for spending on consumer goods or for investing in long-term assets. The growing numbers of cars and buses parked in the streets of Kepahiang's villages were the most obvious sign of increased spending in 1998. But there was also widespread concern to maintain plantations after the 1997 drought and the excessive rainfall of 1998.

Urgently needed herbicides

As already mentioned, coffee farmers in southern Sumatra use little fertiliser but, as coffee does not shade the soil as cocoa does, they use far more herbicide. Herbicide use rose in 1998 (Table 7.8).

Table 7.8 Changes in herbicide use on coffee farms, Kepahiang, 1997-98

Use in 1998 compared to 1997	*No. of farmers*
No. of farmers increasing	17
No. of farmers reducing	9
No. of farmers making no change	12
No. of farmers who never use	2
Total	40

Table 7.9 shows the reasons given by farmers for increasing their use of herbicides. As in the case of the fertilisers applied to cocoa by Sulawesi farmers, their aim was not to maximise yields and hence returns but rather to protect plantations from yield losses caused by the adverse weather of the previous 2 years. After the drought of 1997, the rains of 1998 encouraged weeds to run riot, to the extent that they became extremely difficult to control by hand. At the same time, farmers were short of labour. It was hard to find workers who were prepared to accept a simple day labouring contract to control weeds. The switch to *bagi hasil* contracts meant that few workers were available for piecework.

Table 7.9 Farmers' reasons for increasing herbicide use in 1998

Reasons	*No. of farmers*
Abundant rainfall in 1998 increased weed growth, which was difficult to control by hand	12
Shortage of labour, difficult to find labourers	3
Good prices and high incomes made herbicide purchase easy	1
Wanted to try a new herbicide	1
Total	17

A total of nine farmers said they had reduced their herbicide consumption in 1998. Of these, three cited the high prices of this input as one of their reasons.

Motorcycles and cars

As the *krismon* deepened, numerous second-hand motorcycles and vehicles began arriving for sale in the nearby town of Curup. They came not just from Bengkulu City but from further afield—from Jakarta and Bogor. This was a powerful symbol of the 1998 crisis. While city dwellers suffered and had to sell their status symbols, many villagers became more prosperous, at least if they were involved in export commodities.

Table 7.10 shows how the 40 farmers in our sample spent their money. The list of items bought is similar to that of cocoa farmers, including hand-sprayers, televisions, satellite dishes and trips to Mecca, in addition to motorcycles, cars and even buses.

Daspetah, on the main road to Curup, is a village of some 750 families, most of whom own a coffee plantation or at least make part of their living from coffee. Farmers in the village say that about 300 of them bought motorcycles in 1998. Many share-croppers were among them. Around 25% of these motorcycles were new and 75% second-hand. Daspetah's farmers also bought 50 cars, 47 of them second-hand and 3 new. Rumour has it that one day, during the peak harvesting season, villagers stopped a truck full of motorcycles as it was passing through and bought the entire load. As in the small towns of Sulawesi's cocoa belt, there were not enough motorcycles for sale in the shops of Curup. People had to look further afield, in Bengkulu City or in Lubuk Linggau. Even in a village such as Batu Blarik, which was severely affected by the drought, at least three coffee farmers bought a car and a dozen or so bought second-hand motorcycles.

As we have seen, the high prices benefitted not only farmers but also share-croppers, some of whom bought new motorcycles. A group of share-croppers who ran a high-yielding farm in a forested highland area were able to buy land and build houses in Curup or in villages along the main asphalt road, for example Daspetah.

Table 7.10 Selected purchases of 40 coffee farmers in Kepahiang, 1990-98

	No. of purchases						
Item	*Before 1990*	*1990*	*1991*	*1992*	*1993*	*1994*	*1995*
Bicycle			1			1	1
Motorcycle					1		1
Hand-sprayer	1	3	3	2	2	2	8
Motor-sprayer							
Water pump							
Television	2			1	1	4	2
Satellite dish + television						2	1
Car/bus				1	1		2
Trip to Mecca							1

	No. of purchases					
Item	*1996*	*1997*	*1998*	*Total*	*1997/98 as % of total*	*Average/ farmer*
Bicycle	6	2	7	19	47	0.5
Motorcycle	2		9	13	69	0.3
Hand-sprayer	6	6	3	36	25	0.9
Motor-sprayer						
Water pump						
Television		1	2	13	23	0.3
Satellite dish + television	5	5	4	17	53	0.4
Car/bus			5	9	55	0.2
Trip to Mecca			2	3	66	0.1

In villages such as Bengko, where electricity was about to be introduced, the year 2000 will doubtless witness a bumper crop of new satellite dishes. These are already widespread in several other villages.

Farmers who buy cars mostly do so as a form of investment. They use them first and foremost as a kind of taxi service and secondly to transport coffee to market. This latter use may involve renting the vehicle to other farmers. Only a few farmers use their cars mainly for personal convenience and comfort.

Investment in transport makes sense. Transporting coffee beans from Batu Bandung to Kepahiang, a 38-kilometre drive, cost Rp 25 per kilogramme in 1997 but Rp 40 per kilogramme in 1998. Over the same period the price per passenger doubled from Rp 1000 to Rp 2000. The journey is even more expensive if a farmer starts from a remote hamlet such as Air Punggur, which is around 4-5 kilometres beyond

Batu Bandung. From here to Kepahiang by *kampas*, an old four-wheel drive that can carry about 1 tonne of coffee beans over muddy roads in poor weather, transport cost Rp 1000-1300 per kilogramme in 1998. This was good business for *kampas* drivers who, on a good day, could transport two 1-tonne loads, earning Rp 2 million. During the rains drivers might take 4 days for the round trip, carrying only 1 tonne of coffee—but even then they would still earn Rp 250 000 per day.

Investments in land and marketing

In our 40-farmer sample, the number of *bagi hasil* labourers had stood at 15 in 1996. The figure rose to 20 in 1997 and 29 in 1998. How do we explain the fact that share-cropping contracts have virtually doubled, given that the labour market is relatively tight? Does this make sense in a plantation economy which is no longer at the pioneering stage and in which production seems to have more or less stabilised?

The first question is relatively easy to answer. As in cocoa production, the relative scarcity of labour has translated into a shift into share-cropping arrangements away from other kinds of contract. As we have seen, the rising prices of coffee have made *bagi hasil* contracts more attractive to labourers. The second question is more tricky. It has to do with how the profits from coffee are invested.

Our small sample may not be sufficiently representative, but surveys of this kind remain an effective way of picking up on social changes and the factors affecting farmers' decisions. Of our 40 farmers, 6 were responsible for the increase in the number of *bagi hasil* labourers. All were involved in coffee marketing.

Two of the six had worked as coffee traders since 1989 and 1992 respectively. They invested in both land and plantations in 1997-98. One bought a productive plantation for Rp 9 million (US$ 2250-3000) in late 1997. The other opted for the *sorongan* system, which involved a 7-year rental of a coffee farm at a cost of Rp 1.5 million. As both men were largely taken up with their marketing activities, they put their new farms into the hands of *bagi hasil* workers.

In 1998, two other farmers managed to invest simultaneously in a new trading activity and in planting. Using new variations on the *bagi hasil* theme, they were able to cut their costs substantially by obtaining "labour credit" from their workers. One of them decided to replant his oldest coffee farm. He adopted the new system of handing the entire operation over to share-croppers who, in return for establishing the plantation as well as maintaining and harvesting it, will later receive 50% of the harvest instead of the normal 33%. The other farmer decided to risk clearing forest and planting coffee on a neighbouring concessionary estate. This is another reason for adopting a *bagi hasil* approach. Should problems arise, the share-croppers will be in the front line in more than one sense. They stand to lose more than just their share of the crop.

The last two farmers who contributed to the increase in share-cropping also hired additional *bagi hasil* workers in 1998. They had made their original investments in land and planting in 1996 and were now ready to use the traditional form of the *bagi hasil* contract, leasing their farms out only when the coffee groves started to produce. However, one of these two farmers also had a forest plot cleared in 1998 under the new type of contract.

Despite the anecdotal presentation of these cases, we believe we have identified a new trend, even if we cannot yet quantify it. The *krismon* appears to have stimulated investment in the following:

- Coffee marketing: the number of coffee traders doubled in 1998.
- Established plantations: these were bought mainly by coffee traders. Their purchases are evidence of the sizeable profits made by trading in 1997-98[5].
- Replanting old coffee farms.
- Clearing and planting protected and private forest. This incurs risks which partly explain the increased hiring of share-croppers.

Although the new *bagi hasil* arrangements in part substitute for other types of labour contract, their rising number reflects a positive aspect of the *krismon*: its contribution to job creation.

Conclusions

Coffee farmers described 1998 as the best year of their lives. Although most had experienced other price peaks in the past, and although the drought somewhat reduced yields, their incomes rose to spectacular levels and stayed there over a period of several months. The decline from the peak was slower than in other commodities, with the result that incomes were still relatively high in early 2000. The main factors contributing to the windfall were the sharp rise in the prices of May-June 1998, which coincided with the peak in harvesting, and the delayed rise in other prices.

A further important factor was the liberalisation of the market, which has greatly increased the bargaining power of farmers. Had the national quota system for exporters still existed, as it did in the 1980s, the best year of their lives would probably have passed the farmers by without their even noticing.

All farmers benefitted from the 1998 windfall, as also did landless share-croppers. However, the benefit was substantially greater for those who had higher yields than for farmers who suffered a severe decline in yields as a result of the drought and its aftermath. As usual, the "haves" benefitted more than the "have-nots". Kepahiang is a prime example of a smallholder plantation economy reaching a stage of land shortage and pressure in the labour market. Land is gradually concentrating in fewer hands. Some 20% of farming households are now significantly wealthier than others and are therefore able to invest in coffee marketing, land ownership and share-cropped plantations. The recent switch from *bagi tanah* (land sharing) to *bagi hasil* (product sharing) contracts is strong evidence of land shortage and concentration.

Under these conditions, investments in planting are oriented more towards the replanting of old and "middle-aged" coffee groves than towards conquering new areas of forest, if only because the latter have for the most part long disappeared. However, while private concessions and protected forest areas are still available, increasing pressure from squatters may be expected. That such people are now far less in awe of government and army "muscle" than they used to be is one of the most significant changes wrought by the 1998 crisis.

Investment in planting and replanting leads to job creation, which mostly benefits the next generation of farming families. Despite the obvious enrichment of a few traders and farmers, most families continue to make relatively minor adjustments to the amount of land they own or the amount of labour they employ. These adjustments are, nonetheless, made through market rather than non-market channels.

Kepahiang's coffee farmers have shown themselves to be good technical innovators in the past. They have selected planting material that gives them early returns and established effective replanting systems. Javanese migrants, who have mastered the arts of umbrella pruning and side-grafting, have pioneered the most recent innovations in the area. The technique of umbrella pruning is not new in East Java, where the migrants came from, nor even in the neighbouring province of South Sumatra, where it was already known under the Dutch colonial regime (Coolhas, 1953). However, its recent adoption on farms in Kepahiang, which is related to the growing shortage of land, should help to raise yields and extend the life of plantations. The 1998 windfall seems to have encouraged its adoption.

The most pleasing and visible result of the windfall in Kepahiang's villages was the increased number of motorcycles and cars. The latter were purchased not only for reasons of personal convenience, comfort and prestige but also as a means of investing in off-farm income-earning opportunities, in the form of a transport service. This is a potent example of how windfall benefits from export commodities create much-needed growth elsewhere in the economy.

References

BPS (Biro Pusat Statistik). 1961. Statistical Pocketbook of Indonesia, 1961. Jakarta, Indonesia.

BPS (Biro Pusat Statistik). 1963. Statistical Pocketbook of Indonesia, 1963. Jakarta, Indonesia.

BPS (Biro Pusat Statistik). 1971. Statistical Pocketbook of Indonesia, 1971. Jakarta, Indonesia.

Charras, M. and Pain, M. 1993. *Spontaneous Settlements in Indonesia*. Departemen Transmigrasi and Institut Français de Recherche Scientifique pour le Développement-Centre National de la Recherche Scientifique (ORSTOM-CNRS), Jakarta, Indonesia and Bondy, France.

Clarence-Smith, W.G. 1994. The impact of a forced cultivation system on Java: 1805-1917. *Indonesia Circle* 64: 241-64.

Clarence-Smith, W.G. 1998. The coffee crisis in Asia, Africa and the Pacific, 1870-1914. Paper presented at the Conference on Coffee Production and Economic Development, 10-12 September 1998, St Anthony's College, Oxford, UK.

Coolhas, C. 1953. L'application de greffes de la branche dans la culture du caféier robusta de Java. *Netherlands Journal of Agricultural Science* 1 (2): 130-136.

Cramer, 1957. Review of Literature on Coffee Research in Indonesia. Inter-American Institute of Agricultural Sciences, Turrialba, Costa Rica.

Daviron, B. and Fousse, W. 1994. La compétitivité des cafés Africains. Collection Rapport d'Etude. Ministère de la Coopération, Paris, France.

Godoy, R. and Benett, C. 1989. Diversification among coffee smallholders in the highlands of South Sumatra, Indonesia. *Human Ecology* 16 (4): 397-420.

Levang, P. 1989. Systèmes de production et revenus familiaux. In: Benoit, D., Levang, P., Pain, M. and Sevin, O. (eds), Transmigration et migrations spontanées. Departemen Transmigrasi and Institut Français de Recherche Scientifique pour le Développement-Centre National de la Recherche Scientifique (ORSTOM-CNRS), Jakarta, Indonesia and Paris, France, pp. 193-283.

McStocker, R. 1987. The Indonesian coffee industry. *Bulletin of Indonesian Economic Studies* 23 (1): 40-69.

Ruf, F. 1994. L'Indonésie. In: Etudes de cas sur le compétitivité des principaux pays producteurs. Ministère de la Coopération, Paris, France, pp. 165-245.

Ruf, F. 1995. *Booms et crises du cacao: Les vertiges de l'or brun*. Karthala, Paris, France.

Ruf, F. 1996. Les booms cacao de la Côte d'Ivoire et du Burkina Faso: L'accélération des années 1980-90. CIRAD and Ministère de la Coopération, Montpellier and Paris, France.

Ruf, F. 1997. L'aptitude de l'agriculture familiale à replanter: Le cas du café à Sumatra. In: Hubert, M. (ed.), *Le paysan, l'Etat et le marché: Sociétés paysannes et développement*. Publications de la Sorbonne, Paris, France.

Ruf, F. 1999. Comment et pourquoi la Côte d'Ivoire produit durablement plus d'un million de tonnes de cacao? *Afrique Agriculture* 268: 21-25.

Sevin, O. 1989. Histoire et peuplement. In: Benoit, D., Levang, P., Pain, M. and Sevin, O. (eds), Transmigration et migrations spontanées. Departemen Transmigrasi and Institut Français de Recherche Scientifique pour le Développement-Centre National de la Recherche Scientifique (ORSTOM-CNRS), Jakarta, Indonesia and Paris, France, pp. 13-123.

Shamsher Singh, de Vries, J., Hulley, J. and Yeung, P. 1977. *Coffee, Tea and Cocoa: Market Prospects and Development Lending*. World Bank Staff Occasional Papers No. 22. John Hopkins University Press, Baltimore, USA and London, UK.

Smith, G. and Bouvier, H. 1993. Spontaneous migrants' strategies and settlement processes in mountains and plains. In: Charras, M. and Pain, M. (eds), *Spontaneous Settlements in Indonesia*. Departemen Transmigrasi and Institut Français de Recherche Scientifique pour le Développement-Centre National de la Recherche Scientifique (ORSTOM-CNRS), Jakarta, Indonesia and Bondy, France, pp. 101-186.

Taher, S. 1991. La gestion paysanne du capital caféier à Bengkulu (Indonésie). Centre national d'études agronomiques des régions chaudes (CNEARC), Montpellier, France.

USDA (United States Department of Agriculture). 1999. Indonesia Coffee Annual Report 1999. Foreign Agricultural Service. Website: http://www.fas.usda.gov/scripts/gain_display_report.exe.rep_ID=25454450.0

Notes

1 In the sense of Pareto: A payment to a factor in excess of what is necessary to keep it to its present employment. If 1 hectare of coffee earns US$ 1500 per year when the best alternative crop brings in U$ 1000, the economic rent is US$ 500. In accordance with this definition, coffee is often paid more than what is necessary to keep Indonesian farmers producing it. Competition between buyers is high enough to prevent them from offering low prices compared to those on the world market.

2 Much migration may have been motivated by the need to escape the army or the police force or some other trouble. In the case of coffee, migration to Lampung was associated during the 1960s and 1970s with the repression of PKI members in Java, organized by a government obsessed with the communist threat.

3 Indeed, under the pretext of forest protection, transmigration was sometimes organized in order to expel spontaneous coffee migrants (see Chapter 11).

4 And not only in Indonesia. In Côte d'Ivoire, increased cocoa production since 1994-95 is partly explained by a massive influx of workers from Burkina Faso, who came between 1989 and 1994, while prices were low. They were able to buy land at relatively low prices, especially fallow land and old plantations in already developed areas, where indigenous Ivorian farmers were in urgent need of cash (Ruf, 1994 and 1999).

5 We found a similar trend in the cocoa regions of Sulawesi, independently of the *krismon*. While "normal" migrant farmers bought unused land and planted cocoa, traders tended to buy established plantations at higher prices.

Chapter 8

Rubber Cushions the Smallholder: No Crisis, No Windfall

Eric Penot and François Ruf

A few decades ago, rubber was one of the first tree crops for which new, highly productive clonal planting materials became available. This advance made possible substantial improvements in the productivity and incomes of smallholder farms, but to realise these gains farmers have to change their traditional production systems and practices.

Most smallholders in Indonesia grow unimproved rubber trees in a complex agroforestry system nicknamed "jungle rubber". Clonal rubber, in contrast, is generally grown in monoculture, sometimes with intercrops during the first 3 years. Gouyon (1999) says that "even when computing the cost of the investment and the credit that has to be repaid, the net income per hectare and per labour day from a clonal plantation is at least 50% (sometimes 100%) higher than the income from a jungle rubber plantation."

Before the *krismon*, in 1996, only 15% of smallholders growing rubber had access to new clonal planting materials. Government projects were responsible for most of this limited adoption, which was constrained by lack of information and capital. Many farmers had seen the advantages of clonal material, so the beginnings of a copying effect were detectable. A network of private nurseries marketing the material had begun to develop, at least in two provinces. The smallholder rubber sector was thus becoming more dynamic, but most clonal plantations were still very young. And the vast majority of farmers still relied on ageing jungle rubber, the productivity of which is very low.

In this chapter we ask how the *krismon* affected the jungle rubber and clonal rubber farming systems. Did it accelerate or reduce investment in rubber plantings? Will it speed up the adoption of improved clones?

Did it widen the gap between smallholders with access to clonal technology and those without it?

In 1998, rubber farmers did not benefit from the spectacular windfall enjoyed by cocoa and coffee farmers. Is that because of price movements on the international market, or should we look for the causes in the performances of the two rubber farming systems? Is there a direct relationship between the falling international price of rubber and the effect of the Asian crisis on Indonesian rubber supplies and exports?

In Sumatra and Kalimantan, as in other regions of the country, the economic crisis was compounded by an ecological one. Huge fires, caused partly by drought, destroyed millions of hectares of forests, fallows and crops, including rubber. How did the two crises interact to affect the smallholder rubber sector? Are they likely to reduce future investments in clonal plantings?

During the crises, regions such as West Kalimantan were riven by serious conflicts over land between indigenous groups and immigrants, especially spontaneous migrants[1]. How did these conflicts affect smallholder rubber production? In addition, many traditional rubber areas are threatened with oil palm development—a further potential source of conflict. Did the crisis encourage oil palm development at the expense of rubber?

In this chapter we will address these questions through four sections. The first section is a brief overview of the rubber sector in Indonesia, describing the situation before the *krismon*. In the second section we describe the impact of the *krismon* on rubber smallholdings. Events on the international rubber market are the subject of the third section, while the last section consists of our conclusions, together with a glance at the possible future of the smallholder sector.

Overview

Indonesian smallholders and world rubber supplies

Like cocoa, rubber underwent extraordinary development during the twentieth century. The tree was first transplanted to London from its native continent, South America, in 1876 by a British adventurer called Wickham. Seedlings were then sent to Sri Lanka, Singapore and Malaysia and finally to Bogor. The bulk of development took place in Southeast Asia, with Indonesia a major participant (Figure 8.1). By the 1990s, Malaysia, Thailand and Indonesia accounted for 75% of total world production. Indonesia is now the world's second largest rubber producer, close behind Thailand. The crop is currently the country's fourth largest non-oil export after plywood, pulp/paper and palm oil. In 1996-97, it was even in third place, above palm oil.

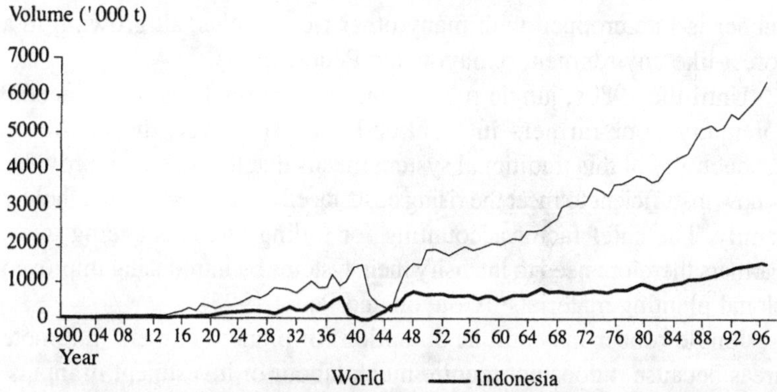

Figure 8.1 Global and Indonesian natural rubber production, 1900-96

Smallholder rubber production overtook estate production in Indonesia as early as the 1930s. This sector now produces 73% of the country's rubber on 85% of the country's total planted rubber area (DGE, 1998). Most of the country's rubber estates were planted before the Suharto era and the number continued to grow only slowly from 1965 to 1990, a period in which the smallholder sector experienced a boom. Since the early 1990s, most rubber estates have switched to oil palm, which is one of the last tree crops to be controlled by large-scale private and government interests.

Natural rubber is mainly used by the tyre industry, which accounts for 70% of global consumption. Demand is thus linked directly to the transport sector, which is expanding rapidly almost everywhere. Rubber farmers can thus rely on strong global demand for the foreseeable future. Indeed, a shortage is predicted to arise at some time between 2003 and 2008 (Burger and Smit, 1994). Indonesia's rubber sector is a source of income for more than 10 million people, 1.2 million of whom are small-scale rubber farmers.

Jungle rubber and clonal plantations

Indonesian smallholders have traditionally grown rubber in an extensive yet complex agroforestry system known as jungle rubber. In this system, rubber is intercropped with many other tree species, all growing in a forest-like environment (Gouyon and Penot, 1995).

Until the 1980s, jungle rubber was an important source of income for many poor farmers in frontier lands. However, the declining productivity of this traditional system means that the income it provides is now insufficient to meet the rising costs faced by an average smallholder family. The chief factor accounting for falling yields is ageing trees. Farmers therefore need to intensify their systems by introducing improved clonal planting materials[2] (Gouyon and Penot,1995).

Jungle rubber may still be an option for pioneer farmers in remote areas because it does not require much labour or investment in inputs. However, this system takes 8-15 years before it begins bringing significant returns—far too long for most farmers. In most areas of West Kalimantan, the only reasonable option is to plant improved clones, which bring returns after only 5 years. This is true even on poor soils with degraded *Imperata* grasslands and in areas of excessive rainfall.

Clonal rubber was developed in the 1970s. Since the early 1980s, the government and international agencies have attached increasing importance to export-oriented tree crops, including rubber[3]. Improved clonal planting materials have been offered to farmers, who have been encouraged to grow them in monoculture. Yet only 15% of smallholders have been able to obtain these materials, usually through government-run development projects[4]. A combination of lack of capital to invest in clonal rubber plantations and lack of technical information and experience in using the clones has slowed adoption (Courbet and Penot, 1997; Kelfoun and Penot, 1997). However, the late 1990s saw the rapid development of private nurseries as demand for clones expanded. This is especially the case in North and South Sumatra, where rubber development projects have had the greatest impact.

North Sumatra used to be Indonesia's primary rubber-producing province, with the bulk of production concentrated in what became known as the "estate belt". But in the 1990s most of the rubber estates here went over to oil palm. Thus South Sumatra has now taken the lead in rubber production. It is followed by Jambi, West Kalimantan and South/Central Kalimantan.

The plains of South Sumatra are highly specialised in rubber production. The province is also a show-case for the long-term positive impact of government rubber projects. A rubber research station, located in Sembawa, was the original source of clonal planting materials and has led research and development efforts over many years. The availability of skilled technicians to provide training and advice, together with the dissemination of planting materials, triggered the development of private nurseries in the late 1990s. These have greatly increased farmers' opportunities to adopt the new technology. In other provinces private nurseries are either non-existent as yet (Bengkulu, Riau and Central Kalimantan) or are just being established (Jambi and West Kalimantan).

The situation before the krismon

Three different types of rubber area can be identified in Indonesia:

- The very remote or pioneer areas. These include Irian Jaya, the Moluccas (Seram) and any remaining undeveloped areas on the edge of the central plains or in the piedmont of Sumatra and Kalimantan (e.g. the East Pasaman area of West Sumatra). In these areas, jungle rubber is generally the only technology immediately accessible to poor farmers[5].
- The traditional jungle rubber areas. In these areas the adoption of clonal rubber is still at a very early stage. Jambi and West Kalimantan are examples.
- The areas where government projects have had a significant impact. Here jungle rubber systems have been largely replaced by more productive clonal rubber plantations. In these areas, a private nursery network has evolved to meet the strong demand for improved planting material, enabling many more farmers outside the projects to invest in clonal rubber. North and South Sumatra are the obvious examples.

Our study areas, in Jambi and West Kalimantan, are located in the second kind of area. The villages we selected are representative of those in which most farmers will sooner or later have to shift from traditional jungle rubber to clonal systems. We estimated that roughly two-thirds of all rubber smallholders are in this position. Those who lack the capital to make the change may find they have no alternative but to accept package offers of credit and planting materials made by private estates. These offers, already common in the oil palm sector, typically involve the exchange of 5-7 hectares of the smallholder's land for 2 hectares of established plantation. The exchange is highly unequal, but the farmers receive a "turnkey" plantation that solves their problems of lack of cash and planting materials. In the past, government projects, including the nucleus estate scheme (NES), have offered such packages in improved rubber.

Within these intermediate areas, a typology of rubber-producing villages can be identified. We will use this typology to assess the impact of the *krismon*. In rubber as in most other tree cropping systems, the impact varied according to the differing access of villages and farmers to land, labour and tree capital. We found five types of village:

- Traditional villages using only jungle rubber (Type 1). These villages are inhabited largely by people who may be considered indigenous. That is, their families came several generations ago and have acquired local rights to land. They are the Malayu in Jambi, found in the village of Seppungur, and the Dayak in Kalimantan, found in the villages of Kopar and Engkayu. Indigenous people are constrained mainly by lack of cash, the shortage of improved planting materials and the absence of technical information about clonal rubber cropping. In the case of Kalimantan, many plantations are already old and less productive than those of Jambi.
- Traditional villages near clonal rubber development schemes (Type 2). The inhabitants of these villages are also "indigenous", either Dayak or Malayu. In Kalimantan this type of village is exemplified by Sanjan and Embaong, where most farmers have 1-2 hectares of clonal rubber. These farmers generally have sufficient cash, mainly from their project plots, to plant a larger area of clonal rubber. In other cases farmers may accept a package offer made by an estate, as has happened at Embaong. Here again the main constraints are lack of

capital and the shortage of high-quality planting materials and technical information. There are still too few private nurseries to meet the demand for materials.

- New villages in tree crop-oriented transmigration schemes (Type 3). These villages are inhabited by Javanese transmigrants, who adopted plantation species provided under the scheme soon after arrival. The villages of Sukamulia and Saptamulia, in Jambi, are examples. They form part of the Rimbo Bujan NES.
- New villages in food crop-oriented transmigration schemes (Type 4). These are also inhabited by Javanese transmigrants, who initially were not allowed to plant tree crops. Examples are the villages of Sukamulia and Trimulia, in Kalimantan. The main constraints faced by these farmers are shortage of good land, a market for which is emerging, coupled with very low incomes, associated largely with the fact that they have not been able to grow tree crops. Grain cropping is not suitable on the poor soils often found on these schemes, which tend to be invaded by *Imperata cylindrica* after 1 or 2 years of cropping. Some of these farmers received 0.4-0.8 hectare of clonal rubber from the Smallholder Rubber Agroforestry Project (SRAP)[6] in 1995.
- Traditional villages reorganised under food crop-oriented transmigration schemes (Type 5). The Dayak farmers on these "local transmigration" (Transmigrasi Lokal) schemes still have ageing jungle rubber in their former villages, but have moved onto the schemes to get access to road transport, technical information and assistance. An example is the village of Pariban Baru, in the Sintang district of West Kalimantan. Some farmers here also acquired 1 hectare of clonal rubber each through the "partial approach" project[7] in 1992.

Note that, for village Types 4 and 5, found on food crop-oriented transmigration schemes, tree cropping was forbidden until 1992. Since then, a few farmers have planted clonal rubber, either on their own initiative or through small projects.

We will now use this typology as the basis for analysing farm incomes.

Farm incomes

Just before the crisis, average farm incomes from rubber in what were historically the main rubber producing areas (village Types 1, 2, 3 and 5) varied greatly, from Rp 0.68 million to Rp 5.5 million (Table 8.1).

In Type 4 villages, income from rubber was much lower, because these Javanese farmers live on food crop transmigration schemes. Since 1992, many of them have planted rubber on their former food crop plots (*lahan* 1 or 2)[8]. This may be clonal but is more often unselected, due to lack of cash or the shortage of clonal planting materials. If they were not burned in the 1997 fires, most of these plantations are still immature or are just beginning to produce. That is why these farmers' average net incomes are the lowest of the five types.

Off-farm activities, mainly retail and rubber trade but also estate jobs, provided an additional income for all types of farmer. In the upper reaches of the Kapuas River, which drains a large area of West Kalimantan, gold mining is also an important seasonal activity. In the Sintang transmigration schemes, for example, 80% of off-farm income is derived from gold mining, while the balance is from work on oil palm estates. In the Sanggau area, also in West Kalimantan, private oil palm estates provide most of the jobs for both local and transmigrant farmers.

The income from rubber directly reflects its yield. Clonal rubber is two to three times more productive than jungle rubber, creating a large yield gap between the two production systems[9]. In addition, the immature period for clonal rubber is only 5-6 years, compared with 8-15 years for jungle rubber. Farmers with clonal rubber plantations, whether or not these were established under projects, thus have a higher income and a better standard of living than those relying on jungle rubber, especially when this is old (as in Type 5). This explains why many Dayak farmers are now attempting to join local transmigration schemes, which also improve their access to roads and markets.

Dayak farmers growing clonal rubber (Type 2) have only 1 hectare of it and are using a clone, GT1, that suffers from a foliar disease (caused by the fungus *Colletrotrichum* sp.). This reduces yields by 30-50%, leading to a relatively low income compared with that of NES farmers growing clonal rubber in Jambi (Type 3). Besides diseases, rubber in Kalimantan also suffers from poorer soils and higher rainfall than in Jambi—conditions to which it is poorly adapted, leading to substantial

Table 8.1 Incomes from rubber, rice and off-farm employment in different village types, July 1997

	Incomes (Rp' 000)					
Province/ villages	*Jambi/ Rimbo Bujang*	*Jambi/ Seppungur*	*Kalimantan/ Sanjan, Embaong*	*Kalimantan/ Kopar, Engkayu*	*Kalimantan/ Trimulia, Sukamulia*	*Kalimantan/ Pariban Baru*
Ethnic group and cropping system	*Javanese transmigrants in NES project with clonal rubber*	*Indigenous Malayu with jungle rubber*	*Indigenous Dayak in SRDP project with clonal rubber*	*Indigenous Dayak with jungle rubber*	*Javanese in food crop transmigration project*	*Dayak in local food crop transmigration project with jungle and clonal rubber*
Type	3	1	2	1	4	5
Income from rubber	5512	3240	2929	1014	96	680
Income from rice	104	42	105	190	557	124
Off-farm income	814	830	330	360	997	450
Total gross income	6700	4139	3704	1815	1932	1484
Cost of inputs	270	27	340	251	282	230
Net income	6430	4112	3364	1564	1650	1254

production losses. Both jungle and clonal rubber are affected. In Jambi, even traditional farmers growing jungle rubber (Type 1) have a relatively high income, due to their younger and more productive trees, which allow higher yields from a small area and hence some share-cropping as an additional source of income.

Even before the *krismon*, it was obvious that clonal rubber brought farmers sizeable yield gains and hence greatly increased the returns to their labour (Table 8.2).

Table 8.2 Returns to labour from various cropping systems in Jambi, July 1997

Main crop	*Cropping system*	*No. of farmers*		*Returns to labour (Rp/person-day)*	
		Jambi	*West Kalimantan*	*Jambi*	*West Kalimantan*
Upland rice	Shifting cultivation	2	16	8000	2100
Irrigated rice	Local varieties	7	14	4800	4100
	Improved varieties	5	8	8200	8100
Rubber	Jungle	24	100	25 300	9600
Rubber	Clonal monoculture (mature plantation)	7	24	61 800	27 200

Most upland rice (*ladang*) produced by rubber smallholders is for their own consumption. They cannot produce enough, however, so use part of their income from rubber and off-farm activities to buy rice. Few farmers own irrigated paddy fields (*sawah*). The limited amount of upland rice cultivation in Jambi appears somewhat more efficient than in Kalimantan. In both cases, the returns to traditional shifting cultivation are three or four times lower than those to jungle rubber. This explains why jungle rubber was the main local tree crop system adopted by farmers on the plains of Sumatra and Kalimantan and why it has spread rapidly throughout the twentieth century.

Since the 1970s, clonal rubber has brought a further leap forward in productivity, providing an important new source of income for those farmers who can adopt it.

The *Krismon* and its Impact

Living dangerously

In 1998, despite rising prices for their commodity, most rubber smallholders displayed little of the jubilation evident among cocoa and coffee farmers. They were grappling with a fourfold crisis:

- An ecological crisis. In 1997-98, huge fires destroyed both natural forest and crops, including rubber. The fires took a high toll on the plains of Sumatra and Kalimantan, where most rubber farmers are concentrated.
- A financial crisis. The *krismon* did not generate a substantial windfall, as it did for coffee and cocoa growers. Whereas the prices of these commodities rose sixfold over the 2-3 months that coincided with the peak harvesting period, rubber prices merely tripled over this period.
- A social crisis. Tensions between indigenous people and Madurese migrants, between Muslims and Christians and between "native" Indonesians and the Indo-Chinese ignited into widespread violence in 1997-98, especially in the rubber producing areas of West Kalimantan.
- A political crisis. The social unrest caused by Indonesia's political and economic crisis further undermined the confidence of the private sector in economic recovery. Because many Indo-Chinese trade in rubber, producers faced the added risk of not being able to find a market.

As rubber smallholders depend on this commodity for 75-90% of their income, trends in rubber prices are an important indicator of their standard of living. The price of rubber on the international market fell from US$ 1.30 per kilogramme in July 1997 to around US$ 0.60 per kilogramme in mid-1998. By mid-1999, it had sunk still lower, to around US$ 0.55 per kilogramme (Figure 8.2). In the second half of 1997, the rupiah price paid to producers remained more or less stable, as the rupiah began to fall. The currency collapse of January 1998 caused the price paid to the smallholder to double or even triple.

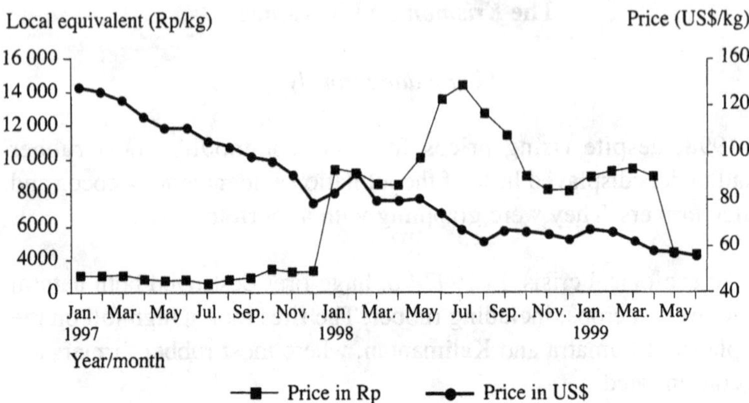

Figure 8.2 International price of rubber and local equivalent, 1997-99. Prices are for cost and freight (CIF), New York, for technically specified rubber grade 20 (TSR 20).

The effects of the crisis on farmers can be analysed over four main periods:

- The first period, July-December 1997. During its first few months the crisis appeared to be having little or no effect. Rubber prices in rupiah increased only slightly, from Rp 1950 to Rp 2265 (+16%) per kilogramme in West Kalimantan and from Rp 2025 to Rp 2630 (+ 30%) per kilogramme in Jambi.
- The second period, January-February 1998. Over these 2 months, rubber prices were high and farmers had an opportunity to profit from the crisis. But the period was far too short to allow most farmers to take advantage of it to any marked degree. Moreover, food prices also soared over this period, especially the price of rice, which tripled in January 1998. This is one of the main differences between rubber farmers and cocoa farmers. The cocoa farmers of Sulawesi enjoyed rice surpluses, enabling them to profit far more and for a much longer period.
- The third period, March-December 1998. This is when rubber smallholders faced real crisis. The prices of agricultural inputs and food rose above those of rubber, leading to a serious short-term fall in income and purchasing power. The price of both imported and local rice peaked in September and remained high for some time

thereafter (Figure 8.3). Most farmers did not understand the reasons for this price volatility.

- The fourth period began in January 1999 and, at the time of writing, is not yet over. It could be defined as a period of adjustment. The rupiah recovered to around Rp 8800 = US$ 1.00 in April 1999, then dipped below Rp 7000 = US$ 1.00 in July 1999 before rising again to Rp 8000 = US$ 1.00 in August 1999. The prices of inputs and food were more or less stable over this period, although some staple foods, such as fish and meat, remained extremely expensive. In mid-1999, rice was still three times dearer than in mid-1997, while the international rubber price was sliding dangerously. Meanwhile, massacres in Aceh and Timor underscored Indonesia's uncertain future.

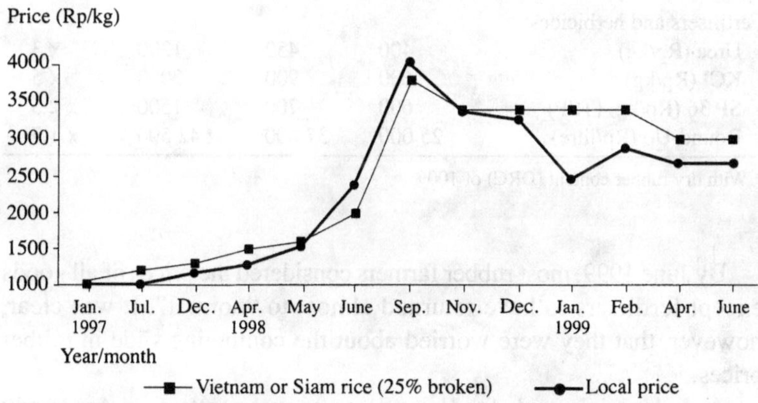

Figure 8.3 Changes in the prices of local and imported rice in West Kalimantan, 1997-99

Table 8.3 shows the prices of rubber, rice and agricultural inputs in West Kalimantan over the *krismon* period. Labour costs in mid-1999 were twice those of mid-1997. Until March 1999, some locally available inputs did not greatly rise in price. Planting materials, for instance, remained at around Rp 500 per stump, eventually rising to Rp 700 per stump by June 1999. Fertilisers, in contrast, rose up to fivefold in price, although here too the price of locally manufactured products such as urea rose less than that of imported products such as KCl. Most rubber farmers do not use fertilisers much, especially during the mature phase.

Table 8.3 Rubber, rice and input prices in West Kalimantan, 1997-99

Item	*Prices*			
	July 1997	*July 1998*	*June 1999*	*Increase 1999/97*
Commodities:				
Rubber at farm gate (Rp/kg)*	2400	4000	3500	x 1.5
Local rice (Rp/kg)	1200	2000	3000	x 2.5
Imported rice (Rp/kg)	1000	2400	2900	x 2.9
Labour and land:				
Labour cost (Rp/person-day)	3500	7000	7500	x 2.1
Fallow land (Rp/ha)	750 000		1 500 000	x 2
Planting materials:				
Stump	300	550	700	x 2.3
Plant in polybag	1000	1500	2000	x 2
Fertilisers and herbicides:				
Urea (Rp/kg)	400	450	1200	x 3
KCl (Rp/kg)	600	900	3000	x 5
SP 36 (Rp/kg) (TSP)	600	700	1500	x 2.5
Round-Up (Rp/litre)	25 000	37 000	42 500	x 1.7

* With dry rubber content (DRC) of 100%.

By June 1999, most rubber farmers considered the prices of all goods except fertilisers to have returned almost to "normal". It was clear, however, that they were worried about the continuing slide in rubber prices.

As Indonesia's staple food, rice deserves special attention. As already mentioned, its price remained extremely high in 1999 (Table 8.4, Figure 8.3). West Kalimantan is far from self-sufficient in rice, importing thousands of tonnes every year from Sulawesi, Java and foreign countries. This explains why, even before the crisis, rice was one of the highest priced necessities of life in Indonesia and why the crisis hit rice prices harder than those of other, entirely home-grown, commodities. During the crisis, the price ratio of rubber to rice moved against rubber farmers (Table 8.4). Many families who grew both crops were able to maintain the amount of rice in their diets, but the poorest, and those who depended most on rice purchases, had to reduce it. In June 1999, as rubber prices continued their slide, these families crossed below the threshold of survival.

Table 8.4 Relative prices of rubber and rice in West Kalimantan, 1997-99

Date	*Exchange rate (Rp/US$)*	*Prices (Rp/kg)* *Rubber**	*Rice*	*Ratio***
July 1997	2400	1500	1200	1.25
January 1998	12 000	4000	4500	0.89
June 1998	10 000	3000	2500	0.86
September 1998	8000	3000	3800	0.79
November 1998	6500	3000	3400	0.88
January 1999	8700	3000	3700	0.76
March 1999	8500	3500	3500	1.00
April 1999	8500	2500	3200	0.78
June 1999	7300	1850	2700	0.69

* Farm gate rubber prices are those of dry sheets with a DRC of 75%. These prices are higher that those of the slab or cup lump rubber produced elsewhere.
** Amount of rice (kg) per 1 kg of wet rubber.
Source: SRAP surveys, 1997-99.

Rubber production incurs few costs other than labour. The main input required is formic acid to stimulate the coagulation of latex. Labour costs are therefore a high proportion of overall production costs, especially when share-cropping is used, as it often is in Sumatra Jambi (Jambi). If rubber and food prices rise at roughly the same pace, the farmer faces few problems.

The main area affected by the *krismon* was farmers' ability to invest. The sharp rise in the prices of imported inputs such as herbicides and fertilisers may have discouraged new plantings. However, improved planting materials, which typically account for 50% of total expenditure during the first 3 years of a clonal rubber plantation, actually fell in price until March-April 1999. Unfortunately, as demand rose the price jumped by 40% in June 1999. Nevertheless, if farmers can combine the use of clonal rubber with relatively low applications of imported inputs, investing in improved planting materials could still prove highly worthwhile. This seems possible in areas without *Imperata cylindrica*, where herbicides are not essential (Ruf et al, 1999).

Unlike other groups, transmigrant Javanese farmers are still at the early stages of entering the rubber market. Many of them are considering buying surrounding land in addition to the 2-hectare plots provided under the NES scheme. The price of land has been rising since 1996. In the Sanggau area, *Imperata* grassland was Rp 350 000 per hectare in July 1997, whereas by June 1999 it had jumped to Rp 1.5 million.

By this stage, it is already clear that rubber, while not nearly as profitable as cocoa or coffee, gave thousands of farmers an advantage in surviving the *krismon* that was not enjoyed by the majority of the population.

Smallholder incomes

We will now analyse in more detail the changes in rubber smallholders' incomes between July 1997 and January 1999 in six villages.

Using July 1997 as the base (100), we calculated an index of incomes in January-March 1999 (Table 8.5). The index varies from 237 to 370, averaging 281. This is similar to the index for the price of all staple foods (288, according to BPS) and slightly more than that for rice (250). This analysis confirms our impression that the crisis has not greatly affected the purchasing power of most rubber producers.

Table 8.5 Changes in incomes from July 1997 to January-March 1999

	*Index**					
Province	*Kalimantan*				*Jambi*	
	Javanese NES project	*Malayu jungle rubber*	*Dayak SRDP project*	*Dayak jungle rubber*	*Javanese food crop transmigration project*	*Dayak local transmigration project*
Rubber income (Rp)	370	300	261	237	256	292
Net farm income (Rp)	345	275	255	236	145	268
Net farm income (US$)	111	88	82	75	46	86

* July 1997 = 100.

Those who had access to clonal rubber, such as Dayak farmers at local transmigration sites, SRDP farmers in Kalimantan and Javanese NES farmers in Jambi, were clearly better able to survive the crisis than the others. This is not surprising, as clonal rubber provides three times the income of jungle rubber. Farmers who have good jungle rubber, such as indigenous Malayu farmers in Jambi and Central Sumatra, also did reasonably well.

Not surprisingly, Javanese transmigrants in food crop schemes, whose rubber plantations are still immature, had the lowest net farm incomes, which were close to those of the wage index (148). However the off-farm job opportunities open to these transmigrants, mostly on oil palm estates and in gold mining, were maintained throughout the *krismon* and may even have increased (see below). Although these incomes often do not cover basic family needs, most Javanese transmigrants in the Sanggau area consider the *krismon* to have had little impact, largely because they were able to keep these jobs. This is probably the main difference between rural Kalimantan and the situation in urban areas or in Java.

Thus, except for some indigenous Dayaks in Kalimantan and a few Javanese on food crop transmigration schemes, most rubber farmers were not badly affected by the *krismon* and managed to maintain their purchasing power. By December-March 1999, consumption patterns had not greatly changed, except in the poorest families. (However, the consumption of meat and fish fell almost everywhere, owing to their high prices.) Discussions with farmers confirmed that the *krismon* was perceived more as a "potentially risky period" than as a real disaster.

Off-farm activities remain essential to the livelihoods of transmigrants in Kalimantan, because their rubber plantations are still immature. Many traditional rubber smallholders also work in plantations for certain periods of the year. The older and less productive their jungle rubber, the more they work off-farm. Job opportunities on estates were maintained or even increased during the *krismon*, with the result that the number of farmers involved in off-farm activities rose (Table 8.6).

Transmigrants increased their off-farm activities from 9.8 months per year in 1997 to 10.1 months per year in 1998. However, the average estate labourer's wage index in January 1999 was only 200. Clearly, wages rose less rapidly than incomes from rubber, as estates reacted to the crisis by reducing their labour costs. In short, although off-farm activities remained stable throughout the crisis, off-farm incomes did not rise as much as input and food costs and incomes from rubber. In June 1999, daily wages in West Kalimantan were Rp 6000-10 000 in gold mining and roughly the same on oil palm estates. The average cost of local labour was thus around Rp 7500 per day (see Table 8.3).

Table 8.6 Off-farm job opportunities among 90 farmers in Sanggau, West Kalimantan, 1996-98

Year	*Proportion of farmers (%)*		
	1996	*1997*	*1998*
Labourers on oil palm estates	20	24	34
Employees in other businesses	10	13	17
With regular off-farm employment	40	48	60

Indonesian rubber production

Owing to the continuous advance of jungle rubber in frontier areas, rubber production in Indonesia has steadily increased. Since the 1980s, clonal rubber from project and some non-project farms has increased its share of total rubber production.

In 1997, despite the drought, total rubber production fell only slightly, to 1.564 million tonnes from 1.574 million tonnes the previous year. According to BPS statistics (DGE, 1998), production was around 1.548 million tonnes in 1998 and was forecast at 1.564 million tonnes in 1999[10]. The London Market Commodities Bulletin provides a slightly higher figure for 1998, of 1.656 million tonnes (a 6% increase over 1997). Dr Budiman, the executive director of the Rubber Association of Indonesia (GAPKINDO), estimates production at 1.6 million tonnes in 1998, a 3% increase over 1997 (Budiman, 1999).

Indonesian domestic rubber consumption fell from 140 000 tonnes in 1996 to 100 000 tonnes in 1997. Most of this (80%) went into tyre production[11], a sector that was seriously affected by the crisis because of its dependence on imported products[12]. Local tyre prices tripled and transporters switched to retread tyres, which are 30% cheaper than new ones. However, the impact on rubber production and prices was not very great, as domestic consumption accounts for a fairly small share of the market (9%) compared to exports.

Farmers enjoyed a relatively high price for 2-3 months in 1998. Did they try to cash in on this by increasing production? In other words, was there a short-term supply response?

In theory, there are two ways in which farmers could have increased their yields almost overnight. First, they could have increased the tapping frequency of mature trees. This technique, which is especially suited to clonal plantations, leads to an immediate increase in production but is not sustainable in the long term and can even kill the trees. Second, farmers in the traditional system could have tapped additional jungle rubber trees. Jungle rubber gardens usually have 250-450 tappable trees per hectare, according to the age of the plantation. But many farmers keep a stock of older trees in reserve, either as land markers or as "security plots", allowing the flexibility to respond to price changes and increase income in the short term to meet specific needs. In Kalimantan, these reserves tend to be limited, but Sumatran farmers frequently have more jungle rubber than they can tap.

As regards the first way, around 70% of farmers surveyed in Kalimantan in May 1999 said that they had not tapped their trees more frequently (Komardiwan and Penot, 1999). Around 30% admitted that they had tried, but not very persistently. Discussions with farmers in the Sintang and Sanggau areas in June 1999 showed that farmers realise that this strategy cannot be used for long without causing serious harm to the trees. As a joke, farmers talk about the "PSM" tapping system (pagi-sore-malam or morning-afternoon-evening system), but nobody really practises it. In Kalimantan, where trees already suffer from foliar diseases, farmers thought increasing tapping frequency would not be advisable. Opinions might be different in South Sumatra, where trees are generally in better condition.

The second way, tapping more jungle rubber trees, would require additional labour. Our surveys in Jambi and Kalimantan did not suggest that the availability of labour had increased in rubber areas as a result of the crisis. Rubber smallholders had a limited labour force before the crisis and that changed little during or after it. Share-cropping, which is common in Sumatra, may have increased locally for a while, in response to the demand for off-farm work from transmigrants on food crop-oriented transmigration schemes.

Moreover, smallholders growing jungle rubber earned 10-20% of their income from off-farm activities, mainly as estate labourers. The fact that this amount was not reduced during the crisis suggests no additional labour was allocated to the tapping of old or distant jungle rubber trees.

What conclusions can we draw from all this? There were some reports, from GAPKINDO and in the newspapers, of farmers pursuing both ways of increasing yields. As in Chapter 2 of this book, these reports have been used to account for increased supplies and exports and hence for the recent fall in international rubber prices. Our surveys suggest that only a few farmers tried to increase their rubber supply in the short term by using either of the two methods, although rather more may have done so in the most dynamic rubber producing areas, such as South Sumatra. We do not, however, believe that this could have had a significant short-term impact on Indonesian rubber supplies and hence on the international price of rubber.

The International Market

The international US dollar price of rubber fell dramatically in the period from mid-1996 to 1999. However, the decline started before the Asian crisis, in the first quarter of 1997. At least at the beginning, it therefore occurred independently of the *krismon*.

After a period of high demand in the early 1980s, the price of rubber fell from 1985 onwards, partly in response to the "second oil shock" and its economic aftermath. The price rose again in 1994-96, due largely to substantial purchases by China, a significant increase in car sales in the USA and a decrease in stockpiled rubber, which led to massive purchases by industry (Loyen, 1998). The price reached a high of US$ 1.60 per kilogramme in 1995, before once again starting to fall in late 1996. By the time of the *krismon*, the slide was well under way. It has since continued, with the price falling to US$ 0.55 per kilogramme[13] by June 1999.

The main factors explaining the slide are:

- World supply has risen by 4% at a time when demand has risen by only 3.5%.
- Mainland China's purchases came to a halt due to overstocking.
- By the end of 1996, world stocks had recovered to some 2 million tonnes (Sulkowski, 1997). These stocks are still depressing prices today.

In summary, the collapse of the Indonesian rupiah led to an increase in rubber prices at farm level. However, there is little evidence to support the hypothesis of an significant short-term supply response to this increase, which could in its turn explain the fall in the international price.

Conclusions

In conclusion, we will consider the implications of events in 1997-99 from three points of view: the real impact of the *krismon* on households that depend on rubber for a living, the hidden impact of the international rubber crisis, and how, in response to both these, rubber-based farming systems are likely to develop in the future. The latter topic can be further subdivided into four components: the outlook for rubber planting, the risk posed by continuing ethnic conflicts, the competition for land with oil palm, and monocropping versus agroforestry as a production strategy. We will end by reviewing the crisis as the logical, indeed inevitable, outcome of the mistaken policies of what we hope is Indonesia's past.

Impact of the krismon *on rubber farmers*

Rupiah-dollar exchange rate movements strongly affected the domestic prices of imported products, and particularly agricultural inputs, in Indonesia over the period 1997-99. The primary effect of the 1998 "price dance", as farmers called it, was to confuse most farmers. Domestic rubber prices kept broadly in line with domestic food prices and the prices of inputs produced in the country (planting materials and fertilisers such as urea). The rupiah price of rubber rose as the currency fell, but to some extent this was offset by the falling international price in US dollars. Producers thus experienced no pronounced gain or loss. Rubber farmers' standards of living remained more or less the same, as incomes were maintained. The poorest farmers, who still rely on old jungle rubber, suffered somewhat, but their standard of living was already low before the crisis. Javanese transmigrants also suffered, particularly those who had given up growing rice and depended only on young rubber plantations whose yield was still low. Farmers who had had access to clonal rubber for several years benefitted most from the *krismon*, but they are still a minority.

Most farmers rode out the crisis quite well. Some, especially transmigrants, went in for non-rubber survival strategies, such as increasing their off-farm activities, selling some cattle and reducing their meat consumption. However, our optimism over their apparent ability to cope should be qualified by the equity and environmental implications of these strategies. To sell cattle is to liquidate resources that may have taken years to accumulate. Rebuilding the herd may take equally long. Farmers who increased their off-farm activities will undoubtedly have been exploited by employers on large oil palm estates, the expansion of which is not good news for Indonesia's remaining forests. That men are daily risking their lives in dangerous gold mines while enduring months of separation from their families courts a public health disaster in the form of mercury poisoning, as well as reduced social cohesion.

The Asian crisis and the rubber crisis

The international price of rubber has fallen steadily since January 1997. In 1997, the slide was hidden by the volatility of the rupiah. And in 1998, the rupiah's collapse allowed farmers, briefly, to achieve relatively good prices. However, this did not trigger a significant short-term supply response. Even if a minority of smallholders attempted such a response, the effect was not significant and could not have greatly influenced Indonesian supplies and international prices.

However, it would be wrong to argue that the Asian crisis as a whole did not influence the international price of rubber. As Thailand, Malaysia and Indonesia account for 80% of the world's rubber supply, what happened to their economies obviously had some impact. We conclude that the Asian crisis acted mainly to lower US dollar costs rather than to increase supplies. End users took the opportunity provided by the crisis to lower the prices they paid. However, we also note that the price of rubber started falling before the crisis and that this appears to have occurred mainly for structural reasons. The Asian crisis was, then, not the only factor influencing the fall.

Having survived the *krismon* in 1998, rubber farmers faced a far more serious crisis in the second half of 1999, as the international rubber price continued its slide. However fragile, the relative stability of the rupiah in 1999 had the opposite effect of its weakness in 1998, which had allowed domestic prices to rise. Farm-gate prices fell rapidly in mid- to late 1999. The partial recovery in the world price that occurred at the very end of the year provided some respite.

Rubber planting

The *krismon* highlighted the vulnerability of the traditional rubber production system, which relies solely on old jungle rubber. It showed just how badly farmers need to rejuvenate their plantations. In June 1999, 86% of farmers in our surveys said they intended to plant or replant within the next 3 years. For farmers who cannot work on oil palm estates, investing in clonal rubber is still the best way of improving their incomes.

As long as rubber prices do not fall through the floor, the decision on whether or not to replant using clonal rubber will continue to depend on a variety of other factors besides price. (In fact, throughout the history of rubber production, prices have never fallen low enough to dissuade farmers from planting.) The moderate rupiah price rise of 1998 did not appear to stimulate a wave of new plantings over and above those already planned by farmers. The trend towards planting improved clones had set in well before the crisis. It was more pronounced in North and South Sumatra than in other provinces, owing to the impact of government projects and the development of a private nursery network to supply planting materials. By the mid-1990s, there were more than 500 nurseries in South Sumatra (Gouyon, 1995) and the number is doubtless far higher by now. In Jambi too, private nurseries are proliferating (Penot and Komardiwan, 1998). Elsewhere, the continuing unavailability of new planting materials may constrain adoption for some years to come.

In many areas, farmers may be less willing to plant clonal rubber in future because of the emergence of a more attractive alternative, oil palm. The pace of smallholder adoption of this commodity began quickening in the early 1990s, slowed down in 1997-98, then speeded up again in 1999. The farmers in our surveys were as keen on moving into oil palm as on switching from jungle rubber to clonal rubber. The crop is obviously becoming a serious alternative to rubber, particularly in provinces such as West Kalimantan, North Sumatra, Riau and Jambi. Nevertheless, farmers' strategies are more oriented towards complementarity of the two crops than to mere substitution.

Ethnic conflict

As we have seen, in 1997 fighting broke out over access to land and other issues, between the indigenous Dayak people of West Kalimantan and migrants from Madura. As a result, many Madura migrants left the province.

It is still too early to evaluate the long-term impact of these conflicts. However, as this book went to press came news that rubber production in West Kalimantan had fallen by 30% in 1999. The exodus of the Madura may well have contributed to this fall, together with other factors such as the switch of land and labour to oil palm.

Competition for land

Indonesia's oil palm sector has grown rapidly over the past 10 years. The new estates have provided local farmers with job opportunities and a new crop into which to diversify. Of the 5.5 million hectares conceded to private and state-owned companies by 1998, 2.4 million had been planted and 1.78 million were already in production (Potter and Lee, 1998). West Kalimantan is the province where oil palm development is most advanced. Given the rate of plantings observed in the late 1990s, there is little prospect of rural job opportunities in this sector drying up over the next few years.

Oil palm estates and the contracts they offer smallholders clearly provide an attractive alternative that competes for land with clonal rubber, especially when farmers decide to replace their old jungle rubber. Oil palm projects provide three main advantages: full credit to fund the planting phase, an income comparable to that of clonal rubber and a shorter immature period (only 3 years). The provision of credit is a welcome form of support for most smallholders, even if the conditions on which it is provided are sometimes not sufficiently clear. More controversial, though not necessarily inequitable provided farmers know what they are getting, is the fact that farmers must exchange around 7.5 hectares of their land for only 2 hectares of productive oil palm. In West Kalimantan, at least, a major outcome of the *krismon* is that many farmers who might previously have hesitated to enter such an arrangement are now willing to do so. Some villages, such as Sanjan (a Dayak village in Sanggau district), have strongly held beliefs about their future that motivate them to keep land for the next generation, but most villages embrace oil palm with enthusiasm if there is a nearby estate.

A role for agroforestry?

The most important lesson of the crisis for rubber farmers is that they must adopt the new high-yielding clones if they are to increase and stabilise their incomes. Farmers desperately need the early maturity and high productivity provided by the clones. In the medium to longer term, the future for rubber smallholders is bright, but the complex agroforestry systems in which jungle rubber is grown are probably now a lost cause. Farmers can no longer afford to wait 10 years before getting a return from their rubber seedlings.

This does not mean that agroforestry is incompatible with the use of improved clones. Under a collaborative project between CIRAD, the International Centre for Research in Agroforestry (ICRAF) and national institutions such as GAPKINDO and the Indonesian Rubber Research Institute (IRRI), researchers have been harnessing the natural curiosity and innovative skills of farmers to experiment with the planting of clones into agroforestry systems as an alternative to monocropping. With its high use of inputs, monocropping is too capital-intensive for many resource-poor farmers during the establishment phase. The researchers hypothesized that a "light" agroforestry system could be used to reduce these costs without sacrificing yields, while maintaining somewhat more biodiversity than a monocropping system (Gouyon, 1993; Penot and Gede Wibaya, 1997). Agroforestry systems could also help rebuild ecologies degraded by the massive forest clearances, droughts and fires of the 1990s. And the increasingly valuable timber they produce could help farmers spread and absorb the costs of replanting.

If agricultural policies change and the fruit sector is entrusted to smallholders rather than estates, combining rubber with a mix of fruit species may prove an appealing option for smallholders in the early years of the new century, especially as new roads improve their links to markets. This type of system is already evolving around some provincial capitals.

Follies of the past

With 2.5 million hectares of jungle rubber that can be replanted with clonal rubber, Indonesia's smallholder rubber sector clearly has enormous potential for productivity gains and so for contributing to equitable rural development. If combined with agroforestry, clonal plantations could also bring long-term environmental benefits.

The state of the rubber sector today demonstrates the common roots of Indonesia's social, economic and environmental crises. Riddled with corruption, the large-scale rubber estates launched by the government in the 1960s were expensive, inefficient and as damaging to social equity as they were to the environment, since they replaced smallholder rubber agroforest with large areas of clonal monoculture. They also suffered from substantial logistical problems, with the result that participating smallholders often received inferior planting materials. Their only positive impact lay in the information they provided about improved rubber clones, which has since spread far and wide in the farming community.

The crisis laid bare the extent of the environmental and social damage done to rubber smallholders by these estates and the logging companies with which they collaborated in land clearance. Several of these estates and companies belonged to the Suharto family, their friends and senior army staff. The damage could thus be laid directly at the door of the government. The crisis may appear to have had a neutral effect on the rubber sector, but what it revealed of the ignorance, corruption and inefficiency that characterised the Suharto regime was far from neutral. It convinced everyone in rural Indonesia of the urgent need for political change. And it showed small-scale producers that they needed to act as a group, forming farmers' associations to defend their interests against the acquisitive behaviour of the private estates.

It may be that, despite farmers' willingness to move forward, the rubber sector has been so badly damaged that its potential in the near future is lower than we think. The case of rubber, like that of most other commodities, demonstrates the imperative of affording priority to smallholders as the key to sustainable, equitable rural development in Indonesia. All aspects of agriculture and natural resources management, from land tenure, through the provision of information and credit, to the support offered to farmers' associations, will need a radical overhaul by the new government.

References

Budiman, A. F. 1999. The Indonesian rubber production and its industry in transition. Paper presented at the International Rubber Marketing Conference, 23-24 June 1999, Hat Yai, Thailand.

Burger, K. and Smit, H.P. 1994. *Natural Rubber Markets – Analysis and Outlook*. Proceedings of the International Rubber Forum, 35th Assembly of the International Rubber Study Group, 26-27 May 1994, Colombo, Sri Lanka.

Colfer, C. J., Newton, B. J. and Herman. 1989. Ethnicity: An important consideration in Indonesian agriculture. *Agriculture and Human Values* 6 (3): 52-66.

Courbet, P. and Penot, E. 1997. Farming systems characterization and innovations adoption process in West Kalimantan. Paper presented at the ICRAF/SRAP Workshop on Rubber Agroforestry Systems, 29-30 September 1997, International Centre for Research in Agroforestry (ICRAF), Bogor, Indonesia.

DGE (Directorate General of Estates). 1998. Statistik karet. Jakarta, Indonesia.

De Foresta, H. 1990. Jungle Rubber: Structural and Floristic Data. Working paper, International Council for Research in Agroforestry (ICRAF), Bogor, Indonesia.

Gouyon, A. 1993. Les plaines de Sumatra-sud: de la forêt aux hévéas. *Tiers Monde* 36 (135): 641-667.

Gouyon, A. 1995. Paysannerie et hévéaculture: dans les plaines orientales de Sumatra: quel avenir pour les systèmes agroforestiers? PhD thesis, Institut national agronomique Paris-Grignon (INA-PG), France.

Gouyon, A. 1999. *Fire in the Rubber Jungle: Fire Prevention and Sustainable Tree Crop Development in South Sumatra*. Idé-Force, Paris, France and Jakarta, Indonesia.

Gouyon, A. and Penot, E. 1995. L'hévéaculture paysanne indonésienne: agroforêts et plantations clonales, des choix pour l'avenir. In: Griffon, M. (ed.), *Succès et limites des révolutions vertes*. CIRAD, Montpellier, France, pp. 169-182.

Gouyon, A., de Foresta, H. and Levang, P. 1993. Does the jungle rubber deserve its name? An analysis of rubber agroforestry systems in Southeast Sumatra. *Agroforestry Systems* 22 (3): 181-206.

Kelfoun, A. and Penot, E. 1997. Farming systems characterization and innovations adoption process in Jambi. Paper presented at the ICRAF/SRAP Workshop on Rubber Agroforestry Systems, 29-30 September 1997, International Centre for Research in Agroforestry (ICRAF), Bogor, Indonesia.

Kheowvongsri, P. 1990. Les jardins à hévéa des contreforts orientaux de bukit Barisan, Sumatra, Indonésie. Diplôme d'Etudes approfondies de Biologie végétale tropicale. Université de Montpellier, France.

Komardiwan, I. and Penot, E. 1999. Socio-economic surveys and prices monitoring in West Kalimantan: Evolution between 1997 and 1999. SRAP working notes, International Centre for Research in Agroforestry (ICRAF), Bogor, Indonesia.

Lawrence, D.C. 1996. Trade-offs between rubber production and maintenance of diversity: The structure of rubber gardens in West Kalimantan, Indonesia. *Agroforestry Systems* 34: 83-100.

Leti Sundawati. 1993. The Dayak garden systems in Sanggau District, West Kalimantan: An agroforestry model. PhD thesis, Göttingen University, Germany.

Loyen G. 1998. Le futur du caoutchouc naturel et l'INRO. *Plantations, recherche et dévéloppement*, July-Aug 1998: 261-269.

Momberg, F. 1993. Indigenous knowledge systems. PhD thesis. Technische Universität Berlin, Germany.

Penot, E. and Gede Wibaya. 1997. Preliminary conclusion summary paper of the SRAP Workshop on Rubber Agroforestry Systems. Paper presented at the ICRAF/SRAP Workshop on Rubber Agroforestry Systems, 29-30 September 1997, International Centre for Research in Agroforestry (ICRAF), Bogor, Indonesia.

Penot, E. and Komardiwan, I. 1998. Rubber Improved Planting Material in the Jambi Province. World Bank report for the Jambi Regional Development Project (JRDP), Jakarta, Indonesia.

Potter, L. and Lee, J. 1998. Tree Planting in Indonesia: Trends, Impacts and Directions. Occasional Paper No. 18. Center for International Forestry Research (CIFOR), Bogor, Indonesia.

Ruf, F., Penot, E. and Yoddang, 1999. After tropical forest, replantation of rubber and cocoa trees: Garden of Eden or chemical inputs? Paper presented at the Planetary Garden, First International Symposium on Sustainable Ecosystem Management, 14-18 March 1999, Chambéry, France, pp. 318-324.

Sulkowski, G. 1997. Natural rubber market outlook: Near and beyond year 2000. Paper presented at the GAPKINDO Rubber Industry Forum, August 1997, Sanur, Bali, Indonesia.

Salafsky, N. 1994. Forest gardens in the Gunung Palung region of West Kalimantan, Indonesia. *Agroforestry Systems* 28: 237-268.

Thiollay, J. 1995. The role of traditional agroforests in the conservation of rain forest bird diversity in Sumatra. *Conservation Biology* 19 (2): 335-353.

Werner, S. 1993. Traditional Land Use systems of Dayaks in West Kalimantan, Indonesia: Ecological Balance or Resource Destruction? A Study of Vegetation Dynamics and Soil Development. Diplomarbeit im Fach Geographie. Geographische Institut, Berlin, Germany.

Notes

1 Migrants from Madura were the group worst affected. They were accused of taking land from the indigenous Dayak peope and of showing a lack of respect for Dayak culture.

2 Other types of improved planting material could also be used, notably polyclonal seedlings. But clones, obtained through grafting, are more homogeneous, more productive and generally better adapted, with resistance or tolerance to a number of diseases.

3 Before then, Indonesian agricultural policy focussed more on rice self-sufficiency, in particular on irrigated rice in Java (see Chapters 9 and 10).

4 Projects of this kind had already been implemented on a much larger scale in Thailand and Malaysia in the 1960s for political reasons (rubber was seen as a reliable source of income for local populations and hence a way of countering local uprisings). Indonesia developed this policy, somewhat belatedly, in the 1970s.

5 The rubber agroforests in Sumatra and Kalimantan have been exhaustively described by Colfer et al (1989), de Foresta (1990), Leti Sundawati (1993), Lawrence (1996), Salafsky (1994), Momberg (1993), Werner (1993), Thiollay (1995) and Kheowvongsri (1990).

6 In this project CIRAD and the International Centre for Research in Agroforestry (ICRAF) are conducting collaborative research with national institutions. Various rubber agroforestry systems are being tested in on-farm trials with farmers.

7 This project, run by the Rubber Association of Indonesia (GAPKINDO) provides farmers with clonal rubber and inputs for the first year only. The project was launched in 1992.

8 In food crop-oriented transmigration projects, farmers are provided with two plots of 1 hectare each, known as *lahan* 1 and 2, and an additional small plot of 0.5 hectare for a house and garden.

9 Smallholder plantations growing the PB 260 clone under the Smallholder Rubber Development Project (SRDP) in South Sumatra yield an average of 1600-2000 kilogrammes per hectare per year, compared to 300-600 kilogrammes per hectare per year in a jungle rubber system, depending on age.

10 Statistics were not officially released in 1999 because of the elections held that year.

11 Indonesia first produced synthetic rubber in 1997. The producer is P.T. Sintetikajaya, a subsidiary of the country's largest tyre producer. The annual capacity is 60 000 tonnes.

12 Natural rubber accounts for only 22% of the production cost of tyres. Around 93% of the other inputs required are imported, at prices set in US dollars.

13 This price is for TSR 20 (technically specified rubber grade 20), the grade most commonly used for tyre production.

PART THREE

SMALLHOLDERS AND FOOD CROPS

Chapter 9

The 1998 Food Crisis: Temporary Blip or the End of Food Security?

Françoise Gérard, Isabelle Marty and Erwidodo

In 1997-98 the international community provided Indonesia with food. It did not, however, succeed in averting a substantial increase in malnutrition. This was caused by a huge increase in the prices of staple foods at a time when real wages were falling sharply.

Indonesia's previous performance in food production had been impressive. By 1996, only 3.34% of the country's population was classified as malnourished (Amang et al, 1996). So was the 1998 food crisis simply a conjunctural event, caused by the coincidence of drought and economic crisis, and therefore only temporary, or did it mark the permanent end of food security for this country of 200 million people?

This question has far-reaching implications. Its answer is inextricably bound up with the future political stability of Indonesia and of Southeast Asia as a whole. In July 1997, Indonesia was hit by a financial storm which quickly led to economic, social and political anarchy. Although there was a time-lag of a few months, every time the exchange rate fell the domestic price of imported rice and other foods eventually reached parity with the international price, triggering riots, looting and ethnic violence as it did so. How did Indonesia arrive at this pass? What was the impact of this price instability on consumers? How was food crop production affected?

To address these questions it is important to see the crisis in a historical context. In the first section we therefore examine the past achievements of the food crop sector and the policy of price stabilisation successfully pursued by the Indonesian government for many years. Besides providing the basis for predicting future trends in food security, this analysis will help explain the unrest when food prices rose in

1998. In addition, it will reveal those areas in which government intervention, now under so much justified criticism, did in fact have a positive impact. In the second section, we will analyse the crisis in terms of the two principal aspects of food security: on the one hand, the production and availability of food, and on the other, consumers' economic access to it. Next, to assess future food security in Indonesia, the third section will address two questions: what was the impact of this unstable period on food crop producers' incomes and assets, and how has the profitability of their enterprises been affected by changes in input and output prices? Finally, in the last section we present our conclusions.

Past Performance of the Food Crop Sector

In the second half of the 1970s, Indonesia was regularly the world's largest rice importer and experts were pessimistic about the country's future ability to feed itself. When Suharto came to power in 1965, he created BULOG, a special agency responsible for implementing food policy, the main aim of which was to protect consumers and producers from sharp fluctuations in the price of rice. During the world food crisis of 1973-74, Indonesia found itself unable to buy enough rice on the world market to maintain domestic price stability. Government intervention in the agricultural sector was subsequently intensified, with impressive results: Indonesia achieved self-sufficiency in rice in the mid-1980s.

Intervention allowed domestic prices to follow world prices, but to avoid sharp fluctuations by storing grain in bulk when the price was low and releasing it when it rose. Such a policy is costly. It was made possible by the huge increases in government revenues associated with the rising oil prices of the 1970s. Since 1987, the policy has had to be relinquished, mainly because government revenues have fallen as oil prices declined but also in response to international pressure from institutions such as the IMF and the World Bank. Agriculture, including food crops, has been progressively liberalised. As a result of rising demand, coupled with a slowdown in yield gains, rice imports once again became necessary in 1996.

Self-sufficiency in rice: A government success story

Rice is Indonesia's most important food crop. It provides 35-67% of total calorie intake and 32-60% of total protein intake, depending on the level of consumer income (Gérard and Versapuetch, 1997). Between 1974 and 1990, domestic rice production doubled (Figure 9.1). The main factors accounting for this achievement were the adoption of high-yielding rice varieties, coupled with the increased use of fertilisers and an expansion of the irrigated area. In other words, this was a classic Green Revolution success story.

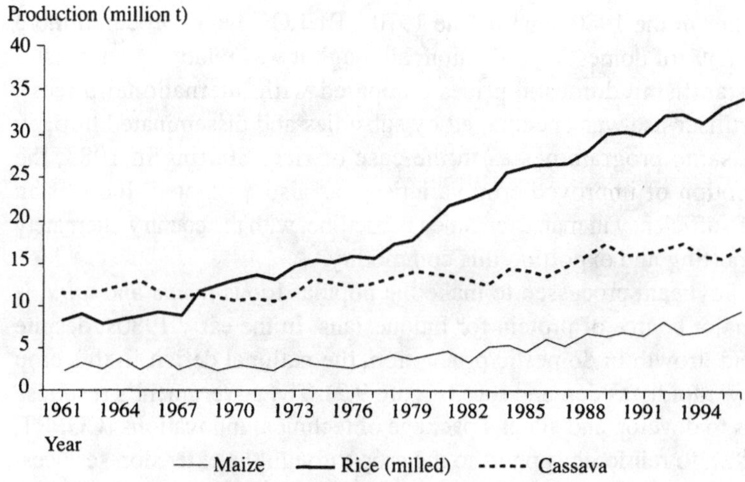

Figure 9.1 Rice, maize and cassava production in Indonesia, 1961-96

The technical components of the Revolution were delivered through various government institutions and programmes established to disseminate improved crop varieties, fertilisers and pesticides at subsidised prices, together with information and training on how to use them (Gérard et al, 1998). At the same time, BULOG provided producers with a favourable policy environment by stabilising rice prices. The domestic market was regulated using a network of public stores, one of which was situated in each district. A floor price was announced before planting time, reducing the risk faced by producers. Yields rose from 2.6 tonnes per hectare in 1973 to 4.3 tonnes per hectare in 1990. This was a quantum leap forward, although it did not match the highest gains achieved elsewhere in Asia, for example in South Korea, where yields reached 6.4 tonnes per hectare in 1990, according to FAO data.

Towards the end of the 1970s, the intervention policy was extended to cover maize, the country's second most important food crop and one on which poor consumers relied greatly. A floor price for maize was established in 1978. However, this measure was largely ineffective because market prices were always higher than the floor price (Rosegrant et al, 1987). Supply and demand rose rapidly, mainly because of the amount consumed by the animal feed industry, which was three times higher in the 1980s than in the 1970s. BULOG never procured more than 3% of domestic production, although it was relatively successful at stabilising domestic prices compared with international prices[1]. Fertiliser use was encouraged by subsidies and disseminated through the same programmes as in the case of rice. Starting in 1983, the adoption of improved crop varieties was also promoted. Indonesian self-sufficiency in maize remained borderline, with the country alternately importing and exporting this commodity.

Soybean, processed to make the popular foods *tempe* and *tahu*, is a major source of protein for Indonesians. In the early 1980s, despite rapid growth in domestic production, the national deficit in this crop grew rapidly as demand rose (Figure 9.2). The government's response was to develop and adapt a package of technical innovations (CGPRT, 1992), to reinforce support to the crop through the extension services, and to allow the price to rise. In 1980, BULOG instituted a floor price combined with import control-measures. The floor price was ineffective because the reduced level of imports drove the domestic price 40-60% higher than the import parity price[2]—well above the level set by BULOG, which was never achieved. The increase in production was almost entirely due to expansion of the area cultivated, only 3% being attributable to yield gains. In Java, cropping patterns favoured the cultivation of soybean during the dry season, when water availability and pest control problems made a third rice crop impossible. Despite this opportunity, most of the increase in national production came from the exploitation of new areas outside Java, associated either with transmigration schemes or with farming by indigenous people.

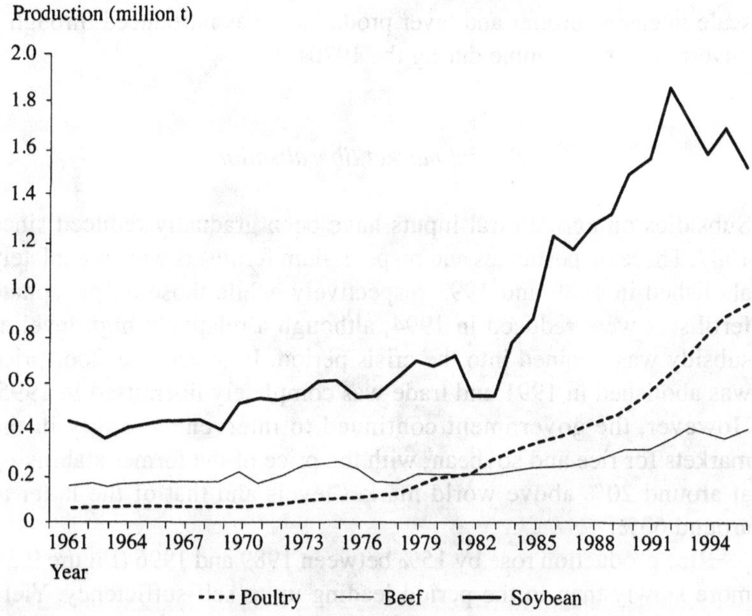

Figure 9.2 Soybean and meat production in Indonesia, 1961-96

Root crops, especially cassava, tend to be consumed by the poor in Indonesia. The average proportion of root crops in the diet has fallen sharply, by around 50%, over the past 20 years as incomes have risen. Nevertheless, by the time the *krismon* struck, root crop consumption was still higher in Indonesia than in other Asian countries at comparable levels of development. Cassava is not an attractive crop for farmers because of the low profit margins it commands. On the other hand, it requires relatively little labour. It is now mainly planted in poor soils or when off-farm activities do not allow enough time to grow other crops.

Indonesians' consumption of animal protein has risen from only 1.40 gram per capita per day in 1969 to 3.77 grams per capita per day in 1994. The amount spent on meat is still low, but was rising rapidly just before the crisis, reflecting rising incomes. Poultry farming, which accounts for 60% of the country's meat production, is the largest component of the livestock sector, forming a profitable source of income for many small-scale producers. Relatively new to Indonesia, large-scale intensive broiler and layer production was introduced through a government programme during the 1970s.

Partial market liberalisation

Subsidies on agricultural inputs have been gradually reduced since 1987. Those on pesticides and on potassium fertilisers were completely abolished in 1989 and 1993 respectively, while those on phosphate fertilisers were reduced in 1994, although a relatively high level of subsidy was retained into the crisis period. In maize, the floor price was abolished in 1991 and trade was completely liberalised in 1995. However, the government continued to intervene strongly in the markets for rice and soybean, with the price of the former stabilising at around 20% above world market levels and that of the latter at around 60%.

Rice production rose by 15% between 1989 and 1996 (Figure 9.3), more slowly than in the period leading up to self-sufficiency. Yield gains were lower than in the early 1980s, with the average yield rising from 4.04 tonnes per hectare in 1987 to 4.42 tonnes per hectare in 1996, according to CBS data. Most of the land suitable for rice production using currently available technologies was already being cultivated, although a further 1 million hectares was earmarked for development in Kalamantan under a government project. Opportunities to increase production by raising the cropping intensity were limited by the problems of pest control (Booth, 1988). Droughts occurred, in 1991 and 1994 for example, bringing with them temporary setbacks in production. Rice consumption is still rising with income, despite consumer diversification into meat, fish, fruit and vegetables. Consequently, imports have again become necessary, starting in 1996.

Between 1991 and 1996, maize production rose by 48%. However, production was outpaced by demand, which according to FAO data rose by 58% for food and 54% for feed, making imports necessary. Soybean yields have levelled off since the late 1980s, after a small gain in the preceding years. This reflects the typical decline in marginal yield gains that occurs once the major components of a package have been adopted by farmers. In addition, it proved difficult to intensify cropping systems any further, particularly in irrigated areas where three

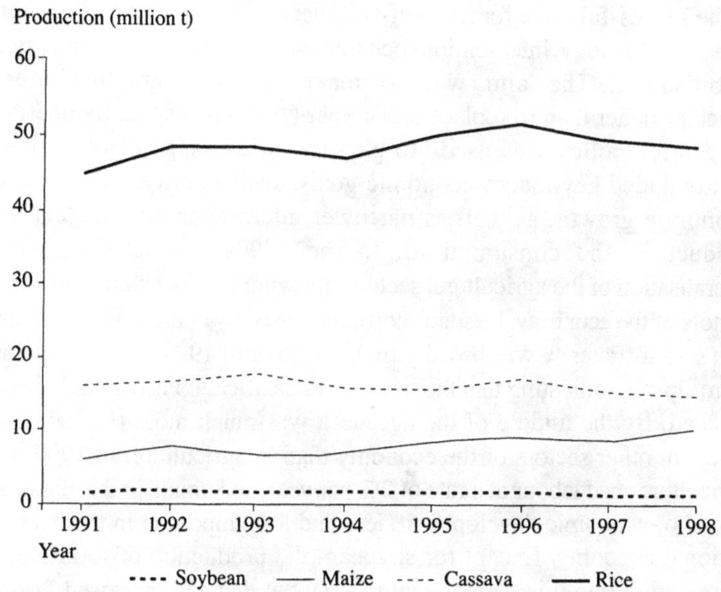

Figure 9.3 Indonesian staple food crop production in the 1990s

crops a year are grown and rice competes for land. Despite valiant efforts to increase both the yield and the area of soybean, national production has increased much more slowly than demand. As a result, imports have risen steadily, at around 8.5% per year.

The poultry industry grew at a phenomenal 20% per year during the 1990s. Egg production alone rose by 12% per year. The domestic broiler market is currently saturated, following the rapid expansion of production under a national campaign to increase non-oil exports. Consequently, broiler prices have fallen drastically in recent years.

In summary, the historical background to the 1998 food crisis was as follows. In the 1980s, not only was self-sufficiency in rice achieved but per capita food consumption also increased sharply. Rice consumption rose from 297 grams per capita per day in 1970 to 411 grams per capita per day in 1990. Indonesia's population rose from 120 million inhabitants in 1970 to more than 203 million in 1998, creating a huge increase in the demand for staple foods, especially rice, soybean and maize. Strong government intervention was a key factor in the successful drive for rice self-sufficiency. Besides the introduction of new technology, intervention focussed on risk reduction through price stabilisation. The aim was to make private marketing more efficient rather than to replace it. Timmer (1989) notes that Indonesian food price policy was used "to pursue a wide range of objectives that included key macro-economic goals, such as price stability and economic growth, as well as narrower micro-economic targets for production and consumption...". The 1990s saw a progressive liberalisation of the agricultural sector, following similar changes in other sectors of the economy. Despite shortfalls caused by climatic fluctuations, rice self-sufficiency was broadly maintained until 1996. Yet yield gains were slower, indicating that the limits to intensification had already been reached. By the middle of the decade it was much more profitable to invest in other sectors of the economy than in agriculture. In 1990-93, agriculture shed labour at a rate of 2% per year, becoming, in the classical model of economic development, less and less important in the overall national economy. Except for soybean, the production of food crops increased during this period (Figure 9.3), but demand increased faster. In the mid-1990s, the country began relying increasingly on food imports. But because the economy as a whole was thought to be performing well, food security did not seem to be an issue.

In the 20 years leading up to the crisis, the rupiah gradually became increasingly overvalued, making things more and more difficult for all sectors producing tradable goods or services, including agriculture. In the food crop sector, these problems were, until the early 1990s, masked by heavy subsidies. When these were substantially reduced, the sector became exposed to the brunt of market forces, suffering considerably in the years leading up to the crisis. In the mid-1990s, lending began growing quickly in all sectors of the economy except agriculture (World Bank, 1996), underlining the fact that agriculture remained outside the speculative bubble.

Food Security during the Crisis

The weather conspired with the laws of economics to push Indonesia into a serious food crisis in early 1998. The primary cause of the fall in production and the subsequent food shortages was the long

El Niño-related drought and its aftermath, the torrential rains associated with La Niña. But the economic and social crisis, which disrupted agricultural input and output markets, was also a serious contributing factor. It is this second crisis that explains why, despite massive food imports, Indonesia's food crisis did so much harm to so many people.

The weather and the need for imports

The El Niño event that began in May-June 1997 was one of the worst of the twentieth century and produced the most severe drought in Indonesia for 50 years. Its impact varied greatly across the country's islands and provinces.

In Java, the onset of the rainy season, which normally extends from October to March, was delayed by up to 2 months. By late 1997, rainfall was far below normal. Water shortages led to a fall in the rice growing area for the main season, in addition to sharply reduced yields. The late first-season harvest meant that planting for the second season had to be delayed, further reducing yields. In Sumatra and Kalimantan, the fires traditionally used to clear bush and forest raged out of control and were put out only by the limited amount of rain falling in late 1997. The fires disrupted grasshopper habitats, causing these insects to inflict considerable damage on crops (FAO/WFP, 1998). No means of control were available, as pesticide prices had rocketed in response to the *krismon*. Fertiliser was also in short supply, not least because of the government's difficulty in maintaining subsidies. All these factors combined to give very low yields.

Total rice production in Indonesia fell by 3% in 1997, the worst affected islands being Sulawesi and Sumatra, where losses approached 8% and 6% respectively. In 1998, it fell still further, by 5.14% compared with 1996. The first rice season of 1998 was the worst, with production down by 18% as water supplies ran out. In most areas, the drought resulted in a delayed rainy season rather than a shortened one, with the result that rainfall was above normal during the following dry season[3]. Unfortunately, the increase in the cutivated area (4.3%) was counterbalanced by low yields due to pest damage and the low use of inputs, including fertiliser as well as herbicides. Increasingly, markets were unable to function properly in the chaos that was Indonesia at the height of the crisis, leading to shortages and high prices of inputs in many areas. These problems were compounded by farmers' lack of cash. As a result, Indonesia experienced one of its lowest average rice yields of the decade, only 4.2 tonnes per hectare for the whole of 1998. Reflecting lower fertiliser applications, the milling rate fell from 65% to 63%, aggravating the harvest shortfall still further. Due to the high price of rice, farmers with sufficient water deviated from their regular rotation practices and planted a third crop of rice, exacerbating the pest problem in several major rice producing regions.

Maize production, which was negatively affected in late 1997, bounced back in 1998, rising by 8% over its 1996 level. Because of water shortages, producers shifted from rice and soybean to maize, which is more resistant to drought. The area devoted to the crop rose by some 500 000 hectares compared with 1997. Yields in 1997 and 1998, amounting to around 2.6 tonnes per hectare, were the highest of the 1990s, due in part to the increased use of hybrid varieties (USDA, 1999). However, the decline in pesticide use led to widespread pest problems, which reduced yields in some areas.

Soybean production was adversely affected by a substantial decrease in both yield and cultivated area. Being highly sensitive to water stress and pests, this crop was not an attractive one for farmers under these difficult climatic conditions. They switched to maize or other crops wherever possible. In some areas the floods of late 1998 caused total crop failure. Production in 1997 and 1998 fell by 10% and 14% respectively against its 1996 level.

Cassava performed as poorly as soybean, with production in 1997 and 1998 falling by 11% and 13% compared with 1996. Unlike soybean, however, production was low not because the crop was vulnerable but because the cultivated area declined, due to the crop's low profitability compared to other crops. Where it was grown, cassava proved, as always, a robust survivor, yielding well under difficult climatic conditions. As such, it was a lifeline to many poor farming families.

Fortunately, the decline in the aggregate supply of staple food crops was largely offset by increased food imports. Imports of rice, at 5.8 million tonnes, soybean, at 700 000 tonnes, and sugar, at 1.7 million tonnes, increased significantly in 1998. The potentially negative effects of El Niño were known in advance, allowing the timely delivery of international aid. As a result, real food shortages were avoided (Figure 9.4).

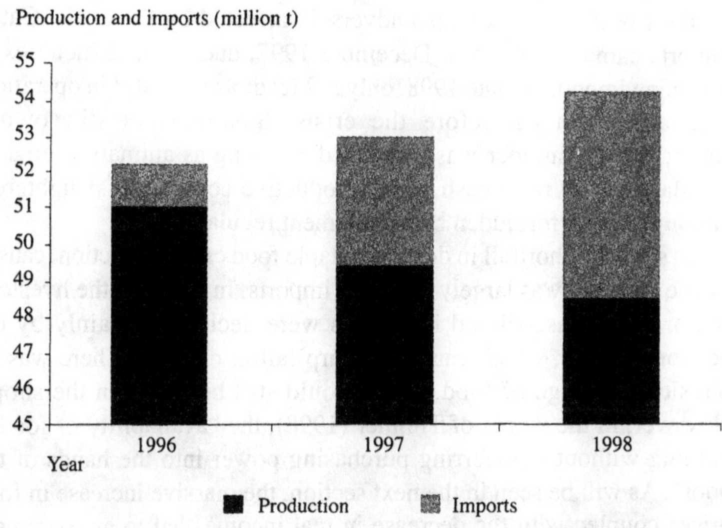

Figure 9.4 Indonesian rice production and imports during the crisis

In contrast, the difficulties faced by the livestock sector came mainly from the demand side. The economic crisis, which reduced real incomes while driving up all prices, caused a sharp fall in demand for livestock products and, consequently, for animal feed. Total broiler production in September 1998 was reduced to approximately 15-20% of its pre-crisis level of 12-13 million birds per week (USDA, 1998). Likewise, egg production fell by 55-60% and remained low until late 1998. Industrial poultry production (broilers and layers), which relies on imported inputs, was more severely affected than the smallholder sector. The rising prices of soybean meal and fish meal resulted in an increase in the price of feeds sold from feed mills, which almost tripled over their 1996 levels. In 1997, only 60% of feed mill capacity was utilised. The 20% fall in production resulted in several mills lying idle and the institution of a 4-day working week in others, with a consequent shake-out of staff. The crisis in the poultry industry had severe and wide-ranging knock-on effects, since the industry was linked to so many others, including the supply of drugs, premixes, additives and equipment, many of them also importing most of their raw materials. Many drug distributors reduced the scale of their operations and had to cut down on staff.

Beef production was also adversely affected by the crisis. Cattle imports came to an end in December 1997, due to the difficulties of financing imports. In late 1998, only 5-7 feedlots were still in operation, compared with 41 before the crisis. Smallholders still owned cattle, but the number was steadily decreasing as animals were sold for slaughter to raise cash. Even productive cows were slaughtered, although this is forbidden by government regulations.

In sum, the shortfall in domestic staple food crop production, caused by the weather, was largely offset by imports. In contrast, the livestock sector and its associated industries were decimated mainly by the economic crisis, which caused a sharp fall in demand. There was no physical shortage of food, which could still be found in the shops. However, in the words of Timmer (1998), the "availability of food is nothing without transferring purchasing power into the hands of the poor". As will be seen in the next section, the massive increase in food prices coupled with the decrease in real incomes led to an extremely painful squeeze in which the majority of the population, and especially the poor, faced major problems in accessing the minimum amount of food they needed in order to survive. Starvation stared many in the face.

Soaring prices, desperate consumers

Food crops are often traded domestically and, even if produced mainly for the domestic market, may sometimes be imported or exported. This means that, in the absence of government intervention, their prices should follow international prices. If domestic prices are lower than international prices (both expressed in US dollars) by more than just transport costs, traders have an incentive to export the product rather than sell it within the country.

Left to their own devices, staple food prices in Indonesia should roughly have doubled at the end of 1997, multiplied by four in January 1998 and then stabilized at around three times their 1996 level by April 1998. As the *krismon* deepened, the government faced a nightmare dilemma: on the one hand, intervening to keep food prices at their pre-crisis level by isolating the domestic market from world prices would unfairly penalize food crop farmers and stifle the potential of agriculture to lead economic recovery; on the other, allowing food prices to rise would mean that poor urban consumers would be unable to survive without a large rise in wages, dissipating the competitive advantage gained through currency depreciation. It might also incur widespread social unrest, reducing people's confidence and encouraging further currency depreciation which, in turn, would push staple food prices still higher.

If domestic production had been sufficient to meet demand, a ban on exports would have succeeded in keeping domestic prices below import parity level. However, this was not the case for Indonesia. Under these circumstances, it was perhaps unwise of the government to adopt such a policy.

Despite the considerable diversity among provinces, the retail prices of rice, maize, soybean and cassava all followed roughly the same course over the 1996-98 period—a course determined largely by trends in the financial market. Prices rose only slowly until December 1997, as BULOG released its stocks (Figure 9.5). During this period, Indonesia's currency was still behaving no worse than the other Southeast Asian currencies caught in the crisis. By December 1997, the price of rice was 32% higher than it had been a year ago, while those of maize and soybean were 17% and 20% higher respectively.

Towards the end of 1997, the health problems of President Suharto caused deepening political uncertainty which, in turn, caused further tremors on the financial markets. This was followed, in early 1998, by the announcement of a budget rejected as unacceptable by the IMF. Investors stampeded out of the rupiah, which in January rose to Rp 17 000 against the US dollar, compared with Rp 2500 = US$ 1.00 in July 1997. Food prices soared, triggering riots and looting in major cities and towns. By February, the price of rice was 67% higher than it had been in the same month in 1996, while maize, soybean and cassava were 84%, 72% and 42% higher. With the value of the rupiah so low, and a huge amount of rice imports necessary because of the drought, a further increase in the price of food became inevitable. If it is difficult at the best of times to hold domestic prices lower than international prices, it is virtually impossible to do so in the context of the extreme political instability faced by Indonesia. Fertiliser subsidies were by this time no longer effective, as supplies had dried up across the country owing to failures in the transport and distribution system, problems in financing subsidies and the diversion of supplies towards large-scale

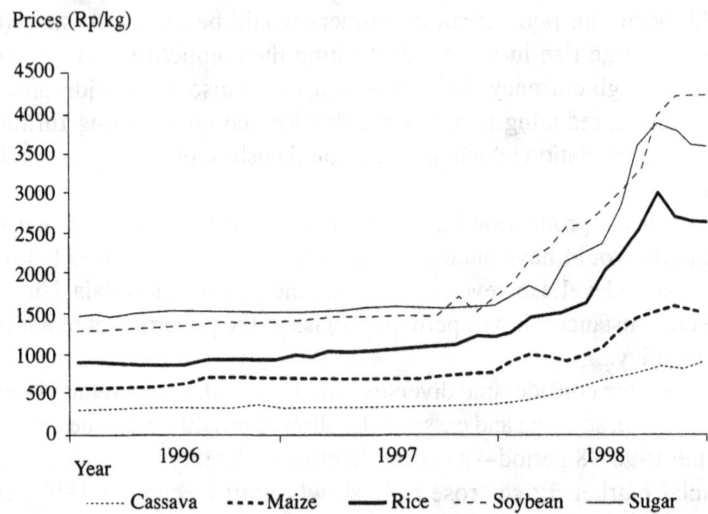

Figure 9.5 Monthly average retail prices for various food staples in Indonesia, 1996-98

plantations, which were able to bribe suppliers by paying over the subsidised price. In addition, illegal exports of rice were regularly reported by the press as businessmen and government officials took advantage of the ailing rupiah to fill their pockets. As people's confidence in the country's institutions sank to an all-time low owing to nepotism and corruption, government policy, now openly criticized by more or less everyone, became more and more difficult to implement.

By June 1998, the price of rice stood 91% above the level of June 1996, but even at this new high it was only 57% of the import parity price. Already, the combination of high prices, a minimal increase in nominal wages and massive unemployment meant that many people, especially in urban areas, had fallen on very hard times, with a reasonable diet increasingly beyond their means. But worse was still to come.

BULOG increased its operations in 1997 and 1998 (Tabor et al, 1999). However, when further riots in May 1998 were followed by the currency crash of June, the government's capacity to avoid a further increase in food prices was stretched to breaking point. In June 1998, the chairman of BULOG was sacked for corruption. Immediately, rumours of empty BULOG warehouses sparked panic buying. During the next few months, food prices went through the roof. The price of rice in September 1998 was 230% higher than during the same month in 1996[4].

Throughout this period, the Chinese were the principal targets of violence, because of the major part they played in trade and business. Traders always take the blame for food price increases, even if no one can actually prove that their profit margins are excessive. The risk of looting added further uncertainty to an already high-risk business, leading to the further disruption of trade, which was already severely hampered by the unavailability of credit and the lack of liquidity.

At this stage of the crisis prices, fueled by panic buying and speculative hoarding, rose more because of pessimistic expectations about future prices than because of an actual shortage of food. Domestic food prices rose above import parity. Rising uncertainty in trade increases costs because the risk premium is high and losses due to riots and looting are factored in. A vicious circle is generated, whereby the failure of the market leads to a speculative increase in food prices, which generates high risk premiums and, hence, further market failures (FAO/WFP, 1998).

Besides the staple food crops, meat and eggs also rose greatly in price during the crisis. The retail prices of broiler meat and beef rose from Rp 4860 and Rp 11 000 per kilogramme in January 1997 to approximately Rp 12 000 and Rp 20 000 per kilogramme respectively in December 1998. Beef continued to rise in price, reaching Rp 22 000 per kilogramme in early 1999, due mainly to higher feed costs, which almost tripled compared with their pre-crisis levels.

The steep rises in food prices became catastrophic when combined with falling real incomes. What began as a financial crisis turned into an economic crisis which spread to all sectors of the economy during the first half of 1998. Almost all businesses were hit by a combination of rising prices of imports, falling domestic demand and a lack of liquidity, the latter caused by a restrictive monetary policy designed to keep inflation at bay. The minimum daily wage remained unchanged between January 1997 and late June 1998, but by mid-June it could buy only 2.6 kilogrammes of rice, compared with 6.3 kilogrammes less than a year-and-a-half ago (ILO, 1999). Within the space of a year, September 1997-98, the price of rice rose by 175% while median wages in the manufacturing, hotel and mining sectors rose by only 26%, 29% and

49% respectively, according to CBS data. Over the same period, the wage of unskilled rural Javanese labourers working in agriculture rose by an average of only 21-43% (Tabor et al, 1999), while unemployment went up by about 20%.

All this had a terrible effect on Indonesia's people. The sudden experience of poverty created a terrifying insecurity, as robbery, rioting and looting broke out in a score of cities across the country, including Jakarta and other cities in East Java, Central Java, West Nusa Tenggara, Aceh and West Kalimantan. Food shortages and even famine were reported in pockets of East Nusa Tenggara, East Kalimantan and even West Java, which is well known as the country's major rice producing province.

The number of poor people multiplied. Estimates of the numbers living below the poverty line range from 32-45 million, according to the IMF, to 100 million (ILO/UNDP, 1998). In May 1998, the Ministry of Food and Horticulture estimated that 50 million rural Indonesians lived in districts classified as food-insecure.

Consumers used different strategies to cope with the simultaneous rise in food prices and fall in incomes. Selling assets was the first strategy, used by 75% of rural and 90% of urban people in Java (ILO, 1999). These "distress" sales, of prized possessions such as motorcycles, televisions and breeding stock in addition to everyday items such as clothes and cooking utensils, increase inequality, since they allow the rich to strip the poor of their assets at knock-down prices. Often, the poor were forced to give up items that were vital to their ability to earn a living, such as a horse-and-cart or a bicycle rickshaw. Other ways in which people tried to make up for their loss of income were to seek jobs in the informal sector, where they worked long hours for low wages at such tasks as hawking newspapers, cigarettes and snacks, collecting scrap metal, quarrying and selling limestone, craftwork, including the weaving of bamboo baskets and other items, and recycling anything and everything from rubber tyres, which were turned into sandals, to old metal cans, which became Kerosene stoves (Jellinek and Rustanto, 1999). All these activities were already well developed in Indonesia before the crisis, but the crisis intensified them, bringing heightened competition at a time when markets were shrinking. By late 1998, an estimated four million displaced employees were working in the informal sector.

City dwellers often returned to their country villages after they had lost their jobs, hoping to start a new life in agriculture or at least to throw themselves on the mercy of their relatives, many of whom they had previously supported with remittances. One strategy resorted to by small communities was to pool resources in order to cut costs or make up for the loss of critical possessions. Examples include sharing buffalo teams for ploughing, sending a small group of youths to the town to sell craft items on behalf of the whole village, and households clubbing together to employ a single cook instead of one each. A few new business opportunities opened up as a result of the crisis. Scrap metal workers did well, as also did traders in second-hand goods. The business start-ups in these areas testified to the resilience of Indonesians, boding well for the country's ability to overcome adversity (Jellinek and Rustanto, 1999). However, these opportunities require capital and were therefore beyond the means of the poorest.

Many consumers changed their diet, giving up more expensive foods in order to meet their basic needs. Maize and cassava regained the place in the diet that they had had 20 years ago, when people were poorer, while rice—the convenience food of the modern city dweller—became less important. Meat became a thing of the past. According to surveys in Central Java (FAO/WFP, 1998), overall protein intake fell drastically, anaemia in children aged less than 35 months rose by 25% cent and 35% of women also suffered from anaemia. Such figures are worrying, not only now but also for the future, as malnourished children become weak adults.

Since August 1998, the government has subsidised a programme to provide rice to poor families at Rp 1000 per kilogramme. Each family was originally entitled to buy 10 kilogrammes per month, but this was subsequently increased to 20. The programme has been expanded to cover more than 15 million families. The government has also extended work capital assistance to 11.5 million families. This comes in the form of a cheap loan, consisting of Rp 20 000-320 000 provided at 6% annual interest. The loan is intended to enable people to maintain their standard of living while waiting for the economy to recover and employment opportunities to become available once again.

Following IMF intervention in early September 1998, BULOG's monopoly on imports of sugar, soybean and wheat flour was axed and subsidies were removed. Private-sector importers were now completely free to import food commodities and were exempt from import duty. The government expressed its commitment to ensuring transparency and competitive bidding in the market place. At least 160 companies, both domestic and foreign, showed an interest in participating in the new, liberalised market. However, continuing political instability, the unresolved debt problem and the inability of the domestic market to function properly, together with general economic uncertainty, tended to limit imports, at least initially. By 1 December 1998, the date on which the government officially allowed the price of imported rice to increase, rice imports were still affected by these factors. It was widely asked whether this was the right time for Indonesia to liberalise its food market.

In sum, the food crisis in Indonesia was the result of a sharp increase in food prices caused by the financial and economic crisis and not by an actual shortage of food. The government's food policy, aimed at maintaining relatively low and stable prices, would have had a better chance of succeeding had it not been for the drought, which made it impossible for the government to isolate the domestic market. In the end, despite all the measures taken to protect the poor, the government was forced to liberalise the food crop sector in late 1998, driving up the numbers of the poor and plunging them into deeper poverty.

Food Crop Producers and Future Food Security

To predict future trends in food crop production it is necessary to determine how profitability has been affected by the price changes brought by the crisis. A further factor to take into account is that, whereas most of the poor lived in rural areas before the crisis, unknown numbers of newly unemployed urban poor have now returned to the rural areas, placing further pressure on the natural resource base and, in areas where there is no land left to settle, creating a new rural proletariat desperately in search of work—a factor that will keep labour costs down but will do little to improve the lot of the rural poor[5]. As we report below, the crisis has precipitated a decrease in equity, with the income of the poorest rural households falling sharply.

This does not necessarily mean that overall food production was, or will be, negatively affected. Indeed, there may even be an improvement in the terms of trade for farmers owning enough land.

The 1998 squeeze

In 1997 and 1998, input and output prices both increased in agriculture, altering the profitability of food crop production. In addition, the inability of markets to function efficiently produced considerable uncertainty and hampered both production and consumption. Uncertainty was a major new factor in farming, since before the crisis the government had minimised it by announcing a guaranteed floor price for each of the major food staples. The effectiveness of this policy in increasing food production was based on confidence and, in particular, confidence in the ability of BULOG to do its job properly. After the crisis broke, BULOG's interventions came under heavy criticism from the IMF, with the result that nobody could be certain how long this institution would last, especially following the resignation of President Suharto in May 1998. This uncertainty became a further factor undermining BULOG's effectiveness. As we have already seen, riots and looting disrupted markets, preventing them from functioning normally. Stockpiling and panic buying became widespread. The FAO/WFP (1998) reported that farmers were holding above-normal levels of food stocks and were reluctant to sell.

Producer price trends for the major food staples—rice, maize, soybean and cassava—generally followed the same pattern as retail prices. For commodities that are imported as well as produced domestically, namely rice and soybean, the percentage rise in producer prices was lower than that in retail prices. The reverse was true for commodities produced and sold domestically but also exported, namely cassava and, in some months, maize. This shows that it was the value of the products on the international market that pushed domestic prices up, rather than any real shortage. At the aggregate level, there is no sign of profiteering on the part of traders.

The price changes brought massive instability to farmers' enterprises. During the crisis the price of pesticides, for which no subsidy was available, increased threefold. Fertiliser subsidies were maintained until

November 1998, but shortages of fertiliser at subsidised prices were reported all over the archipelago (FAO/WFP, 1998; UNDP, 1999 and other reports). Seeds of improved crop varieties were also reported to be in short supply. In fact the entire rural distribution system for both inputs and outputs was severely disrupted by escalating demand coupled with a lack of credit and, in areas riven by violence, mounting insecurity. The government acted simultaneously to curb increases in the prices of outputs while allowing input prices to rise. At the same time, crop yields fell because of the low amounts of inputs applied and the poor climatic conditions. The result was that food crop farmers saw little increase in the profits from their labours, at least until the summer of 1998. Meanwhile, real off-farm incomes fell, as more and more people competed for job opportunities and anxious employers decided not to expand their businesses. The poorest sectors of society were, as always, hardest hit, especially those who did not own enough land to be self-sufficient and who had to sell their labour to other farmers or estate owners.

The price of rice rose sharply during the summer of 1998, but by this time the main rice cropping season was already over. Much of this price rise might have benefitted farmers in the following main season of 1999, but by then prices were already falling. Events such as these underscore the role of a floor price policy in reducing instability. Farmers who were reluctant to sell their harvests and who did not have to do so—in other words, the wealthier farmers—may have been able to benefit from the high prices of the 1998 summer months. Poor farmers will not have had this privilege. And, having sold their assets and borrowed to survive the crisis, they will find their future profitability severely constrained for several years to come.

Despite the need to protect the urban poor, the government tried throughout the crisis to encourage food crop production. In the first 5 months of 1998, BULOG increased the minimum prices at which it bought rice three times: from Rp 600 to Rp 700 and then Rp 1000 per kilogramme. It has been argued that the government should have increased the floor price by 40-50% to close the gap between the prices received by farmers and the import parity price. According to this argument, higher farm-gate prices would have increased farmers' incentives to produce more while reducing rice consumption in the longer term by encouraging households to consume other commodities. In this way the burden of rice self-sufficiency, and the challenge of achieving it, could have been reduced. In practice, whether a higher price increases rural welfare depends greatly on the degree to which farm producers are net sellers or net buyers of rice, and on the elasticity of supply and demand for this commodity in the market place.

During the summer of 1998, the government launched a special programme to encourage self-reliance and domestic food crop production. The programme, which provides subsidised credit for farm inputs and is being applied over a target area of 2.3 million hectares, is reported to have achieved good results in 1999.

In the autumn of 1998, the government announced that all remaining direct subsidies on fertilisers were to be removed and that rice prices would in future be determined largely by market forces. Its intervention would be restricted to guaranteeing a floor price which would, it was hoped, protect farmers from a fall in prices at harvest time. The floor price would be determined for each region instead of at national level, as previously.

Although government intervention in the food crop sector was maintained in 1998, the policy had already been rendered obsolete by events. Policies designed to maintain a price difference between a country's domestic market and the market in neighbouring countries can only be effective if they are enforced by powerful institutions, because producers and traders are tempted to make a quick profit through illegal exports and, if they think they will not be caught, will try to do so. With its reputation for corruption and nepotism, the Indonesian Government did not enjoy the confidence and financial support needed from international institutions in order to implement this policy. This is the real reason why, 9 months after the beginning of the crisis, the government was forced to liberalise the market. With the benefit of hindsight, we conclude that it might have been better to let prices rise from the beginning. This would have allowed farmers to improve their terms of trade considerably, preparing a better basis for economic recovery. The poor could still have been protected through non-market interventions.

How Javanese farmers fared

Javanese lowland farmers produce about 60% of Indonesia's staple food crops, including rice, maize, soybean and cassava. We will now use the results obtained from field surveys, input-output analysis and a simulation model to assess the impact of the price and policy changes on these farmers. The model, which was specially developed for this region (Gérard et al, 1999), allows users to distinguish climatic effects from those resulting from liberalisation. The latter are assumed to be the major determinants of future trends in food crop production, or at least the only predictable ones.

The agriculture of Java is suprisingly diverse. Altitude together with proximity to the sea are the main determinants of agro-climatic conditions and hence of the crops that may be grown. Water availability is the major constraint facing most farmers, influencing not only the number of cropping seasons possible during the year but also the crops grown and the yields achieved. A gulf separates farmers in the irrigated areas, where the Green Revolution was fully implemented, from those in rainfed areas, where conditions are far less predictable and the use of inputs is much risker. The average farm size of 0.5 hectare also masks great diversity, especially in the irrigated areas where larger farms have developed (Figure 9.6)[6].

Given this diversity, which greatly affects farmers' incomes, the crises not surprisingly had very different effects on individual farmers (Figure 9.7). These differences in turn have important implications for the future recovery of agriculture. Three major situations were identified:

- The high-potential irrigated area (with a high level of water control). Three different types of household were distinguished in this area: large landowners, with more than 5 hectares, small tenants, with around 1 hectare, and the landless.

  During the crisis, farmers in this area responded to climatic disturbances and price changes by producing more maize during the second and third seasons and more rice during the third season. They retained their usual rice crop during the first season. Despite the late arrival of the rains in 1997, most farmers managed to plant their second crop, whether rice, maize or soybean, in March, which approximates to the usual planting period. The high level of

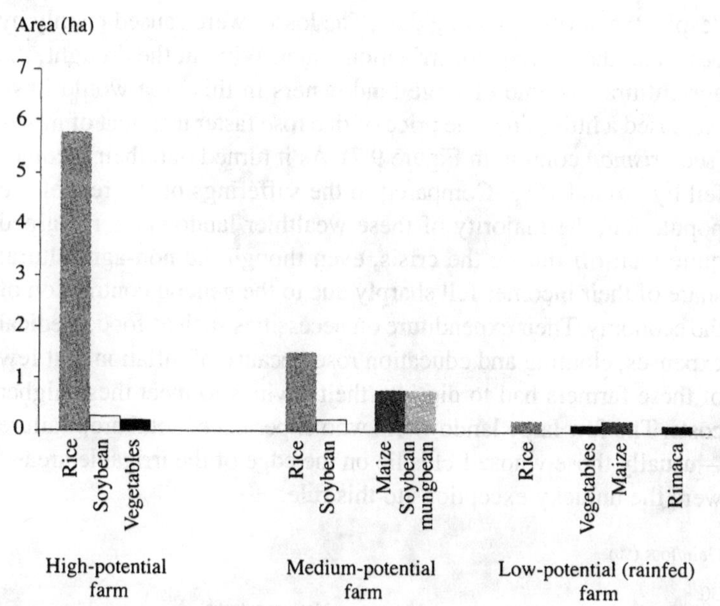

Figure 9.6 Farm size and crops grown on three farms in Java

mechanisation on these farms is an important factor contributing to the quick turn-around time between crops. Although most operations are still done manually, hand-tractors are widely used for land preparation. Usually, rice is not grown in these areas during the third season due to labour shortages and pest problems, but in 1998 farmers took advantage of a wetter than normal third season to plant rice. In so doing they were responding to government incentives as well as making up for the poor harvests obtained during the first season.

Most of the farmers in this area did not achieve their usual target yields of 5.5 tonnes per hectare, but very few of them experienced total crop failure or even serious losses. A survey in the Karawang plains, a major rice growing area near Jakarta, showed that the average yield of rice for the first season was around 4.8 tonnes per hectare, only about 15% lower than usual.

For farmers planting rice as their second crop, yields were far lower than average (about 2.1 tonnes per hectare in our sample), despite the normal planting date. The losses were caused mainly by pests and the shortage of irrigation water. Without the drought, the agricultural income of large landowners in this area would have increased a little, since the price of rice rose faster than that of inputs (see *krismon* column in Figure 9.7). As it turned out, their incomes fell by around 10%. Compared to the sufferings of the rest of the population, the majority of these wealthier landowners remained quite well-off during the crisis, even though the non-agricultural share of their incomes fell sharply due to the general contraction of the economy. Their expenditure on necessities such as food, medical expenses, clothing and education rose because of inflation, but few of these farmers had to dig into their savings to meet these higher costs. The few large landowners who experienced total crop failure —usually those whose fields lie on the edge of the irrigable area— were the unlucky exceptions to this rule.

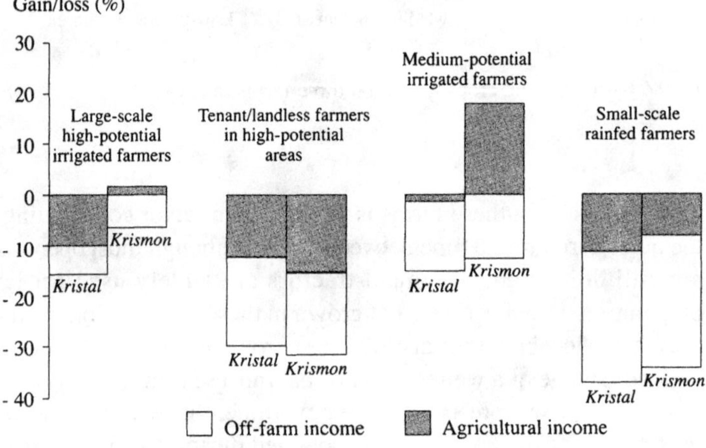

Figure 9.7 Gain or loss of income on farms of different types with and without climatic crisis, Java, 1998. *Krismon*: monetary crisis only. *Kristal*: total crisis, monetary + climatic. Both scenarios were derived using a model and verified in on-farm surveys conducted in January 1999.

The fate of small-time tenant farmers and the landless, although they lived in the same area, was much worse. For them, the fall in real wages from agriculture subtracted greatly from an already low income. With the opportunities for off-farm work also reduced, real incomes fell by about 30%. In 1998, while some tenant farmers still managed to retain some off-farm activities, others had to rely on agriculture alone. These farmers and labourers saw their incomes almost halved. They soon spent their meagre savings on meeting their essential needs. Many drastically altered their diets, reducing the amounts they ate and giving up virtually all forms of protein. For these people, the effects of the crisis lingered long after 1998: their lack of cash meant they were unable to rent sufficient land to feed their families in 1999.

Because non-agricultural jobs were increasingly difficult to find, wealthier farmers used more family labour and therefore hired fewer labourers, further reducing the opportunities for small-time tenants and the landless. At least until 2001, the situation of these people is likely to improve little (Figure 9.8). It will remain very difficult for as long as off-farm opportunities are curtailed by poor economic growth.

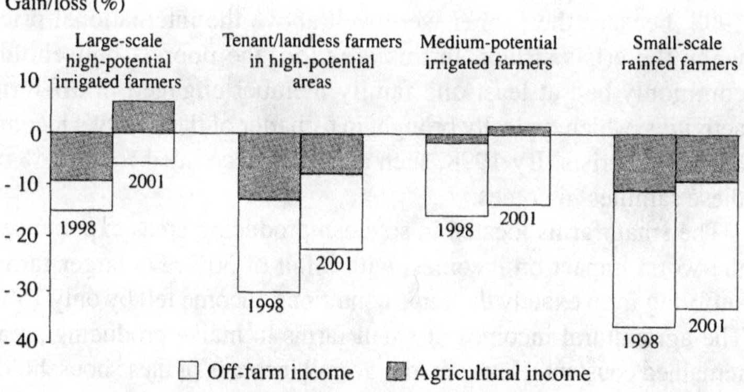

Figure 9.8 Predicted annual gain or loss of income on farms of different types, Java, 1998-2001.Both scenarios were derived using the model, on the basis of the following assumptions: 1. Wages having fallen by 30% in 1998, rise slightly in 1999, to 80% of their pre-crisis level, then grow at 2.5% *per annum* in real terms; 2. Off-farm employment, having fallen by 20% in 1998, does not grow at all until 2001.

- The medium-potential irrigated area (with less control over water). The impact of the crisis in this area ranged from moderate to severe.

The range in farm size, 0.6-1.2 hectare, is lower in this type of area than in areas with the highest potential. Nevertheless, the impact of the crisis on incomes varied greatly from farm to farm. As in high-potential areas, the larger landowners are net sellers of rice and can therefore use hired labour, which is supplied by the tenant farmers. Many farmers in this area grew soybean or maize instead of rice during the second season. In late 1997, because of sparse and late rainfall, farmers began the main rice season later than usual. They managed to reach yields that were close to normal but, due to a late harvest, most of them had to give up the idea of a second rice crop, which is usually squeezed in before the dry-season crop of soybean or maize. Switching to maize for the second crop allowed the larger farmers to increase their incomes, as yields reached their average level while prices also rose. But farmers who chose to switch to soybean had a much harder time, with yields greatly reduced by the crop's sensitivity to waterlogging and by low input use. Some farmers saw the crop completely destroyed by flooding during the autumn of 1998. Moreover, soybean prices rose less than maize prices in 1998, because the former were well above the international price when the crisis struck. In this area too, the poorest households commonly had at least one family member engaged in off-farm activities, which typically brought in a quarter of the family's income before the crisis. By 1998, such activities accounted for 0-15% of these families' incomes.

The small farms located in soybean producing areas experienced the worst impact on incomes, with a fall of 30%. On larger farms suffering from exactly the same conditions, income fell by only 15%. The agricultural incomes of small farms in maize producing areas remained constant. However, the overall incomes of these households fell by around 15%, again because of reduced off-farm income. For the smaller farmer, this fall in an already low income again meant eating into savings to meet essential needs. For larger maize farmers incomes rose by around 10%.

- The low-potential rainfed area. Farmers on rainfed land must wait for the monsoon to grow rice. Despite the drought, all of them managed to grow rice during the first season, but with lower yields than usual (less than 4 tonnes per hectare). Only the larger farms, 1-1.6 hectare, grew any rice during the second season, usually on

> only part of their land. Smaller farms of around 0.3 hectare, which form the vast majority, grew soybean, maize or cassava during the second season, but achieved very low yields.
>
> In response to the crisis, these farmers increased the practice of multiple cropping and diversified away from rice in order to minimise price uncertainties and avoid the risk of crop failure. They applied few inputs because of the price rises, a factor that goes a long way to explain their low yields. When farm size is small, a crisis of this magnitude makes it impossible to meet basic needs. Even before the crisis, farmers in rainfed areas relied heavily on off-farm activities, which accounted for about 40-60% of their incomes. Since the rise in unemployment, these activities have been sharply reduced. These farmers thus faced disaster, having lost around 50% of an income that was already low before the crisis.

In sum, both the climatic and the financial crises have had a negative impact on the income of farmers working in the food crop sector. Nevertheless, agricultural income has risen for those farmers with a sufficiently large area of land. Although this improvement is generally overshadowed by the fall in non-agricultural incomes, these farmers are better placed than many people in other sectors of the economy.

In contrast, small-scale farmers and landless labourers, with their greater reliance on off-farm incomes, are in great distress. By curbing increases in output prices while allowing the cost of inputs to rise, the government asked the country's resource-poor food producers to bear much of the burden of the financial crisis, in effect imposing what amounted to a heavy tax on them (Tabor et al, 1999). In the Javanese lowlands, about 10 million people were severely affected. Forced to sell their assets and increase their borrowing, many smaller farmers face extremely difficult conditions for several years to come. Just one more poor harvest caused by bad weather could force many of those in a weaker position to give up farming and migrate to an urban area.

That said, the overall situation has somewhat improved now that food prices have been allowed to rise. Provided they do not fall again too much at harvest time, profitability has recovered towards its pre-crisis levels. In the longer term, then, food crop production should revert to the gradual upward trend it followed in the pre-crisis years (Figure 9.9).

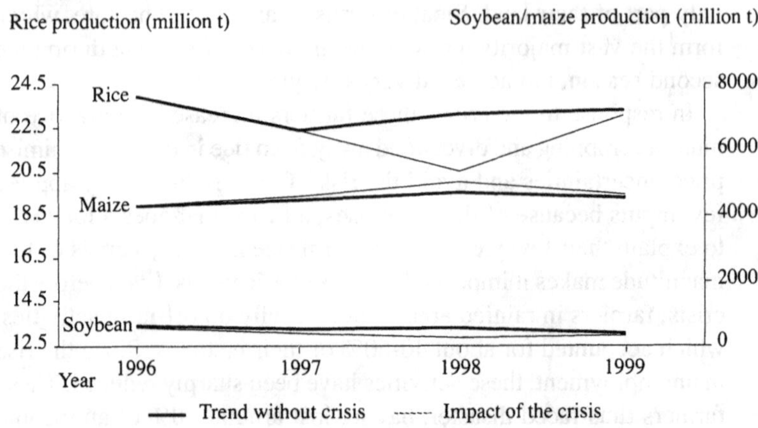

Figure 9.9 Trends in production of basic food staples in Indonesia, with and without the crisis, 1996-99

Conclusions

Indonesia's 1998 food crisis was caused by the huge rise in food prices that occurred when the value of the country's currency fell at a time when massive imports of food were necessary. It was not caused by a decrease in food availability.

Food prices rose approximately threefold, pushing real wages down. At the same time, unemployment increased. The impact was felt by a high proportion of the population, and especially by the poor. However, the poor—resilent as ever—adopted various strategies for coping, which allowed all but the very weakest to survive.

The crisis raises the issue of how the burden of macro-economic adjustment should be shared. When currencies such as the rupiah depreciate, governments are encouraged, as Indonesia was, to apply policies that will reduce external debt and restore investors' confidence. These policies include cutting public expenditure, increasing the cost of borrowing, and so on. At the same time, the rising cost of imports makes life extremely difficult for small businesses, which simultaneously face rising costs, falling demand and reduced liquidity. The countries that implement these policies tend to fall into a deep economic crisis, of just the kind experienced by Indonesia in 1998. Despite the best efforts of the World Bank and other aid agencies, the poor pay the price of these policies, particularly during the adjustment period and sometimes for a long time after it. The need to protect the urban poor from the rise in staple food prices was recognised early in the crisis. As the World Bank (1998) put it, "As costly as it appears to be, the rice price subsidy is probably the most efficient among generalized commodity subsidies for targeting the poor. This makes the effectiveness of BULOG especially important". The government struggled to keep rice affordable by releasing stocks and directing sales into the domestic market. In addition, it implemented a special distribution programme to help the needy. Food subsidies contributed greatly to the government's budget deficit, which amounted to around 8.5% of GDP in 1998. Despite all these efforts, the effects of the crisis on human nutrition were terrible. However, it is worth noting that, with inflation now firmly under control, monetary policy has, with the backing of the IMF, recently become more expansionist, with a lower interest rate and fiscal measures designed to protect the poorest (Severino, 1999).

Besides exacerbating poverty, the crisis has had a negative impact on nutrition, health care and education. Only renewed growth in employment can improve life for the vast majority of Indonesia's people. The one bright spot is that, with the fall in real wages, the high potential for profit should encourage foreign investment to return to Indonesia, provided the country regains political stability.

Was Indonesia's past economic performance so poor as to justify the disastrous fall in incomes experienced by the majority of Indonesians, and especially by those on middle to low incomes? Or did the market overreact and, in so doing, transfer the burden of the losses in the financial sector to the rest of society? Whatever the case, taxes on the international movement of capital have been proposed as one way of attenuating or even preventing financial crises of the kind that triggered Indonesia's sufferings. The funds collected could be used to lighten the burden of financial adjustment and avoid crushing the poor with it.

The future of food production in Indonesia may not have been as adversely affected by the 1997-98 crisis as might at first be supposed. Though the food crop sector suffered, agriculture as a whole was not as badly damaged as other sectors of the economy. Food crop farmers stand to benefit from improved terms of trade in 1999. However, the uncertainties surrounding the sector make predicting its future prone to more than the usual degree of error attaching to such exercises. Although most of the larger landowners located in the irrigated areas managed to maintain their agricultural incomes or even improve them slightly during the crisis, several million farmers, especially the smaller or landless ones and those in the rainfed areas, had to sell their assets and borrow cash in order to meet their immediate needs. Their increased indebtedness will take a long time to overcome, burdening them greatly while the rest of the sector recovers. Some, perhaps many, may have to leave agriculture altogether in the medium to longer term. Clearly, the crisis has already increased inequity in the sector. By forcing the poorest to migrate to the cities, it may also radically alter the structure of farming. However, this scenario is unlikely to depress aggregate production; it may even increase it, as the larger farms that remain invest and become more efficient. Food security will continue to depend mainly on the purchasing power of consumers, which should gradually rise as economic recovery gets under way.

Analysis of Indonesia's food crisis shows that, although the country and the international community managed to avoid mass starvation, food price increases nonetheless caused considerable hardship among the poor, including widespread malnutrition and, in some areas, famine. The fact that food increased in price despite government intervention demonstrates that trying to buck the market—difficult under the best of conditions—is well-nigh impossible for cash-strapped governments facing economic, political and social melt-down. This raises the question of what institutions and interventions might have served Indonesia better and whether these can be developed for future use in such situations.

References

Amang, B., Soetrisno, N. and Sapuan. 1996. Can Indonesia feed itself ? Paper presented at the Second Conference of the Asian Society of Agricultural Economists, 6-9 August 1996, Bali, Indonesia.

Booth, A. 1988. *Agricultural Development in Indonesia*. Allen and Unwin, Sydney, Australia.

CBS (Central Bureau of Statistics). Website: http://www.cbs.go.id

CGPRT (Regional Coordination Centre for Research and Development of Coarse Grains, Pulses, Roots and Tuber Crops in the Humid Tropics of Asia and the Pacific). 1992. Soybean Yield Gap Analysis Project (SYGAP), Final Report. Bogor, Indonesia.

FAO/WFP (UN Food and Agriculture Organization/World Food Programme). 1998. Crop and food supply assessment mission to Indonesia. *Journal of Humanitarian Assistance*. Website: http://www.jha.sps.cam.ac.uk/b/b127.pdf

Gérard, F., Erwidodo, I. and Marty. 1999. Evaluation of the impact of trade liberalization on food crop production and farm income in lowland Java, Indonesia. In: Peters, G.H. and von Braun, J. (eds), *Food Security, Diversification and Resource Management: Refocussing the Role of Agriculture*. Ashgate, Hants, UK.

Gérard, F., Marty, I., Lançon, F. and Versapuech, M. 1998. Measuring the Effects of Trade Liberalization: Multilevel Analysis Tool for Agriculture. Working Paper No. 30. Regional Coordination Centre for Research and Development of Coarse Grains, Pulses, Roots and Tuber Crops in the Humid Tropics of Asia and the Pacific (CGPRT), Bogor, Indonesia.

Gérard, F. and Versapuech, M. 1997. Impact of policy on consumption and employment in Java, Indonesia. In: Gérard, F. (ed.), A Tool for Measuring Policy Impact in Rural Areas: The Multilevel Analysis Tool for Agriculture (MATA). CIRAD and Regional Coordination Centre for Research and Development of Coarse Grains, Pulses, Roots and Tuber Crops in the Humid Tropics of Asia and the Pacific (CGPRT), Bangkok, Malaysia.

ILO/UNDP (International Labour Organisation/United Nations Development Programme). 1998. Employment Challenges of the Indonesian Economic Crisis. ILO, Jakarta, Indonesia.

ILO (International Labour Organisation). 1999. Indonesia's Crisis and Recovery: The Myths and Reality. Occasional Discussion Paper Series No. 1. Jakarta, Indonesia.

Jellinek and Rustanto. 1999. Survival Strategies of the Javanese during the Economic Crisis. World Bank, Jakarta, Indonesia.

Rosegrant, M.W., Kasryno, F. L. A., Gonzales, C., Rasahan and Saefudin, Y. 1987. Price and Investment Polices in the Indonesian Food Crop Sector. International Food Policy Research Institute (IFPRI) and Center for Agro-Economic Research, Washington DC, USA and Bogor, Indonesia.

Severino, J.M. 1999. Asia at the crossroads: An update. Notes prepared for a presentation to the World Bank Board of Executive Directors, 11 February 1999, Washington DC, USA.

Tabor, S.R., Dillon, H.S. and Husein Sawit, M. 1999. Understanding the 1998 food crisis: Supply, demand or policy failure? Paper presented at the International Seminar on the Agricultural Sector During the Turbulence of Economic Crisis: Lessons and Future Directions, 25-27 February 1999, Center for Agro-Socioeconomic Research, Agency for Agricultural Research and Development, Ministry of Agriculture, Bogor, Indonesia.

Timmer, P. 1989. Indonesia: Transition from food importer to exporter. In: Sicular, T. (ed.), *Food Price Policy in Asia: A Comparative Study*. Cornell University Press, Ithaca, USA.

Timmer, P. 1998. Will the Asian financial crisis jeopardize future food security in the region? *2020 Views*: June 1998. International Food Policy Research Institute (IFPRI), Washington DC, USA.

USDA (United States Department of Agriculture). 1998. Foreign Agricultural Service, Jakarta. Website: http://www.fas.usda.gov

USDA (United States Department of Agriculture). 1999. Foreign Agricultural Service, Jakarta. Website: http://www.fas.usda.gov

World Bank. 1996. Indonesia: Dimensions of Growth. Washington DC, USA.

World Bank. 1998. Indonesia in Crisis: A Macroeconomic Update. Washington DC, USA.

Acknowledgements

The authors are grateful to Marie de Lattre-Gasquet, Michel Griffon and Marie-Gabrielle Piketty for their useful comments on previous versions of this chapter, to Marie-France Bellet and Françoise Réolon for their kind and efficient help in the search for references, and to Valérie Hourmant for typing the references.

Notes

1 The coefficient of variation of domestic prices was around half that of international prices.

2 That is, the price farmers would have received if world market prices were fully transmitted to the domestic market.

3 There is usually not enough water to grow rice at this time of the year, even in the high-potential irrigated areas. A third rice crop was in any case strongly discouraged by the government for reasons of pest control. In 1998, however, rainfall was plentiful during the dry season. As a result rice production in May-August of this year increased by 2% over the 1996 level, while production in September-December rose by 19%.

4 Inflated prices were also recorded for maize, soybean and cassava, the levels of which stood 124%, 187% and 174% higher than in 1996 respectively.

5 Breman (1998) underscores the limited capacity of the rural areas to absorb a large influx of urban people.

6 Nine different types of farm were found in the irrigated lowlands alone (Gérard et al, 1999).

Chapter 10

From El Niño to *Krismon*: How Rice Farmers in Java Coped with a Multiple Crisis

Robin Bourgeois and Anne Gouyon

This chapter is a preliminary analysis of the impact of the *krismon* on food crop production in Indonesia. It focusses on irrigated rice farming in Java during the period from July 1997 to the end of 1998. Javanese rice production makes up 55% of national output of this crop, making it of prime importance in the Indonesian agricultural economy (FAO, 1998a).

Using a field survey, newspaper articles, official reports and other published materials, we address the following questions:

- What can be learned from the experiences of rice farmers about the effects of the *krismon* on agriculture?
- Did rice farming benefit from the crisis and can it help pull the national economy out of recession?
- What can policy makers and researchers do to enable rice production to fulfil this role?

Our analysis is in four parts. The first section presents the study areas covered and the data collection methods used in the field survey, before examining the pre-crisis situation in these areas against the background of trends in the overall macro-economic, political and social environment. We pay special attention to the social heterogeneity of the rice sector, presenting a typology of farms based on land tenure, size of holding and income. The second section looks at the varying impacts of the crisis on rice farmers. Again, we put our analysis in perspective by viewing it against the background of overall macro-economic trends, especially those symptomatic of Indonesia's crisis. In the third section, we investigate the possible effects of the crisis on rice farmers in the future, presenting alternative scenarios based on different trends in prices. The last section presents our conclusions.

Rice Farming before the Crisis: A Sector in Decline

The survey

The data used in this chapter come mainly from a socio-economic survey of 400 farmers conducted in September and October 1998 in several of the main irrigated rice areas of West and East Java[1].

Open-ended interviews were conducted in two contrasting areas of West Java:

- Pantura: a flat, lowland area, highly specialised in rice produced on a modern irrigation system.
- Cianjur: a hill area with a more diverse production system including high-quality rice, other food crops and tree crops, using a traditional terraced irrigation system.

Four districts of East Java, representing different agro-ecological conditions, were also covered through open-ended interviews. They were:

- Lamongan and Bojonegoro, consisting mainly of lowland rice areas. Both modern and traditional irrigation systems are found here, together with some non-irrigated wetland fields.
- Ngawi, which is situated at a higher altitude and has a mixture of valley bottom and hillside production systems. This area also has both modern and terraced village irrigation and is well supplied with water. Like Cianjur, it produces high-quality traditional rice varieties grown for their taste and cooking qualities.
- Kediri, which also has a mixture of valley bottom and hillside areas. Agriculture here is diverse, with sugar cane and maize as the main crops. The area's mainly modern irrigation systems are well managed and maintained.

In addition, structured interviews using a questionnaire were conducted in the Pantura area of West Java and in all four districts of East Java. The sample included 16 villages in West Java, 12 of which had participated in Indonesia's Integrated Pest Management Training Program (IPM/TP), and 32 in East Java, 24 of which had participated in the IPM/TP. Interviewees were randomly selected from lists obtained from village officials and IPM/TP technicians. All these villages had access to good irrigation.

In all areas, farmers were asked to compare their financial situation in July 1997 with that of September 1998—in other words, before and during the crisis. The information we obtained on the sequence of events and particularly on the price changes experienced by farmers enabled us to analyse the changing fortunes of agriculture over this period.

One cautionary note: the sample is biased, in that a high proportion of sample farmers had participated in the IPM/TP. These farmers are more likely to be landowners and to have better access to inputs and advice from the extension service than other farmers. Nonetheless, the survey still covered the full range of farm types found in the survey villages.

Before the crisis: The Green Revolution falters

The situation of Javanese rice farmers before July 1997 illustrates the declining role of agriculture in the Indonesian economy.

Because agriculture grew more slowly than other sectors during the 1990s, farmers saw their real incomes fall during the first half of the decade (Table 10.1). Yield gains slowed down, with the result that returns to labour stood still. At the same time, with other sectors offering better incomes, landowners found it increasingly difficult to recruit labourers. Until the crisis, the incomes of landowners grew more slowly than those of urban households, while the income of agricultural labourers actually fell in real terms.

Farmers in our survey reported a massive exodus of young people from the villages during the 1990s. Most people aged 18-25 had sought work in Indonesia's urban areas, in the Middle East or in Malaysia[2]. A recent study of 120 agricultural workers in the Yogyakarta area of central Java indicated that only 7.5% were in the 20-29 age group, while 32.5%

—the largest group—were aged above 50 (EBRI, 1996). These older workers were less well educated, making them less likely to access productivity-increasing technology and information.

Farmers reacted to the shortage of labour by adopting labour-saving practices and technologies, including less labour-intensive rice planting methods (Naylor, 1992) and mechanised land preparation[3]. This increased inequity in the farming community, since not all farmers could afford the capital investment required, particularly for mechanisation (Nehen and Willis, 1985).

Table 10.1 Changes in monthly income by social category, Indonesia, 1975-93

	Year				
	1975	*1980*	*1985*	*1990*	*1993*
Farm labourer:					
Average income (Rp/*capita*)	40.1	103.8	247.4	438.4	502.2
Rate of increase (% per year)		21	19	12	5
Index compared to agricultural employee	1	1	1	1	1
Farmer/landowner (0.5 ha):					
Average income (Rp/*capita*)	43.3	136.4	237.7	566.5	782
Rate of increase (% per year)		26	12	19	11
Index compared to agricultural employee	1.08	1.31	0.96	1.29	1.56
Farmer/landowner (1 ha):					
Average income (Rp/*capita*)	84.8	201.5	567.9	1053.4	1483.1
Rate of increase (% per year)		19	23	13	12
Index compared to agricultural employee	1.96	1.94	2.30	2.40	2.95
Lower level urban household:					
Average income (Rp/*capita*)	97.8	292	554.1	830.4	1054.7
Rate of increase (% per year)		25	14	8	8
Index compared to agricultural employee	1.15	2.81	2.24	1.89	2.10
Higher level urban household:					
Average income (Rp/*capita*)	259.7	548	906.6	1882.2	3105.7
Rate of increase (% per year)		16	11	16	18
Index compared to agricultural employee	6.48	5.28	3.66	4.29	6.18

Source: CBS.

Farm typology and equity

Table 10.2 and Figure 10.1 show a classification of the farmers in our sample according to the size of their land holdings. Size is highly variable, but 42% of farmers cultivate less than 0.5 hectare per household. The variability is correlated with differences in access to land and in land tenure arrangements. Other things being equal, landowners tend to have higher incomes than share-croppers and tenant farmers, since they do not have to share their harvest or rent land. This is especially true in areas with less favourable agro-ecological conditions, where crop yields are low (Bourgeois, 1999).

Table 10.2 Classification of sample farmers by size of farm holding, Java, 1998

Size category (ha)	*No. of farmers in sample*	*Total area (ha)*	*% of sample population*	*% of sample area*
0.05-0.5	167	61.80	42	12
0.5-1	121	104.93	30	20
1-3	78	158.87	20	30
3-6	20	94.07	5	18
6+	12	106.88	3	20
All	398	526.55	100	100

To analyse the impact of the crisis in detail, we established a typology of farms based on variables such as province/district, number of cropping seasons, household size, area cultivated to rice, use of fertilisers and land tenure status. Of the 400 farmers covered, 395 could be grouped into six different categories. Where farm size was highly diverse, subcategories were added. The results are shown in Table 10.3.

This typology confirms the importance of land tenure and size of holding as determining factors in farm income. Location is also important, as this is strongly correlated with the distribution of farm size. Farms in the Pantura area tend to be larger and more specialised in rice production than those in the four districts of East Java. However, yields here are lower than in East Java, partly because soils are inherently less fertile and pest damage is greater and partly because farmers use lower amounts of fertiliser, in particular potash (KCl).

In sum, our analysis of rice farmers in West and East Java before the crisis reveals considerable diversity in farm size, accompanied by

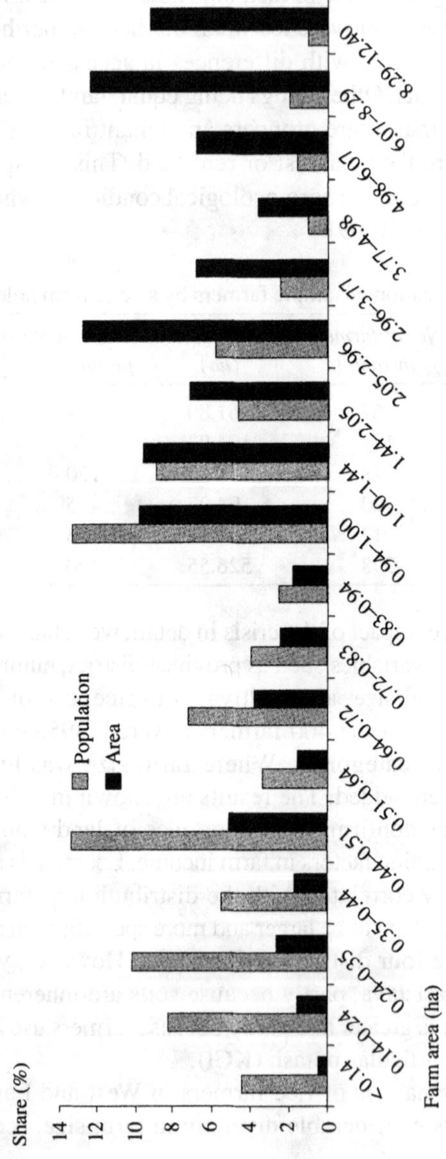

Figure 10.1 Share of sample farming households in total area cultivated and total population, Java, 1998

Table 10.3 Typology of rice farms in Java, 1998

Category and status	*Main region*	*% of sample*	*% of land*	*Characteristics*					
				Rice crops/ year	*Yield (kg/ha)*		*Household size (persons)*	*Cultivated area (ha)*	*Other activities/ inputs*
					Wet season	*First dry season*			
1 and 1b. Tenants	Pantura, East Java	14	9	3	Slightly above average		4	Category 1: 0.32 Category 1b: 0.92	1 or 2/may own a small rice plot
2. Large landowners	Pantura	13	41	2	5000	2700	< 3	4	Usually 0/often own hand tractor, high use of K, low use of N and P
3 and 3b. Small land owners	Pantura	26	18	2	3400	2300	< 3	Category 3: 0.71 Category 3b: 0.25	Some have external activities/low use of P and K
4 and 4b. Share-croppers	Pantura	8	7	2	Similar to category 3 but higher in wet season		< 3	Category 4: 1.1 Category 4b: 0.49	Mostly family labour
5. Highly productive owners	East Java	18	12	3	6100	4400	4	0.75	Typically 2 other farming activities + many off-farm activities/highest use of K
6 and 6b. Small owners	East Java	22	13	3	5400	3600	4.5	Category 6: 0.66 Category 6b: 0.23	No use of K, high use of P and N
7. Landless labourers	Not included in the survey, but this category remains the most numerous in the irrigated rice growing Javanese lowlands (CASER, 1993).								

low or zero growth in productivity and declining real incomes for small-scale and landless farmers. The next section discusses how the crisis affected rice farming in general, before analysing its impact on the different categories of farmers identified through our survey.

How Farmers Perceived the Crisis

A double crisis

While most Indonesians and outsiders define the crisis in economic terms, for farmers it started with freak weather conditions. In a normal year, rice farming in Java is characterised by two main growing seasons. The wet season extends from October to March and produces the largest harvest, while yields in the dry season, from April to August, tend to be lower. In areas with plentiful water, farmers can grow three crops a year, usually diversifying away from rice for the third crop.

In 1997 and 1998, this cropping pattern was severely disrupted by the drought associated with El Niño. Indonesia had already experienced several droughts of this nature over the past decade, especially in 1991 and 1994, but none of them matched the scale and severity of the 1997-98 drought. According to FAO (1998a), the 1997-98 drought was remarkable not just because of its severity, but because it had two distinct phases.

The first phase began around March 1997 and reached its peak in July and August of that year. During this phase, Java was not greatly affected, but there were forest fires and widespread crop losses in Eastern Indonesia, particularly in Kalimantan. The second phase started in the second half of 1997 and lasted until March 1998. The onset of the main rainy season was delayed by 1-2 months throughout the country during this period.

As a result of the delay, planting in Java was late and much reduced in area, leading to losses in production that were all the more serious for occurring during the main cropping season, when high yields can normally be relied on. Farmers prayed that good rains would follow, ensuring good harvests from the second rice season. But when heavy rains finally occurred in 1998, they gave disappointing results.

The main reason was pest attacks. The second and third seasons of 1998 were marred across Java by severe outbreaks of pests, which proliferated in the wet conditions that marked the end of the drought. One of the worst offenders was the brown plant hopper (BPH), which had become common since the start of the Green Revolution, but several new pests, relatively unknown previously, also became serious, including the black bug. Because of pests, the annual production forecast for 1998 was revised downwards from 47.5 million tonnes in April (already 11% below the target) to 45.3 million tonnes in October (FAO, 1998a and b).

Pest outbreaks are determined by a complex of biotic and abiotic factors, so we can only hypothesize as to why they were so severe in this case. On the basis of available reports on the subject, farmers' accounts and our own field observations, we believe the severity of the 1998 infestations can be explained largely by the following circumstances:

- The weather disrupted cropping patterns and planting dates in the 1997-98 main season. Farmers normally limit pest damage by avoiding planting rice more than twice in succession in the same place and by planting at the same time as other farmers in the vicinity. In 1998 many farmers planted rice three times in succession and on different dates from their neighbours (Ministry of Agriculture, 1998).
- Heavy rains brought dense cloud cover and high humidity in mid-year—conditions in which pests flourish (FAO, 1998b).
- The economic crisis raised the prices of KCl fertilisers and pesticides, discouraging farmers from using these inputs (FAO, 1998b).

The latter point illustrates the interactions between the ecological and the economic crises. Between September 1997 and September 1998, the price of urea (N) and phosphate (P) fertilisers remained largely unchanged in Java, owing to heavy government subsidies. But the farm-gate price of KCl more than doubled over this period (Table 10.4). Most farmers had to reduce their inputs of this fertiliser and some stopped using it altogether. This had a significant impact on yields, both directly, as K is needed for grain filling, and indirectly, as K deficiency lowers resistance to pest attacks. Conventional agronomic wisdom, quoted by some of the farmers in our survey, estimates a 40% yield difference

Table 10.4 Breakdown of costs of 1 hectare of irrigated lowland rice production, Java, 1998

Item			*Price*	
	Quantity	*Range*	*September 1997*	*September 1998*
Seeds (kg):				
IR-64	35		1300	3300
Fertilisers:				
Urea	260	0-715	450	500
KCl	30	0-300	850	1700
SP36	130	0-350	650	700
Pesticides:				
Carbofuran (kg)	25	0-40	800	1700
Buprofezin/Fipronil (3 x 1 litre)	3	0-8	12 000	35 000
Herbicides (bag):				
Alli	5	5	1500	4000
Mechanised labour:				
Soil preparation (hand tractor)	1	0-1	140 000	210 000
Manual labour:				
Bund preparation (person-days)	5	5	8000	9000/12 000
Planting (person-days)	30	15-40	5500	9000/12 000
Fertiliser application	8	5-15	5500	9000/12 000
Weeding (x2, person-days)	50	25-80	3500	6000/7000
Spraying (x4, person-days)	8	0-20	5500	9000/12 000
Bund maintenance (person-days)	5		5500	9000/12 000
Harvesting (kg)*	1/10	1/5-1/10	550	1500
Taxes and levies:				
Iuran desa (Rp/ha)	100 000.00		100 000.00	100 000.00
PBB (Rp/ha)	75 000.00		75 000.00	75 000.00
Iuran mitra cai (kg/*gabah*)	25	25	25	25
Other costs:				
Bags (40 kg)			500	800
Drying (person-days)	2	2	10 000	10 000
Share-cropping (% harvest)	50	50		
Rice yield and price:				
Wet season 1997-98 (kg/*gabah*)	4 850.00	0-9800	550	550
Second season 1998 (kg/*gabah*)	3000	0-7840		1500

* One-tenth of harvest.

between a crop with and without the recommended application of KCl.

The distribution of imported pesticides was also disrupted by the crisis. To accumulate the capital they needed, distributors allowed themselves to run out of old stocks before placing new orders. New stocks were priced three to five times higher than in July 1997. Our survey suggested that some distributors sold faked or adulterated pesticides, further compounding farmers' pest problems[4]. Some farmers resorted to alternative, homespun control methods, such as applying diesel oil (*solar*), petroleum (*minyak tanah*) or even washing powder to their fields.

In sum, the combined effect of continuous rice cropping, staggered planting dates, high humidity in the dry season and reduced pesticide and potassium applications allowed insect populations to rise to levels that not only caused severe losses in 1998 but will also threaten future rice crops in Java. Proper monitoring and prompt action by IPM experts will be needed for several years to come.

Changes in price ratios

The *krismon* led to high inflation in 1998. Table 10.4 shows changes in the estimated prices of rice farming inputs and outputs over the year. The higher cost of inputs was offset by an almost threefold rise in the price of rice. This corroborates what some of the farmers in our survey said, namely that the crisis had benefitted them, resulting in higher net incomes. However, the table should be interpreted cautiously since, as we shall see, the crisis affected each category of farmers differently. Furthermore, our survey indicated that the price of inputs rose before the price of rice, with consequent negative effects on farmers' cash flow. Poorer farmers, who had to sell rice while prices were still low in order to buy highly priced inputs for the next season, suffered a loss.

Data on inflation should also be interpreted cautiously. Before the crisis, when inflation was about 10%, different methods of calculating it made little difference to the end result and most experts accepted the government's consumer price index as a reasonable guide. The crisis brought not only a sharp general rise in inflation but also significant differences in the rate of increase for each category of goods and services, depending on whether they are imported or produced domestically, the degree to which they are traded and how their supply was affected by the weather and other factors. Hence, different methods of calculating the prices indicated in the table could alter the results.

Our calculation was based on the official prices of the 12 main items in the rural consumer's shopping basket, according to the CBS. A weighted price index was arrived at by multiplying the price change for each commodity by its share in the expenditures of each population class before the crisis. Comparing these figures with the general consumer price index (CPI) over the same periods (Table 10.5), we concluded that:

- Inflation has hit the rural population of Indonesia more severely than the CPI indicates. The inflation rate we calculated for the rural population as a whole exceeds the official rate by 20-53%.
- Inflation has hit the poor hardest. People in low-expenditure classes consume a higher percentage of goods whose prices have risen faster than the official inflation rate than do people in high-expenditure classes. These goods include rice and other staple foods, the price elasticity of demand for which is lower than for non-essential items.

We therefore revised our calculations, using the following inflation rates:

- From January 1997 to September 1997: 12%
- From January 1997 to January 1998: 30%
- From January 1997 to September 1998: 97-111%, depending on expenditure class.

Impact on equity

As already seen, Table 10.4 shows the costs of producing 1 hectare of irrigated lowland rice, based on our survey data. We calculated different cost structures for each farm category, based on the typology shown in Table 10.3 (Bourgeois, 1999). To compare net incomes in 1997 and 1998, we first used an inflation rate of 97%, then adjusted the results using our own calculation based on expenditure class. Net income was calculated for each farm category according to its consumption of inputs, the size of

Table 10.5 Comparison of the rise in the cost of living by expenditure class with the general consumer price index for 44 cities in Indonesia, 1996-98

Time/place	*General CPI**	*Monthly expenditure class ('000 Rp/capita)*								*ll**
		< 15	*15-20*	*20-30*	*30-40*	*40-60*	*60-80*	*80-100*	*100-150*	
Actual increase in cost of living (%):										
44 cities/November 1998/96	96	144	142	136	132	127	122	118	113	124
Surabaya/November 1998/96	97	128	128	128	128	126	124.	122	119	124
Malang/November 1998/96	117	165	164	158	154	150	146	142	138	147
Bandung/November 1998/96	88	158	157	150	146	140	134	128	122	135
Cirebon/November 1998/96	95	142	137	130	124	118	112	108	104	115
44 cities/November 1998/December 1996	75	99	98	96	94	92	90	87	85	90
Difference between actual increase and official inflation rate (44 cities) (%):										
44 cities/November 1998/96	0	50	48	42	37	32	27	22	18	29
Surabaya/November 1998/96	1	33	34	33	33	32	30	27	24	29
Malang/November 1998/96	22	72	71	65	61	56	52	47	44	53
Bandung/November 1998/96	– 8	65	63	56	52	46	40	33	27	41
Cirebon/November 1998/96	– 1	48	43	35	29	23	17	12	8	20
44 cities/November 1998/December 1996	– 22	32	31	27	25	22	19	16	13	20

* As calculated by the CBS. ** All expenditure classes, including Rp 150 000/month and above.

its land holding, the average yields obtained and the prices at harvest time.

Labour requirements are similar to those found in other lowland rice cropping areas (Suryana dan Kariyasa, 1997; Naylor, 1992). The only exception is that hand-tractors are used for land preparation, reducing the requirement compared to that when this task is done manually. Before the crisis, wages[5] were estimated at Rp 3500 for half a day's work and Rp 5500 for a full day's work. In September 1998, they reached Rp 7000 and Rp 12 000 respectively in West Java (Pantura) and Rp 6000 and Rp 10 000 in East Java.

The official floor price of paddy rice (unhusked and undried) was Rp 1000 per kilogramme in September 1998, but because of the shortage the farm-gate price offered by traders was Rp 1500 per kilogramme. By December the government had raised the floor price to this level. A year earlier, during the wet season of 1997-98, the floor price had stood at only Rp 550 per kilogramme. In the share-cropping systems typical of lowland areas, the rise in the price of rice effectively raised the costs of harvesting. From April 1998 onwards, farmers were obliged to increase the wages paid for other tasks to keep them on a par with those for harvesting.

These increases in farm labourers' wages probably resulted from two coinciding factors: the need for farmers to compete for labourers with other, better paid job opportunities, and pressure for at least nominal wage increases in the face of rising prices for basic commodities. Occurring at a time when other Indonesian industries were laying off millions of workers, this phenomenon is less strange than it at first appears. Recent studies indicate that, during the crisis, the informal economy, including small trades and crafts, prospered as factories laid off staff (Jellinek and Rustanto, 1999).

The other main factor influencing costs is the use of inputs. Fertilisers —mainly urea, superphosphate (SP36) and KCl—are used by nearly all rice farmers. Our survey found that the quantities applied by Pantura farmers in 1998 were very similar to pre-crisis levels of use (Hadnyana et al, 1990). Approximately two-thirds of farmers applied pesticides.

Table 10. 6 and Figure 10.2 summarise net incomes and changes in purchasing power for each category of farmer. Most obvious is the enormous difference in net income between category 2 (large landowners in the Pantura area) and the rest of the sample. In addition, changes in purchasing power show significant differences according to category. Tenants and share-croppers show a sharp decline in net income. The crisis has thus hit the poorest farmers hardest, widening the gap between rich and poor.

Table 10.6 Net incomes and percentage change in purchasing power by category of farmer, Java, 1997-98

Farmer category	*Net income (Rp)*				
	1997 (current)	*1997 (constant)*	*1998 (current)*	*1998 (constant, adjusted)*	*Change in purchasing power (%)*
1. Small tenant	57 105 600	53 805 657	59 922 667	35 046 857	- 35
1b. Tenant	86 277 600	80 963 532	51 934 767	39 063 386	- 52
2. Large owner, Pantura	1 112 050 000	1 039 784 821	1 265 335 000	712 347 240	- 31
3. Small owner, Pantura	17 146 450	109 543 111	148 620 750	76 356 369	-30
3b. Very small owner, Pantura	45 728 750	43 075 759	77 331 250	39 633 738	- 8
4. Share-cropper, Pantura	77 803 000	73 051 589	77 038 500	39 633 738	- 36
4b. Small share-cropper, Pantura	67 977 700	64 076 163	82 584 600	46 342 250	- 28
5. Highly productive owner, East Java	283 944 375	266 347 667	453 698 438	231 763 793	- 13
6. Small owner, East Java	179 787 300	169 301 079	304 748 400	160 406 249	- 5
6b. Very small owner, East Java	78 293 150	73 801 004	125 980 200	66 363 929	- 10
7. Landless labourer	72 000 000	68 142 857	108 000 000	42 667 509	- 37

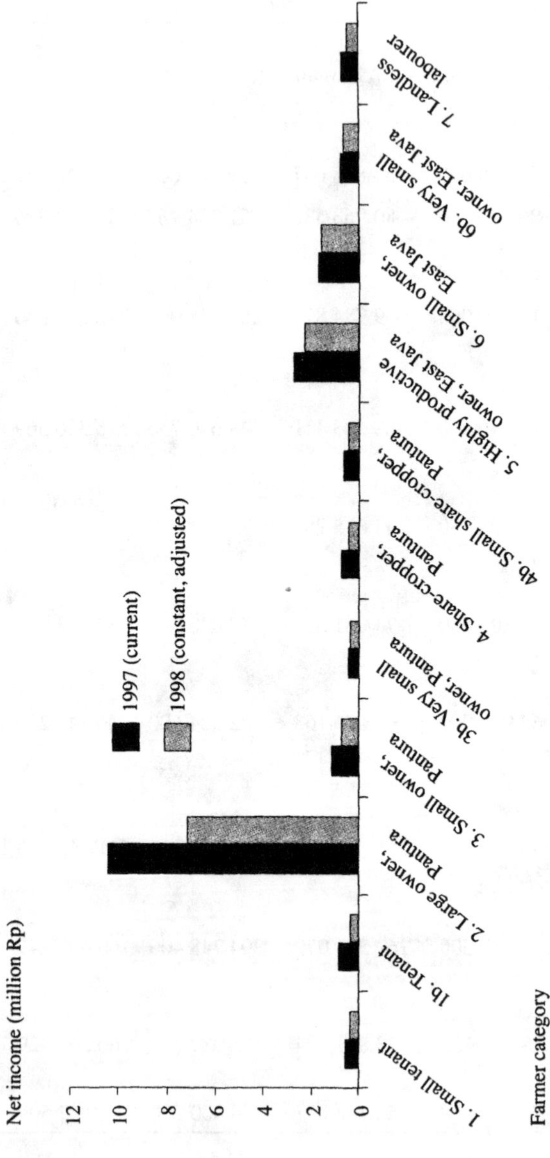

Figure 10.2 Net annual incomes from rice per category of rice farmer, Java, 1997-98

In the table, net income has been adjusted according to the expenditure class to which each farmer category belongs. The general decline in incomes is due to the combination of two factors:

- The producer price of rice paid was still low in early 1998, while inflation had already increased other prices by 30%.
- Although rice prices had risen by September 1998, the effect was counteracted by low yields and high inflation of 97-111%.

These farmers are highly unlikely to have been able to improve their management practices or invest in more inputs in order to increase rice yields. However, a shift into other crops is a possibility. This was observed in several of Indonesia's outer islands, including Sulawesi, where farmers moved into cocoa, and Sumatra, where shrimps and spices proved popular. In Java, however, these shifts are likely to have been limited due to farmers' lack of capital and the island's more difficult agro-ecological conditions. The poorer categories, especially landless labourers, had —and still have—an income barely above the official poverty line (according to CBS data). This means that they are only just surviving and in no position to start accumulating wealth. It also suggests that, contrary to some reports, people from urban areas are unlikely to have come to the rural areas during the crisis unless they were desperate.

Nevertheless, some farmers were able to benefit from the crisis by storing the 1998 wet season's harvest and selling it later at higher prices. Only the wealthier farmers were in a position to do this. Their relative wealth originated either from large cultivated area (category 2) or from high yields (category 5 and, to a lesser extent, category 6). These categories represent no more than 40-45% of the total sample population. And, given the bias of our sample group, the proportion is likely to be much lower when the whole rice farming population is considered.

Sales of rice surpluses in September 1998 brought in a potential additional income of Rp 13.5 million, 3 million and 1.8 million respectively for categories 2, 5 and 6. At the time of the survey, it was too early to estimate the full impact of this additional income on spending patterns. The farmers who benefitted were adopting a "wait-and-see" attitude, preferring to keep their surplus income as a hedge against possible future rises in the prices of inputs and consumer goods.

These calculations indicate that small changes in assumptions with regard to prices can lead to very different conclusions as to what happened to farmers' net incomes. The prices of different items such as labour, rice, physical inputs and consumer goods changed greatly at different times during the crisis. In addition, the overall impact of price changes on farmers differed according to their income and the items they bought. It is clear that, in future situations of this kind, calculations of income should take these differences into account and should therefore be based on real information on prices obtained from field surveys, not on official statistics.

Future Scenarios

Assumptions and unknowns

In the light of recent changes in the government's economic policy, we will now explore three different scenarios for the future of food production in Indonesia, analysing the impact of each on farmers' incomes. The scenarios are based on the following assumptions:

- Since most farmers are not in a position to store rice and sell it later at a better price, they will face cash flow problems, especially at planting time. This will affect their consumption of inputs, especially pesticides and potash. These farmers risk seeing their yields fall to levels similar to those of the second season of 1998. If this happens in the Pantura area the effect on food supplies could be particularly severe, since this area normally produces about 20% of Indonesia's rice.
- If supplies of fertilisers and pesticides continue to be disrupted, as seems likely for as long as traders lack capital to restock, even farmers who can afford to buy inputs may be forced to cut back on them.
- Price increase will average 142% between December 1999 and September 1997. This figure is kept constant for the three scenarios.

The scenarios also reflect the question-marks that surround government food policy. The government's decision to increase the floor price of rice in December 1998 from Rp 1000 to Rp 1500 per kilogramme brought this price into line with the real price paid to farmers in September 1998, as revealed in our survey data. Higher rice prices in the short term will certainly ease the situation of farmers and provide them with incentives to grow rice. However, they will also hit not only urban consumers but also the most vulnerable segment of the rural population, landless labourers. In the longer term, the situation could once again become very difficult for Javanese rice farmers. International prices are low at the moment due to surpluses from Thailand and Vietnam. Massive imports of cheap rice would benefit poor consumers, provided price reductions are passed on to the consumer, but they would also put pressure on the farm-gate price of domestically produced rice. This could lead to the exact opposite of the trend observed during the crisis, since farmers' net incomes would fall while their costs remained the same.

Here again, the crucial point is the quantity and quality of inputs available. Rising floor prices will not lead to increased production unless farmers have access to inputs. In certain areas, producers may be able to switch to other more lucrative crops for the second growing season, as has already been observed in some East Javan villages[6]. However, in areas such as Pantura, where it is difficult or impossible to find alternatives to rice, farmers will remain extremely vulnerable to price changes.

Scenarios

Our three scenarios are as follows:

- Scenario 1, optimistic: good prices, good weather. Government intervention succeeds in maintaining the price of paddy at or above Rp 1500 per kilogramme. Fertilisers are available at reasonable prices (urea at Rp 1200 per kilogramme, SP36 at Rp 1200 per kilogramme and KCl at Rp 1700 per kilogramme). Adequate amounts of fertiliser and pesticide are applied to control pests, and good weather conditions lead to two good harvests, with yields returning to 1997 levels (Figure 10.3 and Table 10.7).

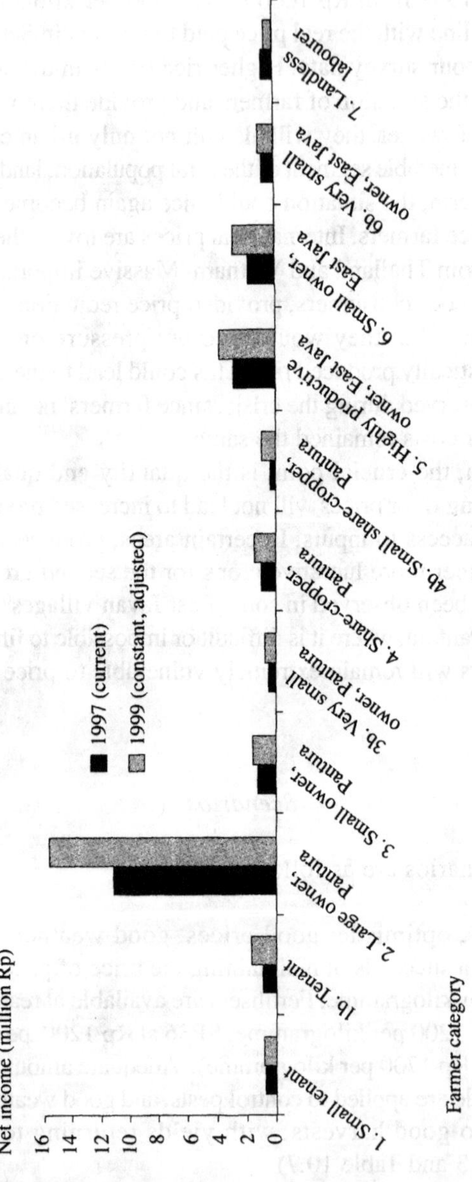

Figure 10.3 Net annual income from rice by category of rice farmer under Scenario 1, 1997-99

Table 10.7 Net annual income and percentage change in purchasing power by category of farmer under Scenario 1, Java, 1997-99

Farmer category	*Net income (Rp)*				
	1997 (current)	*1997 (constant)*	*1999 (current)*	*1999 (constant, adjusted)*	*Change in purchasing power (%)*
1. Small tenant	571 056	538 057	1 926 144	767 755	43
1b. Tenant	862 776	809 635	4 008 624	1 626 877	101
2. Large owner, Pantura	11 120 500	10 397 848	37 180 000	15 440 199	48
3. Small owner, Pantura	1 171 465	1 095 431	3 820 510	1 550 532	42
3b. Very small owner, Pantura	457 288	430 758	1 675 250	667 750	55
4. Share-cropper, Pantura	805 255	756 282	3 658 160	1 484 643	96
4b. Small share-cropper, Pantura	358 705	336 889	2 276 344	915 518	172
5. Highly productive owner East Java	2 839 444	2 663 477	4 821 675	3 874 486	45
6. Small owner, East Java	1 797 873	1 693 011	6 868 884	2 852 527	68
6b. Very small owner, East Java	782 932	738 010	2 632 902	1 058 921	43
7. Landless labourer*	720 000	681 429	1 440 000	568 900	- 17

* Based on 72 working days per season for two cropping seasons at Rp 5000/day in 1997 and Rp 10 000/day in 1999. Meals included in 1997.

Figure 10.4 Net annual income from rice by category of rice farmer under Scenario 2, 1997-99

Table 10.8 Net annual income and percentage change in purchasing power by category of farmer under Scenario 2, Java, 1997-99

Farmer category	*Net income (Rp)*				
	1997 (current)	*1997 (constant)*	*1999 (current)*	*1999 (constant, adjusted)*	*Change in purchasing power (%)*
1. Small tenant	571 056	538 057	970 731	380 142	- 29
1b. Tenant	862 776	809 635	1 255 601	496 050	
2. Large owner, Pantura	11 120 500	10 397 848	19 770 840	8 210 482	- 21
3. Small owner, Pantura	1 171 465	1 095 431	1 744 669	695 420	- 37
3b. Very small owner, Pantura	457 288	430 758	944 320	369 799	- 14
4. Share-cropper, Pantura	778 030	730 516	1 161 204	458 756	- 37
4b. Small share-cropper, Pantura	679 777	640 762	1 323 608	522 917	- 18
5. Highly productive owner, East Java	2 839 444	2 663 477	2 496 173	2 187 117	- 18
6. Small owner, East Java	1 797 873	1 693 011	3 796 373	1 540 736	- 9
6b. Very small owner, East Java	782 932	738 010	1 562 178	622 680	- 16
7. Landless labourer*	720 000	681 429	1 224 000	483 565	- 29

* Based on 72 working days per season for two cropping seasons at Rp 5000/day in 1997 and Rp 10 000/day in 1999. Meals included in 1997.

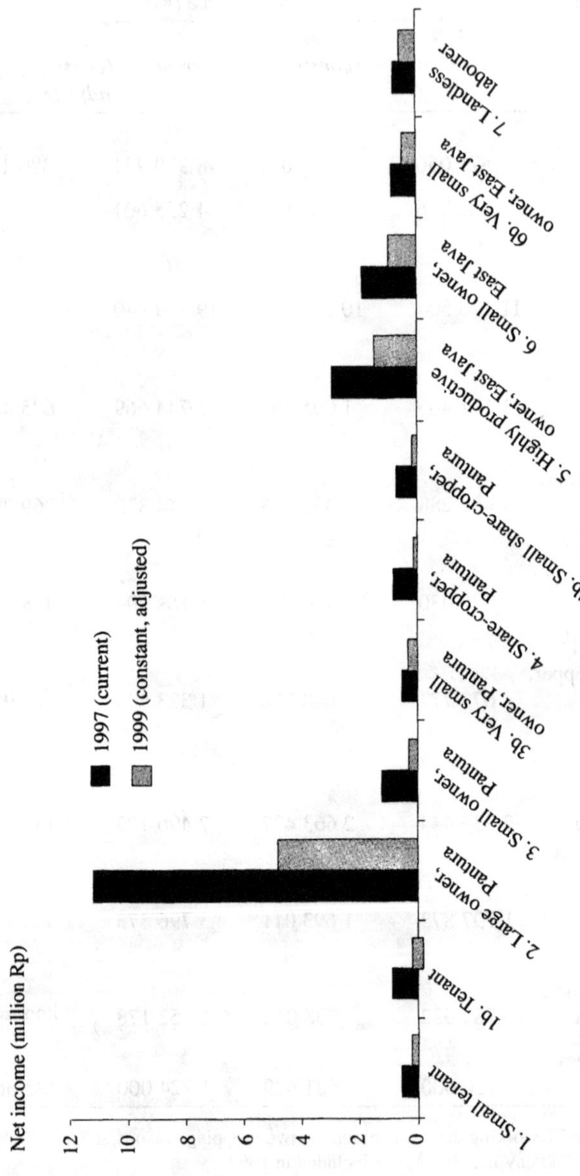

Figure 10.5 Net annual income from rice by category of rice farmer under Scenario 3, 1997-99

Table 10.9 Net annual income and percentage change in purchasing power by category of farmer under Scenario 3, Java, 1997-99

Farmer category	*Net income (Rp)*				
	1997 (current)	*1997 (constant)*	*1999 (current)*	*1999 (constant, adjusted)*	*Change in purchasing power (%)*
1. Small tenan	571 056	538 057	393 173	153 296	- 72
1b. Tenant	862 776	809 635	(413 157)	(161 087)	- 120
2. Large owner, Pantura	11 120 500	10 397 848	11 537 060	4 791 138	- 54
3. Small owner, Pantura	1 171 465	1 095 431	672 015	263 164	- 76
3b. Very small owner, Pantura	457 288	430 758	568 155	222 492	- 48
4. Share-cropper, Pantura	778 030	730 516	98 846	38 539	- 95
4b. Small share-cropper, Pantura	679 777	640 762	155 604	60 669	- 91
5. Highly productive owner, East Java	2 839 444	2 663 477	1 631 269	1 412 296	- 47
6. Small owner, East Java	1 797 873	1 693 011	2 229 097	896 516	- 47
6b. Very small owner, East Java	782 932	738 010	1 016 007	397 872	- 46
7. Landless labourer*	720 000	681 428,5714	1152 000	455120.1011	-33

* Based on 72 working days per season for two cropping seasons at Rp 5000/day in 1997 and Rp 10 000/day in 1999. Meals included in 1997.

- Scenario 2, moderate difficulties: good harvests, low prices. The farm-gate price of paddy cannot be maintained at its current level due to competition from imported rice at harvest time. It falls to Rp 1100 per kilogramme. Fertilisers are available at reasonable prices (urea at Rp 1200 per kilogramme, SP36 at Rp 1200 per kilogramme and KCl at Rp 1700 per kilogramme). Pests are controlled during the first season but not during the second season, when falling incomes reduce the use of inputs. Yields are equal to those of 1997 for the first season but decline by 15% for the second season. The lower yields and falling price of rice reduce the income of share-croppers by 15% (Figure 10.4 and Table 10.8).
- Scenario 3, extreme difficulties: crisis returns. The farm-gate price of rice cannot be maintained at its current level and falls to Rp 1000 per kilogramme. Fertilisers are not sufficiently available and their prices rise (urea at Rp 1700 per kilogramme, SP36 at Rp 1700 per kilogramme and KCl at Rp 2000 per kilogramme), with fake products infiltrating the market. Small-scale farmers reduce their consumption of both fertilisers and pesticides. Despite good weather, yields fall by 10% in the first season and by 25% in the second. Share-croppers' incomes fall by 20% (Figure 10.5 and Table 10.9).

Discussion

The three scenarios described above show that rice farmers' incomes are highly sensitive to price changes. Only in Scenario 1, where good yields combine with good farm-gate prices for farmers, is it possible for all farmers to see an improvement over 1997. Even tenants and share-croppers stand to benefit from this scenario. The only category who may not are landless labourers, who seem likely to experience a continuing decline in their incomes.

If the price of rice were to fall, the prospects for farmers would deteriorate. In Scenario 2, despite an increase in net income, the purchasing power of all categories of farmer would decline by around 30-50%. If, as in Scenario 3, the fall in the price of rice is accompanied by continuing input supply problems, large numbers of farmers would not even be able to produce enough rice for their own consumption. Tenants and share-croppers would be hardest hit. Paradoxically, although landless labourers would suffer more than in previous scenarios, they would nonetheless suffer less than the other categories.

Should Scenario 1 prevail, the rice economy in Indonesia would recover rapidly, compensating farmers for the losses of 1998. Scenario 2 would maintain the status quo, whereby the wealthier farmers would survive but the smaller and poorer would have to readjust by reducing their domestic consumption and/or turning to other crops. In this case shortages of rice would continue during 1999 and possibly into 2000. Scenario 3 could lead to a sharp fall in the income of many rice farmers, with severe economic and social consequences. Special measures are needed to prevent its occurrence, and these are discussed below.

Conclusions

Combining macro-economic and secondary data with farm-level survey data, our study has allowed us to test some hypotheses about the impact of Indonesia's crisis on food crop farmers and to examine in more detail some of the issues raised by the crisis. We draw the following conclusions.

Grounds for optimism

While the rise in the prices of inputs since January 1997 appears to have been more than offset by the rise in the price of rice, adverse weather conditions wiped out the potential gains for most farmers. Only wealthier farmers who owned large farms or had high yields were able to take advantage of the situation by storing rice and selling it when prices were at their peak.

Indonesia's rice farmers produce an essential commodity for the domestic market which may be considered an import substitute. Given the small size of the international market, shortages of rice in Indonesia could lead to higher international prices. The price elasticity of demand for rice is among the lowest of all products available on the domestic market. This is reflected in the difficulties encountered by the government in promoting alternatives to rice. Other food crops, such as maize and cassava, suffered less than rice as a result of the drought, and in some cases their production actually increased (FAO, 1998a and b). But these commodities are not accepted by consumers as replacements for rice. Should this taste for rice sustain farm-gate paddy prices at, say, Rp 1500 per kilogramme, farmers can be expected to recover relatively quickly from the crisis.

What happens will depend greatly on the ratio of input to output prices in the near future. The price of rice could level off or even fall, as food aid programmes increase supplies, but the prices of imported inputs are unlikely to fall. Even if the rupiah appreciates in 1999, traders may well decide to keep supplies of rice low in order to maintain prices and limit the risks of currency losses. If the political and social environment does not improve, this could lead to further hoarding. The government's recent decision to cancel the subsidies on nitrogen and phosphorus fertilisers available to estates has had the unfortunate side-effect of increasing prices to smallholders. Although in theory farmers are supposed to be able to continue buying these inputs at subsidised prices, some traders are willing to buy the farmers' quota at a higher price in order to sell at a profit to the estates, which means that the real opportunity cost of these fertilisers to farmers has risen. This policy can only aggravate the current confusion and further disrupt trade in inputs, to the detriment of staple food supplies.

While all farmers, including landless labourers, appear better off than the urban unemployed, only some categories of farmers are clear winners. Wealthier landowners possessing land and capital have benefitted from the crisis. At the other end of the spectrum, tenant farmers and share-croppers are those who have suffered most—the former because the ecological crisis meant that their yields were worth less than the rent they had agreed to pay, and the latter because of the rise in the price of inputs, which they normally pay for. In other words, the crisis affected most seriously those categories of farmer most exposed to risk.

The situation of landless labourers is the most problematic. Their wages, which had lagged well behind those of urban employees before the crisis, doubled in nominal terms between October 1997 and October 1998. Despite this, they experienced a net decline in purchasing power. Meanwhile, the incomes of urban employees showed at best only modest increases and often actually fell as companies stopped paying overtime and bonuses. Their situation was thus even worse than that of rural labourers. The different fate of the two groups indicates that Indonesia's rural and urban labour markets for the most part function separately, so that dismissed urban workers were not in fact available for agricultural work, even in rural areas close to urban centres. Our discussions with workers in Jakarta confirmed this view. Many of them indicated that they would be unable to carry out even the simplest agricultural tasks and that they would be ashamed to return to their villages in their current straitened circumstances. Thus, a return to the villages is seen by urban workers only as a last-ditch solution when all else has failed.

Farmers in our survey made no mention of the return of urban workers in significant numbers. This study, however, was conducted in October 1998. Since then, the economic situation in the urban areas has worsened. There has been a steady increase in the numbers of unemployed, fewer and fewer of whom have any savings left to fall back on. This trend can be expected to continue at least into the first half of 1999. Interviews conducted at the end of 1998 suggested that an exodus into the rural areas was beginning. Many city dwellers who return to their villages for *Id al-Fitr* in January 1999 may decide to stay there. An exodus would have negative implications for existing agricultural labourers, who may have to accept lower wages, while easing the pressures in urban areas and increasing the benefits to landowners, who will have a larger workforce at their disposal. (Nevertheless, many landowners may find themselves sharing their higher yields and incomes with a larger number of dependants.) As other surveys have shown, however, returning urban workers would not necessarily be employed directly in agriculture, but are more likely to become small-scale traders or to start a cottage industry.

Causes for concern

Looking ahead to 1999, we see several reasons for tempering our optimism.

Poorer rice farmers, particularly those in East Java and similar climactic areas, may decide to switch to more lucrative crops during the second season, leading to a reduced area cultivated to rice. At the same time, higher prices of inputs could result in lower yields as farmers reduce their applications. The combined effect could be a new rice production crisis. As a result a high level of imports would be needed, placing a heavier burden on the trade balance and on foreign currency reserves. A first indicator of whether or not this is happening will be the figures for rice production for the last 4 months of 1998. If these show a decrease on the 1997 figures, this will mean that farmers have not been able to benefit from the higher prices of rice.

A further concern is the continuing disruption of trade in both inputs and outputs. Disruption is caused by inappropriate government price policies (such as the different prices of fertilisers for estates and small-scale farmers), traders' lack of cash, political and social instability, and farmers' lack of information (for example, on fake pesticides). The government will need to address these factors through public information programmes and specific measures to restore confidence.

Landless labourers are estimated to account for 40-50% of the working rural population (Susilowati, 1997). If Scenarios 2 or 3 materialise, their plight will worsen considerably. Smaller areas cultivated and lower yields will reduce both their opportunities to work and their incomes when they do work, since these are paid in rice. The government will need to monitor the situation closely over the coming months, so as to be ready to intervene promptly with an emergency food-for-work programme targetted to this group should the need arise. The following areas will need special attention:

- The quantity and quality of inputs available, changes in price ratios, and the different effect of inflation on different expenditure classes.
- The long-term effects of the reduced or disrupted use of fertilisers and pesticides, including the combined effects of the ecological and economic crises on pest population levels.
- The capacity of agriculture and the rural economy to absorb and sustain workers migrating from urban areas.

In conclusion, the results of our field study suggest that food crop farmers may well be able to contribute to renewed growth and stability in Indonesia. There are, however, major areas of concern. The role of the new government will be crucial in avoiding further difficulties: policies will need to be put in place to ensure that farmers have access to inputs, so that they are able to maintain and increase production both in the short and in the long term. The right policies can only be designed and implemented by people who know how rural markets work and who have the necessary sympathy and respect for the small-scale farming community.

References

Bourgeois, R. 1999. Javanese irrigated rice farmers and the Indonesian crisis. In: Simatupang, P., Pasaribu, S., Bahri, S., and Stringer, R. (eds), *Indonesia's Economic Crisis: Effects on Agriculture and Policy Responses*. Center for Agricultural Socio-Economic Research (CASER), Bogor, Indonesia.

Cremer, G. 1988. Deployment of Indonesian migrants in the Middle East: Present situation and prospects. *Bulletin of Indonesian Economic Studies* 24 (3): 73-86.

EBRI (Economic and Business Review Indonesia). 1996. Growing pains: Farmers face an uncertain future. Issue 232: 6-11.

FAO (Food and Agriculture Organization) 1998a FAO/WFP Crop and Food Supply Assessment Mission to Indonesia, 17 April 1998. Global Information and Early Warning System on Food and Agriculture, Food and Agriculture Organization/World Food Programme (FAO/WFP), Rome, Italy.

FAO (Food and Agriculture Organization) 1998b. FAO/WFP Crop and Food Supply Assessment Mission to Indonesia, 6 October 1998. Global Information and Early Warning System on Food and Agriculture, Food and Agriculture Organization/World Food Programme (FAO/WFP), Rome, Italy.

Guinness, P. 1990. Indonesian migrants in Johor: An itinerant labour force. *Bulletin of Indonesian Economic Studies* 26 (1): 117-131.

Hadnyana, M. O., Aten, M. H. and Adimesna, D. 1990. Perubahan struktur usahatani padi sebagai dampak penerapan teknologi supra insus di jalur Pantura. *Penelitian Pertanian* 10 (1): 46-53.

Jellinek, L. and Rustanto, B. 1999. Survival Strategies of the Javanese during the Economic Crisis. World Bank, Jakarta, Indonesia.

Ministry of Agriculture. 1996. Agricultural Development in Indonesia. Paper presented at the 1996 World Food Summit, Food and Agriculture Organization of the United Nations (FAO), Rome, Italy.

Ministry of Agriculture. 1998. Position Paper on the Food Crisis in Indonesia. International Cooperation Bureau, Ministry of Agriculture, Jakarta, Indonesia.

Naylor, R. 1992. Labour-saving technologies in the Javanese rice economy: Recent developments and a look into the 1990s. *Bulletin of Indonesian Economic Studies* 28 (3): 71-91.

Nehen, I.K. and Willis, I.R. 1985. Efficiency and distribution: The case of tractors in Sawah land preparation in West Java, Indonesia. *Bulletin of Indonesian Economic Studies* 23 (3): 34-51.

Suryana, A. and Kariyasa. K. 1997. Efisiensi usahatani padi melalui pengembangan SUTPA. *Forum Agro Ekonomi* 15 (1 and 2): 67-81.

Susilowati, S.H. 1997. Struktur dan distribusi pemilikan lahan pertanian, studi di pedesaan Jawa Tengah. In: Prosiding Agribisnis Dinamika Sumberdaya dan Pengembangan Sistem Usaha Pertanian, Buku I. Center for Agricultural Socio-Economic Research (CASER), Bogor, Indonesia.

Acknowledgements

We are grateful to the World Bank for allowing us to use the survey data in this book. In particular, we would like to thank Dr. Dely Gapasin of the World Bank and Daniel Deybe and Gabriel de Taffin of CIRAD for their support and encouragement. Irene Myrtasanty of the University of Indonesia collaborated in organising the survey and collecting the qualitative data. The interviews in East Java were conducted by Hania Rahma of the Center for Policy and Implementation Studies (CPIS). Frank Jesus of CIRAD contributed substantially to the high quality of the data analysis. We also wish to thank Dr Pantjar Simatupang of CASER, Bogor, for his many helpful comments and for sharing his field knowledge with us.

Notes

1 The survey was originally designed as a means of evaluating the impact of Indonesia's Integrated Pest Management Training Program (IPM/TP). It was funded by the World Bank and the French Trust Fund, and was conducted by CIRAD under the leadership of Dr Daniel Deybe.

2 From 1984 onwards, the Department of Labour encouraged migration to the Middle East as a response to lower oil prices and export revenues (Cremer, 1988). This programme was especially popular in the Muslim areas of West Java, including Cianjur. On Indonesian migrants to Malaysia, see Guinness (1990).

3 Between 1984 and 1994, the number of hand-tractors in Indonesia rose more than fivefold, from 8880 to 50 220 (Ministry of Agriculture, 1996). Our field

surveys indicated that motorised land preparation was the technology most in demand among farmers in the 1990s.

4 Farmers said that some of their usual pesticides were ineffective in 1998, especially when purchased at low prices from itinerant vendors. When farmers obtained new supplies of the same brand from the government, the effect returned to normal.

5 Including the cost of meals, coffee and cigarettes provided to workers.

6 For instance, almost all farmers interviewed in the Kediri district have, since the crisis, grown soybean instead of rice as a second crop.

Chapter 11

It never Rains but it Pours: Food Crop Farmers barely Survive in Transmigration Areas

Patrice Levang, Baslian K. Yoza, Etty Diana and Haryati

In 1998, while the financial and political crisis crippled most other sectors of the Indonesian economy, the agricultural sector as a whole proved surprisingly robust. For 30 years, government policy had kept the prices of staple food crops artificially low, providing urban consumers with stability but doing no favours to farmers. Monetary depreciation had the effect of forcing the government to liberalise prices, enabling the farmer to get his own back.

As seen previously, many export crops, whose commodity prices are fixed in US dollars on the world market, benefitted from the crisis. In contrast, the food crop sector, already inefficient before the crisis, went into further decline. Food crops in densely populated Java were, as we have seen, badly affected. But what was the impact on the transmigration sites in the outer islands? Here the availability of land is less of a constraint, but its quality is uneven and government services to agriculture are often poor. Were the transmigrants able to take advantage of rising food crop prices?

To answer these questions, we surveyed three transmigration sites in Northern Lampung, Sumatra. The villages chosen were Tri Tunggal Jaya (transmigration unit SP8, Manggala C), Kebun Dalam (transmigration unit SP4, Mesuji E) and Sumber Agung (transmigration unit SP1, Rawa Pitu). The two first villages (hereafter referred to as Manggala and Mesuji) are on upland food crop sites. Manggala was opened in 1994 and is still under the supervision of the Ministry of Transmigration. Mesuji is part of an older scheme opened in 1982. Comparison of these two schemes gives us a good idea of how transmigration units have evolved. Rawa Pitu is a lowland scheme, opened in 1990. It is part of the huge area of tidal marshes in Northern Lampung reclaimed by the government and settled by local transmigrants as part of what is known as the Translok Programme. In the three villages, a randomised sample of 97 farmers was interviewed during the first week of January 1999, when data on agricultural prices were also collected. Prices were surveyed again in June 1999.

This chapter is in seven sections. The first section provides background information on the three transmigration sites. In the second and the third we describe the events of 1997-98 and their general effects, while the fourth and the fifth provide a more detailed typology of farming households and an analysis of the impact of the crisis on each. The sixth section describes the strategies people adopted to survive the crisis. And the last section presents our conclusions.

Setting the Scene

The resettlement of forest squatters

In the early 1980s, the provincial government of Lampung decided to give the Ministry of Forestry its full support in its bid to free all forest land from squatters.

Since before independence, encroachment on land officially classified as state forest had become commonplace. In some areas, especially in the mountainous south and west of the province, illegal clearances had taken place so long ago that farmers had forgotten the fact that they were, in fact, squatters[1]. Suddenly, these relatively wealthy coffee growers were told to vacate the lands they were cultivating so that these could be reforested. In compensation, the farmers were offered the opportunity to join transmigration schemes in Northern Lampung, where they were each allotted a 2-hectare food crop plot (Figure 11.1). Although they were not forced to join the schemes, they effectively had no choice as all their assets were taken over by the government[2]. This is how the Translok Programme was implemented in Lampung, where 70 000 families were resettled in the north of the province between 1980 and 1995 (Levang, 1997).

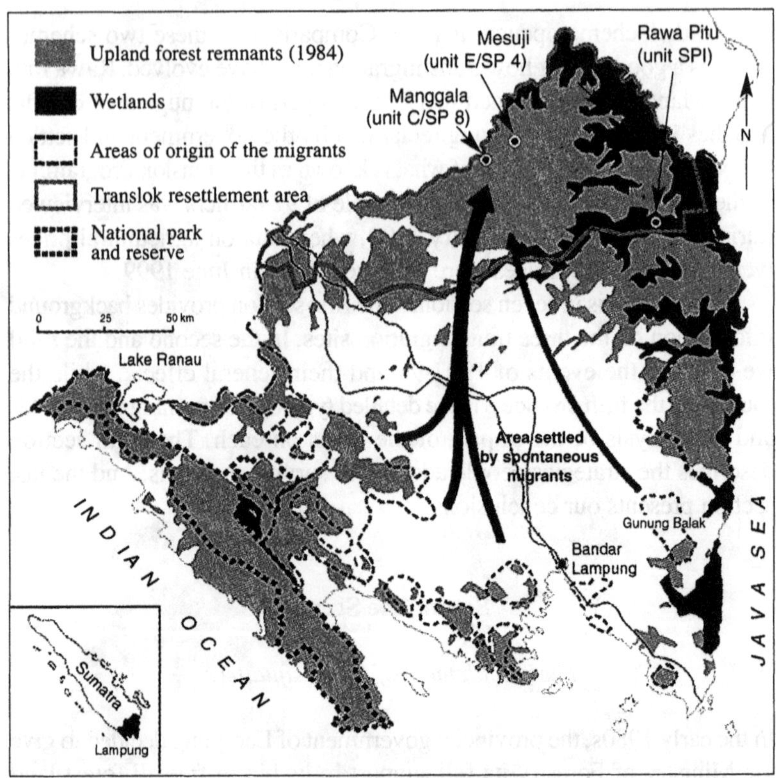

Figure 11.1 The Translok Programme in Lampung Province. (© IRD-Orstom, 1999). Source: IRD-Orstom 1999 survey.

Out of the frying pan...

The transmigrants found that their new home consisted largely of inaccessible yet overlogged forest land, much of which had been reclassified as "conversion" forest—land scheduled for conversion to estates and food crop schemes. Suffering from very low chemical fertility, the soils were marginal for cropping[3]. Hundreds of destructive Sumatran elephants still roamed the area, adding to the already considerable risk of trying to grow a crop. Heavy pest infestation compounded the problems, resulting in low yields even at the outset. As the years went on, yields declined even further and the rising population of elephants became a major hazard. To feed their families, farmers had no alternative but to look for off-farm work. At first, illegal logging was the most popular and profitable activity. Later, when the forests became too depleted, the settlers sought work as day labourers for neighbouring plantation companies[4]. Food crop production became a part-time activity. Cassava was the main crop grown, as it was the only one that could be relied on to provide food and some extra income without the need to purchase seed and fertiliser. Many transmigrants lost hope and left the area for good, only to be replaced by other, spontaneous settlers[5].

One of the farmers we interviewed at the upland crop scheme at Mesuji had arrived with the first settlers in 1982. Mr Sarmin was born in Southern Lampung, where his father, an immigrant from Java, had settled in the 1960s. One morning he awoke to find that his coffee plantation, together with those of his neighbours, had been completely destroyed during the night. Having lost everything, he decided to volunteer for the Translok Programme. On arrival in Mesuji, he found that his allocated plot of land was still covered with bush. During the first 2 years, Mr Sarmin harvested nothing, as rice bugs devoured his ripening crop. During the third and fourth years he was able to harvest upland rice and cassava. However, from the fifth year onwards, elephants regularly destroyed his crops. Most of his friends returned to Southern Lampung, but he stayed and became a regular day labourer at the Gunung Madu Plantation. From 1989 to 1994 his village benefitted from aid provided under the World Food Programme, which helped to clear the bush and wasteland around the village where the elephants hid during the daytime. In 1994, the elephants were finally driven out of the area and Mr Sarmin returned to farming. For 3 consecutive years he made a living without having to leave the village, by growing upland rice, cassava and maize. He was even able to invest in a young rubber plantation, but during the 1997 drought all the trees died.

The first settlers arrived at Manggala, the other upland scheme in our survey, in 1994, by which time elephant herds were no longer in the area. Today the settlers are still struggling to make a living from agriculture while the scheme remains under the supervision of the Ministry of Transmigration. Although they have not so far experienced the severe problems of the Mesuji transmigrants, the settlers of Manggala are already suffering the consequences of declining soil fertility on their small plots. Most have given up trying to grow upland rice, soybean and maize and have reverted to cassava monoculture. Still relative newcomers to the area, they prefer for the time being to remain in the village and to supplement their income by working as day labourers for wealthier neighbours. Some have already been contacted by manpower suppliers for plantation companies[6]. Manggala is a decade behind, but it is treading the same downhill path as Mesuji.

Rawa Pitu, our lowland site, forms part of the huge marshland reclamation scheme on the east coast of Northern Lampung. In comparison with Mesuji and Manggala, the soils of this area are reasonably fertile and, formed from marine alluvium with a shallow covering of peat, not liable to acid sulphate problems. Prone to constant flooding, these tidal wetlands are not coveted by local people. Because they are free of local land claims, they are ideal for development under transmigration schemes. The key to successful development is to ensure proper flood control. It was for this purpose that the government built a 6-kilometre primary canal perpendicular to the area's main river, the Way Pedada. Along the canal were regularly spaced sluice gates, allowing water levels in adjacent fields to be controlled. At first, Rawa Pitu enjoyed some good harvests, at least during the rainy season (the second, dry-season crop was regularly destroyed by rats and other pests). Unfortunately, the government has not allocated any funding for the maintenance of the canal and gates. With each passing year the primary canal silts up, the gates fall into disrepair and the evacuation of excess water takes longer. During the rainy season of 1998-99, the settlers experienced a 3-month long flood during which some families had to be evacuated while others lived up to their knees in water.

The first harvests at Rawa Pitu were so promising that many spontaneous migrants were attracted to the site. The 500 original families settled in 1990 have since been joined by 636 others. Mr Sunari arrived in 1994, after hearing that irrigated rice fields were available at bargain prices. Officially, migrants get access to 1.25 hectare of land free-of-charge under what is known as the Transmigrasi Swakarsa Mandiri (TSM) programme[7]. However, Mr Sunari found he had to pay Rp 500 000 in "administrative fees" to the head of the village. He lived together with his wife and child in a shack for a year while he waited for building materials to arrive. For 3 years he cultivated a 0.25-hectare home plot, the rest of the land being made available to him only in 1997. He grew two crops a year, harvesting an average of 800-1000 kilogrammes of paddy rice during the first season. However, his second crop was invariably destroyed by rats, wild boars, bugs or birds. In 1997-98, for the first time, he managed to grow more rice than he needed to feed his family. He was just thinking of giving up day labouring when his land was flooded. Despite this new setback, he feels that he was lucky, since his house is still above water while most of his neighbours had to abandon theirs, taking refuge with relatives in the south.

The early years of a transmigration scheme are always difficult. Organising and supporting agricultural colonisation in remote areas is a complex logistical challenge. Food crop schemes are especially liable to run into problems when soil fertility is as marginal as it is in Northern Lampung. However, transmigrants, with their pioneering spirit, are very resilient. Those who survive quickly learn how to adapt and to minimise risk. Most become part-time farmers, producing food mainly for their own consumption while earning the bulk of their income from off-farm activities. Yet the maintenance of farming activities, whether profitable or not, plays an important psycho-social role, as the status of a farmer is much higher than that of a labourer. Even though he spends most of his time engaged in off-farm activities, the transmigrant always refers to himself as a farmer.

The Worst is Yet to Come

The drought of 1997

By 1997 the economic situation looked as though it was about to improve, when the whole Indonesian archipelago was affected by the freak weather patterns associated with El Niño. Northern Lampung was hit by the worst drought for 50 years. Generally, average rainfall in this area may fall below 100 mm per month during July, August or September every second year or so, although it is rare to have 3 consecutive months all with less than 100 mm. However, in 1997, no rain fell at all for 5 consecutive months, from June until October. The upland and lowland transmigration schemes coped with this prolonged drought differently.

In Manggala and Mesuji the wells rapidly dried up, and finding drinkable water kept most family members busy from August onwards. Apart from cassava, no food crops survived. Many tree crops, especially young plantations, wilted. In Manggala, charcoal sellers offered credit to the hungry transmigrants, who in return cut down all the remaining trees on their plots and turned them into charcoal. Within 3 months the whole area had been cleared and burned. A day's work earned Rp 2000: just enough to repay the credit. In Mesuji, where all the remaining forest had already been cleared by the early 1990s in order to get rid of the elephants, the transmigrants had no choice but to leave the village to seek a daily wage on neighbouring estates. However, in both these upland villages the drought also had some positive effects. Transmigrants generally wait 10 years or more before opening their second plot of land. In Manggala, thanks to charcoal making, all the plots were cleared and ready for cultivation by the end of the third year. In Mesuji, all the weeds and shrubs on fallow land wilted and could be cleared using fire, the easiest and cheapest way. The area cultivated in the two villages almost doubled in the year following the drought.

In Rawa Pitu the effects of the drought were entirely positive. In this lowland area no wells dried up, while the absence of floods enabled the transmigrants to grow upland crops such as soybean, maize and groundnut[8]. As they were the only farmers to enjoy harvests during this period, they got the highest possible prices for their crops.

In November 1997, the first rains fell. The hard times were over. The farmers had taken advantage of the prolonged drought. By clearing all their plots they had considerably expanded their cropping area. For the first time in years, the invasive weed *Imperata cylindrica* had been pushed back to make way for food crops. Transmigrants were able to feel optimistic again.

The krismon: *prices go crazy*

The drought was not yet over when the monetary crisis—the infamous *krismon*—began to make news headlines. Speculators' attacks on the Thai baht began in July 1997, causing a crisis in the financial markets which quickly spread to other Southeast Asian countries. After a long period of stability, the Indonesian rupiah began to lose ground against the US dollar.

At first, the transmigrants were not affected. Most of them had never even seen a "greenback" in their lives. However, when the financial markets panicked, the rupiah's decline turned into a free fall. Indonesian manufacturers were no longer able to import raw materials. Hyperinflation set in and prices began to soar.

The prices of the *sembako*[9], the shopping basket of nine basic necessities monitored by the government to determine inflation rates, poverty lines and the minimum wage, began rising sharply in early 1998 and soared during the second half of the year (Table 11.1). The transmigrants were most affected by the rising prices of rice, sugar and cooking oil. Commodities such as wheat flour, coffee, tea and milk also became very expensive, but this affected the transmigrants less than other sections of the community as their consumption of these products was already low. During the first half of 1999 the situation improved somewhat, with the price of sugar falling by 50% and rice and cooking oil easing back by 10%. The prices of higher-value foods such as fish, meat and eggs continued to rise, however.

Table 11.1 Movements of *sembako* prices, 1998-99

Item	*Prices (Rp/unit)*			
	January 1998	*April 1998*	*December 1998*	*June 1999*
Rice (white) (kg)	900	1200	3000	2700
Sugar (kg)	1600	2000	6000	3000
Salt (100 g)	300	300	300	600
Dried fish (kg)*	3000	3000	3500	7500
Kerosene (litre)	350	350	400	500
Soap (kg)	700	1000	1000	1000
Wheat flour (kg)	750	1600	4000	3200
Cooking oil (litre)	1600	3500	4000	3600
Textiles (piece)	5000	5000	5000	5000

* Prices for lowest quality available on the market. Source: Departemen Tenaga Kerja, Lampung.

The prices of agricultural commodities lagged slightly behind the overall trend. Figure 11.2 compares the movements of farm-gate prices for paddy rice, cassava (fresh peeled tuber), maize (grain) and soybean. The price of cassava rose most, reaching an unprecedented high of Rp 275 per kilogramme in February 1998[10]. Prices remained high until September 1998, but fell quickly thereafter. During the first half of 1999, cassava remained relatively low in price, fluctuating at around Rp 125-150 per kilogramme. The prices of paddy rice, maize and soybean behaved similarly, rising slowly between October 1997 and April 1998 and then sharply until September 1998. From October 1998 prices for these commodities tended to fall, but not by as much as cassava. During the first few months of 1999, the price of paddy rice remained stable at Rp 1800 per kilogramme, while maize stood at Rp 1000 per kilogramme. Except in the case of cassava, farmers benefitted little from the price rises, as prices were highest when they had nothing to sell. As the harvest approached, most prices fell once more.

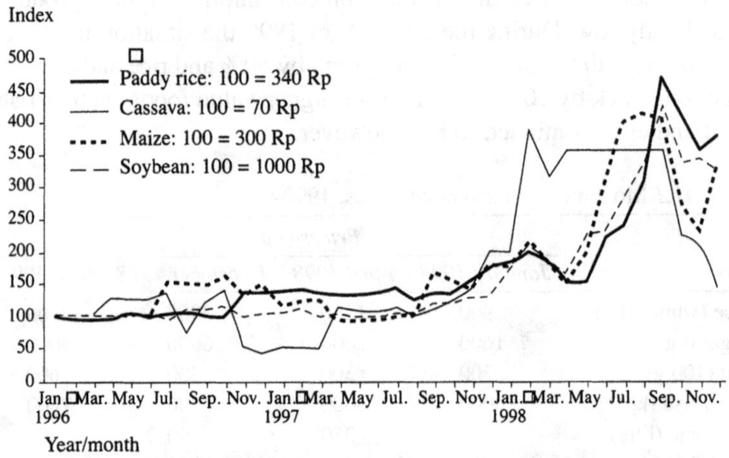

Figure 11.2 Farm-gate prices of agricultural commodities in Lampung, 1996-98 (© IRD-Orstom 1999). Source: Departemen Pertanian, Lampung.

The prices of agricultural inputs rose fourfold in response to the *krismon* and, unlike those of commodities, remained high in 1999 (Table 11.2). Supplies dried up as local middlemen did not have enough capital to restock at the new prices. The problem was exacerbated as wholesalers (and producers) began hoarding in anticipation of further price rises. Some fertilisers, including KCl, were not available locally for months on end. Indeed, KCl has only reappeared in Northern Lampung since March 1999, and sporadically at that. Its price can be as high as Rp 3000 per kilogramme. However, most farmers are unable to buy at these inflated prices, so most other agricultural inputs remained available for those who could afford them.

Table 11.2 Movements of agricultural input prices, 1997-99

Item	*Prices (Rp/unit)*		
	1997	*1998*	*1999*
Seeds (kg):			
Paddy Way Rarem	600	1200	2200
Maize Pioneer 4	2400	4400	8400
Fertiliser (kg):			
Urea	300	340	1200
TSP/SP36	500	640	2000
KCl	500	640	2200
Herbicide/pesticide (litre):			
Round-Up	12 000	20 000	50 000
Polaris	7000	15 000	27 000
Vastrax	60 000	95 000	240 000

Source: IRD-Orstom field survey.

Labour costs followed the same trends as the prices of basic goods, with a time-lag of a few months. In the villages, the daily wage remained at Rp 3000 until April 1998, when it rose to Rp 4000. It rose again, to Rp 6000, over the period September-October 1998. The *kebutuhan hidup minimum pekerja* (KHMP), the workers' minimum monthly cost of living as calculated by the Ministry of Manpower, showed a rapid increase between April and August 1998 (Figure 11.3). In theory calculated monthly, the KHMP figures are in fact manipulated in order to make industrial labour costs appear low. Officially, minimum wage costs did not even double between January and December 1998, a period in which the prices of basic commodities rose threefold.

How the Villages Fared

Even to an experienced observer, the upland villages of Northern Lampung did not appear to have changed much by late 1998. They still contained a majority of poorly built shacks and huts interspersed with the few more solid and attractive houses of the relatively affluent, while the roads along which they are scattered were as poorly maintained as ever. The most striking change lay not in the village centres but in

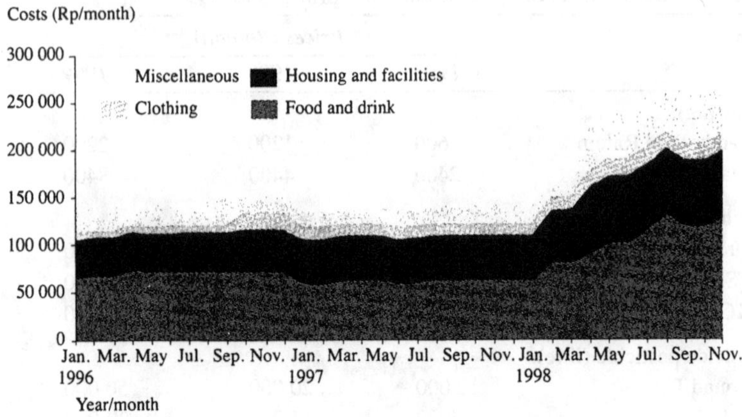

Figure 11.3 Official cost of living in Lampung, 1996-98 (© IRD-Orstom 1999). Source: Departemen Tenaga Kerja, Lampung.

the cultivated appearance of the surrounding land: as far as the eye could see, cassava had replaced *Imperata*.

It was tempting to conclude that the economic crisis had made agriculture profitable again. But in fact the *krismon* had had little effect. Rather, it was the prolonged drought of the previous year that had helped farmers push back the boundaries of cultivation, enabling them to clear their plots cheaply by firing the land. In Manggala, the migrants who produced charcoal during the drought took advantage of the clearings left by this operation to plant upland rice and cassava. In Mesuji, grass and shrubs wilted on land that had lain fallow for many years. These were easily burned, preparing the land for cassava cropping.

At first sight the vast fallow areas of the lowlands formed a disappointing contrast to the cultivated uplands. The once promising rice fields of Rawa Pitu, which had lain flooded for nearly 3 months, looked like a disaster area. Alongside the silt-filled main canal, all the village roads were under water. Most of the inhabitants had already fled some of the hamlets, while in others people had rebuilt their houses closer to the dyke. But appearances can be misleading. Despite the floods the economic situation in the lowlands is in fact better than in the uplands. Figure 11.4 compares activities and average incomes for 1998 in upland and lowland villages.

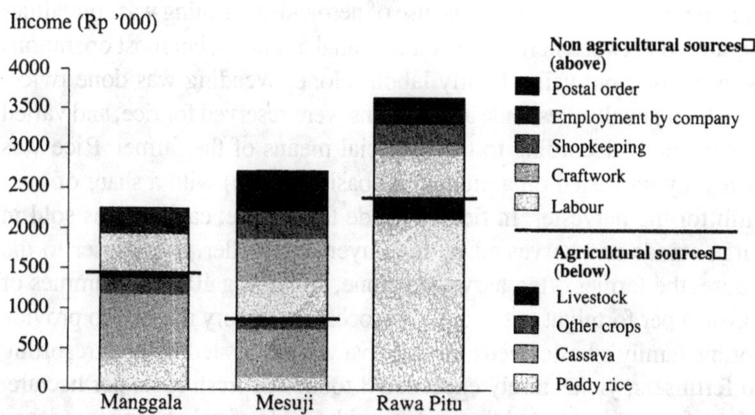

Figure 11.4 Comparison of average incomes in three villages, North Lampung, 1998 (© IRD-Orstom 1999). Source: IRD-Orstom field survey.

Activities and incomes

In Manggala, the average annual income per household in 1998 was Rp 2.3 million, 65% of which came from agriculture. Cassava was the main income-earning crop, followed by upland rice, maize and a few others. Animal husbandry (goats and chickens) was an important source of cash for some farmers, but did not contribute much at overall village level. Off-farm work was mainly restricted to day labouring in the neighbourhood. Only a very few farmers sought work away from the village. An additional source of cash for some families were the postal orders sent by their grown-up children, generally girls working as housemaids in Jakarta. A few craftsmen and shopkeepers also benefitted from additional income.

Virtually all the land granted to transmigrants and suitable for arable crops was cultivated. The 0.25-hectare house plot and the original 1-hectare field plot were generally planted with cassava only, while newly cleared plots, usually 0.75 hectare, were devoted to upland rice intercropped with cassava. Following the major locust attacks of 1997-98, most farmers gave up trying to grow maize.

The soil in the plots already cultivated was tilled with a hoe, or with the help of a single draught animal. In the newly opened plots zero tillage was the rule, with or without the use of herbicides. Planting was sometimes organised between neighbours on a mutual aid basis, but most operations were carried out using family labour alone. Weeding was done twice, usually manually. Pesticide applications were reserved for rice, and varied considerably according to the financial means of the farmer. Rice was generally harvested on a mutual aid basis (*bawon*) with a share of one-fifth for the harvester. In fields outside the village, cassava was sold in large stands and harvested by the buyer. In smaller plots closer to the house, the farmer often harvested alone, delivering 100 kilogrammes of cassava per fortnight to the closest processing factory in order to provide for his family's basic needs. As cassava was cultivated without resorting to fertilisers, yields rarely exceeded 8 tonnes of fresh roots per hectare. Many farmers contented themselves with yields of only 5 tonnes, as they sold their crop at 6 months instead of the more usual 8. They claimed that the loss of earnings was offset by more frequent harvesting. In fact, being up against it, they usually had no choice but to sell their crop before maturity. Upland paddy rice yields were low, around 1250 kilogrammes per hectare. Depending on the area cultivated, on average a family harvested 880 kilogrammes per year—not enough to meet its needs. Rice was supplemented to varying degrees with cassava. All the same, most families barely survived. The only ones who were somewhat better off were those who still owned coffee plantations in Southern Lampung and therefore had capital to invest.

In Mesuji, the average annual income per household was slightly higher than in Manggala, reaching Rp 2.7 million. Agriculture contributed only 33% to this total. Cassava was again the main income-earner, while rice and other crops contributed little as the cropped areas were small, usually only 0.25 hectare. Paddy rice yields were around 1100 kilogrammes per hectare. Cattle, goats and poultry provided an income, but again the contribution of livestock was insignificant when considered at village level. Off-farm activities constituted the bulk of family incomes, with most families engaged in wage labouring, crafts and trade. Farming was merely a part-time activity.

At 1.23 hectare, the average size of holdings was smaller than in Manggala, many plots having been sold to spontaneous migrants over the years. Usually the whole holding was under cultivation. The house plots were planted to perennial crops and could no longer accommodate food crops. Plots in the lower lying parts were reserved for rice, whereas those on higher ground were given over to cassava monoculture. The soil was tilled using a team of oxen, although there was some manual soil preparation in the lowlands. Planting was often organised between neighbours on a mutual aid basis. Weeding was carried out manually, by family labour in poor families while wealthier ones hired labour. As a rule, cassava was sold in the field and harvested by the buyer. As only the wealthier families —shopkeepers or wage earners—were able to use fertilisers, yields were low, rarely exceeding 5 tonnes per hectare. Only half of all families had a paddy rice harvest of 450 kilogrammes—a level still far from sufficient for their needs. Wealthier families were able to buy the extra rice they needed, while others had to make do with cassava. Despite having been settled over a decade longer, Mesuji's economic situation was little better than that of Manggala. Sadly, this does not mean that Manggala is likely to overtake Mesuji but rather that both villages will endure a roughly similar standard of living in the longer term.

In Rawa Pitu, average household income in 1998 was Rp 3.7 million —considerably higher than in Manggala and Mesuji. Agriculture accounted for 65% of the total, with the income from rice alone close to the average total income in Manggala. No crops other than rice were grown. Animal husbandry contributed significantly to agricultural income in this crisis year, with two families in our sample deciding to sell all their cattle at the same time. These farmers were able to use livestock as a buffer against adversity.

Once the rice was planted, most heads of family left the village to look for additional income on neighbouring estates or in distant coffee plantations in Southern Lampung. During the first cropping season, most farmers cultivated the whole of their holdings. These varied considerably in size, from 0.25 to 4 hectares, since the wealthier farmers were able to buy plots from neighbours in financial difficulties. The spontaneous transmigrants received only the standard 1.25 hectare under the TSM programme, and many more newcomers were still waiting for their plots.

Small plots were prepared manually with hoes. On plots larger than 1 hectare, soil preparation was mechanised. Some farmers earned an appreciable sum by renting out their hand-tractor. Depending on the water level, rice farmers either transplanted or seeded rice directly, generally carrying out the operation on a mutual aid basis. Although direct seeding is quickest and cheapest, this is not possible when fields are flooded.

Most farmers applied fertilisers in 1998 and some also used herbicides. Weeding was generally carried out manually using family labour, while harvesting was done collectively (*bawon*), with the harvester taking one-fifth. Farmers' yields[11] averaged 2.5 tonnes of paddy rice per hectare for the first cropping season. The second season was, as always, more problematic. As many farmers had followed their usual practice of reducing the area they cropped, pests tended to concentrate on the few plots that were cultivated, increasing the risk of losing the entire crop. Because the risk of income loss was higher, farmers avoided using fertilisers and pesticides. As a result the failure rate was alarmingly high, with only one farmer in four achieving a net yield of 2000 kilogrammes of paddy rice per hectare. Three out of four experienced total crop failure, so the overall average yield for the second season was low, at around 500 kg.

We found the economic situation in Rawa Pitu to be much better than in Manggala and Mesuji. In Manggala, nearly all families are poor, while in Mesuji, only shopkeepers, craftsmen and wage earners are relatively well off. However, in Rawa Pitu, income levels are highly variable according to farm size, available capital and management skills. In contrast to other villages, farming families here can earn more than shopkeepers. Though most people remain poor, agriculture at least has potential, provided the water supply can be properly controlled.

Typology of Households

At first glance everybody on a transmigration scheme looks poor[12]. A more searching appraisal quickly reveals sizeable financial differences between families, despite the fact that everybody is supposed to begin on the same basis, with equal plot size and similar labour availability. Figure 11.5 plots every household in the three villages surveyed, by annual income and by the percentage of income derived from agriculture. From these data, we were able to group families into four types:

- Poor farmers. Living in Manggala or Mesuji, these households, which constituted 21% of our sample, rely on agriculture alone for their survival. The heads of these families are typically either too old to look for off-farm work or too proud to do so, refusing to become day labourers. These stubborn farmers persist in their attempt to make a living from agriculture, against all the odds. They cultivate small plots of land, working the soil manually and using as few

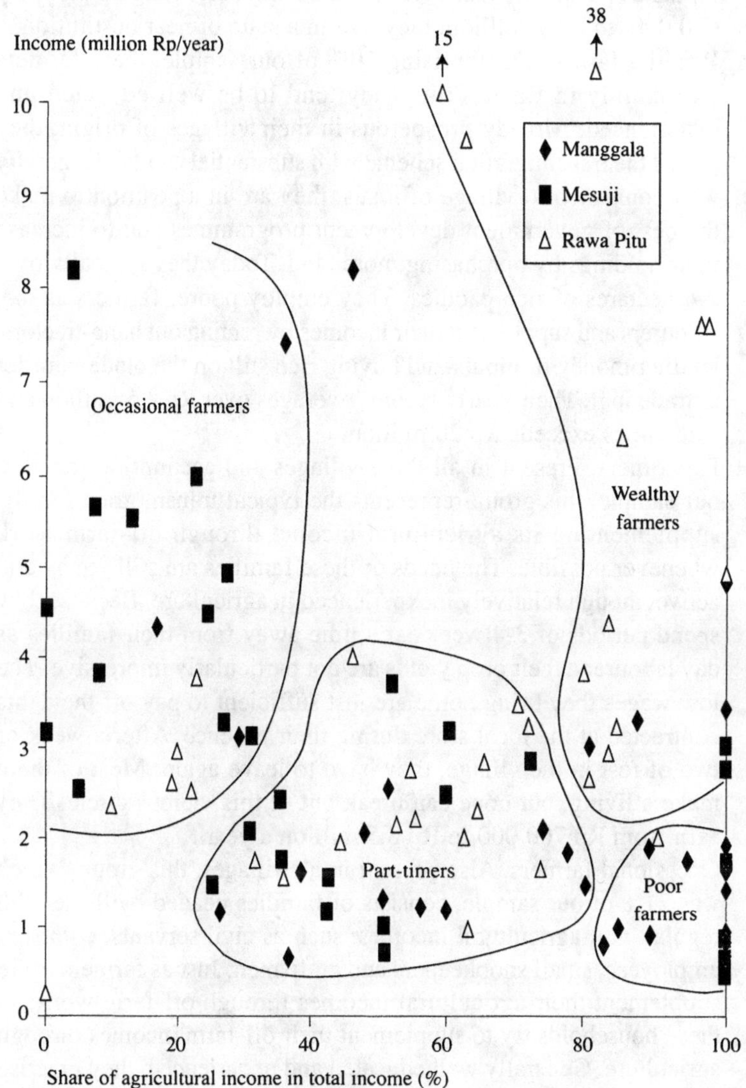

Figure 11.5 Typology of households on three transmigration schemes, North Lampung (© IRD-Orstom 1999).
Source: IRD-Orstom field survey.

inputs as possible. With average yearly incomes ranging from Rp 600 000 to Rp 2 million, they live in a state of near destitution.

- Wealthy farmers. Comprising 19% of our sample, these farmers live mainly in Rawa Pitu. They tend to be well educated and experienced. Already prosperous in their villages of origin, they joined the transmigration scheme with substantial capital. Generally well connected to village officials, they are in a position to make the best of government development programmes and to increase their holdings by purchasing more land. Today they typically own 2-4 hectares of rice paddies. They employ poorer farmers as day labourers and supplement their incomes by renting out hand-tractors, lending money or inputs and buying rice still on the blade in order to trade in it. Their yearly income averages over Rp 2.5 million and sometimes exceeds Rp 20 million.
- Part-timers. Present in all three villages and accounting for 38% our sample, this group represents the typical transmigrant family, supplementing its agricultural income through off-farm work whenever possible. The heads of these families are still young and active, though relatively inexperienced in agriculture. Because they spend periods of 3-4 weeks at a time away from their families as day labourers, their crop yields are not particularly impressive. The low wages they bring home are just sufficient to pay off the debts contracted at the local store during their absence. After a week or two of rest in the village, they have to leave again. Most of them make a living, but none can break out of this vicious circle. They earn from Rp 700 000 to Rp 3.5 million a year.
- Occasional farmers. Also present in all villages, this group, which was 21% of our sample, consists of families headed by those with regular, non-agricultural incomes, such as civil servants, company employees, small shopkeepers and craftsmen. Just as farmers try to supplement their agricultural incomes through off-farm work, so these households try to supplement their off-farm incomes through agriculture. Generally well educated and experienced, they practise a relatively capital-intensive form of farming. They are the main employers of day labourers in the village. They generally achieve good results in terms of yields, but low returns to the capital they invest. However, as the only employers in the village, they enjoy high social status and are highly regarded by their neighbours.

What was obvious from our survey was that, no matter what class they belonged to, all farming families had been severely hit by the *krismon*. Only a very few were in a position to take advantage of it.

The Impact of the Crisis

Impact on farming systems

The impact of the crisis on farming systems depended on the changing ratios between input and output prices. Tables 11.3, 11.4 and 11.5 show the figures for the production of lowland rice, upland rice and cassava respectively.

Table 11.3 Input and output prices for lowland rice production, 1996-97 and 1998-99

Item	*Prices (Rp/ha)*		
	1996/97	*1998/99*	*Increase (times)*
Materials:			
Seed (40 kg)	24 000	88 000	3.67
Urea (200 kg)	60 000	240 000	4.00
SP 36 (100 kg)	50 000	200 000	4.00
KCl (50 kg)	25 000	100 000	4.00
Herbicide	20 000	67 500	3.38
Pesticide	30 000	120 000	4.00
Sub-total	209 000	815 500	3.90
Labour:			
Soil tillage (tractor)	100 000	145 000	1.45
Seeding/planting	22 000	50 000	2.27
Fertiliser application/ pest control	12 000	24 000	2.00
Weeding (x 1)	60 000	120 000	2.00
Sub-total	194 000	339 000	1.75
Total costs	403 000	1 154 500	2.86
Gross return (2500 kg)	875 000	3 450 000	3.94
Net return	472 000	2 295 500	4.86
Input/output ratio (%)	46	33	0.72
Return to labour	666 000	2 634 500	3.96

Source: IRD-Orstom field survey.

Table 11.4 Input and output prices for upland rice production, 1996-97 and 1998-99

Item	*Prices (Rp/ha)*		
	1996/97	*1998/99*	*Increase (times)*
Materials:			
Seed (30 kg)	28 000	120 000	4.29
Urea (100 kg)	30 000	120 000	4.00
SP 36 (50 kg)	25 000	100 000	4.00
KCl (50 kg)	25 000	100 000	4.00
Pesticide	15 000	60 000	4.00
Sub-total	123 000	500 000	4.07
Labour:			
Soil tillage (draught animals)	100 000	160 000	1.60
Seeding/planting	50 000	100 000	2.00
Fertiliser application/ pest control	12 000	24 000	2.00
Weeding (x 1)	60 000	120 000	2.00
Sub-total	222 000	404 000	1.82
Total costs	345 000	904 000	2.62
Gross return (1250 kg)	437 500	1725 000	3.94
Net return	92 500	821 000	8.88
Input/output ratio	79	52	0.66
Return to labour	314 500	1 225 000	3.90

Source: IRD-Orstom field survey.

On average, the price of material inputs increased fourfold, while that of labour merely doubled. As the price of rice also increased fourfold, the crisis should, in theory, have had little impact on rice cropping systems. Farmers employing labourers should even have benefitted, since the cost of labour rose less than the cost of materials.

However, these figures are only theoretical. With each new cropping season the farmer had to pay more for inputs, while his income still reflected yesterday's prices. For instance, at the time of writing, no farmer had earned the current price of Rp 1380 per kilogramme for his paddy rice. At the last harvest, the average price was still around Rp 500 per kilogramme. Moreover, by increasing input prices, the crisis also increased the risk faced by farmers. A total crop failure, which as we have seen is far from unusual in transmigration areas, would place an intolerable burden on the already vulnerable smallholder.

Table 11.5 Input and output prices for cassava production, 1996-97 and 1998-99

Item	*Prices (Rp/ha)*		
	1996/97	*1998/99*	*Increase (times)*
Materials:			
Stakes (free)			
Urea (50 kg)	15 000	60 000	4.00
P 36 (50 kg)	25 000	100 000	4.00
Sub-total	40 000	160 000	4.00
Labour:			
Soil tillage			
(draught animals)	100 000	160 000	1.60
Planting	25 000	50 000	2.00
Weeding (x 2)	100 000	200 000	2.00
Sub-total	225 000	410 000	1.82
Total costs	265 000	570 000	2.15
Gross return (5000 kg)	350 000	750 000	2.14
Net return	85 000	180 000	2.12
Input/output ratio	0.76	0.76	1.00
Return to labour	310 000	590 000	1.90

Source: IRD-Orstom field survey.

Furthermore, the figures are based on the assumption that yields remain at the same level, which may well not be the case. In response to the soaring prices of inputs, most farmers reduced their fertiliser and pesticide applications. Some of those who formerly used tractors for land preparation could no longer afford the cost and reverted to manual preparation, reducing the area they cropped. These measures will certainly lead to lower production and may have greatly increased the risk of total crop failure, as pests devour the smaller remaining stands. Already risky, the growing of food crops could well become a dangerous gamble for the farmers of Northern Lampung.

Cassava farmers were not greatly affected by the rising prices of inputs since they seldom apply fertilisers. However, with the prices at which they must buy other basic commodities tripling while the selling price of fresh tubers merely doubled, cassava farmers definitely suffered a net financial loss[13]. Their already low incomes fell dramatically in real terms.

Indisputably then, the crisis had a negative impact on food crop farming systems in Northern Lampung. In the uplands, poor soils and a lack of cash gave farmers no choice but to grow cassava, although this is the crop that rose least in price. In the lowlands, farmers either did not have the means to maintain their use of inputs at the same level or were not prepared to take the risk of doing so. The steady loss of control over flooding partly influenced their decisions.

A tremendous increase in poverty

It is clear that, far from being able to benefit from the *krismon*, many transmigrants had become trapped by their poverty. Indonesia's Central Bureau of Statistics, the BPS, set the rural poverty line at an income of Rp 27 413 per capita per month in 1996, but raised it to Rp 41 588 in 1998 (*Suara Pembaharuan*, 1998). If we compare the incomes of the families in our sample with these levels, we find that poverty rose to disturbingly high levels in all three villages. If we use the KHMP as our yardstick the results are even worse, with two-thirds or more of the population of the three villages living below the poverty line (Table 11.6).

Table 11.6 Percentage of households living below the poverty line in three survey villages, 1996 and 1998

Location	*Percentage according to:*			
	BPS		*KHMP*	
	1996	*1998*	*1996*	*1998*
Manggala	48	71	48	81
Mesuji	33	45	33	67
Rawa Pitu	9	36	12	64

Sources: BPS, Departemen Tenaga Kerja (Lampung) and IRD-Orstom field survey.

Strategies for Coping

To cope with the crisis, the transmigrants of all three villages developed similar strategies designed to reduce their outgoings. No one dared take risks in order to profit from the new opportunities that the crisis also brought. The only ones who were able to benefit were those who took advantage of other people's distress.

Reducing production costs

In response to the soaring prices of agricultural inputs, most farmers opted to cut their production costs drastically. In the uplands, the already low amounts of pesticides and fertilisers used by farmers were further reduced. The percentage of farmers using fertilisers on upland rice fell from 69% to 27% in Manggala and from 75% to 20% in Mesuji. In Rawa Pitu, the percentage of farmers using fertilisers on lowland rice fell from 94% to 26%. Only 10% of Manggala farmers and 29% of Mesuji farmers applied fertilisers to their cassava crop. The use of pesticides also fell sharply, from 73% to 24% in Rawa Pitu.

As we have seen, another way of reducing production costs is to reduce the area cultivated. In Rawa Pitu, for instance, 48% of farmers substantially reduced their rice area. Some had to do so, resorting to manual soil preparation because they could no longer afford to rent a hand-tractor. For others, the deep flooding on part of their plots had a similar effect.

Reducing production costs is only worthwhile if returns remain at the same level. In all the cases we examined, the returns were lower. The only advantage gained was reduced financial losses in the event of crop failure. Paradoxically, however, reducing the area cultivated and lowering the use of pesticides had the effect of heavily increasing the risk of crop failure.

Reduction of other expenditures

For most of the farmers in our survey, reducing the purchase of inputs was not enough to enable them to cope with the crisis, since most of them had never used large amounts of inputs in the first place. People's next reaction to the squeeze was to postpone non-essential expenditures, on items such as leisure, housing and clothes, and also expensive social occasions such as circumcisions, weddings and entertaining. Craftsmen had a hard time, as nobody wanted them to carry out home improvements. Many families in our survey confessed that, for the first time for many years, they were unable to buy new clothes for the coming Lebaran[14].

After cutting non-essential expenditures, the next stage was to reduce essential ones. Traditional drugs and remedies made a surprising comeback, as many families could no longer afford expensive modern medicines. School-related expenditures also had to be drastically reduced; poor families could no longer afford to buy new uniforms[15]. Fortunately, because teachers agreed to accept even those pupils whose uniforms had worn out, no child had to leave school for financial reasons.

Spending rapidly became limited to the purchase of basic goods (*sembako*). In our sample, 72% of families did not reduce their daily food consumption. However, they typically found themselves spending three times as much on cooking oil, sugar, coffee, tea and cooking ingredients. Whereas Rp 3000 a day was sufficient for these purchases before the crisis, now Rp 10 000 was not enough. Before the crisis, civil servants and most people in employment had been able to save one-third of their monthly salary, typically Rp 300 000. Now, 28% of families had to cut back on cooking oil, sugar, coffee, tea, onions, chilli and, with the utmost reluctance, on cigarettes.

Finally, when there was no other way to economise, people were forced to save on food staples. Even in rice producing areas, rice stopped being the staple food of transmigrants. As they could buy 10 kilogrammes of cassava for the price of 1 kilogramme of rice, rice growers preferred to sell their rice and buy cassava instead. Except in a few rich families, *tiwul*, a mixture of rice and cassava, became everyday fare. This was already a part of most families' diet before the *krismon*. The difference now lay in the proportions of rice and cassava mixed: one glass of rice for 3 kilogrammes of cassava. Some families chose to give the rice to their small children only, with the other family members eating cassava tubers supplemented with cassava leaves.

Borrowing

When times are hard people can still obtain credit—or at least they can try. After a while most families found they could no longer borrow, as the shopkeepers had already reached their lending limits. The notorious *ijon* system, whereby the farmer sells his crop at rock-bottom prices long before the harvest, made a worrying comeback. A new practice thrived: *yarnen*. This is short for *bayar sesudah panen* or "paid at harvest". The purchase of agricultural inputs, the renting out of hand-tractors and even the purchase of staple food—all were done on a *yarnen* basis. At harvest, if they had not experienced crop failure, the farmers made just enough to repay their debts before beginning the vicious circle all over again.

Increasing off-farm work

Off-farm work was the only way to earn cash quickly. Fortunately, there were still local opportunities for such work. Northern Lampung's export crop producing estates continued to employ day labourers throughout the *krismon*. However, these opportunities were open only to families with a young, strong labour force, most of whom had already taken on as much off-farm work as they could by the time the crisis began. The only other option was to give up farming altogether and become a full-time estate worker. However, the estates do not wish to employ full-time workers, since in doing so they incur additional costs in sickness benefits, housing, sick and home leave and government taxes. Full-time workers have to be paid, even if there is no work; they always ask for more facilities; and they might even organise trade unions. For the estates, it is far more economical to treat employees as proletarian peasants.

Opportunities for off-farm work outside the province were few. Some families sent their grown-up daughters to Jakarta to work as housemaids. Malaysia became a favourite destination, but for the most part only in people's dreams.

Return to the mountains

Most transmigrants lost all their possessions when they were expelled from Southern Lampung and forced to join the Translok Programme. Some, however, were able to save their coffee plantations. Either the plantation was not located in the area registered for reforestation, or it was considered too remote by the foresters, or reforestation simply failed and the coffee shrubs survived. In Manggala, for instance, about 30% of the transmigrants still "owned" a coffee plantation in their area of origin. During their first years on the scheme they gave little attention to this left-over asset. Once a year, at harvest time, they paid a short visit to the plantation to reap its fruits. As the plantations were poorly maintained, the harvests barely paid the travel costs, but the visit was also a good opportunity to strengthen ties with relatives and former neighbours.

This attitude changed radically with the advent of the *krismon*. The tremendous rise in the rupiah price of coffee rekindled the transmigrants' interest in their plantations. Although still officially resident at Manggala, plantation owners regularly spent a fortnight tending their coffee shrubs in Southern Lampung. There they were joined by a mass exodus of other transmigrants looking for waged labour. The sudden wealth of the Lampung coffee growers had made headlines all over the country. The exceptionally high price of coffee had both created job opportunities for day labourers and encouraged former owners to think that reopening their plantations might be worth the risk.

All this is a sign of changing times. Farmers are no longer subservient and the Forestry Department officials responsible for policing state forest land are keeping a lower profile. Most transmigrants still hesitate to exchange their poor but relatively secure lives in the north for the risky pursuit of riches in the south. But if the conditions for food crop farming do not improve soon, many more may have no choice but to abandon their Translok villages for good.

Selling assets

Assets offered for sale at a relatively early stage of the crisis included bicycles, household utensils, furniture and a wide range of other items.

In Northern Lampung as elsewhere in Indonesia and the developing world, farmers store wealth in the form of livestock. As the crisis intensified, many farmers sold cattle, often sacrificing most or all of a herd built up slowly over the years. Some farmers also sold land, either voluntarily or in forced sales when loans were recalled (see below).

Selling land was considered a last resort, since effectively it meant giving up farming.

Taking advantage of the crisis

When crisis strikes, there are always a few people who, in theory at least, are in a position to take advantage of it. In Northern Lampung, these people consisted mainly of relatively affluent money lenders, shopkeepers and employers. Each of these groups fared somewhat differently.

Money lenders did particularly well, as farmers were forced to sell their crops long before harvest. Some became loan sharks, requiring farmers to hand over their land certificates as collateral for loans. If the farmers prove unable to pay back their loans in the coming months, they will be forced to sell their land at the price fixed by the loan shark. Shopkeepers and larger retailers were less badly hit by the crisis than others, as they could pass price increases on to the customer. However, as the purchasing power of their customers decreased, they had to sell more on credit. Many reached their lending limits and were no longer sure they would be repaid. On the other hand, to refuse credit to a customer ran the risk of offending him—a dangerous thing to do in these times of *reformasi*. Employers were in theory well placed to take advantage of the crisis, which had reduced labour costs in real terms. But this would have meant borrowing money from the bank and investing it—too risky in these troubled times. As a result, many chose not to expand their businesses.

Conclusions

In 1998, all the reports written about Indonesia forecasted a worst-case scenario. The country was about to run out of a host of basic commodities including rice, soybean, meat, eggs and medicines. Surprisingly, this was one disaster that did not happen. By the end of the year, these and other goods were still to be found in local stores. This provided enough "evidence" for the next crop of reports to swing to the opposite extreme, replacing the predictions of doomsday with an equally naïve over-optimism (Lingle and Larsson, 1999).

According to a recent and controversial World Bank report, the Indonesian economy "had proven to be very resilient and its population far more resourceful than expected". Similar views found their way into the popular press. "While Indonesia is suffering a severe crisis, it is not the universal disaster some would have it" reported the *Los Angeles Times* in January 1999 (Iritani, 1999). No doubt the forecasts of a dramatic increase in poverty, unemployment and school drop-out rates were inflated, based as they were on inadequate data and false assumptions about the nature of the crisis. Desperately looking for international aid, the Indonesian Government probably also exaggerated the situation. However, the fact that basic commodities could still be found in local stores does not prove that the Indonesian economy performed better than predicted. These commodities remained available only because the vast majority of Indonesia's people could no longer afford to buy them.

Both the transmigrants and the Indonesian peasantry as a whole proved to be very resilient. They always have been. But what of their hopes that they would never go hungry again? Thanks to cassava, they have survived. But, for the majority, bare survival is all they are ever likely to achieve. They are in no position to benefit by the present economic turmoil. The soaring prices of inputs have forced even the most progressive farmers to revert to subsistence farming. Falling back into the poverty trap has left people in a state of shock. To cope with the crisis, all the farmers in our sample developed survival strategies. However, none of these strategies—low-input farming, reducing the cropping area, increasing off-farm labour, borrowing money—will help them spring the trap. Rather, these desperate measures are likely to mire them even more deeply in poverty.

Even before the crisis hit the transmigrants, the rationale behind the government's resettlement programme in Lampung Province was questionable. In the name of reforestation, thousands of moderately well-off people were displaced from the fertile Barisan mountains to the marginal soils of the Northern Lampung plains, where thousands of hectares of forest were cleared without providing any real social benefit. Was the programme really motivated purely by environmental concerns, as the government claimed? The Gunung Balak area—one of the largest areas to be reforested—was opened in the early 1960s by the

Indonesian Communist Party (PKI). The nearby Barisan mountains became a haven for members of the Barisan Tani Indonesia (BTI)[16] fleeing the post—1965 persecutions in Java. Given the government's obsession with the so-called "latent communist danger", it is conceivable that environmental concerns were used as the pretext for dispersing alleged former communists over a wider area and into more easily controlled settlements.

The Indonesian food crop sector is not about to collapse, but it badly needs help if it is to avoid reverting to subsistence agriculture. Our prediction is that the present trend towards low-input cropping will, if nothing is done to arrest it, result in lower yields and eventually in permanent food shortages at a national level. Unless the government subsidizes inputs, at least for a while, Indonesia is highly unlikely to become self-sufficient in rice again, as it was in the late 1980s and the first half of the 1990s. The maintenance of irrigation networks is another priority. Rawa Pitu has the potential to become Northern Lampung's rice granary, but only if primary canals are properly maintained.

Many of the former forest squatters now living in the Northern Lampung Translok area remember the good times they experienced in their mountain homes. Their relatives who have remained in Southern Lampung are now enjoying peak prices for their coffee. Some transmigrants have heard rumours that the areas from which they were forcibly evacuated have been recolonised by newcomers. In the flooded houses of Rawa Pitu, desperate families dream of returning to their villages of origin. In these times of *reformasi* they are no longer afraid of guns. They may well be tempted to turn that dream into a reality.

References

Iritani, E. 1999. Indonesian fiscal crisis now seen as less severe. *Los Angeles Times*, 23 January. Los Angeles, California, USA.

Levang, P. 1997. La terre d'en face: La transmigration en Indonésie. Institut français de la recherche scientifique pour le développement en coopération (ORSTOM), Paris, France.

Lingle, C. and Larsson, T. 1999. Indonesia's economy is doing reasonably well. *Journal of Commerce* (Washington DC), January 21.

Suara Pembaharuan. 1998. Akhir 1998 penduduk miskin jadi 118 juta. 3 July issue.

Notes

1 For example, the Gunung Balak sub-district in the southwest of Lampung was opened in 1963 and the government has been collecting taxes there ever since. In 1983, local farmers watching television learned that they were forest squatters and would have to leave the sub-district immediately.

2 Recalcitrants saw their houses burnt or even elephant-dozed. The intimidation and violence orchestrated by the local authorities were widely publicised, persuading the squatters to join the Translok Programme en masse.

3 Soils had very low cation exchange capacity, a pH of 4.2-4.5, and were deficient in phosphorus (Levang, 1997).

4 A plethora of oil palm, pineapple and coconut estates had been established, possibly on purpose, close to the transmigration schemes. The transmigrants represented a plentiful source of cheap labour.

5 In Mesuji, 16 years after the village had been founded, only one-third of the original settlers remained, all others having returned to the area from which they had been expelled, the Barisan mountain range in the southwest. The total population of the village had risen only slowly, from 600 to 823 families.

6 The large plantation estates do not directly employ workers, but subcontract most operations to contractors who are in charge of recruiting, supervising and paying the labourers. The estate management monitors the work and pays the contractor.

7 The objective of this programme is to reduce the costs of transmigration by attracting spontaneous migrants to already developed sites. Upon arrival these migrants receive a 1.25-hectare plot, a few seeds, and some tools and building materials.

8 Because of the risk of unexpected floods, the second cropping season in Rawa Pitu is usually also devoted to rice.

9 *Sembako* stands for *Sembilan bahan pokok*, or nine basic commodities. These commodities are: rice, sugar, salt, dried fish, kerosene, soap, wheat flour, cooking oil and textiles.

10 This peak was probably caused by the temporary intervention of a new buyer, Indofood, on the local market.

11 The farmers always announce their yields net of the harvester's share. The total yield in this case was thus 3 tonnes of paddy rice per hectare.

12 The differences between rich and poor may seem minute, especially to outsiders. But even the slightest difference may translate into a huge difference in social status.

13 Based on the price of cassava in January 1999. Given the substantial amount of cassava produced in Northern Lampung, the price probably had some way further to fall at the time of going to press.

14 Poor families generally buy new clothes only once a year, for Lebaran (*Id-al-Fitr*).

15 School uniforms (three per year) represent the bulk of schooling costs at primary level.

16 The Indonesian Peasant Front, which was closely linked to the PKI.

SYNTHESIS

Chapter 12

What Role for Agriculture in Indonesia's Recovery?

François Ruf and Françoise Gérard

Agriculture is often thought of as a lever of economic growth, particularly after a country's currency has depreciated. Because the output of agriculture is tradable, currency depreciation implies a rapid increase in producer prices. Costs, however, should increase more slowly, because of the importance of labour and land in production. These production factors are relatively non-tradable and therefore, in theory at least, less affected by inflation. East Asia's recent currency depreciations should thus make its agriculture more competitive, abroad as well as at home. Exports in tradable agricultural sectors should rise, while imports from developed countries should decline, because of increased competition as well as reduced demand (Mohan, 1998).

In 1998, a number of success stories in Indonesia's agricultural exports, for example coffee, cocoa and spices, seemed to bear out this hypothesis. While the rest of the country was suffering, hundreds of thousands of farmers in Sumatra and Sulawesi enjoyed spectacular windfalls. However, 1999 told a different story. The domestic prices of these commodities fell again. This new setback was not caused merely by the slow recovery of the rupiah. International prices also fell heavily. For example, CIF prices[1] of cocoa in New York fell from US$ 1600 per tonne in July 1998 to less than US$ 900 in late 1999.

Is there a relationship between the Asian crisis and the decline in world prices? In other words, does the crisis act in the longer term to reduce its early positive impact on the nominal incomes enjoyed by farmers? According to economic theory, a currency devaluation or depreciation in a major commodity producing country could indeed trigger a decline in world prices (see Chapter 2). The decline would occur through two mechanisms. First, outside the country, devaluation makes exports cheaper for buyers paying in foreign currency. That may well increase the demand for exports, but market forces intervene to reduce prices still further, capturing part of the surplus at the expense of the producing country. Second, inside the country, the producer usually benefits from higher prices in local currency, so there is an incentive to increase short-term supplies by either expanding the area under cultivation or increasing yields.

Increasing the area of export crops may mean more forest is cleared. If unsustainable production systems are put in its place, there could be a short-term gain in production that has a negative impact on the environment and hence on development in the long term. In the words of Stiglitz (1999), "Some of the so-called revival of exports is little more than a shipment of the productive assets of the country abroad—hardly a victory for economic recovery! The goal should be to ensure that these productive assets continue to produce and that the assets are not stripped away".

Indonesia's multi-dimensional crisis has had a profound impact on its peoples' lives. This impact stems not only from economic recession but also from the social and political turmoil that the *krismon* unleashed. The crisis brought to boiling point all the frustration, the resentments and the spoiled relationships that had for so long simmered in Indonesian society. Against this background, Indonesia's new leaders must sieze the opportunity they now have to reappraise the country's apparent past economic successes and to begin again, this time with better economic and social policies. What should those policies be?

This final chapter synthesizes all that we now know about the role of agriculture in Indonesia's economic recovery. We draw from previous chapters to discuss the country's major crops for the export and domestic markets. We also include a few commodities not covered previously but on which we have some secondary data. The first section deals with the potential and actual impact of agricultural exports, focussing on how world prices reacted to the currency crisis. The second section examines the impact of the crisis on farmers' incomes. In the third section, we summarise the chief factors affecting the outcome of the crisis for different farmers. Lastly, we present our conclusions.

Recovery through Export-led Growth

The classic course of action following currency devaluation or depreciation is to relaunch the economy by means of exports, which should have become more competitive. This works well provided international prices do not fall, which they should not do if the country has only a small share of a market. It is likely to work less well if the country is already a major producer. Especially in the commodities market, being a major producer is not the same as being a price maker.

Severe monetary depreciation drives down domestic prices when these are expressed in foreign currency. In so doing it generates a kind of unearned profit or "rent". How the rent is shared is then negiotated through the marketing chain. The negotiation "game" is played by everyone in the chain, from producers to international buyers, through middlemen and exporters. Buyers, however, tend to have the last word. The fewer the international buyers, the more powerful their bargaining position and the greater the risk that export prices and, eventually, world prices will decline. This is the first and most direct mechanism of world price decline triggered by currency depreciation. The mechanism may also apply to countries that export a substitute commodity. For instance, the 50% depreciation of the Brazilian Real in 1999 put heavy downward pressure on world oil palm prices because of its direct impact on the price of soybean oil, which is widely used as a substitute for palm oil.

A second and indirect mechanism is farmers' tendency to respond positively to rising prices in the national currency by increasing production and hence exports. If the country has a large market share, this too may push world prices down (see Chapter 2). For example, this is what Mr. Budiman, President of GAPKINDO, said in August 1999, according to the Jakarta Post (12 August 1999):

"Indonesia increased its rubber exports by 15% last year from 1.4 million tonnes in 1997, largely because the falling rupiah's exchange rate made the commodity more competitive.... Rubber production increased last year because cash-pressed smallholders, who run most of the country's rubber plantations, worked double shifts to augment their income."

A third mechanism causing a decline in world prices may be falling domestic demand. Countries affected by currency depreciation may reduce their consumption of a commodity because of its higher price and/or because the domestic industry that consumes it has been weakened. For instance, although it was always of limited importance, the 1998 collapse of the car assembly industry in Indonesia reduced the domestic demand for rubber.

Currency depreciation and the 1999 fall in commodity prices

Figures 12.1-12.4 show how international prices for Indonesia's principal agricultural export commodities moved in the period 1997-99. Several, but not all, commodities show a decline in 1999:

- Cocoa. The world price of cocoa fell from a high of US$ 1700 per tonne in July 1998 to below US$ 1000 per tonne in August 1999. The explanation would seem at first to lie in Indonesia. However, the increase in production in Indonesia was not related to a short-term supply response but rather to planting decisions taken before the crisis (see Chapters 5 and 6). And in any case Indonesia produces barely 15% of global cocoa supplies, whereas Côte d'Ivoire accounts for 42%. International buyers certainly tried to get their share of the spoils of Indonesian monetary depreciation, but if we want to explain the fall in prices properly we must look first at supplies from Côte d'Ivoire and at overall world demand in 1999.

  The 50% devaluation of the CFA franc in 1994 had a positive effect on supplies from Côte d'Ivoire. Combined with structural factors, especially new plantings in the 1980s and replantings in the 1990s, the devaluation triggered a recovery of the market, since exporters suddenly needed half the French francs to buy a tonne of cocoa. This made the market in Côte d'Ivoire more attractive to foreign companies. In both 1994 and 1995, farmers benefitted from cash payments by middlemen—something that had not occurred for many years. Regular cash payments gave farmers the incentive to take more care of their plantations and to apply pesticides again. This short-term farmer response to more stable prices increased yields on the back of the structural changes that had preceded it—migrations, new plantings that replaced forests in the 1980s and, perhaps more important, replantings since 1983, after the El Niño drought of that year had led to plantation fires (Ruf, 1996 and 1999). However, devaluation of the CFA franc and increased production in Côte d'Ivoire did not immediately trigger a fall in the world price, which went on rising until 1998, falling only in 1999. The reasons were twofold: production in Brazil and Malaysia, two other major producing countries, fell over the same period, while world demand continued to increase.

Despite the lack of a direct link, it is difficult not to regard with suspicion the "coincidence" between the world price decline of 1999 and the liberalisation of the cocoa sector in Côte d'Ivoire, which produced more than 40% of world supplies in 1998-99. Liberalisation officially occurred in August 1999, but under pressure from the World Bank was prepared for, and anticipated by, increases in the nominal prices paid to producers in 1997 and 1998. It is possible that the oligopsony of international cocoa buyers anticipated the production increases that were to result from new plantings in previous years and, more directly, from these producer price increases (Ruf and Cebron, 1999). One thing is sure: the 1999 fall in price coincided with a fall in world demand—the first for 20 years. Having risen by 2-6% per year for over two decades, demand fell by 0.2% in 1998-99.

One factor accounting for this fall in demand was reduced consumption in Russia, which was strongly related to impoverishment and the decline of the rouble. Consumption also fell in most Eastern European countries, for similar reasons. A second factor was the strategy employed by one or two international companies, which reduced their processing activities in order to widen the margin between whole beans and semi-processed products such as cocoa butter and powder. This strategy was facilitated by the reduced number of firms involved in trading and processing.

- Coffee. World prices of robusta coffee have been more volatile than those of cocoa in recent years. They peaked in 1994, fell in 1996, climbed again in 1997 and then, in 1998, obliged coffee farmers with a new peak. However, since June 1998 they have gone into a decline, falling to some US$ 1.3 per kilogramme from over US$ 1.9. Meanwhile, Indonesian production and exports have shown a slight increase, but the resulting extra 20 000 to 30 000 tonnes could not have been enough to influence the international market (see Chapter 7). If any Asian country played a significant part in determining prices it was Vietnam, whose production doubled in a decade, reaching 400 000 tonnes in 1999 compared with 200 000 tonnes in 1990 and almost nothing in 1980. The 1999 devaluation of the Real in Brazil, from CR 1-1.2 = US$ 1.00 in 1998 to around CR 1.9 = US$ 1.00 in 1999, was certainly one of the driving forces behind the fall in coffee prices.

- Rubber. The sharp fall in world rubber prices to US$ 0.55 per kilogramme in July 1999 from a previous high of US$ 1.30 in January 1997 was related to increases in production that outstripped demand in the three major rubber producing countries of Southeast Asia: Thailand, Malaysia and Indonesia. The price of rubber began falling rapidly in 1995-96—well before the *krismon*. The steady decline in prices explains why Indonesian rubber producing smallholders did not share the 1998 windfall enjoyed by cocoa and coffee farmers. The rupiah depreciated by just enough to offset the impact on producer prices of the fall in world prices (see Chapter 8).

The tyre market is the world's major consumer of rubber. Before the Asian crisis, the American and European tyre markets were considered to be saturated and the Asian market was seen as the most promising. Since the crisis, although world demand has increased it has done so less rapidly than expected. The Asian crisis has had a negative impact on demand, reinforcing the existing trend towards lower prices.

As far as Indonesia is concerned, exports certainly increased. However, this increase was related less to short-term decisions to increase tapping than to new plantations coming into production and to the recovery of existing plantations from drought. As in the case of cocoa, it therefore reflected investment decisions taken well before the crisis[2].

The decline in rubber prices may also be the symptom of a powerful global oligopoly. Demand now comes almost entirely from three giant buyers on the market, the major tyre companies Michelin, Goodyear and Bridgestone. As an official of the Association professionelle du caoutchouc en Afrique (ACNA) put it, "Even though the buyers do not deliberately lower prices, producers (scattered in many factories and export companies) find it difficult to defend their rights" (*Afrique Agriculture*, 1999). Today's market is lacking in transparency.

- Palm oil. The prices of this commodity fell by more than half in 1999, to US$ 320 per tonne in July of that year from US$ 680 a year previously. The finger may be pointed at the greatly increased supplies from Indonesia and Malaysia, where exports rose 9% and 16% respectively. In Indonesia the increase came when a ban and heavy taxes on exports, imposed in 1997, were suddenly lifted. A further factor explaining the fall was that importers stopped worrying about the impact of the drought on Indonesian supplies. In addition, the USA and Brazil enjoyed bumper harvests of soybean, the major commodity which can be substituted for oil palm in the processing of cooking oil (see Chapter 3). The 50% monetary depreciation in Brazil also helped.

- Plywood. The trend for this commodity is an interesting exception, moving in the opposite direction to that of all the other major export commodities. World prices fell in 1998, reflecting the collapse of Asian demand and, more specifically, the recession in the construction sectors of Japan and Korea. This early fall was thus directly associated with the impact of the Asian crisis on demand. However, 1999 was a year of slow recovery for plywood. This recovery was again explained by a change in Asian demand, in the form of unexpected new demand from China. This country had faced problems in domestic production caused by La Niña-related floods, which had forced it to stop exploiting its own timber resources (see Chapter 4).

  China managed to avoid devaluing its currency throughout the region's crisis. Together with the size of its economy and the scale of its demand for imports, this provided significant help to the Indonesian timber sector. Demand for Indonesian plywood also picked up in the Japanese and European economies, themselves recovering from recession.

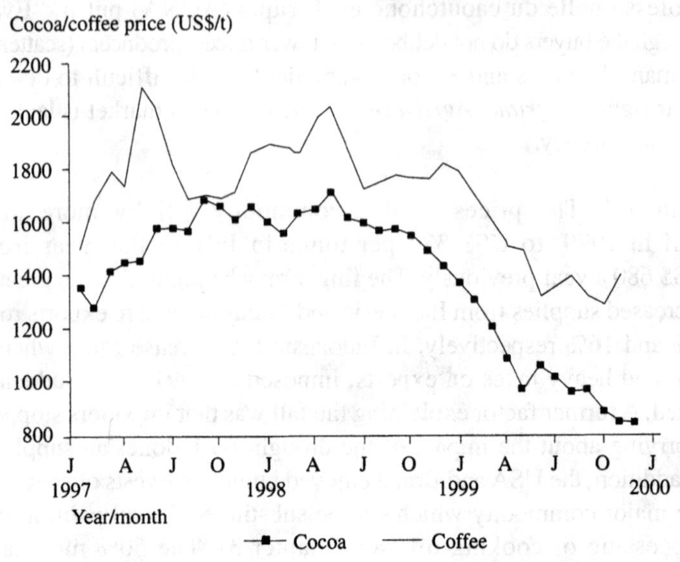

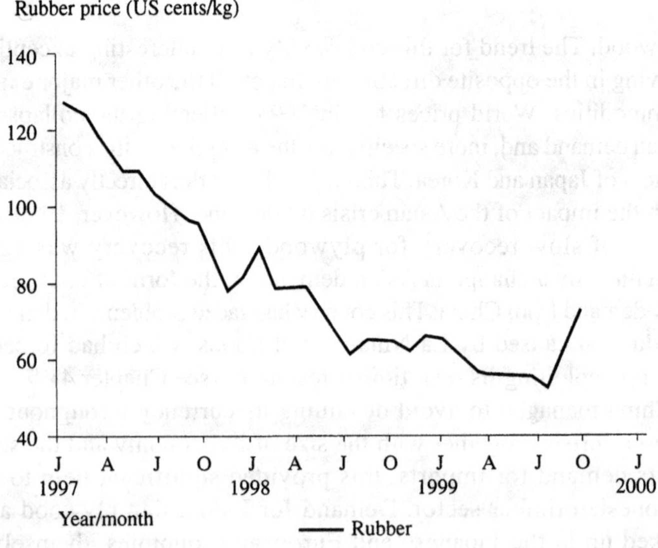

Figure 12.1 International prices of cocoa, coffee and rubber, 1997-99. Sources: USDA (1999), GAPKINDO.

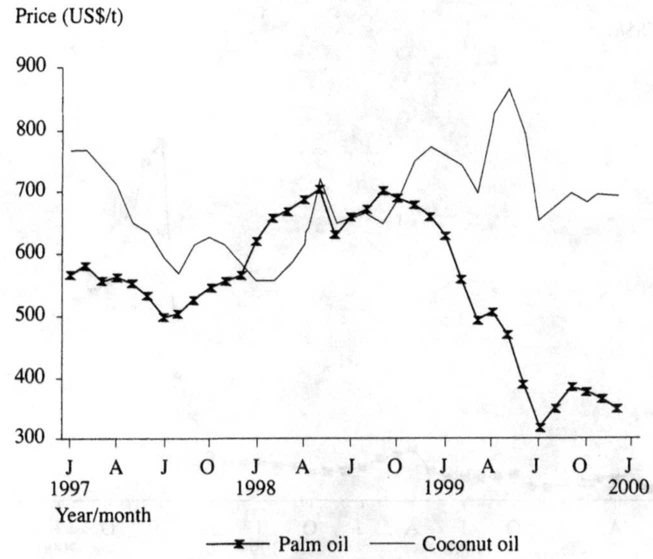

Figure 12.2 International prices of palm and coconut oil, 1997-99. Sources: *Oil World* (various issues).

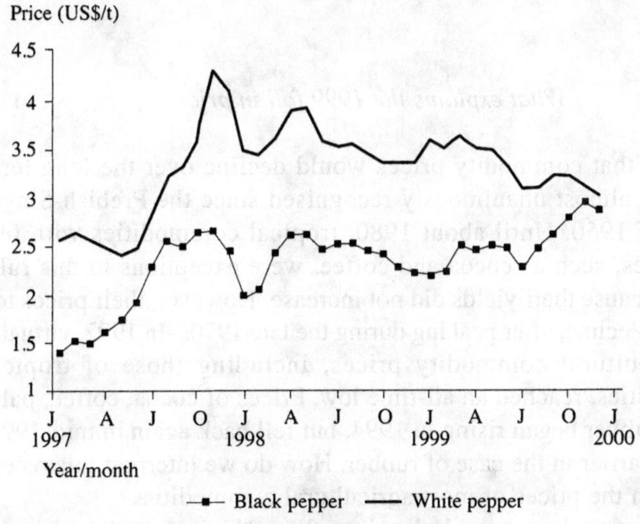

Figure 12.3 International prices of pepper, 1997-99. Source: USDA (1999).

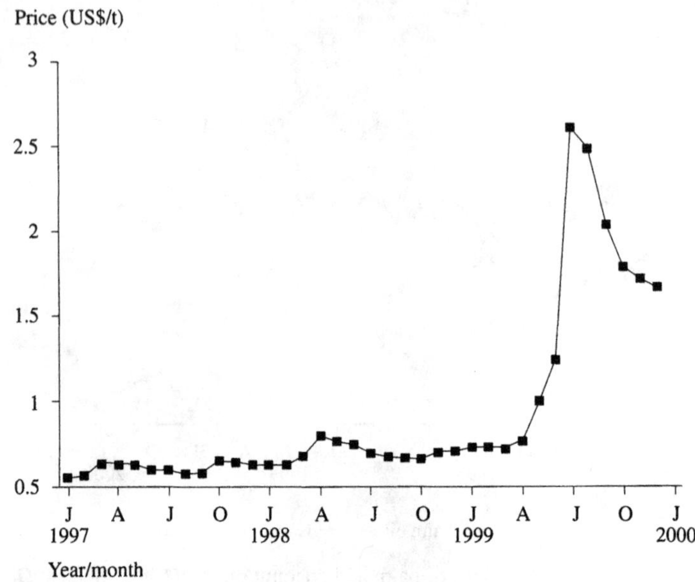

Figure 12.4 International prices of cloves, 1997-99. Source: USDA (1999).

What explains the 1999 fall in prices?

The fact that commodity prices would decline over the long term has been almost unanimously recognised since the Prebish-Singer works of 1950. Until about 1980, tropical commodities with few substitutes, such as cocoa and coffee, were exceptions to this rule, partly because their yields did not increase. However, their prices too began to decline, after peaking during the late 1970s. In 1992, virtually all agricultural commodity prices, including those of tropical commodities, reached an all-time low. Prices of cocoa, coffee, palm oil and rubber began rising in 1994, but fell back again in mid-1998, or even earlier in the case of rubber. How do we interpret this recent decline in the prices of most agricultural commodities?

Much of the long-term decline is explained by increased production. This has four major sources:

- Progress in tropical tree crop breeding. Before the 1970s, relatively poor progress was made in this field—at least in comparison with the sizeable gains made in cereals in developed countries. However, in the 1970s that began to change. In several commodities new planting materials began becoming available to farmers. In tropical tree crop farming, the tree is often the main productive asset in the farming system, so major improvements in tree genotypes can lead to major yield gains. Inevitably, these push prices lower in the long term.

  One of the best examples of this is cocoa. In Côte d'Ivoire, improved trees such as Upper-amazons and hybrids were widely adopted by migrant cocoa farmers in the 1970s on account of their early maturity. The trees bear their first pods in the second or third year after planting, instead of the fourth or fifth. The resulting higher yields, together with higher incomes within a few years of planting, led to a rapid expansion of cocoa-driven migration and hence to a sudden increase of several hundred thousand tonnes in the amount of cocoa traded on the international market. This increase was clearly a factor in the decline of prices in the 1980s and 1990s.

  In Indonesia, other yield-increasing technologies, including fertiliser applications and improved pruning practices, have augmented the impact of improved cocoa planting materials. The intensive farming systems of Sulawesi, whose trees produce 250 kilogrammes per hectare at 2 years of age and 2000 kilogrammes per hectare at 5, have helped keep prices low since around 1990. A further factor has been technological progress in other sectors. The advent of labour-saving technologies in rice production led to a mass exodus of rice farmers and labourers, who migrated to the cocoa pioneer fronts (see Chapter 5).

  Unless its cost is too high, the adoption of new technology can be very rapid. As farmers observe the returns obtained by early adopters, they become convinced that large and rapid yield gains are possible. Information then circulates quickly and the demand for the new planting material and other inputs escalates. This is what is now happening in Indonesia's rubber sector (see Chapters 2 and 8).

  The importance of yield-increasing technology is highlighted by the contrast between oil palm and coconut, which is particularly instructive in Indonesia's case. Oil palm has benefitted from substantial genetic improvement, with early-maturing trees now producing at the age of 3 instead of 5. Coconut, in contrast, still takes 5 years before it enters production. Farmers therefore have less incentive to plant or replant coconut. Despite the efforts made by national research and extension services in the 1980s, Indonesia's coconut sector, like that of the Philippines, faces a huge backlog in replanting.

- Infrastructural development. After the Second World War, logging companies resumed and intensified their activities in the tropics, including Indonesia. The roads, bridges and tracks they built for their trucks opened up new areas of forest to migrant farmers who had hitherto used rivers and mule paths. Vast numbers of new farmers migrated and soon there were many plots in scattered forest clearings.

  In the 1960s and 1970s, pioneer fronts developed, with huge numbers of farmers adopting mixed tree-crop or commercial tree cropping systems. A few years later, when the increased output reached the international market, prices began falling. The effect was magnified by the fact that a similar process was taking place in several countries at the same time, in both Asia and Africa.

  The process of forest conversion continued through the 1980s and into the 1990s. It is a major factor explaining the 1999 decline in prices, at least in the cases of oil palm, cocoa and rubber in Indonesia (see Chapters 3, 5 and 8).

- Lack of alternative opportunities. In theory, when the price of a commodity falls, farmers tend to reduce the care devoted to their established farms and, unless they believe the market will recover in the near future, to stop investing in new plantings. This is the basic mechanism that explains why prices tend to rise again a few years later. A rise of this kind may take place in the first decade of the twenty-first century. In the meantime, however, the prices of most commodities remain low, with the trough of the mid- to late-1990s continuing longer than expected. Our micro-economic data in Indonesia and Côte d'Ivoire lead us to believe the explanation lies in the fact that population continues to rise while alternative employment opportunities, both in agriculture and in other sectors, remain extremely limited. In practice there are still few alternatives to rubber in the peneplains of South Sumatra. Even fewer are the alternatives to cocoa in coastal Sulawesi or southern Côte d'Ivoire. In the case of Côte d'Ivoire, the number of cocoa migrants rose rapidly in the 1990s as the worsening economic situation of the

Sahelian countries drove new waves of economic refugees southwards. The result is more new plantings and more cocoa on the world market, whatever the price.

- Drought and environmental degradation. Paradoxically, these factors may drive a short-term increase in the production of certain commodities, as people migrate away from stricken areas. Deforestation on the massive scale that has occurred in Southeast Asia has almost certainly had a negative effect on the region's rainfall patterns and intensified the impact of its periodic droughts. Drought strikes worst in the drier areas, which have been deforested the longest. For example, drought in the far south of Sulawesi is one of the factors that has led to increased migration to the cocoa pioneer fronts of the island's central region. Similarly, recurrent droughts in Sahelian zone of Burkina Faso during the 1980s and 1990s greatly increased the flow of cocoa migrants to southern Côte d'Ivoire.

Two short-term factors on the supply side also contributed to the 1999 fall in prices. These are:

- The weather. The prices of most agricultural commodities in 1998-99 were affected by climate. In early1998 the market was apprehensive about the possible continuing impact of El Niño, with the result that, for the first few weeks of the year, prices rose. When buyers were reassured that yields were normal, prices fell to below their previous levels.
- Currency depreciation. Having occurred in Indonesia and much of the rest of Southeast Asia, in Brazil and, with delayed effects, in West Africa, currency depreciation may also be thought to have influenced the 1999 decline in prices, via increased supplies. However, although it is tempting to believe that farmers responded to domestic price rises with a short-term increase in supplies, this does not in fact seem to have been the case.

It is true that cocoa farmers in Indonesia increased their harvesting frequency, used more fertilisers and weeded their plots more often in 1998 than in previous years. But these practices were motivated more by the need to deal with the drought and to ward off pest attacks than by price increases. They did not increase production in the short term. However, it is also true that, had farmers not tried to save their trees by using more fertilisers, the negative effects of the drought on yields would have been more keenly felt (see Chapter 5).

The decline in prices is partly explained by interactions between the *krismon* and factors on the demand side. The two most important interactions are:

- Currency depreciation and buyer oligopolies. The liberalisation of commodity markets during the 1990s led to a reduction in the number of buyers on international markets. This has accelerated the decline in prices triggered by the monetary crisis.

  The fact that there are only three main buyers on the international rubber market, and barely more on the cocoa market, has helped these buyers negotiate, or rather impose, lower prices. They are well placed to take advantage of the downward pressure on prices in developing countries.
- Currency depreciation and falling Asian demand. The regional economic recession associated with the collapse of most national currencies was a secondary factor in the decline of global prices. All export commodities except timber were affected. In 1999, Indonesian timber prices actually recovered as demand from China began pulling the sector out of recession.

From Boom to Bust

Figures 12.5-12.10 show what happened to producer prices for various commodities in the period 1997-99. In most cases, prices show the typical boom-to-bust pattern, closely associated with exchange rate movements.

Whatever crop the farmer grew, he or she was almost bound to have been affected either by the 1997 drought or by the 1998 floods, or by both. However, the impact of the crisis on farmers' incomes in 1998-99 varied according to location in the archipelago, crops grown and size of farm. Early in the crisis, export-oriented farms began experiencing an increase in incomes, leading to a windfall during the summer of 1998 in coffee, cocoa and pepper (see Chapters 5 to 7).

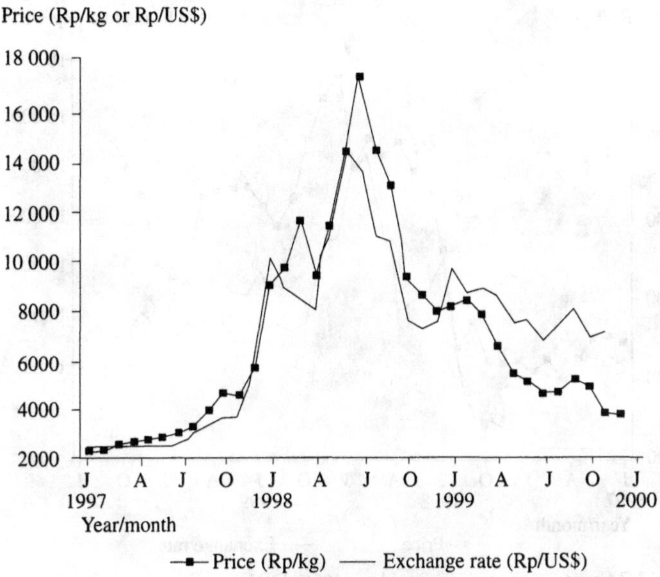

Figure 12.5 Producer price of cocoa at Noling market, South Sulawesi, 1997-99, compared with exchange rate movements

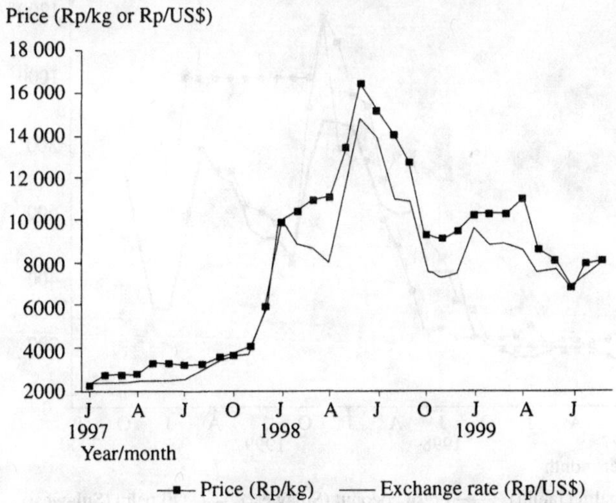

Figure 12.6 Producer price of coffee in southern Sumatra, 1997-99, compared with exchange rate movements

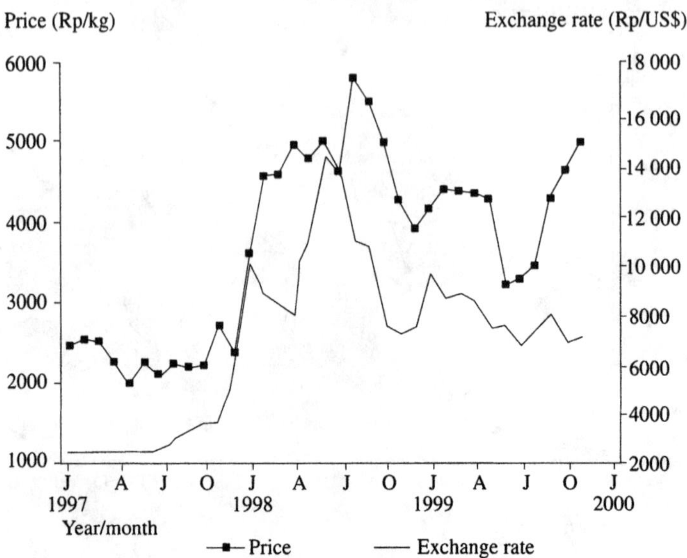

Figure 12.7 Factory gate price of rubber (100% DRC) in Pontianac, South Kalimantan, 1997-99, compared with exchange rate movements

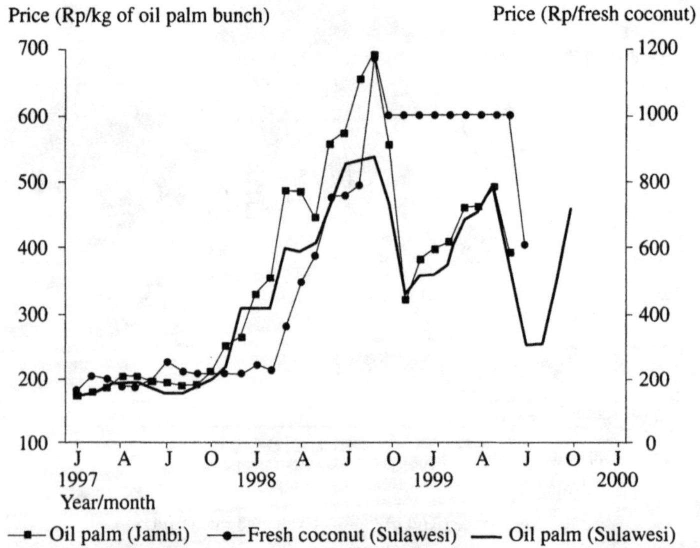

Figure 12.8 Producer prices of oil palm and fresh coconut in Sumatra and South Sulawesi, 1997-99

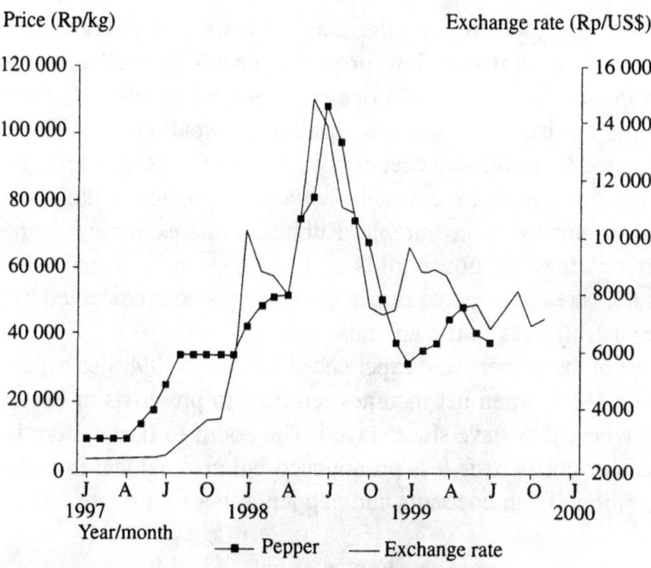

Figure 12.9 Producer price of pepper in South Sulawesi, 1997-99, compared with exchange rate movements. Source: USDA (1999).

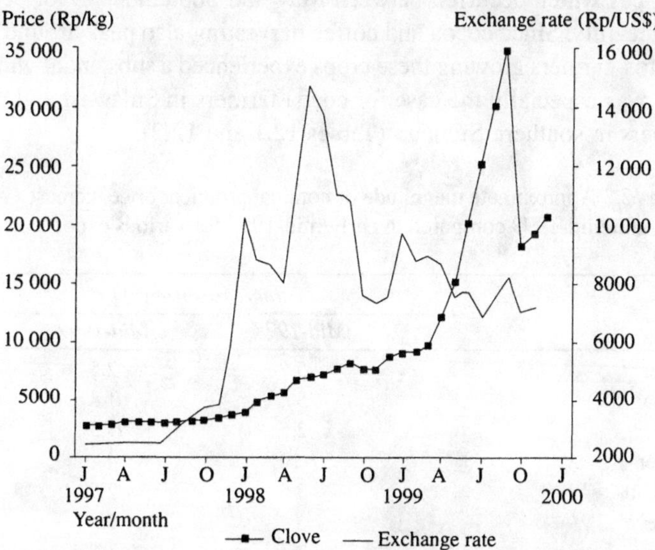

Figure 12.10 Producer price of clove in South Sulawesi, 1997-99, compared with exchange rate movements. Source: USDA (1999).

Farms growing food crops for the domestic market, in contrast, continued to experience relatively low producer prices in real terms, as the government held staple food prices in check while allowing the prices of inputs to rise. Combined with adverse weather conditions, this precipitated their fall into deeper poverty (see Chapters 9 to 11). There were also intermediate cases, in which the impact of the crisis was neutral or somewhat favourable. Rubber is one example (Chapter 8). Another is the few households and villages in Java that possess a reasonable area of irrigated rice in the lowlands complemented by a few coffee or fruit trees in the uplands.

Most of the farmers who experienced a boom in 1998 also experienced a bust in 1999, when net incomes returned to pre-crisis or even lower levels, where they have since stayed. The boom-to-bust pattern is most marked for cocoa. It is less pronounced but also evident in coffee, oil palm, rubber, fresh coconuts and pepper, at least until late 1999.

Export crops

Farmers producing coffee, cocoa and spices benefitted from a sharp rise in prices which occurred between May and September 1998, peaking in June-July. Since cocoa and coffee harvesting also peak around these months, farmers growing these crops experienced a substantial windfall. This was especially the case for cocoa farmers in Sulawesi and coffee farmers in southern Sumatra (Tables 12.1 and 12.2).

Table 12.1 Approximate magnitude of nominal producer price increases in mid-1998 and mid-1999 compared to early/mid-1997 for various export commodities

	Increases (times)	
	Mid-1998	*Mid-1999*
Coffee*	5	2.5
Cocoa*	5	1.8
Rubber	2.5	1.5
Pepper	7-10	4
Palm oil	3	2.5
Clove	3	6
Rice	2	1.5

Table 12.2 Approximate average gross incomes of different types of farmer in 1996, 1997 and 1998

Commodity/location	*Incomes (Rp)*			
	1996	*1997*	*1998*	*Increase in 1998/1996/97 (times)*
Coffee in Bengkulu	8 672 800	7 514 000	33 089 650	3.8
Cocoa:				
Mostly in hills of Sulawesi*	7 894 000	7 751 000	27 161 000	3.4
Mostly in plains of Sulawesi*	13 827 000	17 211 000	49 400 000	3.6
Pepper in South Sulawesi**	3 000 000	7 200 000	30 400 000	4-10
Oil palm in South Sulawesi**	n.av.	7 500 000	21 000 000	3
Food crops in Lampung	n. av.	1 500 000	2 800 000	1.9

* The house is based in the hills but one of the farm-plots may be on the plain. The reverse applies to households "mostly in plains": one of the farm plots may be in the hills.
** Indicative figures from farms in Sulawesi (which is not the main centre of production for these two crops).n.av. = data not available.

* For coffee and cocoa the most relevant comparison is not average yearly prices but rather mid-year prices, since mid-year is when production peaks occur. This is what is used here.

For export-oriented farmers the *krismon* had a positive effect on incomes almost from the start of 1998. In the January to March period the prices of rubber, cocoa and coffee rose sharply at a time when those of food and other items sold in local stores had not yet begun to increase. Coffee farmers were not able to harvest much during this period, but some possessed stored coffee and therefore had something to sell. With production regular throughout the year, rubber farmers in theory had a better deal. In Sumatra and Kalimantan, farmers began saving up to buy motorcycles and other consumer goods. In Sulawesi, the rise in cocoa prices had started even earlier, in or around September 1997, and was already helping farmers overcome the negative impact of the drought, especially in the hills. By January or February 1998, however, farmers in the hills were jealous of their neighbours on the alluvial plains. Whereas the drought had not left many pods on the trees in the hills, lowland farmers had much larger amounts for sale. These farmers benefitted greatly from the January price hike, when prices rose to nearly Rp 10 000 per kilogramme compared with around Rp 2500 per kilogramme 6 months earlier. Men and women who took their cocoa to the middlemen came back home with bags of bank notes. They had never seen so much money in their lives and did not know how to spend it. The next 3 months (February-April 1998) were quieter. Prices fluctuated, rising in March but returning to their February level in April. There was not yet much cocoa for sale. During this period the exchange rate stabilised for a short time before starting to rise rapidly once again. The price of cocoa did likewise, confirming the overriding impact of exchange rates on prices.

During the summer of 1998, as the crisis reached its nadir for urban dwellers, farmers producing coffee, cocoa, pepper and other exportable spices enjoyed spectacular profits. The highest earnings came to pepper farmers in Kalimantan, close to the Malaysian border, who in July were able to sell 1 kilogramme of pepper for around Rp 100 000. A year previously the price had been less than Rp 5000. Coffee provided the second biggest windfall, with the peak harvesting season coinciding with an increase in the international price and with further depreciation of the rupiah. Thousands of coffee farmers were able to buy cars, trucks and buses. Cocoa farmers, who have to spend somewhat more on inputs than coffee farmers, also benefitted greatly, investing their extra cash in four-wheel drives and other vehicles. Other windfalls occurred on a lesser scale. For example, betel nut farmers in Aceh earned Rp 16 000 per kilogramme of their pruduct, a twentyfold increase over its previous price of Rp 800 per kilogramme (McBeth, 1998). At the same time, food prices also increased sharply, but not nearly enough to cancel out the increases in farmers' incomes.

For rubber farmers, the *krismon* was more neutral in its effects (see Chapter 8). These farmers did not experience a peak in prices during July-September 1998. The international price had been declining since 1997. Local prices roughly doubled, but this was hardly enough to offset the increase in food prices. The only real winners were farmers with improved clones, situated in favourable growing areas with good market access, such as South Sumatra. Most other rubber farmers experienced only a slight rise in incomes. More motorcycles were seen in the villages, but there was no real windfall in 1998 or at least nothing to compare with those for coffee, cocoa, pepper and even palm oil. However, when they compared their lot with that of most Indonesians, rubber farmers felt lucky. They knew that rubber had helped them escape the worst effects of the crisis.

In theory, oil palm smallholders benefitted from the crisis in 1998, since local prices rose more than threefold in the 12-month period from mid-1997, from Rp 200 to Rp 700 per kilogramme. In practice, however, most smallholders laboured under the tight control of the estates that bought their produce. Their profits were, therefore, reduced by the hidden costs of credit and fertilisers, knocked off the farm-gate price by the estate. This somewhat reduced the attractiveness of oil palm to smallholders in 1998. For instance, farmers in Sulawesi who grew cocoa, pepper and oil palm ranked the latter as being the crop of least benefit to them that year. Their assessment might have been different if the survey had been repeated in 1999 and 2000 (see below).

After the erratic policy towards clove production pursued over the years by the Suharto regime, the sudden rise in prices that occurred when the policy was abandoned may have helped some farmers. However, in provinces such as Central Sulawesi, the rise came too late, since many clove farmers had already left their farms (see Box 1.3).

In the timber sector (see Chapter 4), the crisis had an entirely different impact to that on tree crops. The effect here was much more typical of the effects observed in the Indonesian economy as a whole, namely a slump in 1998 followed by a slow recovery in 1999. The market began to deteriorate in 1997, with a massive fall in demand from the building sector, which was directly involved in the "bubble" of the mid-1990s and the first sector to feel the pain, in Japan and Korea as well as Indonesia. The price of plywood fell sharply and 30% of capacity fell idle. The recovery of 1999 was, as we have seen, related mainly to unexpected demand from China. This Asian giant suffered its own ecological crisis in 1997-98 and had to rethink its policy of massive deforestation and dam construction. As a result it suddenly began importing whole timber and plywood. China managed to avoid devaluing its currency and in many ways was actually strengthened by the crisis affecting its neighbours.

In sum, a rough classification of 1998 winners and losers looks as follows:

Major winners:	Most pepper farmers Coffee farmers Cocoa farmers
Slightly improved situation	Rubber farmers with improved planting materials Oil palm smallholders
Neutral	Farmers with jungle rubber
Losers	Most clove farmers Most food crop farmers.

Not surprisingly, most winners became avid consumers. But they also spent their money on investments, including what can be termed "social investments"—things that improved their standing in the community (Table 12.3).

In cocoa, coffee and pepper villages, motorcycles and cars appeared in droves. Stone, wood, cement, sand and other building materials began accumulating in backyards, to be used to improve an existing house or build a new one. Balinese transmigrants proved their Hindu faith by building splendid temples (see Chapter 6). Bugis, who are fervent Muslims, filled otherwise empty planes flying to Mecca.

Cocoa farmers in South and Southeast Sulawesi experienced their windfall against a background of abundant land in neighbouring districts, mostly in Central Sulawesi. Cocoa planting material is plentiful and cheap, so they did what South American and African cocoa farmers did before them when prices and incomes suddenly rose: they reinvested a larger share of their profits in land purchases and new plantations (Hill, 1964; Berry, 1976; Ruf, 1995). From a farmer's point of view, the tree and the plantation are still the easiest and safest forms of storing savings, insuring against adversity and building a family heritage (Dupraz and Lifran, 1995). This is especially true during a time of economic crisis, when liquidity is a risk.

Table 12.3 How smallholders used their windfalls

	Expenditures			
Smallholder type	*Consumer items*	*Agricultural investments*	*Non-agricultural investments*	*Social investments*
Coffee in Bengkulu	Satellite-dish + TV	• Purchase of land and old plantations • Replanting and regenerations of old plantations	• Thousands of motocycles • Cars and buses for hire	Pilgrimage to Mecca
Cocoa in Sulawesi	Satellite-dish + TV	• Massive purchases of forests and plantations • Forest clearings • Fertilisers to save farms affected by drought • Water pumps (same objective) • Motor-sprayers	• Thousands of motocycles • Personal cars	Pilgrimage to Mecca
Rubber in Kalimantan	Radios	• Clonal planting materials (some areas only)	• Bicycles • A few motorcycles	
Clove in Sulawesi		Disinvestment: farmers leave their farms and let trees die		

Most rubber farmers did not experience a windfall in 1998. The early profits made in January and February petered out as the year went on. As already explained, this was mainly because, after March, there was little, if any, increase in real prices. In addition, rubber smallholders faced a shortage of land and lacked the capital with which to buy relatively expensive improved planting materials. There was strong competition for land with oil palm, mainly because many estates were willing to exchange a ready-made plantation for new land. The terms of exchange were appalling-typically 7 hectares of new land for only 2 hectares of mature plantation, which would have to be paid for over a period of years-but to many rubber farmers such exchanges seemed to be a ready-made solution to their problems (see Chapter 8). The farmer gained immediate access to an income and to a technologically superior production system that, could lead to higher incomes in the future.

Most coffee farmers in more intensively developed South Sumatra and Lampung provinces, and also in some districts of Bengkulu, lacked access to land. Many of them decided to invest in rehabilitating their existing coffee plantations (see Chapter 7).

Following the 1998 windfall, 1999 was a time of recession which saw the collapse of rupiah prices and hence producers'incomes in the export-oriented tree-crop sector. The first factor contributing to the collapse was the partial recovery of the rupiah, which was good news for city dwellers but not for export farmers, since it lowered commodity prices in local currency. More importantly, however, the international prices of most export commodities either declined steadily or fell sharply in late 1998 and 1999.

Cocoa farmers faced what amounted to a slump in 1999. They had not expected such a catastrophic fall in prices. Many cocoa farmers were squeezed between the slide in cocoa prices and the high prices of fertilisers and pesticides. To add to their troubles, the CBP, a severe pest in Southeast Asia, began spreading rapidly throughout Sulawesi, requiring heavy expenditures on pesticides and other means of pest control. In some places the situation has become critical and could trigger a shift of production into new areas. This is a classical scenario in cocoa production. As pioneer fronts open up increasingly remote new areas, allowing the development of new plantations over thousands of hectares, older areas fall into decline, afflicted by a combination of falling prices, increasing pressure from pests and lack of maintenance. The latter occurs because farmers actually prefer to move to new frontier land. This "shifting production" system, often observed elsewhere, was already emerging in Sulawesi before the crisis, but was probably accelerated by it. The 1997 drought and the 1998 flooding may also have been contributory factors (see Chapters 5-7).

The price of coffee declined less than that of cocoa in 1999, but the decline continues in 2000 and may well have a long way further to run. In rubber, the decline in international prices began earlier than in other commodities, dating back to 1996. By 1999, many small-scale rubber farmers faced severe difficulties (see Chapter 8). However, since the turn of the new century rubber has started looking as if it may become the first tree-crop commodity to show a modest recovery. Oil palm, which is produced for the domestic as well as the export market, is dealt with in the next section.

Clove stands apart from the other tree crops for two reasons. The first is that Indonesia is both the world's largest producer and its largest consumer of this crop. Indonesian clove farmers mostly produce for the domestic market because Indonesians are great smokers of clove cigarettes, an item which features prominently in weekly family budgets. During the *krismon* poor families in both urban and rural areas cut back their consumption of this item, albeit reluctantly (see Chapter 11). The second reason is an extraordinary initiative by one of the sons of President Suharto, who took over the clove marketing chain by setting up a trade monopoly, ostensibly to protect farmers against price fluctuations. The monopoly in fact led to the pinning of producer prices at their lowest level for years, with the result that many farmers gave up growing the crop. In 1999, Indonesia lacked sufficient cloves to supply its cigarette factories, which is probably why both domestic and international prices skyrocketed during the year (see Box 1.3 and Figures 12.4 and 12.10).

Crops for the domestic market

For the producers of commodities sold mainly on the domestic market, such as palm oil and food crops, the potentially positive impact of currency depreciation was at least partially offset by government policy. This policy was intended to keep prices low for urban consumers. Indonesia has a long tradition of intervention in the domestic commodity market. Stable food prices was part of the "social contract" in place during the Suharto era. The violence that accompanied each rise in food prices during the crisis illustrates the difficulties faced by a country in which a switch to free trade implied a threefold rise in domestic food prices at a time of painful economic adjustment.

The dilemma facing countries such as Indonesia is truly terrible. On the one hand, hikes in staple food prices have a devastating impact on the poor, as well as a strong overall inflationary effect. Targetting the most vulnerable social groups with food programmes is expensive and difficult, especially when, as in Indonesia's case, confidence in the institutions of government has been damaged by years of corruption. Without such programmes social unrest is almost inevitable, given rising unemployment and deepening poverty. On the other hand, intervening to keep the price of staple foods low can also be too expensive, even when an international institution provides assistance, and is, in addition, difficult to police. Maintaining low output prices when input prices have increased also penalises farmers, preventing them from contributing to the country's economic recovery.

This is the classical dilemma of food price policy. In the circumstances faced by Indonesia—strong currency depreciation, a large deficit in rice production, the flight of foreign capital and a deepening socio-political crisis to add to the economic one—the dilemma became a nightmare.

In the early stages of the crisis, the government was able to intervene to minimise increases in the price of food. However, price regulation broke down in the summer of 1998, owing to a combination of drought-induced shortages, the country's financial difficulties and the lack of confidence in government institutions. Each round of price rises triggered violence and insecurity, increasing the risk of trading. This pushed prices up still further, leading to panic buying during the summer of 1998. Food prices soared, leading to further widespread social unrest and a deepening of the political and economic crisis (see Chapter 9). In September, the domestic prices of several food items, including rice, were higher than import parity prices.

Under these chaotic conditions, the impact of the crisis on food crop producers varied greatly. Some farmers maintained or even increased their incomes, while others faced ruin.

The location of a farm, together with its size, were major determinants of the impact of the crisis. Farmers on rainfed land were harder hit by drought than were those in irrigated areas, who suffered more from floods. Farm size determined whether a farmer was a net buyer or a net seller of rice. Some farmers, for instance transmigrants in Sumatra (see Chapter 11) or Javanese farmers without adequate irrigation water supplies (see Chapter 9), experienced a sharp fall in production. Already poor before the crisis, these farmers were not able to grow enough rice to support themselves and their families. Early in the crisis, they faced a rise in the price of inputs, forcing them to reduce the quantities they applied, which in turn reduced yields still further. Even when food prices rose, these farmers did not benefit since they had little or no surplus to sell. Their troubles were compounded by reduced off-farm employment opportunities. Most of them barely survived.

Larger food crop farmers growing a surplus of rice or maize were more fortunate. After a neutral period at the beginning of the crisis, they enjoyed higher incomes or at least greater income stability, as the rising prices made their crops more profitable (see Chapter 10). In 1998, many farmers in irrigated areas experienced good yields and good prices. The delayed season, which led to a later than usual harvest, allowed those who were not too short of cash to wait for a price rise before selling their rice. Inflation quickly swallowed up their additional profits, however, and in 1999 prices actually fell at harvest time.

Government intervention also seems to have been unsuccessful in the case of palm oil. Exports of this commodity were banned from December 1997 to January 1998. After the ban was lifted, export taxes were increased, to 40% in April-June 1998 and then to 60% in July 1998-January 1999 (see Chapter 3). The idea behind these moves was to prevent oil palm estates from exporting their produce at high international prices and so to avoid shortages and rising prices on the domestic market. However, the domestic retail price of palm oil rose rapidly in 1998 — earlier and more sharply than that of rice. Intervention clearly failed to keep prices under control. How smallholders fared is difficult to assess, primarily because they are relatively few in number. This sector is still dominated by estates and most smallholders are tied to nucleus/plasma schemes[3]. The price paid to the smallholder is, in any case, not the whole story. Smallholders have to apply large amounts of fertiliser and, during much of the crisis, paid a higher than market price for this and other necessary inputs. However, oil palm production as a whole did become more profitable and smallholders had some share in the profits. Net incomes from oil palm in 1998 showed a smaller increase than those from cocoa, coffee and pepper, but they still rose significantly.

The export tax was reduced to 30% in April 1999 and then to 10% in July of that year. Because the prices of all cooking oils had fallen on the world market, it was considered that the cut would do no harm to the domestic market.

Producer prices of palm oil rose less in 1998 than those of other commodities such as pepper, cocoa and coffee, but they held up better in

1999. As a result, farmers' interest in the crop quickened as the crisis wore on. Oil palm appeared an attractive alternative into which to diversify in rubber producing areas (see Chapter 8). By 1999, oil palm trees had shaken off the effects of the 1997 drought, allowing yields and hence gross incomes to rise. Farmers' main complaint throughout this year was that the nucleus schemes were charging them exorbitant prices for inputs.

Another major impact of the crisis on the oil palm sector was to intensify conflicts over land. Impoverished smallholders, intent on reclaiming the land from which they had been displaced by the rapid spread of the estates in previous years, vented their anger by rioting, stealing from plantations and setting them on fire. In some cases they were aided and abetted by army personnel, who either sympathised with their cause or wanted a share of the loot. The result was that the foreign companies involved in the country's oil palm sector lost confidence, bringing their investments to an abrupt halt. In 1999-2000, a degree of confidence returned, with some companies renewing their investments, sometimes at the expense of rubber (see Chapter 8). It is impossible to attach a figure to this, but we believe that the crisis may have proved useful to small-scale oil palm producers. The frustration that erupted into violence was accompanied by a loosening of the estates' grip on the sector, providing an opportunity for some producers to free themselves altogether from the estates and extend their own small oil palm farms. Indonesia may be about to discover that oil palm can be a very good smallholder crop.

Diverse impact

We will now explore the diverse impact of the crisis on farmers in the different commodity sectors. Four main factors explain this diversity. The first is the relationship between farm-gate prices and international prices, which is greatly affected by the market the farmer is selling into, domestic or export, and the degree of competition in the market. The second factor, which concerns tree crop farmers only, is the age structure of their orchards at the time of the crisis. Relatively young orchards nearing or at the peak of their productive life brought farmers very high profits indeed. The third factor is the opportunities for farmers to respond to rising prices by increasing production in the short term. This opportunity is different for tree crops and annual crops, but did it really materialise in either case?

The fourth factor is demand. We have already discussed the 1999 global decline in prices and the possible reasons for it. Now we will try to explain the different trends for different commodities. Why did a few commodities earn better incomes than others in 1998 and/or show better "resistance" than others to the pressure for price reduction in 1999?

Market factors

Two major market factors explain the different impacts of the crisis on farmers:

- Destination market. Exports are essential if a country is to recover economically when its currency falls apart. In 1998, clove farmers and most food crop farmers in Indonesia were ham-strung by a market that was entirely domestic and isolated from world prices by government interventions. However, commodity sectors relying on exports alone are more vulnerable than those also benefitting from a domestic market, for which the risks are spread. Compared with cocoa and rubber farmers, oil palm, coconut and pepper producers experienced less traumatic price falls in 1999, probably because they also sell into the domestic market. Clove producers, who sell mainly to the domestic market, even experienced a rise in prices in 1999 as the effects of liberalisation finally kicked in.
- Liberalisation and competition. An entirely free market and plenty of competition between numerous middlemen and exporters are the ideal conditions if farmers are to cash in on a currency crisis. For cocoa and coffee farmers in 1998, these conditions were more or less met.

  There was less competition between middlemen in the rubber sector, at least in Kalimantan. The main signs of this were the range in prices paid to farmers and their dependency on middlemen for credit to buy food.

  Oil palm is the sector in which there was least competition. Smallholder production in this sector is almost entirely controlled by the big estates, through the nucleus/plasma system. We need not comment further on the degree of competition in the clove industry before 1999, but that market has now been liberalised.

Age of orchards

Whatever the price fetched by a tree crop, the age of the orchard is by far and away the most important factor affecting farmers' yields and hence incomes. In aggregate terms, Indonesia's different tree crops can be dated to different periods.

The country's clove orchards were planted mainly in the 1970s. This means that clove trees planted on good soil are in theory still relatively young[4], but they have been "made old" by years of poor maintenance by farmers—caused mainly by the extremely low prices they were paid.

For the rubber industry, the crisis came too early. Apart from a few areas in which improved planting materials have been made available, the trees in most rubber plantations and traditional jungle rubber systems are old. Five years into the new century, when increasing numbers of high-yielding clonal rubber trees will have come into production, the crisis would have had a more positive effect on smallholders' incomes. Young clonal rubber would have allowed incomes to rise owing to its higher average yields and higher returns to labour.

In contrast, the age of many cocoa, coffee, oil palm and pepper plantations was just right to turn a price rise into a windfall. Many cocoa and coffee orchards, in particular, are still relatively young and highly productive. For example, cocoa is still a new crop in Sulawesi, while coffee farmers in southern Sumatra know how to optimise their favourable climate and soils by regularly replanting their trees (Ruf, 1997). The situation for oil palm is more complex, but increasing numbers of large-scale producers and smallholders have gone into the crop over the past decade, so many new plantations were coming into production when the crisis struck. In several regions of Indonesia, including Sulawesi, pepper farmers also enjoyed the fruits of recently established and now fully productive creepers.

Taken together, the age of orchards in each sector and the degree of competition within it are good indicators of how well it performed during the 1998 boom (Figure 12.11).

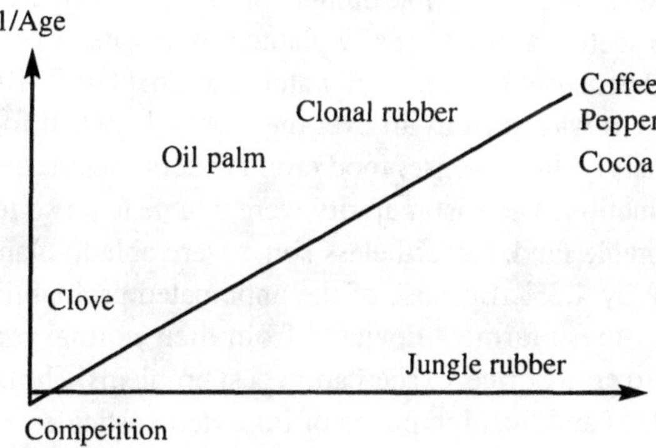

Figure 12.11 Age of orchards and degree of competition as explanations of tree crop performance during the crisis

Potential for supply response

Sooner or later almost all commodities go through a period in which their real prices rise, creating incentives to increase production. A major feature of most agricultural commodities, however, is the difficulty of increasing supplies in the short term. This difficulty goes a long way to explain the price instability that typically afflicts agriculture.

In tree crops, deliberate short-term (within-season) increases in production are difficult if not impossible to achieve. Let us take rubber as an example. Virtually the only way of increasing production from a jungle rubber plot is by tapping previously abandoned trees, but few farmers do this since they know how poor the yields will be. Where farmers are growing improved clones, production can be increased by tapping the trees more frequently, but at high risk of tree damage and mortality a few months later. Again, our field research showed that very few farmers do this. In the case of cocoa, already discussed, farmers attempted to resuscitate their trees after the 1997 drought by using more inputs, but they did not succeed in actually increasing production.

In annual food crops, which respond to inputs faster and have shorter cyclesthe opportunities to increase both yields and cultivated areas quickly in response to market signals are in theory greater. In practice, however, they seldom materialise for small-scale producers.

In Indonesia's case, the terrible drought of late 1997 severely damaged the food crop sector. Areas normally planted to irrigated rice had to be left unplanted because of the lack of water (see Chapters 9, 10 and 11). By early 1998, it was obvious all over the archipelago that food prices would rise sharply. In response, food crop farmers tried desperately to increase production. The vast majority were unable to do so for lack of water and suitable land. Nevertheless some were able to plant and the rice area rose by 4.3%. Because of the anticipated profitability of the crop, some of these farmers deviated from their normal practice by planting a third crop of rice, exacerbating pest problems. The disruption of input markets and the high prices of imported pesticides, combined with continuing climatic constraints, kept yields low, minimising any positive effect from increased area. The general insecurity made farmers reluctant to sell their produce and stocks well above the usual level were reported in producing areas (see Chapter 9). All these factors combined to minimise any short-term increase in food crop production that might have resulted from price incentives.

Demand effects

Besides the degree of competition, dealt with above, two other major factors on the demand side may have affected the different outcome of the crisis for different farmers:

- Falling international demand. Some economists consider the impact of the Asian crisis on international demand to have been marginal. It is true that rubber prices, for example, started falling before the Asian crisis (see Chapter 8). Nevertheless, as already explained, it is our belief that the Asian, Russian and Brazilian crises combined had more than a marginal impact on the international demand for rubber and cocoa.
- Product substitution. A further complication in understanding the impact of demand is the potential for product substitution. High yields of soybean in the USA and Brazil and currency depreciation in Brazil played a major part in the 1999 collapse of crude palm oil prices in Rotterdam.

Conclusions

The economic crisis in Indonesia brought about a windfall for a minority, but plunged the vast majority into deeper poverty, raising the spectre of renewed hunger and malnutrition. Much progress has since been made towards democracy and freedom of speech. There is also progress, albeit slow, towards economic reform. However, the road ahead will be difficult indeed. The stakes are extremely high. Indonesia is a huge country of major strategic importance. As the linchpin of ASEAN, it plays a critical role in regional security and trade. Recent developments, including the emergence of a plethora of political parties and several secessionist movements, instill fears of a return to a period of weak government, divisive party politics and administrative anarchy—a situation remembered by some from the post-independence 1950-57 period.

At that time, Indonesians were poorly equipped to manage their own affairs. Political scientists, economists and competent administrators were in short supply. This is no longer the case. In addition, the crisis has provided compelling evidence that totalitarianism is not compatible with harmonious development and the pursuit of prosperity for the many, once a certain level of development has been attained. It seems unlikely that Indonesia's new leaders will turn their backs on this truth.

Much concern remains about the approach to development that the country will now adopt. Perhaps Indonesia can learn from its neighbours. Whereas the other four Southeast Asian countries that were strongly affected by crisis in 1998 have emerged from it more rapidly and relatively unscathed, the multiple crisis in Indonesia dragged the country far lower and greatly delayed its recovery. In contrast to Indonesia, the political systems of at least three of these other countries have been evolving towards democracy since the late 1980s.

Indonesia and its people have suffered greatly from their lack of legal rights and the lack of transparency and accountability of government — things that can be achieved only with democracy. Suharto's Indonesia had many institutions, but their purposes and activities were often obscure and they were frequently controlled by Suharto's family and friends. This cosy situation was exploded by the *krismon*. To some extent the crisis may have been perpetrated, indeed deliberately stoked up, both within the country and from the outside, in order to provoke the necessary political changes.

The fall in the rupiah was one of the steepest currency depreciations ever recorded. Whereas moderate currency depreciations allow salutary adjustments to occur in the economy, this was no longer the case in Indonesia, where the total disruption of import prices led to thousands of bankruptcies. Some features of Indonesian development may explain the crisis (Krugman, 1994), but the financial market seems to have overreacted, raising the question of what regulatory mechanisms should be put in place to prevent such a melt-down happening again. The crisis was strongly linked to the rapid liberalisation of capital markets and the deregulation of the banking system throughout the region in the early to mid-1990s, which led to huge flows of speculative capital and highly volatile stock markets (Stiglitz, 1999). If liberalisation can wreak such havoc on the financial markets, what will happen if the same medicine is meted out to agricultural commodities? Huge price fluctuations in this sector are far more damaging to ordinary producers and consumers than are most stock market crashes (Boussard and Gérard, 1992; Boussard, 1994).

In many ways, agriculture in pre-crisis Indonesia suffered from the same weaknesses as the rest of the economy. The clove saga, for which the presidential family can be held directly responsible, was an extreme example of the corruption and nepotism that enriched the few while impoverishing the many, but it was far from the only one. The regulation of the oil palm sector, in which farmers are forced into nucleus/plasma systems, was and still is a barrier that prevents smallholders from participating as they should do in the wealth created by the industry. It permits high incomes for investors, while depriving plantation workers of all but a risible share of the profits (see Chapter 3). Smallholders were in a better position, but their share of the added value also remained very low. Transmigration programmes were another instrument by which the government impoverished food crop producers while denying the land rights of indigenous forest dwellers (see Chapter 11). The allocation of forest concessions led to billions of dollars worth of bribes (see Chapter 4).

During the crisis of 1998, the agricultural sector nevertheless performed better than other sectors. This was because of the tradable nature of its products, because it had not participated in the speculative bubble of the mid-1990s and because it was not for the most part overburdened by debt. The terms of trade experienced by farmers differed greatly according to the type and location of their crops. The potentially positive impact of the crisis on farmers' incomes was considerably offset by government intervention in the staple food market and by the impact of the drought on crop yields. However, the windfalls experienced by export-oriented farmers in some areas of the outer islands were an important factor in keeping parts of the country's economy alive. Their positive influence was felt in several ways.

First, by greatly increasing consumption, the windfalls helped maintain active trade and hence reasonable prices in certain sectors. For example, the prices of second-hand cars and other vehicles remained surpisingly buoyant for most of the crisis. The cocoa, coffee and pepper growing regions sucked in motorcycles, cars and trucks from throughout the country. This helped vehicle traders and other people who needed to sell their assets, who might otherwise have had a much harder time. It also helped keep public transport costs relatively low, a real boon for an economy in which many were forced to travel in search of work.

Second, the 1998 windfalls also helped keep the building industry active. Thousands of carpenters and masons were invited to build houses in Sulawesi and southern Sumatra. Many Balinese architects and artists were engaged to build and decorate Hindu temples in the transmigration schemes of Central Sulawesi.

Third, in provinces such as Sulawesi, the 1999 recession did not slow down the rush to plant new areas to cocoa. Provided the world price recovers in 2002 or 2003, the new plantings should bring huge returns, although the costs of the accelerated deforestation that accompanies them will eventually have to be reckoned with.

Fourth, we argue tentatively that the windfalls were probably helpful in preserving national unity[5]. When cocoa farmers in Sulawesi experienced their windfall, they did not talk about independence. When coffee farmers in Sumatra benefitted, there were few complaints about estates stealing land. The oil palm sector, which dispossessed a large segment of the smallholder population, stands in marked contrast, disrupted as it was by riots and looting. Separatism and conflict loom when farmers are prevented from participating in the wealth of the nation by a political system that is morally and financially bankrupt.

Destructive though they were, the riots and squatter movements that challenged the corporate plantations during the crisis years may have a positive impact in the longer term. Both during and since the

Dutch colonial era, Indonesia has suffered greatly as a result of its governments' policy of promoting large-scale estate development at the expense of smallholders. This was not merely a social error. In economic terms, most tree and cash crop sectors perform much better when managed by smallholders than by estates, owing to diseconomies of scale (Clarence-Smith, 1995). The cocoa, coffee and rubber sectors have already demonstrated this truth. It should not be too long before the oil palm sector discovers it too.

The liberalisation that proved advantageous for so many export-oriented farmers in 1998 somewhat backfired on them in 1999. It is clear that oligopolies of international buyers in sectors such as cocoa and rubber captured part of the surplus generated by currency depreciation and in so doing hastened the 1999 price collapse, which was also caused by a fall in demand.

Nevertheless, we should not forget that at least 40 million Indonesian people directly or indirectly depend on the production of rubber, oil palm, coffee, cocoa, pepper and a few other spices—and that they were able to continue doing so during the crisis that engulfed their country. Their relative prosperity and security, amidst a population of 210 million most of whom suffered greatly, served as a tremendous safety valve for society and the economy as a whole. Although the prices of cocoa and coffee remain at new lows in early 2000, the partial recovery of rubber and oil palm confirms that export commodities will constitute a precious resource with which to relaunch Indonesia's economy in the twenty-first century.

Under what conditions will agriculture really pull its weight as the engine of Indonesia's recovery in the coming years? We conclude with some recommendations for the country's policy makers:

- It will be essential to build on and enhance the inherent efficiency of smallholders. This applies to all commodities, but particularly to oil palm. Smallholders in this sector have already begun to free themselves from the yoke of the anachronistic and inefficient nucleus/plasma system. They must be further encouraged. And, in every sector, the rights of smallholders to land, to management of the local resource base, to credit and to the other support services provided by government and the private sector need to be enshrined in new laws and promoted through new institutions.

- Access to new technology will be imperative if smallholders are to rise to the challenge of restoring the agricultural sector's productivity and efficiency. High-quality, certified planting materials are especially needed in clonal rubber, oil palm and the timber sector. Smallholders could become the best customers of estates given over to the production of such materials. For tree crops subject to high pest pressure, such as cocoa, the priority should be to help farmers get access to the most efficient pesticides and organise to spray all together at the right time. In food crops, it will be necessary to enable poor or indebted farmers to buy the inputs they need to improve and sustain the productivity of rice and other crops. If this is done and there is renewed investment in the development of higher-yielding rice plants, Indonesia may be able to regain the self-sufficiency in rice of earlier years.
- Although economic theory says that free markets are a condition for maximum efficiency, care must be taken not to allow the demand side an unhealthy degree of concentration while the supply side becomes an unfettered free-for-all. If inefficient or corrupt state intervention is used as the pretext for banning all forms of producers' organisations while the buyers in a market number only three or four international companies, an imbalance will be created, allowing the companies to dictate prices that strongly disadvantage the small producer. This is a familiar problem that long pre-dates the Asian crisis. Between 1975 and 1993, for example, the price of coffee on the world market declined by 18%, but the consumer price for it in the USA rose by 240% (Morisset, 1997). Nevertheless, the need to avoid such inequitable price movements is one of the clearest lessons to emerge from the Asian crisis. Unlike those of non-agricultural goods, the prices of virtually all tropical agricultural commodities fell heavily between the second half of 1998 and 2000. In Indonesia, these falls virtually stifled at birth the export-led economic recovery launched in 1998 by the country's tree crop sector. As we have seen, the falls cannot be explained by short-term supply responses, nor by reduced demand from the rest of Asia, although this is a minor contributory factor. The major determinant of declining prices is structural—the lack of alternative opportunities for resource-poor farmers, not only in Indonesia but in all poor countries. These farmers

have no choice but to migrate and to plant export crops such as cocoa and rubber, whatever their market prices, because there is no other legitimate way in which they can earn a living. Against this background, currency devaluations or depreciations such as Indonesia's intensify the decline in prices. They always do, of course: the basic principle of competitive devaluation is that a country hopes to gain market share by offering international buyers lower prices in US dollars. However, when buyers are few in number, competition between them is reduced, exerting a further downward pressure on prices that enables them to capture part of the surplus created by devaluation. What the Asian crisis shows is that the trend of price decline in agricultural commodities is accelerated by economic globalisation.

- Thus, while getting rid of the public or private monopolies that have performed so poorly in the past, Indonesia will probably need to provide support to the formation of producers' organisations, either at the national or at the international level. Such organisations have long been suggested and are regarded by some as merely a Utopian pipe-dream. Nevertheless, the Asian crisis has provided a sharp reminder of how greatly they are needed.

References

Afrique Agriculture. 1999. Caoutchouc: Un cours très bas mais qui devrait rebondir à court terme. Issue 273: 26-27.

Berry, S. 1976. Supply response reconsidered: Cocoa in western Nigeria, 1909-44. *Journal of Development Studies* 13 (1): 4-17.

Boussard, J.M. and Gérard, F. 1992. Risk Aversion and Chaotic Motion in Agricultural Markets. Working Document 17. Unité de recherche pour les politiques agricoles, CIRAD, Paris, France.

Boussard, J.M. 1994. Revenus, marchés et anticipation de la dynamique de l'offre agricole, *Economie rurale* 220-221: 61-68.

Cayrac-Blanchard, F. 1998. Faillite fracassante pour la dictature Indonésienne. *Le Monde Diplomatique*, February issue.

CBS (Central Bureau of Statistics). Website: http://www.cbs.go.id

Clarence-Smith, W. 1995. Cocoa plantations in the Third World, 1870s-1914: The political economy of inefficiency. In: Harris, Hunter, J. and Lewis, C.M. (eds), *The New Institutional Economics and Third World Development*. Routledge Economics, London, UK and New York, USA, pp. 157-171.

Cohen, M. 1998. How sweet it is. *Far Eastern Economic Review*, 3 December issue.

Dupraz, P. and Lifran, R. 1995. The economic complementarity of cocoa and coconut intercropping: Asset strategies of smallholders in Malaysia and implications for cocoa supply. In: Ruf, F. and Siswoputranto, P.S. (eds), *Cocoa Cycles: The Economics of Cocoa Supply*. Woodhead, Cambridge, UK, pp. 281-289.

FAO/WPF (Food and Agriculture Organisation/World Food Programme) 1998. Crop and food supply assessment mission to Indonesia. *Journal of Humanitarian Assistance*. Website: http://www.jha.sps.cam.ac.uk/b/b127.pdf

Hill, P. 1964. *Migrant Cocoa Farmers of Southern Ghana: A Study in Rural Capitalism*. Cambridge University Press, UK.

ILO/UNDP (International Labour Organization/United Nations Development Programme). 1998. Employment Challenges of the Indonesian Economic Crisis. ILO, Jakarta, Indonesia.

Jacquemard, J.C. and Jannot, C. 2000. Indonésie: Quel avenir pour le palmier à huile? 2: Indonésie dans la tourmente. *Plantations, recherche, développement* (in press).

Krugman, P. 1994. The Myth of the Asian Miracle. Website: http://web.mit.edu/krugman

McBeth, J. 1998. Crisis, what crisis? *Far Eastern Economic Review*, 3 December issue.

Mohan, U. 1998. East Asia crisis and the poor. News and Views, 2020 Vision for Food, Agriculture and the Environment (June). International Food Policy Research Institute (IFPRI), Washington DC, USA.

Morisset, J. 1997. Unfair Trade? Empirical Evidence in World Commodity Markets over the Past 25 Years. Website: http://wbln0018.worldbank.org.

Prebish, R. 1950. *The Economic Development of Latin America and its Principal Problems*. United Nations, New York, USA.

Ruf, F. 1995. *Booms et crises du cacao: Les vertiges de l'or brun*. Karthala, Paris, France.

Ruf, F. 1996. Les booms cacao de la Côte d'Ivoire...et du Burkina Faso: L'accélération des années 1980-90. CIRAD and Ministère de la Coopération, Montpellier and Paris, France.

Ruf, F. 1997. L'aptitude de l'agriculture familiale à replanter: Le cas du café à Sumatra. In: Hubert, M. (ed.), *Le paysan, l'Etat et le marché: Sociétés paysannes et développement*. Publications de la Sorbonne, Paris, France, pp. 278-293.

Ruf, F. 1999. Comment et pourquoi la Côte d'Ivoire produit durablement plus d'un million de tonnes de cacao? *Afrique Agriculture* 268: 21-25.

Ruf, F. and Cebron, D. 1999. La libéralisation du cacao en Côte d'Ivoire sur fonds de crise du marché international. *Afrique Agriculture* 275: 55-57.

Singer, H. 1950. The distribution of gains between investing and borrowing countries. *American Economic Review* 40.

Stiglitz, J.E. 1999. Lessons from East Asia. *Journal of Policy Modelling* 21 (3): 311-380.

Tabor, S.R., Dillon, H.S. and Husein Sawit, M. 1999. Understanding the 1998 food crisis: Supply, demand or policy failure? Paper presented at the International Seminar on the Agricultural Sector during the Turbulence of Economic Crisis: Lessons and Future Directions. Center for Agro-Socioeconomic Research, Agency for Agricultural Research and Development, Ministry of Agriculture, Bogor, Indonesia.

USDA (United States Department of Agriculture). 1999. Website: http://www.Fas.usda.gov (Commodities/Tropical Products).

Notes

1 That is, the price of the product delivered to the port of destination, including all transport and insurance costs.

2 Our conclusions, drawn from the empirical evidence presented in Chapters 5 to 8, confirm the theory presented in Chapter 2, that currency depreciations lead to declining world prices. However, we disagree with the second mechanism used by the authors of Chapter 2 to explain the decline, namely producers' short-term supply responses.

3 In these schemes, a central private or public factory and estate—the nucleus—was established to grow and process a commercial crop such as rubber, oil palm or sugar. The plasma consisted of small family farms established round the outside of the estate to increase supplies to the factory. Nucelus/plasma schemes were often associated with transmigration schemes, with transmigrants being settled on the new farms.

4 If well managed, clove trees can be harvested into their fifties and beyond.

5 We must remain cautious about this hypothesis, since the windfalls also accelerated the rush for land in the outer islands, a factor that played a part in the "religious" conflicts between indigenous Christians and Muslim migrants in Sulawesi and elsewhere. Nevertheless, we believe that, in Sulawesi at least, most farmers can resolve these conflicts peacefully if left to do so without external manipulation.

For Product Safety Concerns and Information please contact our EU representative GPSR@taylorandfrancis.com
Taylor & Francis Verlag GmbH, Kaufingerstraße 24, 80331 München, Germany

www.ingramcontent.com/pod-product-compliance
Lightning Source LLC
Chambersburg PA
CBHW060131280326
41932CB00012B/1482

* 9 7 8 1 1 3 8 8 6 2 5 9 3 *